## Get the eBook FREE!

(PDF, ePub, Kindle, and liveBook all included)

We believe that once you buy a book from us, you should be able to read it in any format we have available. To get electronic versions of this book at no additional cost to you, purchase and then register this book at the Manning website.

Go to https://www.manning.com/freebook and follow the instructions to complete your pBook registration.

That's it!
Thanks from Manning!

*Cloud Native Patterns*

# Cloud Native Patterns

## DESIGNING CHANGE-TOLERANT SOFTWARE

CORNELIA DAVIS
FOREWORD BY GENE KIM

MANNING
SHELTER ISLAND

For online information and ordering of this and other Manning books, please visit www.manning.com. The publisher offers discounts on this book when ordered in quantity. For more information, please contact

> Special Sales Department
> Manning Publications Co.
> 20 Baldwin Road
> PO Box 761
> Shelter Island, NY 11964
> Email: orders@manning.com

Manning Publications Co.
20 Baldwin Road
PO Box 761
Shelter Island, NY 11964

| | |
|---|---|
| Development editor: | Christina Taylor |
| Technical development editor: | Raphael Villela |
| Review editor: | Ivan Martinović |
| Production editor: | Deirdre Hiam |
| Copyeditor: | Sharon Wilkey |
| Proofreader: | Carol Shields |
| Technical proofreader: | Neil Croll |
| Typesetter: | Gordan Salinovic |
| Cover designer: | Marija Tudor |

ISBN 9781617294297
Printed in the United States of America

*To my husband, Glen.*
*The day I met you, my whole life changed.*


*To my son, Max.*
*The day you were born, my whole life changed.*

# brief contents

# contents

# *foreword*

For six years, I've had the privilege of working with Nicole Forsgren and Jez Humble on the "State of DevOps Report," which has collected data from more than 30,000 respondents. One of the biggest revelations for me was the importance of software architecture: high-performing teams had architectures that enabled developers to quickly and independently develop, test, and deploy value to customers, safely and reliably.

Decades ago, we could joke that software architects were expert only at using Visio, creating UML diagrams, and generating PowerPoint slides that no one ever looked at. If that were ever true, that is certainly not the case now. These days, businesses win and lose in the marketplace from the software they create. And nothing impacts the daily work of developers more than the architecture that they must work within.

This book fills a gap, spanning theory and practice. In fact, I think only a handful of people could have written it. Cornelia Davis is uniquely qualified, having spent years as a PhD student studying programming languages, having developed a love of functional programming and immutability, working for decades within large software systems, and helping large software organizations achieve greatness.

Over the past five years, I've reached out to her for help and advice many times, often about topics such as CQRS and event sourcing, LISP and Clojure (my favorite programming language), the perils of imperative programming and state, and even simple things like recursion.

What makes this book so rewarding to read is that Cornelia doesn't just start with patterns. She starts with first principles, and then proves their validity through argumentation, sometimes through logic, and sometimes through flowcharts. Not satisfied with just theory, she then implements those patterns in Java Spring, iteration after iteration, incorporating what you've learned.

I found this book entertaining and educational, and learned an incredible amount on topics that I formerly had only a cursory understanding of. I am now committed to implementing her examples in Clojure, out of a desire to prove that I can put this knowledge into practice.

I suspect you'll connect concepts that will delight and maybe even startle you. For me, one of those concepts was the need to centralize cross-cutting concerns, whether through aspect-oriented programming, Kubernetes sidecars, or Spring Retry injections.

I hope you find this book as rewarding to read as I did!

—GENE KIM, RESEARCHER AND COAUTHOR OF
*THE PHOENIX PROJECT, THE DEVOPS HANDBOOK,*
AND *ACCELERATE*

# *preface*

I started my career in image processing. I worked in the Missile Systems Division of Hughes Aircraft on infrared images, doing things like edge detection and frame-to-frame correlation (some of the things that you can find in any number of applications on your mobile phone today—this was all the way back in the 80s!).

One of the calculations we perform in image processing a lot is standard deviation. I've never been particularly shy about asking questions, and one that I often asked in those early days was around that standard deviation. Invariably, a colleague would write down the following:

$$\sigma = \sqrt{\frac{1}{N} \sum_{i=1}^{N} (x_i - \mu)^2}$$

But I knew the formula for standard deviation. Heck, three months in I had probably already coded it half a dozen times. I was really asking, "What is knowing the standard deviation telling us in this context?" Standard deviation is used to define what is "normal" so we can look for outliers. If I'm calculating standard deviation and then find things outside the norm, is that an indication that my sensor might have malfunctioned and I need to throw out the image frame, or does it expose potential enemy actions?

What does all of this have to do with cloud-native? Nothing. But it has everything to do with patterns. You see, I knew the pattern—the standard deviation calculation—

but because of my lack of experience at the time, I was struggling with when and why to apply it.

In this book, I'll teach you the patterns for cloud-native applications, and yes, I'll show you many "formulas," but I spend far more time on the *context*—the when and why of applying these patterns. In fact, the patterns aren't generally that hard (for example, a request retry, covered in chapter 9, is a simple concept that's easy to implement). But choosing when to apply a pattern, and exactly how to do it—that can be tricky. There's so much to understand about the context in which you'll be applying these patterns, and frankly, that context can be complex.

What is that context, then? It's fundamentally one of distributed systems. When I started my career more than 30 years ago, I didn't know many people who worked on distributed systems, and I didn't take a distributed systems class in college. Yes, people were working in this space but, honestly, it was pretty niche.

Today the vast majority of software is a distributed system. Some parts of your software are running in the browser, and other parts on a server, or dare I say, a whole bunch of servers. Those servers could be running in your corporate data center, or they might be in a dark data center running in Prineville, Oregon, or both. And all of those pieces are communicating over a network, probably the internet, and likely your software's data is also widely distributed. Simply put, cloud-native software is a distributed system. In addition, things are in a constant state of change—servers are moving out from under you, networks have frequent outages, even if brief, and storage devices may go belly up with no warning—yet your software is expected to remain running. That's a pretty challenging context.

But it's totally tractable! My goal with this book is to help you understand this context and supply you the tools to become a proficient cloud-native software architect and developer.

I've never been more intellectually stimulated than I am right now. This is in large part because the technology landscape is shifting in significant ways, and cloud-native is at the core. I absolutely *love* what I do for a living and I want nothing more than for everyone, you in particular, to enjoy writing software as much as I do. And that's why I've written this book: I want to share with you the crazy cool problems we are working on as an industry and help you on your journey to being able to solve these problems. I am so honored to have the opportunity to play even a small part in your flight to the cloud.

# *acknowledgments*

My cloud-native journey began in earnest in 2012 when my boss at the time, Tom Maguire, asked me to start looking into this PaaS (Platform as a Service) thing. As a member of the Architecture group in the EMC CTO office, looking at emerging technology was not new for us—but boy, did this one pan out! I will forever be grateful to Tom for the impetus and for giving me the space to explore.

By early 2013, I had learned enough to know that this was the space for me to work in for the foreseeable future, and with the creation of Pivotal Software, I had a place to do that work. I have Elisabeth Hendrickson to thank, first for welcoming me to the Cloud Foundry party—even while I was still at EMC—and for introducing me to James Watters. I often say that the best career move I ever made was going to work for James. I thank him for the many opportunities that he presented me, for trusting me in a way that allowed me to do my best work, for countless high-bandwidth conversations in which we collectively learned about this cloud-native thing, and for the deep friendship we've created over the last six years.

I'm grateful that I've been a part of Pivotal since its inception, where I have learned alongside so many bright, dedicated, and kind colleagues. I'd like to thank Elisabeth Hendrickson, Joshua McKenty, Andrew Clay-Shafer, Scott Yara, Ferran Rodenas, Matt Stine, Ragvender Arni, and so many others (please forgive me for any omissions) for helping me learn and for sharing the best six years of my life! I'd also like to thank Pivotal, Ian Andrews and Kelly Hall in particular, for sponsoring the *Cloud-Native Foundations* minibook.

I've learned so much from more industry colleagues than I can ever begin to list—thank you to each of you. But I would like to single out Gene Kim. I recall the night we met (and again thank Elisabeth Hendrickson for the part she played in making that meeting all that it could be) and knew right away that we'd be collaborators for a long time. I thank Gene for the opportunity to work with him on the DevOps Enterprise Summit, through which I've met so many innovative people working at a broad range of companies. I thank him for some of the most invigorating, mind-expanding conversations. And I thank him for writing the foreword to this very book.

Of course, I thank Manning Publications for the opportunity to write this book, starting with Mike Stephens, who helped me go from idle curiosity about book writing to actually taking the plunge. I owe such a debt of gratitude to my development editor, Christina Taylor. She took a novice author who started with a 20-chapter mess of ideas and an early chapter that rambled on for 70 or so pages, and helped me produce a book that has structure and a real story line. She stuck with me for more than two and a half years, encouraging me when I was in my valleys of despair and celebrating me when I was at my peaks of accomplishment. I also thank the production team, including Sharon Wilkey, Deirdre Hiam, Neil Croll, Carol Shields, and Nichole Beard, who are responsible for getting this thing over the finish line. And thank you to my reviewers—Bachir Chihani, Carlos Roberto Vargas Montero, David Schmitz, Doniyor Ulmasov, Gregor Zurowski, Jared Duncan, John Guthrie, Jorge Ezequiel Bo, Kelvin Johnson, Kent R. Spillner, Lonnie Smetana, Luis Carlos Sanchez Gonzalez, Mark Miller, Peter Paul Sellars, Raveesh Sharma, Sergey Evsikov, Sergio Martinez, Shanker Janakiraman, Stefan Hellweger, Win Oo, and Zorodzayi Mukuya. Your feedback had a marked impact on the finished product.

And most of all, I thank my husband, Glen, and son, Max, for their patience, encouragement, and unfailing faith in me. They, more than any others, are the two people who have made this possible, not only by giving me support over the last nearly three years, but also by helping me lay a foundation over several decades before that. The two of you have my deepest gratitude. And that you, Max, have fallen in love with computing as much as I, and have allowed me to be a spectator on that ride, that is double-chocolate icing on a death-by-chocolate cake—thank you!

# about this book

## Who should read this book

Going to "the cloud" is more about how you design your applications than where you deploy them. *Cloud-Native Patterns: Designing Change-Tolerant Software* is your guide to developing strong applications that thrive in the dynamic, distributed, virtual world of the cloud. This book presents a mental model for cloud-native applications, along with the patterns, practices, and tooling that support their construction. In it, you'll find realistic examples and expert advice for working with apps, data, services, routing, and more.

Fundamentally, this is an architecture book, with code examples to support the design-related discussions contained therein. You'll find that I often make reference to differences between the patterns I cover here and the way that we might have done things in the past. Having experience or even knowledge of the patterns of the prior era is, however, not required. Because I'm covering not only the patterns themselves, but also the motivations for them and the nuances of the context in which they're applied, you should find significant value regardless of your number of years in software.

And although many code examples appear throughout the book, this is not a programming book. It won't teach you how to program if you don't already know the basics. The code examples are in Java, but experience in any language should allow you to follow along with no trouble. Having a basic understanding of client/service interactions, especially over HTTP, is also helpful, but not essential.

## *How this book is organized: A roadmap*

This book has 12 chapters divided into two parts.

Part 1 defines the cloud-native context and presents the characteristics of the environment into which you'll deploy your software:

- Chapter 1 defines *cloud-native* and differentiates it from the cloud. It presents a mental model around which the patterns that come later can be built: the entities of that model are *apps/services, interactions* between services, and *data*.
- Chapter 2 covers cloud-native operations—the patterns and practices used to keep cloud-native software running in production through all of the inevitable disruptions that are thrust upon it.
- Chapter 3 introduces the cloud-native platform, a development and runtime environment that provides support for and even implementations of many of the patterns presented in the second part of the book. Although it's important for you to understand all the patterns that are to come, you needn't implement them all yourself.

Part 2 dives deep into the cloud-native patterns themselves:

- Chapter 4 is about cloud-native *interactions*, also touching a bit on *data*, introducing event-driven communication as an alternative to the familiar request/response style. Although the latter is all but ubiquitous in most software today, event-driven approaches often offer significant advantages to highly distributed cloud-native software, and it's important to consider both protocols as you study the patterns to follow.
- Chapter 5 is about cloud-native *apps/services* and their relationship to *data*. It covers how apps are deployed as redundant instances, often at significant scale, why and how to make them stateless, and how to bind them to a special stateful service.
- Chapter 6 is about cloud-native *apps/services*, covering how application configuration can be consistently maintained when many, many instances are deployed across a widely distributed infrastructure. It also covers how application configurations are properly applied when the environment that they're running in is constantly changing.
- Chapter 7 is about cloud-native *apps/services*, covering the application lifecycle and numerous zero-downtime upgrade practices, including rolling upgrades and blue/green upgrades.
- Chapter 8 is about cloud-native *interactions*. It focuses both on how apps can find the services they need (service discovery), even while those services are constantly moving about, and on how requests ultimately find their way to the right services (dynamic routing).
- Chapter 9 is about cloud-native *interactions*, focusing on the client side of an interaction. After explaining the need for interaction redundancy, and presenting

retries (in which requests are repeated if they initially fail), the chapter covers both problems that can result from the naïve application of retries and ways to avoid those troubles.

- Chapter 10 is about cloud-native *interactions*, focusing on the service side of an interaction. Even if clients initiating interactions are doing so responsibly, the service must still protect itself from misuse and from being overwhelmed with traffic. This chapter covers API gateways and circuit breakers.
- Chapter 11 is about both *apps* and *interactions*, covering a means for observing the behaviors and performance of the distributed system that makes up your software.
- Chapter 12 is about *data*, and has substantial implications on the *interactions* between the services that make up your cloud-native software. It covers patterns for breaking up what was once a monolithic database into a distributed data fabric, ultimately circling back to the event-driven patterns covered at the beginning of this second part of the book.

## About the code

This book contains many examples of source code, both in numbered listings and in line with normal text. In both cases, source code is formatted in a `fixed-width font like this` to separate it from ordinary text. Sometimes code is also **in bold** to highlight portions to draw your attention to.

In many cases, the original source code has been reformatted; we've added line breaks and reworked indentation to accommodate the available page space in the book. In rare cases, even this was not enough, and listings include line-continuation markers (➡). Additionally, comments in the source code have often been removed from the listings when the code is described in the text. Code annotations accompany many of the listings, highlighting important concepts.

The code for the examples in this book is available for download from the Manning website at https://www.manning.com/books/cloud-native-patterns and from GitHub at https://github.com/cdavisafc/cloudnative-abundantsunshine.

## liveBook discussion forum

Purchase of *Cloud-Native Patterns* includes free access to a private web forum run by Manning Publications, where you can make comments about the book, ask technical questions, and receive help from the author and from other users. To access the forum, go to https://livebook.manning.com/#!/book/cloud-native-patterns. You can also learn more about Manning's forums and the rules of conduct at https://livebook .manning.com/#!/discussion.

Manning's commitment to our readers is to provide a venue where a meaningful dialogue between individual readers and between readers and the author can take place. It is not a commitment to any specific amount of participation on the part of the author, whose contribution to the forum remains voluntary (and unpaid). We suggest you try asking the author some challenging questions lest her interest stray! The forum and the archives of previous discussions will be accessible from the publisher's website as long as the book is in print.

## Other online resources

You can find Cornelia online through Twitter (@cdavisafc), Medium (https://medium.com/@cdavisafc), or her blog at http://corneliadavis.com.

# *about the author*

Cornelia Davis is vice president of technology at Pivotal, where she works on the technology strategy for both Pivotal and Pivotal customers. Currently she is working on ways to bring the various cloud-computing models of Infrastructure as a Service, Application as a Service, Container as a Service, and Function as a Service together into a comprehensive offering that allows IT organizations to function at the highest levels.

An industry veteran with almost three decades of experience in image processing, scientific visualization, distributed systems and web application architectures, and cloud-native platforms, Cornelia has a BS and MS in computer science from California State University, Northridge, and further studied theory of computing and programming languages at Indiana University.

A teacher at heart, Cornelia has spent the last 30 years making better software and better software developers.

When not doing these things, you can find her on the yoga mat or in the kitchen.

# *about the cover illustration*

The figure on the cover of *Cloud-Native Patterns* is captioned "Habit of a Russian Midwife in 1764." The illustration is taken from Thomas Jefferys' *A Collection of the Dresses of Different Nations, Ancient and Modern* (four volumes), London, published between 1757 and 1772. The title page states that these are hand-colored copperplate engravings, heightened with gum arabic.

Thomas Jefferys (1719–1771) was called "Geographer to King George III." He was an English cartographer who was the leading map supplier of his day. He engraved and printed maps for government and other official bodies and produced a wide range of commercial maps and atlases, especially of North America. His work as a map maker sparked an interest in local dress customs of the lands he surveyed and mapped, which are brilliantly displayed in this collection. Fascination with faraway lands and travel for pleasure were relatively new phenomena in the late 18th century, and collections such as this one were popular, introducing both the tourist as well as the armchair traveler to the inhabitants of other countries.

The diversity of the drawings in Jefferys' volumes speaks vividly of the uniqueness and individuality of the world's nations some 200 years ago. Dress codes have changed since then, and the diversity by region and country, so rich at the time, has faded away. It's now often hard to tell the inhabitants of one continent from another. Perhaps, trying to view it optimistically, we've traded a cultural and visual diversity for a more varied personal life—or a more varied and interesting intellectual and technical life.

At a time when it's difficult to tell one computer book from another, Manning celebrates the inventiveness and initiative of the computer business with book covers based on the rich diversity of regional life of two centuries ago, brought back to life by Jefferys' pictures.

# *The cloud-native context*

Although it may sound cliché, this first part of the book really sets the stage. I suppose I could have jumped right into the patterns that I'm sure you're eager to learn about (service discovery, circuit breakers, and more), but I want you to understand these patterns at such a deep level that these first chapters are essential. Understanding the context in which your apps will run, the infrastructure as well as the more human elements, will allow you to apply the patterns in the most effective way. Your customers' expectations of your digital offerings (constant evolution and zero downtime) and the way you and your colleagues deliver those offerings (empowered teams and no tickets) have relationships to the design patterns that you might not expect.

One of the main things I do in the first chapter is define *cloud-native*, differentiating it from *cloud* (spoiler alert: the latter is about *where*, whereas the former is about *how* and is the really interesting part). I also establish a mental model around which part 2 of the book is organized.

The second chapter is all about operating cloud-native apps. I can hear some of you thinking "I'm dev—I don't need to worry about that," but please suspend your disbelief for a moment. The operational practices that deliver on some of your customers' demands immediately translate to requirements on your software.

And finally, in the third chapter, I cover platforms that serve both development and production needs. Many of the patterns I cover in the second part of the book, although absolutely essential for generating top-quality software, needn't be entirely implemented by you; the right platform can provide you a great deal of assistance.

So, if you're tempted to skip these chapters, please don't. I promise that your investment here will pay dividends later.

# *You keep using that word: Defining "cloud-native"*

*It's not Amazon's fault.* On Sunday, September 20, 2015, Amazon Web Services (AWS) experienced a significant outage. With an increasing number of companies running mission-critical workloads on AWS—even their core customer-facing services—an AWS outage can result in far-reaching subsequent system outages. In this instance, Netflix, Airbnb, Nest, IMDb, and more all experienced downtime, impacting their customers and ultimately their business's bottom lines. The core outage lasted about five hours (or more, depending on how you count), resulting in even longer outages for the affected AWS customers before their systems recovered from the failure.

If you're Nest, you're paying AWS because you want to focus on creating value for your customers, not on infrastructure concerns. As part of the deal, AWS is responsible for keeping its systems up, and enabling you to keep yours functioning as well. If AWS experiences downtime, it'd be easy to blame Amazon for your resulting outage.

But you'd be wrong. Amazon isn't to blame for your outage.

Wait! Don't toss this book to the side. Please hear me out. My assertion gets right to the heart of the matter and explains the goals of this book.

First, let me clear up one thing. I'm not suggesting that Amazon and other cloud providers have no responsibility for keeping their systems functioning well; they obviously do. And if a provider doesn't meet certain service levels, its customers can and will find alternatives. Service providers generally provide service-level

3

agreements (SLAs). Amazon, for example, provides a 99.95% uptime guarantee for most of its services.

What I'm asserting is that the applications you're running on a particular infrastructure can be more stable than the infrastructure itself. How's that possible? That, my friends, is exactly what this book will teach you.

Let's, for a moment, turn back to the AWS outage of September 20. Netflix, one of the many companies affected by the outage, is the top internet site in the United States, when measured by the amount of internet bandwidth consumed (36%). But even though a Netflix outage affects a lot of people, the company had this to say about the AWS event:

> *Netflix did experience a brief availability blip in the affected Region, but we sidestepped any significant impact because Chaos Kong exercises prepare us for incidents like this. By running experiments on a regular basis that simulate a Regional outage, we were able to identify any systemic weaknesses early and fix them. When US-EAST-1 became unavailable, our system was already strong enough to handle a traffic failover.*[1]

Netflix was able to quickly recover from the AWS outage, being fully functional only minutes after the incident began. Netflix, still running on AWS, was fully functional even while the AWS outage continued.

**NOTE**  How was Netflix able to recover so quickly? Redundancy.

No single piece of hardware can be guaranteed to be up 100% of the time, and, as has been the practice for some time, we put redundant systems are in place. AWS does exactly this and makes those redundancy abstractions available to its users.

In particular, AWS offers services in numerous regions; for example, at the time of writing, its Elastic Compute Cloud platform (EC2) is running and available in Ireland, Frankfurt, London, Paris, Stockholm, Tokyo, Seoul, Singapore, Mumbai, Sydney, Beijing, Ningxia, Sao Paulo, Canada, and in four locations in the United States (Virginia, California, Oregon, and Ohio). And within each region, the service is further partitioned into numerous availability zones (AZs) that are configured to isolate the resources of one AZ from another. This isolation limits the effects of a failure in one AZ rippling through to services in another AZ.

Figure 1.1 depicts three regions, each of which contains four availability zones. Applications run within availability zones and—here's the important part—may run in more than one AZ and in more than one region. Recall that a moment ago I made the assertion that redundancy is one of the keys to uptime.

In figure 1.2, let's place logos within this diagram to hypothetically represent running applications. (I have no explicit knowledge of how Netflix, IMDb, or Nest have deployed their applications; this is purely hypothetical, but illustrative nevertheless.)

---

[1] See "Chaos Engineering Upgraded" at the Netflix Technology blog (http://mng.bz/P8rn) for more information on Chaos Kong.

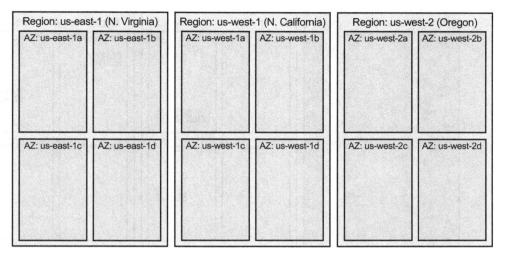

**Figure 1.1  AWS partitions the services it offers into regions and availability zones. Regions map to geographic areas, and AZs provide further redundancy and isolation within a single region.**

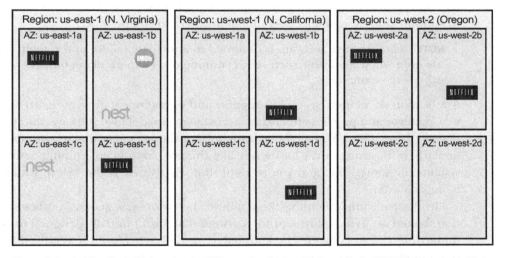

**Figure 1.2  Applications deployed onto AWS may be deployed into a single AZ (IMDb), or in multiple AZs (Nest) but only a single region, or in multiple AZs and multiple regions (Netflix). This provides different resiliency profiles.**

Figure 1.3 depicts a single-region outage, like the AWS outage of September 2015. In that instance, only us-east-1 went dark.

In this simple graphic, you can immediately see how Netflix might have weathered the outage far better than others companies; it already had its applications running in other AWS regions and was able to easily direct all traffic over to the healthy instances. And though it appears that the failover to the other regions wasn't automatic, Netflix

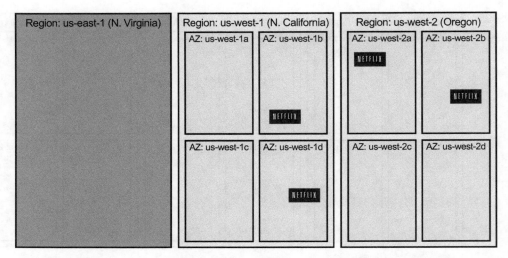

**Figure 1.3   If applications are properly architected and deployed, digital solutions can survive even a broad outage, such as of an entire region.**

had anticipated (even practiced!) a possible outage such as this and had architected its software and designed its operational practices to compensate.[2]

> **NOTE**   Cloud-native software is designed to anticipate failure and remain stable even when the infrastructure it's running on is experiencing outages or is otherwise changing.

Application developers, as well as support and operations staff, must learn and apply new patterns and practices to create and manage cloud-native software, and this book teaches those things. You might be thinking that this isn't new, that organizations, particularly in mission-critical businesses like finance, have been running active/active systems for some time, and you're right. But what's new is the way in which this is being achieved.

In the past, implementing these failover behaviors was generally a bespoke solution, bolted on to a deployment for a system that wasn't initially designed to adapt to underlying system failures. The knowledge needed to achieve the required SLAs was often limited to a few "rock stars," and extraordinary design, configuration, and testing mechanisms were put in place in an attempt to have systems that reacted appropriately to that failure.

The difference between this and what Netflix does today starts with a fundamental difference in philosophy. With the former approaches, change or failure is treated as an exception. By contrast, Netflix and many other large-scale internet-native companies, such as Google, Twitter, Facebook, and Uber, *treat change or failure as the rule.*

---

[2]See "AWS Outage: How Netflix Weathered the Storm by Preparing for the Worst" by Nick Heath (http://mng.bz/J8RV) for more details on the company's recovery.

These organizations have altered their software architectures and their engineering practices to make designing for failure an integral part of the way they build, deliver, and manage software.

> **NOTE** Failure is the rule, not the exception.

## 1.1 Today's application requirements

Digital experiences are no longer a sidecar to our lives. They play a major part in many or most of the activities that we engage in on a daily basis. This ubiquity has pushed the boundaries of what we expect from the software we use: we want applications to be always available, be perpetually upgraded with new whizbang features, and provide personalized experiences. Fulfilling these expectations is something that must be addressed right from the beginning of the idea-to-production lifecycle. You, the developer, are one of the parties responsible for meeting those needs. Let's have a look at some key requirements.

### 1.1.1 Zero downtime

The AWS outage of September 20, 2015, demonstrates one of the key requirements of the modern application: it must always be available. Gone are the days when even short maintenance windows during which applications are unavailable are tolerated. The world is always online. And although unplanned downtime has never been desirable, its impact has reached astounding levels. For example, in 2013 *Forbes* estimated that Amazon lost almost $2 million during a 13-minute unplanned outage.[3] Downtime, planned or not, results in significant revenue loss and customer dissatisfaction.

But maintaining uptime isn't a problem only for the operations team. Software developers or architects are responsible for creating a system design with loosely coupled components that can be deployed to allow redundancy to compensate for inevitable failures, and with air gaps that keep those failures from cascading through the entire system. They must also design the software to allow planned events, such as upgrades, to be done with no downtime.

### 1.1.2 Shortened feedback cycles

Also of critical importance is the ability to release code frequently. Driven by significant competition and ever-increasing consumer expectations, application updates are being made available to customers several times a month, numerous times a week, or in some cases even several times a day. Exciting customers is unquestionably valuable, but perhaps the biggest driver for these continuous releases is the reduction of risk.

From the moment that you have an idea for a feature, you're taking on some level of risk. Is the idea a good one? Will customers be able to use it? Can it be implemented in a better-performing way? As much as you try to predict the possible outcomes, reality

---

[3] See "Amazon.com Goes Down, Loses $66,240 Per Minute" by Kelly Clay at the Forbes website for more details (http://mng.bz/wEgP).

is often different from what you can anticipate. The best way to get answers to important questions such as these is to release an early version of a feature and get feedback. Using that feedback, you can then make adjustments or even change course entirely. Frequent software releases shorten feedback loops and reduce risk.

The monolithic software systems that have dominated the last several decades can't be released often enough. Too many closely interrelated subsystems, built and tested by independent teams, needed to be tested as a whole before an often-fragile packaging process could be applied. If a defect was found late in the integration-testing phase, the long and laborious process would begin anew. New software architectures are essential to achieving the required agility in releasing software to production.

### 1.1.3   Mobile and multidevice support

In April 2015, Comscore, a leading technology-trend measurement and analytics company, released a report indicating that for the first time, internet usage via mobile devices eclipsed that of desktop computers.[4] Today's applications need to support at least two mobile device platforms, iOS and Android, as well as the desktop (which still claims a significant portion of the usage).

In addition, users increasingly expect their experience with an application to seamlessly move from one device to another as they navigate through the day. For example, users may be watching a movie on an Apple TV and then transition to viewing the program on a mobile device when they're on the train to the airport. Furthermore, the usage patterns on a mobile device are significantly different from those of a desktop. Banks, for example, must be able to satisfy frequently repeated application refreshes from mobile device users who are awaiting their weekly payday deposit.

Designing applications the right way is essential to meeting these needs. Core services must be implemented in a manner that they can back all of the frontend devices serving users, and the system must adapt to expanding and contracting demands.

### 1.1.4   Connected devices—also known as the Internet of Things

The internet is no longer only for connecting humans to systems that are housed in and served from data centers. Today, billions of devices are connected to the internet, allowing them to be monitored and even controlled by other connected entities. The home-automation market alone, which represents a tiny portion of the connected devices that make up the Internet of Things (IoT), is estimated to be a $53 billion market by 2022.[5]

The connected home has sensors and remotely controlled devices such as motion detectors, cameras, smart thermostats, and even lighting systems. And this is all extremely affordable; after a burst pipe during a −26-degree (Fahrenheit) weather

---

[4]See Kate Dreyer's April 13, 2015 blog at the Comscore site (http://mng.bz/7eKv) for a summary of the report.
[5]You can read more about these findings by Zion Market Research at the GlobeNewswire site (http://mng.bz/mm6a).

spell a few years ago, I started with a modest system including an internet-connected thermostat and some temperature sensors, and spent less than $300. Other connected devices include automobiles, home appliances, farming equipment, jet engines, and the supercomputer most of us carry around in our pockets (the smartphone).

Internet-connected devices change the nature of the software we build in two fundamental ways. First, the volume of data flowing over the internet is dramatically increased. Billions of devices broadcast data many times a minute, or even many times a second.[6] Second, in order to capture and process these massive quantities of data, the computing substrate must be significantly different from those of the past. It becomes more highly distributed with computing resources placed at the "edge," closer to where the connected device lies. This difference in data volume and infrastructure architecture necessitates new software designs and practices.

### 1.1.5   *Data-driven*

Considering several of the requirements that I've presented up to this point drives you to think about data in a more holistic way. Volumes of data are increasing, sources are becoming more widely distributed, and software delivery cycles are being shortened. In combination, these three factors render the large, centralized, shared database unusable.

A jet engine with hundreds of sensors, for example, is often disconnected from data centers housing such databases, and bandwidth limitations won't allow all the data to be transmitted to the data center during the short windows when connectivity is established. Furthermore, shared databases require a great deal of process and coordination across a multitude of applications to rationalize the various data models and interaction scenarios; this is a major impediment to shortened release cycles.

Instead of the single, shared database, these application requirements call for a network of smaller, localized databases, and software that manages data relationships across that federation of data management systems. These new approaches drive the need for software development and management agility all the way through to the data tier.

Finally, all of the newly available data is of little value if it goes unused. Today's applications must increasingly use data to provide greater value to the customer through smarter applications. For example, mapping applications use GPS data from connected cars and mobile devices, along with roadway and terrain data to provide real-time traffic reports and routing guidance. The applications of the past decades that implemented painstakingly designed algorithms carefully tuned for anticipated usage scenarios are being replaced with applications that are constantly being revised or may even be self-adjusting their internal algorithms and configurations.

---

[6]Gartner forecasts that 8.4 billion connected things will be in use worldwide in 2017; see the Gartner report at www.gartner.com/newsroom/id/3598917.

These *user* requirements—constant availability, constant evolution with frequent releases, easily scalable, and intelligent—can't be met with the software design and management systems of the past. But what characterizes the software that can meet these requirements?

## 1.2    Introducing cloud-native software

Your software needs to be up, 24/7. You need to be able to release frequently to give your users the instant gratification they seek. The mobility and always-connected state of your users drives a need for your software to be responsive to larger and more fluctuating request volumes than ever before. And connected devices ("things") form a distributed data fabric of unprecedented size that requires new storage and processing approaches. These needs, along with the availability of new platforms on which you can run the software, have led directly to the emergence of a new architectural style for software: cloud-native software.

### 1.2.1    Defining "cloud-native"

What characterizes *cloud-native software*? Let's analyze the preceding requirements a bit further and see where they lead. Figure 1.4 takes the first few steps, listing requirements across the top and showing causal relationships going downward. The following list explains the details:

- Software that's always up must be resilient to infrastructure failures and changes, whether planned or unplanned. As the context within which it runs experiences those inevitable changes, software must be able to adapt. When properly constructed, deployed, and managed, composition of independent pieces can limit the blast radius of any failures that do occur; this drives you to a modular design. And because you know that no single entity can be guaranteed to never fail, you include redundancy throughout the design.

- Your goal is to release frequently, and monolithic software doesn't allow this; too many interdependent pieces require time-consuming and complex coordination. In recent years, it's been soundly proven that software made up of smaller, more loosely coupled and independently deployable and releasable components (often called *microservices*) enables a more agile release model.

- No longer are users limited to accessing digital solutions when they sit in front of their computers. They demand access from the mobile devices they carry with them 24/7. And nonhuman entities, such as sensors and device controllers, are similarly always connected. Both of these scenarios result in a tidal wave of request and data volumes that can fluctuate wildly, and therefore require software that scales dynamically and continues to function adequately.

Some of these attributes have architectural implications: the resultant software is composed of redundantly deployed, independent components. Other attributes address the management practices used to deliver the digital solutions: a deployment must

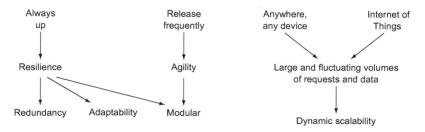

**Figure 1.4   User requirements for software drive development toward cloud-native architectural and management tenets.**

adapt to a changing infrastructure and to fluctuating request volumes. Taking that collection of attributes as a whole, let's carry this analysis to its conclusion; this is depicted in figure 1.5:

- Software that's constructed as a set of independent components, redundantly deployed, implies distribution. If your redundant copies were all deployed close to one another, you'd be at greater risk of local failures having far-reaching consequences. To make efficient use of the infrastructure resources you have, when you deploy additional instances of an app to serve increasing request volumes, you must be able to place them across a wide swath of your available infrastructure—even, perhaps, that from cloud services such as AWS, Google Cloud Platform (GCP), and Microsoft Azure. As a result, you deploy your software modules in a highly distributed manner.

- Adaptable software is by definition "able to adjust to new conditions," and the conditions I refer to here are those of the infrastructure and the set of interrelated software modules. They're intrinsically tied together: as the infrastructure changes, the software changes, and vice versa. Frequent releases mean frequent change, and adapting to fluctuating request volumes through scaling operations represents a constant adjustment. It's clear that your software and the environment it runs in are constantly changing.

   **DEFINITION**   Cloud-native software is highly distributed, must operate in a constantly changing environment, and is itself constantly changing.

Many more granular details go into the making of cloud-native software (the specifics fill the pages of this volume). But, ultimately, they all come back to these core characteristics: highly distributed and constantly changing. This will be your mantra as you progress through the material, and I'll repeatedly draw you back to extreme distribution and constant change.

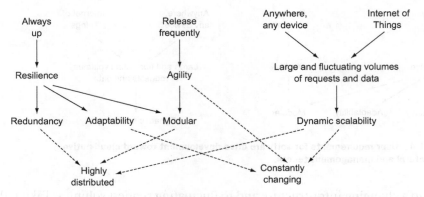

**Figure 1.5   Architectural and management tenets lead to the core characteristics of cloud-native software: it's highly distributed and must operate in a constantly changing environment even as the software is constantly evolving.**

### 1.2.2  A mental model for cloud-native software

Adrian Cockcroft, who was chief architect at Netflix and is now VP of Cloud Architecture Strategy at AWS, talks about the complexity of operating a car: as a driver, you must control the car and navigate streets, all while making sure not to come into contact with other drivers performing the same complex tasks.[7] You're able to do this only because you've formed a model that allows you to understand the world and control your instrument (in this case, a car) in an ever-changing environment.

Most of us use our feet to control the speed and our hands to set direction, collectively determining our velocity. In an attempt to improve navigation, city planners put thought into street layouts (God help us all in Paris). And tools such as signs and signals, coupled with traffic rules, give you a framework in which you can reason about the journey you're taking from start to finish.

Writing cloud-native software is also complex. In this section, I present a model to help bring order to the myriad of concerns in writing cloud-native software. My hope is that this framework facilitates your understanding of the key concepts and techniques that will make you a proficient designer and developer of cloud-native software.

I'll start simple, with core elements of cloud-native software that are surely familiar to you, shown in figure 1.6.

An *app* implements key business logic. This is where you'll be writing the bulk of the code. This is where, for example, your code will take a customer order, verify that items are available in a warehouse's inventory, and send a notification to the billing department.

The app, of course, depends on other components that it calls to either obtain information or take an action; I call these *services*. Some of the services store *state*—the warehouse inventory, for example. Others may be apps that implement the business logic for another part of your system—customer billing, for example.

---

[7] Hear Adrian talk about this and other examples of complicated things at http://mng.bz/5NzO.

Introducing cloud-native software

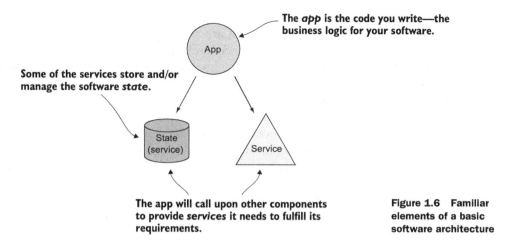

The *app* is the code you write—the business logic for your software.

Some of the services store and/or manage the software *state*.

The app will call upon other components to provide *services* it needs to fulfill its requirements.

**Figure 1.6  Familiar elements of a basic software architecture**

Taking these simple concepts, let's now build up a topology that represents the cloud-native software you'll build; see figure 1.7. You have a distributed set of modules, most of which have multiple instances deployed. You can see that most of the apps are also acting as services, and further, that some services are explicitly stateful. Arrows depict where one component depends on another.

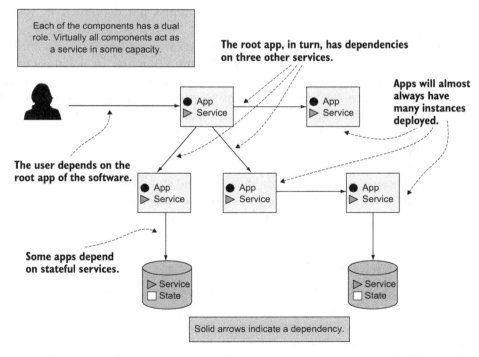

Each of the components has a dual role. Virtually all components act as a service in some capacity.

The root app, in turn, has dependencies on three other services.

Apps will almost always have many instances deployed.

The user depends on the root app of the software.

Some apps depend on stateful services.

Solid arrows indicate a dependency.

**Figure 1.7  Cloud-native software takes familiar concepts and adds extreme distribution, with redundancy everywhere, and constant change.**

This diagram illustrates a few interesting points. First, notice that the pieces (the boxes and the database, or storage, icons) are always annotated with two designations: apps and services for the boxes, and services and state for the storage icons. I've come to think of the simple concepts shown in figure 1.7 as roles that various components in your software solution take on.

You'll note that any entity that has an arrow going to it, indicating that the component is depended upon by another, is a service. That's right—almost everything is a service. Even the app that's the root of the topology has an arrow to it from the software consumer. Apps, of course, are where you're writing your code. And I particularly like the combination of *service* and *state* annotations, making clear that you have some services that are devoid of state (the stateless services you've surely heard about, annotated here with "app"), whereas others are all about managing state.

And this brings me to defining the three parts of cloud-native software, depicted in figure 1.8:

- *The cloud-native app*—Again, this is where you'll write code; it's the business logic for your software. Implementing the right patterns here allows those apps to act as good citizens in the composition that makes up your software; a single app is rarely a complete digital solution. An app is at one or the other end of an arrow (or both) and therefore must implement certain behaviors to make it participate in that relationship. It must also be constructed in a manner that allows for cloud-native operational practices such as scaling and upgrades to be performed.

- *Cloud-native data*—This is where state lives in your cloud-native software. Even this simple picture shows a marked deviation from the architectures of the past, which often used a centralized database to store state for a large portion of the software. For example, you might have stored user profiles, account details, reviews, order history, payment information, and more, all in the same database. Cloud-native software breaks the code into many smaller modules (the apps), and the database is similarly decomposed and distributed.

- *Cloud-native interactions*—Cloud-native software is then a composition of cloud-native apps and cloud-native data, and the way those entities interact with one another ultimately determines the functioning and the qualities of the digital solution. Because of the extreme distribution and constant change that characterizes our systems, these interactions have in many cases significantly evolved from those of previous software architectures, and some interaction patterns are entirely new.

Notice that although at the start I talked about services, in the end they aren't one of the three entities in this mental model. In large part, this is because pretty much everything is a service, both apps and data. But more so, I suggest that the interactions between services are even more interesting than a service alone. Services pervade through the entire cloud-native software model.

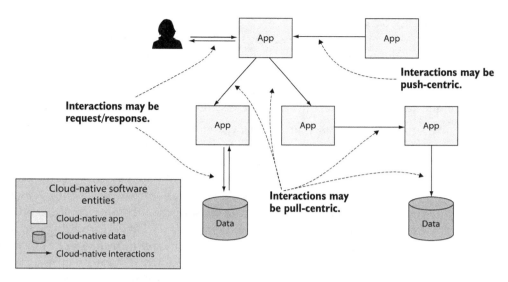

**Figure 1.8  Key entities in the model for cloud-native software: apps, data, and interactions**

With this model established, let's come back to the modern software requirements covered in section 1.1 and consider their implications on the apps, data, and interactions of your cloud-native software.

### CLOUD-NATIVE APPS

Concerns about cloud-native apps include the following:

- Their capacity is scaled up or down by adding or removing instances. We refer to this as *scale-out/in*, and it's far different from the scale-up models used in prior architectures. When deployed correctly, having multiple instances of an app also offers levels of resilience in an unstable environment.
- As soon as you have multiple instances of an app, and even when only a single instance is being disrupted in some way, keeping state out of the apps allows you to perform recovery actions most easily. You can simply create a new instance of an app and connect it back to any stateful services it depends on.
- Configuration of the cloud-native app poses unique challenges when many instances are deployed and the environments in which they're running are constantly changing. If you have 100 instances of an app, for example, gone are the days when you could drop a new config into a known filesystem location and restart the app. Add to that the fact that these instances could be moving all over your distributed topology. And applying such old-school practices to the instances as they are moving all over your distributed topology would be sheer madness.
- The dynamic nature of cloud-based environments necessitates changes to the way you manage the application lifecycle (not the software *delivery* lifecycle, but rather the startup and shutdown of the actual app). You must reexamine how you start, configure, reconfigure, and shut down apps in this new context.

## CLOUD-NATIVE DATA

Okay, so your apps are stateless. But handling state is an equally important part of a software solution, and the need to solve your data-handling problems also exists in an environment of extreme distribution and constant change. Because you have data that needs to persist through these fluctuations, handling data in a cloud setting poses unique challenges. The concerns for cloud-native data include the following:

- You need to break apart the data monolith. In the last several decades, organizations invested a great deal of time, energy, and technology into managing large, consolidated data models. The reasoning was that concepts that were relevant in many domains, and hence implemented in many software systems, were best treated centrally as a single entity. For example, in a hospital, the concept of a patient was relevant in many settings, including clinical/care, billing, experience surveys, and more, and developers would create a single model, and often a single database, for handling patient information. This approach doesn't work in the context of modern software; it's slow to evolve and brittle, and ultimately robs the seemingly loosely coupled app fabric of its agility and robustness. You need to create a distributed data fabric, as you created a distributed app fabric.
- The distributed data fabric is made up of independent, fit-for-purpose databases (supporting polyglot persistence), as well as some that may be acting only as materialized views of data, where the source of truth lies elsewhere. Caching is a key pattern and technology in cloud-native software.
- When you have entities that exist in multiple databases, such as the "patient" I mentioned previously, you have to address how to keep the information that's common across the different instances in sync.
- Ultimately, treating state as an outcome of a series of events forms the core of the distributed data fabric. Event-sourcing patterns capture state-change events, and the unified log collects these state-change events and makes them available to members of this data distribution.

## CLOUD-NATIVE INTERACTIONS

And finally, when you draw all the pieces together, a new set of concerns surface for the cloud-native interactions:

- Accessing an app when it has multiple instances requires some type of routing system. Synchronous request/response, as well as asynchronous event-driven patterns, must be addressed.
- In a highly distributed, constantly changing environment, you must account for access attempts that fail. Automatic retries are an essential pattern in cloud-native software, yet their use can wreak havoc on a system if not governed properly. Circuit breakers are essential when automated retries are in place.
- Because cloud-native software is a composite, a single user request is served through invocation of a multitude of related services. Properly managing

cloud-native software to ensure a good user experience is a task of managing a composition—each of the services and the interactions between them. Application metrics and logging, things we've been producing for decades, must be specialized for this new setting.

- One of the greatest advantages of a modular system is the ability to more easily evolve parts of it independently. But because those independent pieces ultimately come together into a greater whole, the protocols underlying the interactions among them must be suitable for the cloud-native context; for example, a routing system that supports parallel deploys.

This book covers new and evolved patterns and practices to address these needs.

Let's make all of this a bit more concrete by looking at a specific example. This will give you a better sense of the concerns I'm only briefly mentioning here, and will give you a good idea of where I'm headed with the content of this text.

### 1.2.3 *Cloud-native software in action*

Let's start with a familiar scenario. You have an account with Wizard's Bank. Part of the time you engage with the bank by visiting the local branch (if you're a millennial, just pretend with me for a moment ;-)). You're also a registered user of the bank's online banking application. After receiving only unsolicited calls on your home landline (again, pretend ;-)) for the better part of the last year or two, you've finally decided to disconnect it. As a result, you need to update your phone number with your bank (and many other institutions).

The online banking application allows you to edit your user profile, which includes your primary and any backup phone numbers. After logging into the site, you navigate to the Profile page, enter your new phone number, and click the Submit button. You receive confirmation that your update has been saved, and your user experience ends there.

Let's see what this could look like if that online banking application were architected in a cloud-native manner. Figure 1.9 depicts these key elements:

- Because you aren't yet logged in, when you access the *User Profile* app, **①** it will redirect you to the *Authentication* app. **②** Notice that each of these apps has multiple instances deployed and that the user requests are sent to one of the instances by a router.
- As a part of logging in, the Auth app will create and store a new *auth token* in a stateful service. **③**
- The user is then redirected back to the User Profile app, with the new auth token. This time, the router will send the user request to a different instance of the User Profile app. **④** (Spoiler alert: sticky sessions are bad in cloud-native software!)
- The User Profile app will validate the auth token by making a call to an *Auth API service*. **⑤** Again, there are multiple instances, and the request is sent to one of them by the router. Recall that valid tokens are stored in the stateful Auth Token service, which is accessible from not only the Auth app, but also any instances of the Auth API service.

- Because the instances of any of these apps (the User Profile or Auth apps) can change for any number of reasons, a protocol must exist for continuously updating the router with new IP addresses.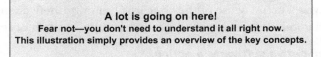
- The User Profile app then makes a downstream request to the *User API service* ❻ to obtain the current user's profile data, including phone number. The User Profile app, in turn, makes a request to the user's stateful service.
- After the user has updated their phone number and clicked the Submit button, the User Profile app sends the new data to an *event log* ❼.
- Eventually, one of the instances of the User API service will pick up and process this change event ❽ and send a write request to the Users database.

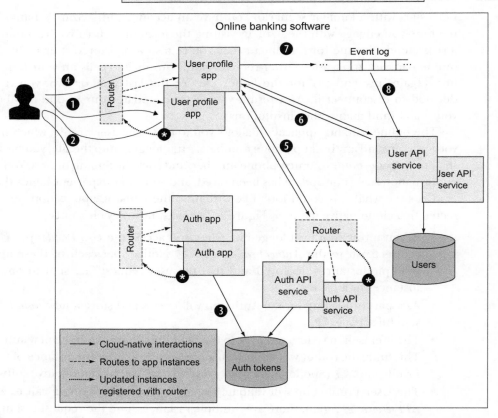

**Figure 1.9    The online banking software is a composition of apps and data services. Many types of interaction protocols are in play.**

Yes, this is already a lot, but I want to add even more.

I haven't explicitly stated it, but when you're back at the bank branch and the teller verifies your current contact information, you'll expect the teller to have your updated phone number. But the online banking software and the teller's software are two different systems. This is by design; it serves agility, resilience, and many of the other requirements that I've identified as important for modern digital systems. Figure 1.10 shows this product suite.

The structure of the bank teller software isn't markedly different from that of the online banking software; it's a composition of cloud-native apps and data. But, as you can imagine, each digital solution deals with and even stores user data, or shall I say, *customer* data. In cloud-native software, you lean toward loose coupling, even when you're dealing with data. This is reflected with the Users stateful service in the online banking software and the Customers stateful service in the bank teller's software.

The question, then, is how to reconcile common data values across these disparate stores. How will your new phone number be reflected in the bank teller software?

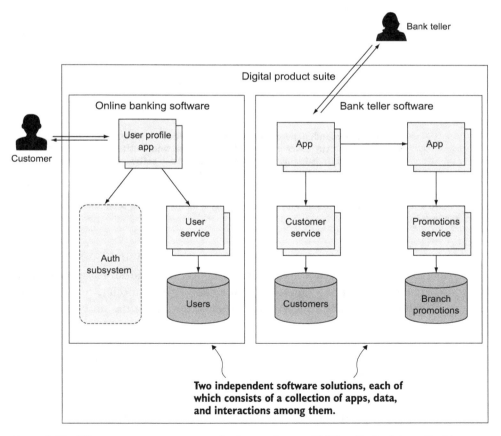

**Figure 1.10   What appears to a user as a single experience with Wizard's Bank is realized by independently developed and managed software assets.**

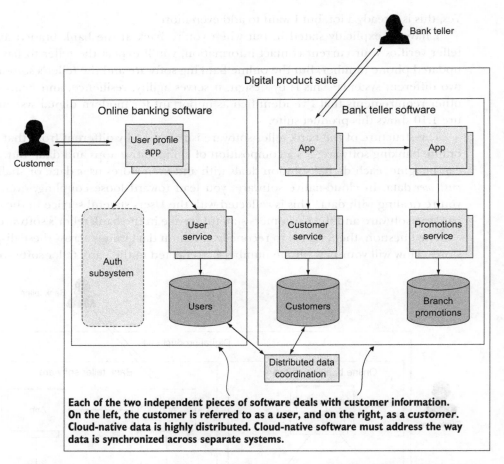

Figure 1.11   A decomposed and loosely coupled data fabric requires techniques for cohesive data management.

In figure 1.11, I've added one more concept to our model—something I've labeled "Distributed data coordination." The depiction here doesn't imply any implementation specifics. I'm not suggesting a normalized data model, hub-and-spoke master data management techniques, or any other solution. For the time being, please accept this as a problem statement; I promise we'll study solutions soon.

That's a lot! Figures 1.9, 1.10, and 1.11 are busy, and I don't expect you to understand in any great detail all that's going on. What I do hope you take from this comes back to the key theme for cloud-native software:

- The software solution comprises quite a distribution of a great many components.
- Protocols exist to specifically deal with the change that's inflicted upon the system.

We'll get into all the details, and more, throughout the following chapters.

## 1.3 Cloud-native and world peace

I've been practicing in this industry long enough that I've seen several technological evolutions promise to solve *all* problems. When object-oriented programming emerged in the late 1980s, for example, some people acted as if this style of software would essentially write itself. And although such bullish predictions wouldn't come to pass, many of the hyped technologies, without question, brought improvements to many elements of software—ease of construction and management, robustness, and more.

Cloud-native software architectures, often referred to as microservices,[8] are all the rage today—but spoiler alert, they also won't lead to world peace. And even if they did come to dominate (and I believe they will), they don't apply to everything. Let's look at this in more detail in a moment, but first, let's talk about that word, *cloud*.

### 1.3.1 Cloud and cloud-native

The narrative around the term *cloud* can be confusing. When I hear a company owner say, "We're moving to the cloud," they often mean they're moving some or maybe even all of their apps into someone else's data center—such as AWS, Azure, or GCP. These clouds offer the same set of primitives that are available in the on-premises data center (machines, storage, and network), so such a "move to the cloud" could be done with little change to the software and practices currently being used on premises.

But this approach won't bring much improved software resilience, better management practices, or more agility to the software delivery processes. In fact, because the SLAs for the cloud services are almost always different from those offered in on-prem data centers, degradation is likely in many respects. In short, moving to the cloud doesn't mean your software is cloud-native or will demonstrate the values of cloud-native software.

As I reasoned through earlier in the chapter, new expectations from consumers and new computing contexts—the very ones of the cloud—force a change in the way software is constructed. When you embrace the new architectural patterns and operational practices, you produce digital solutions that work well in the cloud. You might say that this software feels quite at home in the cloud. It's a native of that land.

> **NOTE** *Cloud* is about *where* we're computing. *Cloud-native* is about *how*.

If cloud-native is about how, does that mean you can implement cloud-native solutions on premises? You bet! Most of the enterprises I work with on their cloud-native journey first do so in their own data centers. This means that their on-premise computing infrastructure needs to support cloud-native software and practices. I talk about this infrastructure in chapter 3.

As great as it is (and I hope that by the time you finish this book, you'll think so too), cloud-native isn't for everything.

---

[8]Although I use the term microservice to refer to the cloud-native architecture, I don't feel that the term encompasses the other two equally important entities of cloud-native software: data and interactions.

### 1.3.2   *What isn't cloud-native*

I'm certain it doesn't surprise you to hear that not all software should be cloud-native. As you learn the patterns, you'll see that some of the new approaches require effort that otherwise might not be necessary. If a dependent service is always at a known location that never changes, you won't need to implement a service discovery protocol. And some approaches create new problems, even as they bring significant value; debugging program flow through a bunch of distributed components can be hard. Three of the most common reasons for not going cloud-native in your software architecture are described next.

First, sometimes the software and computing infrastructure don't call for cloud-native. For example, if the software isn't distributed and is rarely changing, you can likely depend on a level of stability that you should never assume for modern web or mobile applications running at scale. For example, code that's embedded in an increasing number of physical devices such as a washing machine may not even have the computing and storage resources to support the redundancy so key to these modern architectures. My Zojirushi rice cooker's software that adjusts the cooking time and temperature based on the conditions reported by on-board sensors needn't have parts of the application running in different processes. If some part of the software or hardware fails, the worst that will happen is that I'll need to order out when my home-cooked meal is ruined.

Second, sometimes common characteristics of cloud-native software aren't appropriate for the problem at hand. You'll see, for example, that many of the new patterns give you systems that are eventually consistent; in your distributed software, data updated in one part of the system might not be immediately reflected in all parts of the system. Eventually, everything will match, but it might take a few seconds or even minutes for everything to become consistent. Sometimes this is okay; for example, it isn't a major problem if, because of a network blip, the movie recommendations you're served don't immediately reflect the latest five-star rating another user supplied. But sometimes it's not okay: a banking system can't allow a user to withdraw all funds and close their bank account in one branch office, and then allow additional withdrawals from an ATM because the two systems are momentarily disconnected. Eventual consistency is at the core of many cloud-native patterns, meaning that when strong consistency is required, those particular patterns can't be used.

And, finally, sometimes you have existing software that isn't cloud-native, and there's no immediate value in rewriting it. Most organizations that are more than a couple of decades old have parts of their IT portfolio running on a mainframe, and believe it or not, they may keep running that mainframe code for another couple of decades. But it's not just mainframe code. A lot of software is running on a myriad of existing IT infrastructures that reflect design approaches that predate the cloud. You should rewrite code only when there's business value in doing so, and even when there is, you're likely to have to prioritize such efforts, updating various offerings in your portfolio over several years.

### 1.3.3    *Cloud-native plays nice*

But it's not all or nothing. Most of you are writing software in a setting filled with existing solutions. Even if you're in the enviable position of producing a brand-new application, it will likely need to interface with one of those existing systems, and as I just pointed out, a good bit of the software already running is unlikely to be fully cloud-native. The brilliant thing about cloud-native is that it's ultimately a composition of many distinct components, and if some of those components don't embody the most modern patterns, the fully cloud-native components can still interact with them.

Applying cloud-native patterns where you can, even while other parts of your software employ older design approaches, can bring immediate value. In figure 1.12, for example, you see that we have a few application components. A bank teller accesses account information via a user interface, which then interfaces with an API that fronts a mainframe application. With this simple deployment topology, if the network between that Account API service and the mainframe application is disrupted, the customer will be unable to receive their cash.

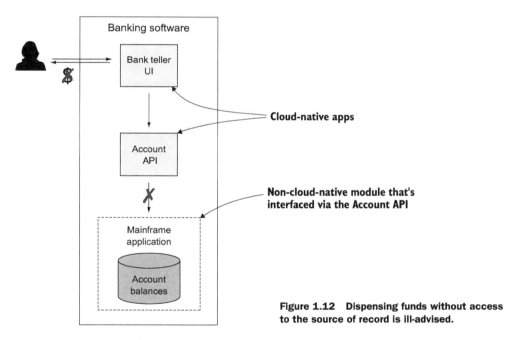

Figure 1.12    **Dispensing funds without access to the source of record is ill-advised.**

But now let's apply a few cloud-native patterns to parts of this system. For example, if you deploy many instances of each microservice across numerous availability zones, a network partition in one zone still allows access to mainframe data through service instances deployed in other zones (figure 1.13).

It's also worth noting that when you do have legacy code that you wish to refactor, it needn't be done in one fell swoop. Netflix, for example, refactored its entire

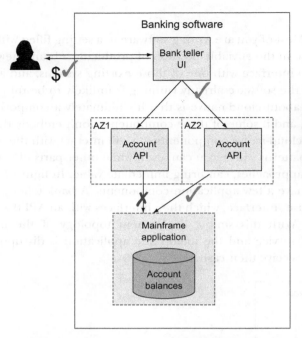

**Figure 1.13   Applying some cloud-native patterns, such as redundancy and properly distributed deployments, brings benefit even in software that isn't fully cloud-native.**

customer-facing digital solution to a cloud-native architecture as a part of its move to the cloud. Eventually. The move took seven years, but Netflix began refactoring *some* parts of its monolithic, client-server architecture in the process, with immediate benefits.[9] As with the preceding banking example, the lesson is that even during a migration, a partially cloud-native solution is valuable.

Whether you're building a net, new application that's born and bred in and for the cloud, where you apply all of the newfangled patterns, or you're extracting and making cloud-native portions of an existing monolith, you can expect to realize significant value. Although we weren't using the term *cloud-native* then, the industry began experimenting with microservices-centric architectures in the early 2010s, and many of the patterns have been refined over several years. This "new" trend is well enough understood that its embrace is becoming significantly widespread. We've seen the value that these approaches bring.

I believe that this architectural style will be the dominant one for a decade or two to come. What distinguishes it from other fads with less staying power is that it came as a result of a foundational shift in the computing substrate. The client-server models that dominated the last 20 to 30 years first emerged when the computing infrastructure moved from the mainframe to one where many smaller computers became available,

---

[9]For more details, see "Completing the Netflix Cloud Migration" by Yury Izrailevsky (http://mng.bz/6j0e).

and we wrote software to take advantage of that computing environment. Cloud-native has similarly emerged as a new computing substrate—one offering *software-defined* compute, storage, and networking abstractions that are highly distributed and constantly changing.

## Summary

- Cloud-native applications can remain stable, even when the infrastructure they're running on is constantly changing or even experiencing difficulties.
- The key requirements for modern applications call for enabling rapid iteration and frequent releases, zero downtime, and a massive increase in the volume and variety of the devices connected to it.
- A model for the cloud-native application has three key entities:
    - The cloud-native app
    - Cloud-native data
    - Cloud-native interactions
- *Cloud* is about where software runs; *cloud-native* is about how it runs.
- Cloud-nativeness isn't all or nothing. Some of the software running in your organization may follow many cloud-native architectural patterns, other software will live on with its older architecture, and still others will be hybrids (a combination of new and old approaches).

# Running cloud-native
# applications in production

---

**This chapter covers**

- Recognizing why developers should care about operations
- Understanding obstacles to successful deployments
- Eliminating those obstacles
- Implementing continuous delivery
- Impact of cloud-native architectural patterns on operations

As a developer, you want nothing more than to create software that users will love and that will provide them value. When users want more, or you have an idea for something you'd like to bring to them, you'd like to build it and deliver it with ease. And you want your software to run well in production, to always be available and responsive.

Unfortunately, for most organizations, the process of getting software deployed in production is challenging. Processes designed to reduce risk and improve efficiency have the inadvertent effect of doing exactly the opposite, because they're slow and cumbersome to use. And after the software is deployed, keeping it up and running is equally difficult. The resulting instability causes production-support personnel to be in a perpetual state of firefighting.

Even given a body of well-written, completed software, it's still difficult to

- Get that software deployed
- Keep it up and running

As a developer, you might think that this is someone else's problem. Your job is to produce that well-written piece of code; it's someone else's job to get it deployed and to support it in production. But responsibility for today's fragile production environment doesn't lie with any particular group or individual; instead, the "blame" rests with a system that has emerged from a set of organizational and operational practices that are all but ubiquitous across the industry. The way that teams are defined and assigned responsibility, the way that individual teams communicate, and even the way that software is architected all contribute to a system that, frankly, is failing the industry.

The solution is to design a new system that doesn't treat production operations as an independent entity, but rather connects software development practices and architectural patterns to the activities of deploying and managing software in production.

In designing a new system, it behooves you to first understand what is causing the greatest pains in the current one. After you've analyzed the obstacles you currently face, you can construct a new system that not only avoids the challenges, but also thrives by capitalizing on new capabilities offered in the cloud. This is a discussion that addresses the processes and practices of the entire software delivery lifecycle, from development through production. As a software developer, you play an important role in making it easier to deploy and manage software in production.

## 2.1 The obstacles

No question—handling production operations is a difficult and often thankless job. Working hours usually include late nights and weekends, either when software releases are scheduled or when unexpected outages happen. It isn't unusual for a fair bit of conflict to arise between application development groups and operations teams, with each blaming the other for failure to adequately serve consumers with superior digital experiences.

But as I said, that isn't the fault of the ops team nor of the app-dev team. The challenges come from a system that inadvertently erects a series of barriers to success. Although every challenging situation is unique, with a variety of detailed root causes playing a part, several themes are common across almost all organizations. They're shown in figure 2.1 and are summarized as follows:

- *Snowflakes*—Variability across the software development lifecycle (SDLC) contributes to trouble with initial deployments as well as to a lack of stability after the apps are running. Inconsistencies in both the software artifacts being deployed and the environments being deployed to are the problem.

- *Risky deployments*—The landscape in which software is deployed today is highly complex, with many tightly coupled, interrelated components. As such, a great risk exists that a deployment bringing a change in one part of that complex network will cause rippling effects in any number of other parts of the system. And fear of the consequences of a deployment has the downstream effect of limiting the frequency with which you can deploy.

- *Change is the exception*—Over the last several decades, we generally wrote and operated software with the expectation that the system where it ran would be stable. This philosophy was probably always suspect. But now, with IT systems being complex and highly distributed, this expectation of infrastructure stability is a complete fallacy.[1] As a result, any instability in the infrastructure propagates up into the running application, making it hard to keep running.

- *Production instability*—And finally, because deploying into an unstable environment is usually inviting more trouble, the frequency of production deployments is limited.

Let's explore each of these factors further.

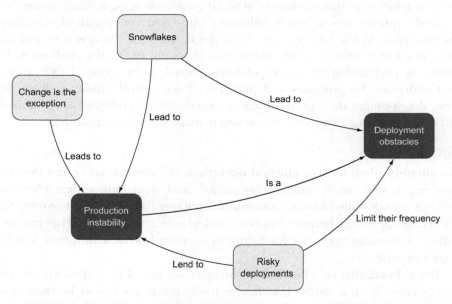

**Figure 2.1    Factors that contribute to the difficulty in deploying software and keeping it running well in production**

---

[1] Wikipedia's "Fallacies of Distributed Computing" entry (http://mng.bz/pgqw) provides more details.

### 2.1.1 *Snowflakes*

"It works on my machine" is a common refrain when the ops team is struggling to stand up an application in production and reaches out to the development team for help. I've spoken with professionals at dozens of large enterprises who've told of six-, eight-, or even ten-week delays between the time that software is ready for release and the time it's available to the user. One of the primary reasons for this delay is variability across the SDLC. This variability occurs along two lines:

- A difference in environments
- A difference in the artifacts being deployed

Without a mechanism for providing exactly the same environment from development through testing, staging, and production, it's easy for software running in one environment to inadvertently depend on something that's lacking or different in another one. One obvious example of this occurs when differences exist in the packages that the deployed software depends on. A developer might be strict about constantly updating all versions of the Spring Framework, for example, even to the point of automating installs as a part of their build scripts. The servers in the production environment are far more controlled, and updates to the Spring Framework occur quarterly and only after a thorough audit. When the new software lands on that system, tests no longer pass, and resolution likely requires going all the way back to the developer to have them use the production-approved dependencies.

But it isn't only differences in environment that slow deployments. All too often the artifact being deployed also varies through the SDLC—even when environment-specific values aren't hardcoded into the implementation (which none of us would ever do, right?). Property files often contain configurations that are directly compiled into the deployable artifact. For example, the JAR file for your Java application includes an application.properties file and, if certain configuration settings are made directly in that file—ones that vary across dev, test, and prod—the JAR files must be different for dev, test, and prod too. In theory, the only differences between each of those JAR files are the contents of the property files, but any recompiling or repackaging of the deployable artifact can, and often does, end up inadvertently bringing in other differences as well.

These snowflakes don't only have a negative impact on the timeline for the initial deployment; they also contribute greatly to operational instability. For example, let's say you have an app that has been running in production with roughly 50,000 concurrent users. Although that number doesn't generally fluctuate too much, you want room for growth. In the user acceptance testing (UAT) phase, you exercise a load with twice that volume, and all tests pass. You deploy the app into production, and all is well for some time. Then, on Saturday morning at 2 A.M., you see a spike in traffic. You suddenly have more than 75,000 users, and the system is failing. But, wait, in UAT you tested up to 100,000 concurrent users, so what's going on?

It's a difference in environment. Users connect to the system through sockets, socket connections require open file descriptors, and a configuration setting limits the number of file descriptors. In the UAT environment, the value found in /proc/sys/fs/file-max is 200,000, but on the production server it's 65,535. The tests you ran in UAT didn't test for what you'd see in production, because of the differences between the UAT and production environments.

It gets worse. After diagnosing the problem and increasing the value in the /proc/sys/fs/file-max file, all of the operations staff's best intentions for documenting this requirement are trumped by an emergency; and later, when a new server is configured, it has the file-max value set to 65,535 again. The software is installed on that server, and the same problem will eventually once again rear its ugly head.

Remember a moment ago when I talked about needing to change property files between dev, test, staging, and production, and the impact that can have on deployments? Well, let's say you finally have everything deployed and running, and now something changes in your infrastructure topology. Your server name, URL, or IP address changes, or you add servers for scale. If those environment configurations are in the property file, then you must re-create the deployable artifact, and you risk having additional differences creep in.

Although this might sound extreme, and I do hope that most organizations have reigned in the chaos to some degree, elements of snowflake generation persist in all but the most advanced IT departments. The bespoke environments and deployment packages clearly introduce uncertainty into the system, but accepting that deployments are going to be risky is itself a first-class problem.

### 2.1.2  Risky deployments

When are software releases scheduled at your company? Are they done during "off hours," perhaps at 2 A.M. on Saturday morning? This practice is commonplace because of one simple fact: deployments are usually fraught with peril. It isn't unusual for a deployment to either require downtime during an upgrade, or cause unexpected downtime. Downtime is expensive. If your customers can't order their pizza online, they'll likely turn to a competitor, resulting in direct revenue loss.

In response to expensive outages, organizations have implemented a host of tools and processes designed to reduce the risks associated with releasing software. At the heart of most of these efforts is the idea that we'll do a whole bunch of up-front work to minimize the chance of failure. Months before a scheduled deployment, we begin weekly meetings to plan the "promotion into upper environments," and change-control approvals act as the last defense to keep unforeseen things from happening in production. Perhaps the practice with the highest price tag in terms of personnel and infrastructure resources is a testing process that depends on doing trial runs on an "exact replica of production." In principle, none of these ideas sound crazy, but in practice, these exercises ultimately place significant burdens on the deployment process itself. Let's look at one of these practices in more detail as an example: running test deployments in an exact replica of production.

A great deal of cost is associated with establishing such a test environment. For starters, twice the amount of hardware is needed; add to that double the software, and capital costs alone grow twofold. Then there are the labor costs of keeping the test environment in alignment with production, complicated by a multitude of requirements such as the need to cleanse production data of personally identifiable information when generating testing data.

Once established, access to the test environment must be carefully orchestrated across dozens or hundreds of teams that wish to test their software prior to a production release. On the surface, it may seem like it's a matter of scheduling, but the number of combinations of different teams and systems quickly makes it an intractable problem.

Consider a simple case in which you have two applications: a point-of-sale (PoS) system that takes payments, and a special order (SO) application that allows a customer to place an order and pay for it by using the PoS application. Each team is ready to release a new version of their application, and they must perform a test in the preproduction environment. How should these two teams' activities be coordinated? One option is to test the applications one at a time, and although executing the tests in sequence would extend the schedule, the process is relatively tractable if all goes well with each of the tests.

Figure 2.2 shows the following two steps. First, version 4 of the SO app is tested with version 1 (the old version) of the PoS app. When it's successful, version 4 of the

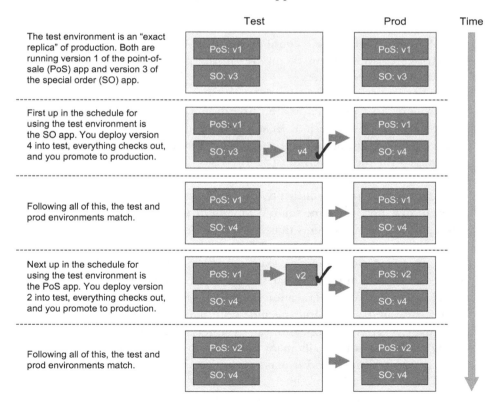

**Figure 2.2  Testing two apps in sequence is straightforward when all tests pass.**

SO application is deployed into production. Both test and production are now running v4 of SO, and both are still running v1 of PoS. The *test* environment is a replica of *prod*. Now you can test v2 of the PoS system, and when all the tests pass, you can promote that version into production. Both application upgrades are complete, with the test and prod environments matching.

But what happens if tests fail for the upgrade to the SO system? Clearly, you can't deploy the new version into production. But now what do you do in the test environment? Do you revert to version 3 of SO (which takes time), even if PoS doesn't depend on it? Was this a sequencing problem, with SO expecting PoS to already be on version 2 before it began its test? How long before SO can get back into the queue for using the test environment?

Figure 2.3 shows a couple of alternatives, which get complicated quickly, even in this toy scenario. In a real setting, this becomes intractable.

My goal isn't to solve this problem here, but rather to demonstrate that even an oversimplified scenario can quickly become extraordinarily complicated. I'm sure you can imagine that when you add more applications to the mix and/or try to test new versions of multiple applications in parallel, the process becomes completely intractable. The environment that's designed to ensure that things go well when software is deployed in production becomes a substantial bottleneck, and teams are caught between the need to get finished software out to the consumer as quickly as possible and doing it with complete confidence. In the end, it's impossible to test exactly the scenarios that will present themselves in the production environment, and deployments remain risky business.

Risky enough, in fact, that most businesses have time periods in the year when new deployments into production aren't permitted. For health insurance companies, it's the open-enrollment period. In e-commerce in the United States, it's the month between Thanksgiving and Christmas. That Thanksgiving-to-Christmas time frame is also sacred for the airline industry. The risks that persist despite efforts to minimize them make it difficult to get software deployed.

And because of this difficulty, the software running in production right now is likely to stay there for some time. We might be well aware of bugs or vulnerabilities in the apps and on the systems that are driving our customer experiences and business needs, but we must limp along until we can orchestrate the next release. For example, if an app has a known memory leak, causing intermittent crashes, we might preemptively reboot that app at regular intervals to avoid an emergency. But an increased workload against that application could cause the out-of-memory exception earlier than anticipated, and an unexpected crash causes the next emergency.

Finally, less-frequent releases lead to larger batch sizes; a deployment brings with it many changes, with equally many relationships to other parts of the system. It has been well established, and it makes intuitive sense, that a deployment that touches many other systems is more likely to cause something unexpected. Risky deployments have a direct impact on operational stability.

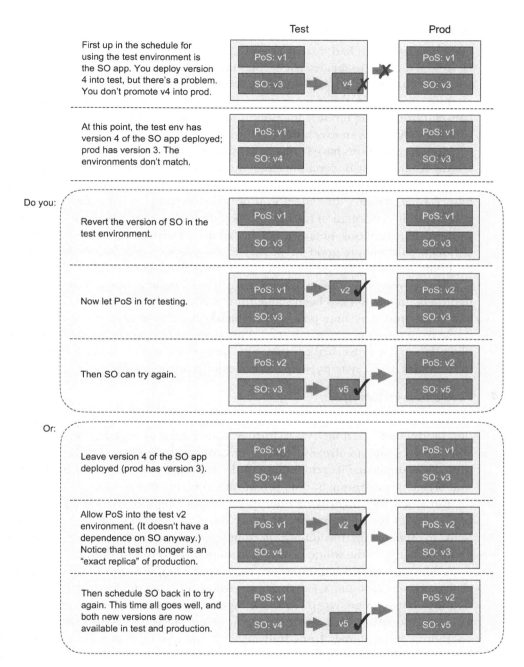

**Figure 2.3  A failing test immediately complicates the process for preproduction testing.**

### 2.1.3   *Change is the exception*

Over the years, I've had dozens of conversations with CIOs and their staff who have expressed a desire to create systems that provide differentiated value to their business and their customers, but instead they're constantly facing emergencies that draw their attention away from these innovation activities. I believe the cause of staff being in constant firefighting mode is the prevailing mindset of these long-established IT organizations: change is an exception.

Most organizations have realized the value of involving developers in initial deployments. A fair bit of uncertainty exists during fresh rollouts, and involving the team that deeply understands the implementation is essential. But at some point, responsibility for maintaining the system in production is completely handed over to the ops team, and the information for how to keep things humming is provided to them in a *runbook*. The runbook details possible failure scenarios and their resolutions, and although this sounds good in principle, on deeper reflection it demonstrates an assumption that the failure scenarios are known. But most aren't!

The development team disengaging from ongoing operations when a newly deployed application has been stable for a predetermined period of time subtly hints at a philosophy that some point in time marks the end of change—that things will be stable from here on out. When something unexpected occurs, everyone is left scrambling. When the proverbial constant change persists, and I've already established that in the cloud it will, systems will persist in experiencing instability.

### 2.1.4   *Production instability*

All the factors I've covered until now inarguably hinder software from running well, but production instability itself further contributes to making deployments hard. Deployments into an already unstable environment are ill-advised; in most organizations, risky deployments remain one of the leading causes of system breakage. A reasonably stable environment is a prerequisite to new deployments.

But when the majority of time in IT is spent fighting fires, we're left with few opportunities for deployments. Aligning those rare moments where production systems are stable with the timing of completing the complex testing cycles I talked about earlier, and the windows of opportunity shrink even further. It's a vicious cycle.

As you can see, writing the software is only the beginning of bringing digital experiences to your customers. Curating snowflakes, allowing deployments to be risky, and treating change as an exception come together to make the job of running that software in production hard. Further insight about how these factors negatively impact operations today comes from studying well-functioning organizations—those from born-in-the-cloud companies. When you apply the practices and principles as they do, you develop a system that optimizes the entire software delivery lifecycle, from development to smooth-running operations.

## 2.2 The enablers

A new breed of companies, those that came of age after the turn of the century, have figured out how to do things better. Google has been a great innovator, and along with some of the other internet giants, has developed new ways of running IT. With its estimated two million servers running in worldwide data centers, there's no way that Google could've managed using the techniques I just described. A different way exists.

Figure 2.4 presents a sketch of a system that's almost an inverse of the bad system I described in the previous section. The goals are as follows:

- Easy and frequent releases into production
- Operational stability and predictability

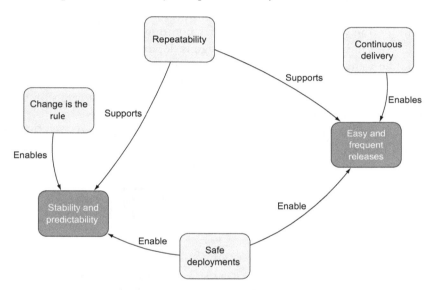

**Figure 2.4  Explicit attention to these four factors develops a system of efficiency, predictability, and stability.**

You're already familiar with the inverses of some of the factors:

- Whereas snowflakes had previously contributed to slowness and instability, repeatability supports the opposite.
- Whereas risky deployments contributed to both production instability and challenging deployments, the ability to deploy safely drives agility and stability.
- Replacing practices and software designs that depend on an unchanging environment with ones that expect constant change radically reduces time spent fighting fires.

But looking at figure 2.4, you'll notice a new entity labeled "Continuous delivery" (CD). The companies that have been most successful with the new IT operations model have redesigned their entire SDLC processes with CD as the primary driver.

This has a marked effect on the ease with which deployments can happen, and the benefits ripple through the entire system.

In this section, I first explain what CD is, how basic changes in the SDLC enable CD, and the positive outcomes. I then return to the other three key enablers and describe their main attributes and benefits in detail.

### 2.2.1   Continuous delivery

Amazon may be the most extreme example of frequent releases. It's said to release code into production for www.amazon.com on average every second of every day. You might question the need for such frequent releases in your business, and sure, you probably don't need to release software 86,000 times per day. But frequent releases drive business agility and enablement—both indicators of a strong organization.

Let me define *continuous delivery* by first pointing out what it isn't. Continuous delivery doesn't mean that every code change is deployed into production. Rather, it means that an as-new-as-possible version of the software is *deployable* at any time. The development team is constantly adding new capabilities to the implementation, but with each and every addition, they ensure that the software is ready to ship by running a full (automated!) test cycle and packaging the code for release.

Figure 2.5 depicts this cycle. Notice that there's no "packaging" step following the "test" phase in each cycle. Instead, the machinery for packaging and deployment is built right into the development-and-test process.

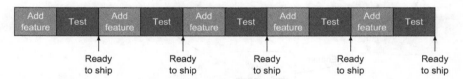

**Figure 2.5   Every dev/test cycle doesn't result in a ship; instead, every cycle results in software that's ready to ship. Shipping then becomes a business decision.**

Contrast this with the more traditional software development practice depicted in figure 2.6. A far longer single cycle is front-loaded with a large amount of software development that adds a great many features to an implementation. After a predetermined set of new capabilities has been added, an extensive test phase is completed and the software is readied for release.

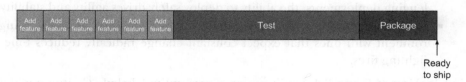

**Figure 2.6   A traditional software delivery lifecycle front-loads a lot of development work and a long testing cycle before creating the artifacts that can then be released into production.**

Let's assume that the time spans covered by figures 2.5 and 2.6 are the same, and that the start of each process is on the left, and the Ready to Ship point is on the far right. If you look at that rightmost point in time alone, you might not see much of a difference in outcome; roughly the same features will be delivered at roughly the same time. But if you dig under the covers, you'll see significant differences.

First, with the former approach, the decision of when the next software release happens can be driven by the business rather than being at the mercy of a complex, unpredictable, software development process. For example, let's say you learn that a competitor is planning a release of a product similar to yours in two weeks, and as a result, the business decides that you should make your own product immediately available. The business says, "Let's release now!" In figure 2.7, overlaying that point in time over the previous two diagrams shows a stark contrast.

Using a software development methodology that supports CD allows the Ready to Ship software of the third iteration (shown in italics) to be immediately released. True, the application doesn't yet have all of the planned features, but the competitive advantage of being first to market with a product that has some of the features may be significant. Looking at the lower half of the figure, you see that the business is out of luck. The IT process is a blocker rather than an enabler, and the competitor's product will hit the market first!

The iterative process also affords another important outcome. When the Ready to Ship versions are frequently made available to customers, it gives you an opportunity to gather feedback used to better the subsequent versions of the product. You must be deliberate about using the feedback gathered after earlier iterations to correct false assumptions or even change course entirely in subsequent iterations. I've seen many Scrum projects fail because they strictly adhere to plans defined at the beginning of a project, not allowing results from earlier iterations to alter those plans.

Finally, let's admit it: we aren't good at estimating the time it takes to build software. Part of the reason is our inherent optimism. We usually plan for the happy path,

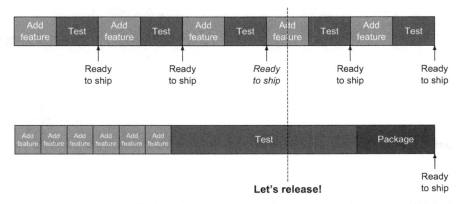

**Figure 2.7 Continuous delivery is concerned with allowing business drivers, not IT readiness, to determine when software is shipped.**

where the code works as expected immediately after the first write. (Yeah, when put like that, we see the absurdity of it right away, huh?) We also make the assumption that we'll be fully focused on the task at hand; we'll be cutting code all day, every day, until we get things done. And we're probably getting pressured into agreeing to aggressive time schedules driven by market needs or other factors, usually putting us behind schedule even before we begin.

Unanticipated implementation challenges always come. Say you underestimate the effect of network latency on one part of your implementation, and instead of the simple request/response exchange that you planned for, you now need to implement a much more complex asynchronous communication protocol. And while you're implementing this next set of features, you're also getting pulled away from the new work to support escalations on already released versions of the software. And it's almost never the case that your stretched goals fit within an already challenging time schedule.

The impact these factors have on the old-school development process is that you miss your planned release milestone. Figure 2.8 depicts the idealized software release plan in the first row. The second row shows the actual amount of time spent on development (longer than planned for), and the final two rows show alternatives for what you can do. One option is to stick with the planned release milestone, by compressing the testing phase, surely at the expense of software quality (the packaging phase usually can't be shortened). A second option is to maintain the quality standards and move the release date. Neither of these options is pleasant.

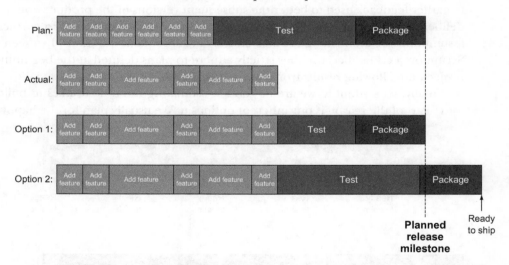

Figure 2.8   When the development schedule slips, you need to decide between two unpalatable options.

Contrast this to the effects that "unanticipated" development delays have on a process that implements many shorter iterations. As depicted in figure 2.9, you again see that your planned release milestone is expected to come after six iterations. When the

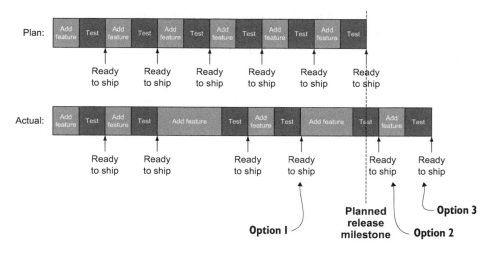

**Figure 2.9** Shorter iterations designed for continuous delivery allow for an agile release process while maintaining software quality.

actual implementation takes longer than expected, you see that you're presented with some new options. You can either release on schedule with a more limited set of features (option 1), or you can choose a slight or longer delay for the next release (options 2 and 3). The key is that the business is presented with a far more flexible and palatable set of options. And when, through the system I'm presenting in this section, you make deployments less risky and therefore deploy more frequently, you can complete those two releases in rapid succession.

To net it all out, lengthy release cycles introduce a great deal of risk into the process of bringing digital products to consumers. The business lacks the ability to control when products are released to the market, and the organization as a whole is often in the awkward position of trading off near-term market pressures with long-term goals of software quality and ability to evolve.

> **NOTE** Short iterations release a great deal of tension from the system. Continuous delivery allows business drivers to determine how and when products are brought to market.

I've talked about continuous delivery first, and at relative length, because it truly is at the core of a new, functional system of software development and operations. If your organization isn't yet embracing practices such as these, this is where your initial efforts should be placed. Your ability to change the way that you bring software to market is hindered without such changes. And even the structure of the software you build, which is what this book is about, is linked to these practices in both subtle and direct ways. Software architecture is what this book is about, and we'll cover that in depth throughout.

Now let's go back to figure 2.4 and study the other factors that support our operational goals of easy, frequent releases and software stability.

### 2.2.2 Repeatability

In the previous section, I talked about the detrimental effect of variability, or as we often call them, *snowflakes*, on the workings of IT. They make things hard to deploy because you must constantly adjust to differences in both the environments into which you're deploying, and in the variability of the artifacts you're deploying. That same inconsistency makes it extremely difficult to keep things running well once in production, because every environment and piece of software gets special treatment anytime something changes. Drift from a known configuration is a constant threat to stability when you can't reliably re-create the configuration that was working before a crash.

When you turn that negative into a positive in your enabling system, the key concept is repeatability. It's analogous to the steps in an assembly line: each time you attach a steering wheel to a car, you repeat the same process. If the conditions are the same within some parameters (I'll elaborate on this more in a moment), and the same process is executed, the outcome is predictable.

The benefits of repeatability on our two goals—getting things deployed and maintaining stability—are great. As you saw in the previous section, iterative cycles are essential to frequent releases, and by removing the variability from the dev/test process that happens with each turn of the crank, the time to deliver a new capability within the iteration is compressed. And once running in production, whether you're responding to a failure or increasing capacity to handle greater volumes, the ability to stamp out deployments with complete predictability relieves tremendous stress from the system.

*How do we then achieve this sought-after repeatability?* One of the advantages of software is that it's easy to change, and that malleability can be done quickly. But this is also exactly what has invited us to create snowflakes in the past. To achieve the needed repeatability, you must be disciplined. In particular, you need to do the following:

- Control the environments into which you'll deploy the software
- Control the software that you're deploying—also known as the *deployable artifact*
- Control the deployment processes

#### CONTROL THE ENVIRONMENT

In an assembly line, you control the environment by laying out the parts being assembled and the tools used for assembly in exactly the same way—no need to search for the three-quarter-inch socket wrench each time you need it, because it's always in the same place. In software, you use two primary mechanisms to consistently lay out the context in which the implementation runs.

First, you must begin with standardized machine images. In building up environments, you must consistently begin with a known starting point. Second, changes applied to that base image to establish the context into which your software is deployed *must be coded.* For example, if you begin with a base Ubuntu image and your software requires the Java Development Kit (JDK), you'll script the installation of the JDK into the base image. The term often used for this latter concept is *infrastructure as code.* When you need a new instance of an environment, you begin with the base image and apply the script, and you're guaranteed to have the same environment each time.

Once established, any changes to an environment must also be equally controlled. If operations staff routinely ssh into machines and make configuration changes, the rigor you've applied to setting up the systems is for naught. Numerous techniques can be used to ensure control after initial deployment. You may not allow SSH access into running environments, or if you do, automatically take a machine offline as soon as someone has ssh'd in. The latter is a useful pattern in that it allows someone to go into a box to investigate a problem, but doesn't allow for any potential changes to color the running environment. If a change needs to be made to running environments, the only way for this to happen is by updating the standard machine image as well as the code that applies the runtime environment to it—both of which are controlled in a source code control system or something equivalent.

Who is responsible for the creation of the standardized machine images and the infrastructure-as-code varies, but as an application developer, it's essential that you use such a system. Practices that you apply (or don't) early in the software development lifecycle have a marked effect on the organization's ability to efficiently deploy and manage that software in production.

### CONTROL THE DEPLOYABLE ARTIFACT

Let's take a moment to acknowledge the obvious: there are always differences in environments. In production, your software connects to your live customer database, found at a URL such as http://prod.example.com/cutomerDB; in staging, it connects to a copy of that database that has been cleansed of personally identifiable information and is found at http://staging.example.com/cleansedDB; and during initial development, there may be a mock database that's accessed at http://localhost/mockDB. Obviously, credentials differ from one environment to the next. How do you account for such differences in the code you're creating?

I know you aren't hardcoding such strings directly into your code (right?). Likely, you're parameterizing your code and putting these values into some type of a property file. This is a good first step, but often a problem remains: the property files, and hence the parameter values for the different environments, are often compiled into the deployable artifact. For example, in a Java setting, the application.properties file is often included in the JAR or WAR file, which is then deployed into one of the environments. And therein lies the problem. When the environment-specific settings are compiled in, the JAR file that you deploy in the test environment is different from the JAR file that you deploy into production; see figure 2.10.

As soon as you build different artifacts for different stages in the SDLC, repeatability may be compromised. The discipline for controlling the variability of that software artifact, ensuring that the only difference in the artifacts is the contents of the property

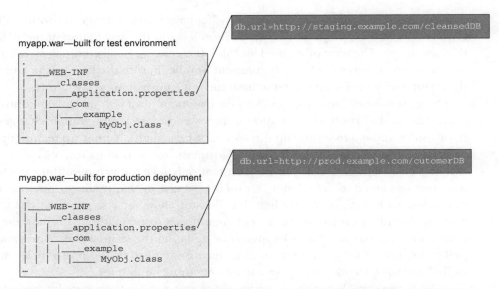

```
                                              db.url=http://staging.example.com/cleansedDB

myapp.war—built for test environment

 .
 |_____WEB-INF
 |  |_____classes
 |  |  |_____application.properties
 |  |  |_____com
 |  |  |  |_____example
 |  |  |  |  |_____ MyObj.class
 ...
```

```
                                              db.url=http://prod.example.com/cutomerDB

myapp.war—built for production deployment

 .
 |_____WEB-INF
 |  |_____classes
 |  |  |_____application.properties
 |  |  |_____com
 |  |  |  |_____example
 |  |  |  |  |_____ MyObj.class
 ...
```

**Figure 2.10    Even when environment-specific values are organized into property files, including property files in the deployable artifact, you'll have different artifacts throughout the SDLC.**

files, must now be implanted into the build process itself. Unfortunately, because the JAR files are different, you can no longer compare file hashes to verify that the artifact that you've deployed into the staging environment is exactly the same as that which you've deployed into production. And if something changes in one of the environments, and one of the property values changes, you must update the property file, which means a new deployable artifact and a new deployment.

For efficient, safe, and repeatable production operations, it's essential that a single deployable artifact is used through the entire SDLC. The JAR you build and run through regression tests during development is the *exact* JAR file deployed into the test, staging, and production environments. To make this happen, the code needs to be structured in the right way. For example, property files don't carry environment-specific values, but instead define a set of parameters for which values may later be injected. You can then bind values to these parameters at the appropriate time, drawing values from the right sources. It's up to you as the developer to create implementations that properly abstract the environmental variability. Doing this allows you to create a single deployable artifact that can be carried through the entire SDLC, bringing with it agility and reliability.

**CONTROL THE PROCESS**

Having established environment consistency, and the discipline of creating a single deployable artifact to carry through the entire software development lifecycle, what's left is ensuring that these pieces come together in a controlled, repeatable manner. Figure 2.11 depicts the desired outcome: in all stages of the SDLC, you can reliably stamp out exact copies of as many running units as needed.

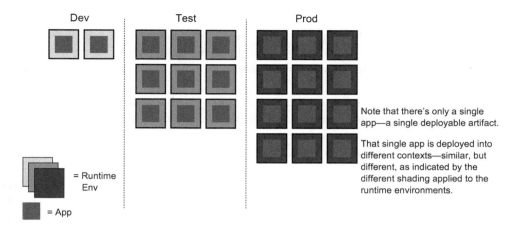

**Figure 2.11  The desired outcome is to be able to consistently establish apps running in standardized environments. Note that the app is the same across all environments; the runtime environment is standardized within an SDLC stage.**

This figure has no snowflakes. The deployable artifact, the app, is exactly the same across all deployments and environments. The runtime environment has variation across the different stages, but (as indicated by the different shades of the same gray coloring) the base is the same and has only different configurations applied, such as database bindings. Within a lifecycle stage, all the configurations are the same; they have exactly the same shade of gray. Those antisnowflake boxes are assembled from the two controlled entities I've been talking about: standardized runtime environments and single deployable artifacts, as seen in figure 2.12.

A whole lot is under the surface of this simple picture. What makes a good base image, and how is it made available to developers and operators? What is the source of

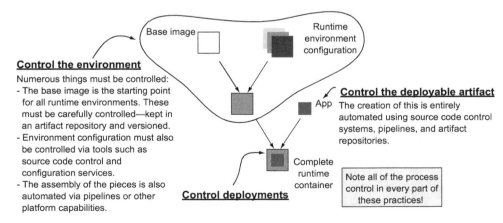

**Figure 2.12  The assembly of standardized base images, controlled environment configurations, and single deployable artifacts is automated.**

the environment configuration, and when is it brought into the application context? Exactly when is the app "installed" into the runtime context? I'll answer these questions and many more throughout the book, but at this juncture my main point is this: the only way to draw the pieces together in a manner that ensures consistency is to automate.

Although the use of continuous integration tools and practices is fairly ubiquitous in the development phase of writing software (for example, a build pipeline compiles checked-in code and runs some tests), its use in driving the entire SDLC isn't as widely adopted. But the automation must carry all the way from code check-in, through deployments, into test and production environments.

And when I say it's all automated, I mean *everything*. Even when you aren't responsible for the creation of the various bits and pieces, the assembly must be controlled in this manner. For example, users of Pivotal Cloud Foundry, a popular cloud-native platform, use an API to download new "stem cells,"[2] the base images into which apps are deployed, from a software distribution site, and use pipelines to complete the assembly of the runtime environment and the application artifact. Another pipeline does the final deployment into production. In fact, when deployments into production also happen via pipelines, servers aren't touched directly by humans, something that'll make your chief security officer (and other control-related personnel) happy.

But if you've totally automated things all the way to deployment, how do you ensure that these deployments are safe? This is another area that requires a new philosophy.

### 2.2.3   *Safe deployments*

Earlier I talked about risky deployments and that the most common mechanism that organizations use as an attempt to control the risk is to put in place expansive and expensive testing environments with complex and slow processes to govern their use. Initially, you might think that there's no alternative, because the only way to know that something works when deployed into production is to test it first. But I suggest that it's more a symptom of what Grace Hopper said was the most dangerous phrase: "We've always done it this way."

The born-in-the-cloud-era software companies have shown us a new way: they experiment in production. Egad! What am I talking about?! Let me add one word: they *safely* experiment in production.

Let's first look at what I mean by *safe experimentation* and then look at the impact it has on our goals of easy deployments and production stability.

When trapeze artists let go of one ring, spin through the air, and grasp another, they most often achieve their goal and entertain spectators. No question about it, their success depends on the right training and tooling, and a whole load of practice. But acrobats aren't fools; they know that things sometimes go wrong, so they perform over a safety net.

---

[2]See Pivotal's API Documentation page at https://network.pivotal.io/docs/api for more information.

When you experiment in production, you do it with the right safety nets in place. Both operational practices and software design patterns come together to weave that net. Add in solid software-engineering practices such as test-driven development, and you can minimize the chance of failure. But eliminating it entirely isn't the goal. Expecting failure (and failure will happen) greatly lessens the chances of it being catastrophic. Perhaps a small handful of users will receive an error message and need to refresh, but overall the system remains up and running.

> **TIP** Here's the key: everything about the software design and the operational practices allows you to easily and quickly pull back the experiment and return to a known working state (or advance to the next one) when necessary.

This is the fundamental difference between the old and the new mindset. In the former, you tested extensively before going to production, believing you'd worked out all the kinks. When that delusion proved incorrect, you were left scrambling. With the new, you plan for failure, intentionally creating a retreat path to make failures a non-event. This is empowering! And the impact on your goals, easier and faster deployments, and stability after you're up and running is obvious and immediate.

First, if you eliminate the complex and time-consuming testing process that I described in section 2.1.2, and instead go straight to production following basic integration testing, a great deal of time is cut from the cycle and, clearly, releases can occur more frequently. The release process is intentionally designed to encourage its use and involves little ceremony to begin. And having the right safety nets in place allows you to not only avert disaster, but to quickly return to a fully functional system in a matter of seconds.

When deployments come without ceremony and with greater frequency, you're better able to address the failings of what you're currently running in production, allowing you to maintain a more stable system as a whole.

Let's talk a bit more about what that safety net looks like, and in particular, the role that the developer, architect, and application operators play in constructing it. You'll look at three inextricably linked patterns:

- Parallel deployments and versioned services
- Generation of necessary telemetry
- Flexible routing

In the past, a deployment of version $n$ of some software was almost always a replacement of version $n - 1$. In addition, the things we deployed were large pieces of software encompassing a wide range of capabilities, so when the unexpected happened, the results could be catastrophic. An entire mission-critical application could experience significant downtime, for example.

At the core of your safe deployment practices is parallel deployment. Instead of completely replacing one version of running software with a new version, you keep the known working version running as you add a new version to run alongside it. You start out with only a small portion of traffic routed to the new implementation, and you watch what happens. You can control which traffic is routed to the new implementation based on a variety of available criteria, such as where the requests are coming from (either geographically or what the referring page is, for example) or who the user is.

To assess whether the experiment is yielding positive results, you look at data. Is the implementation running without crashing? Has new latency been introduced? Have click-through rates increased or decreased?

If things are going well, you can continue to increase the load directed at the new implementation. If at any time things aren't happy, you can shift all the traffic back to the previous version. This is the retreat path that allows you to experiment in production.

Figure 2.13 shows how the core practice works.

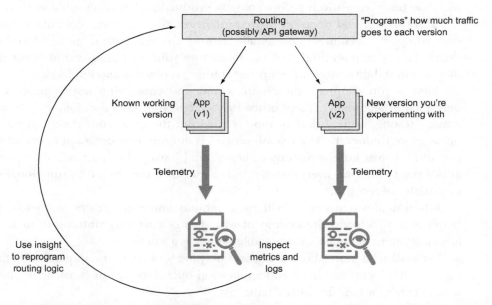

**Figure 2.13   Data tells you how parallel deployments of multiple versions of your apps are operating. You use that data to program control flows to those apps, supporting safe rollouts of new software in production.**

None of this can be done if proper software engineering disciplines are ignored, or applications don't embody the right architectural patterns. Some of the keys to enable this form of A/B testing are as follows:

- Software artifacts must be versioned, and the versions must be visible to the routing mechanism to allow it to appropriately direct traffic. Further, because you'll be analyzing data to determine whether the new deployment is stable and achieving the desired outcomes, all data must be associated with the appropriate version of the software in order to make the proper comparisons.

- The data used to analyze how the new version is functioning takes a variety of forms. Some metrics are completely independent of any details of the implementation; for example, the latency between a request and response. Other metrics begin to peer into the running processes, reporting on things such as the number of threads or memory being consumed. And finally, domain-specific metrics, such as the average total purchase amount of an online transaction, may also be used to drive deployment decisions. Although some of the data may automatically be provided by the environment in which the implementation is running, you won't have to write code to produce it. The availability of data metrics is a first-class concern. I want you to think about producing data that supports experimentation in production.

- Clearly, routing is a key enabler of parallel deployments, and the routing algorithms are pieces of software. Sometimes the algorithm is simple, such as sending a percentage of all the traffic to the new version, and the routing software "implementation" can be realized by configuring some of the components of your infrastructure. Other times you may want more-sophisticated routing logic and need to write code to realize it. For example, you may want to test some geographically localized optimizations and want to send requests only from within the same geography to the new version. Or perhaps you wish to expose a new feature only to your premium customers. Whether the responsibility for implementing the routing logic falls to the developer or is achieved via configuration of the execution environment, routing is a first-class concern for the developer.

- Finally, something I've already hinted at is creating smaller units of deployment. Rather than a deployment encompassing a huge portion of your e-commerce system—for example, the catalog, search engine, image service, recommendation engine, shopping cart, and payment-processing module all in one—deployments should have a far smaller scope. You can easily imagine that a new release of the image service poses far less risk to the business than something that involves payment processing. Proper componentization of your applications—or as many would call it today, a microservices-based architecture—is directly linked to the operability of digital solutions.[3]

Although the platform your applications run on provide some of the necessary support for safe deployments (and I'll talk more about this in chapter 3), all four of these factors—versioning, metrics, routing, and componentization—are things that you, as a developer, must consider when you design and build your cloud-native application. There's more to cloud-native software than these things (for example, designing bulkheads into your architecture to keep failures from cascading through the entire system), but these are some of the key enablers of safe deployments.

---

[3]Google provides more details in its "Accelerate: State of DevOps" report, available at http://mng.bz/vNap.

### 2.2.4    *Change is the rule*

Over the last several decades, we've seen ample evidence that an operational model predicated on a belief that our environment changes only when we intentionally and knowingly initiate such changes doesn't work. Reacting to unexpected changes dominates the time spent by IT, and even traditional SDLC processes that depend on estimates and predictions have proven problematic.

As we're doing with the new SDLC processes I've been describing throughout this chapter, building muscle that allows you to adapt when change is thrust upon you affords far greater resilience. What's subtle is identifying what those muscles are when it comes to stability and predictability for production systems. This concept is a bit tricky, a bit "meta" if you will; please bear with me a moment.

The trick isn't to get better at predicting the unexpected or allocating more time for troubleshooting. For example, allocating half of a development team's time to responding to incidents does nothing to address the underlying cause of the firefighting. You respond to an outage, get everything in working order, and you're done—until the next incident.

*"Done."*

This is the root of the problem. You believe that after you're finished with a deployment, responding to an incident, or making a firewall change, you've somehow completed your work. The idea that you're "done" inherently treats change as something that causes you to become not done.

**TIP**    You need to let go of the notion of ever being done.

Let's talk about *eventual consistency.* Rather than creating a set of instructions that brings a system into a "done" state, an eventually consistent system never expects to be done. Instead, the system is perpetually working to achieve equilibrium. The key abstractions of such a system are the desired state and the actual state.

The *desired state* of a system is what you want it to look like. For example, say you want a single server running a relational database, three application servers running RESTful web services, and two web servers delivering rich web applications to the users. These six servers are properly networked, and firewall rules are appropriately set. This topology, as shown in figure 2.14, is an expression of the desired state of the system.

You'd hope that, at some point, even most of the time, you have that system entirely

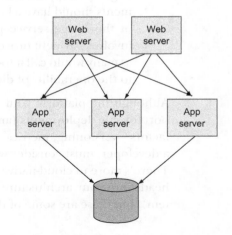

**Figure 2.14    The desired state of your deployed software**

established and running well, but you'll never assume that things remain as you left them immediately following a deployment. Instead, you treat the *actual state*, a model of what's currently running in your system, as a first-class entity, constructing and maintaining it by using some of the metrics you already considered in this chapter.

The eventually consistent system then constantly compares the *actual state* to the *desired state*, and when there's a deviation, performs actions to bring them back into alignment. For instance, let's say that you lose an application server from the topology laid out in figure 2.14. This could happen for any number of reasons—a hardware failure, an out-of-memory exception coming from the app itself, or a network partition that cuts off the app server from other parts of the system.

Figure 2.15 depicts both the desired state and the actual state. The actual state and desired state clearly don't match. To bring them back into alignment, another application server must be spun up and networked into the topology, and the application must be installed and started thereon (recall earlier discussions around repeatable deployments).

For those of you who previously might not have done much with eventual consistency, this might feel a bit like rocket science. An expert colleague avoids using the term *eventual consistency* because he worries that it'll invoke fear in our customers. But systems built on this model are increasingly common, and many tools and educational materials can assist in bringing such solutions to fruition.

And I'll tell you this: it's absolutely, totally, completely essential to running applications on the cloud. I've said it before: things are always changing, so better to embrace that change than to react to it. You shouldn't fear eventual consistency. You should embrace it.

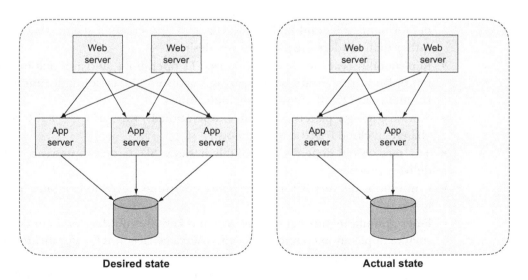

**Desired state**          **Actual state**

**Figure 2.15   When the actual state doesn't match the desired state, the eventually consistent system initiates actions to bring them back into alignment.**

Let me clarify something. Although the system I'm referring to here isn't necessarily entirely automated, having a platform that implements the core portions of the paradigm is required (I'll say more about the role of the platform in the next chapter). What I want you to do is design and build your software in a manner that allows a self-healing system to adapt to the constant change inflicted upon it. Teaching you how to do this is the aim of this book.

Software designed to remain functional in the face of constant change is the Holy Grail, and the impact on system stability and reliability is obvious. A self-healing system maintains higher uptime than one that requires human intervention each time something goes wrong. And treating a deployment as an expression of a new desired state greatly simplifies it and reduces risk. Adopting a mindset that change is the rule fundamentally alters the nature of managing software in production.

## *Summary*

- In order for value to be realized from the code you write, you need to be able to do two things: get it deployed easily and frequently, and keep it running well in production.
- Missing the mark on either of these tasks shouldn't be blamed on developers or operators. Instead, the "blame" rests with a failing system.
- The system fails because it allows bespoke solutions, which are hard to maintain; creates an environment that makes the act of deploying software inherently risky; and treats changes in the software and environment as an exception.
- When deployments are risky, they're performed less frequently, which only serves to make them even riskier.
- You can invert each of these negatives—focusing on repeatability, making deployments safe, and embracing change—and create a system that supports rather than hinders the practices you desire.
- Repeatability is at the core of optimized IT operations, and automation applies not only to the software build process, but also to the creation of runtime environments and the deployment of applications.
- Software design patterns as well as operational practices expect the constant change in cloud-based environments.
- The new system depends on a highly iterative SDLC that supports continuous delivery practices.
- Continuous delivery is what a responsive business needs to compete in today's markets.
- Finer granularity throughout the system is key. Shorter development cycles and smaller application components (microservices) account for significant gains in agility and resilience.
- Eventual consistency reigns supreme in a system where change is the rule.

# The platform for cloud-native software

---

## This chapter covers

- A brief history of cloud platform evolution
- Foundational elements of the cloud-native platform
- The basics of containers
- Use of a platform throughout the entire SDLC
- Security, compliance, and change control

---

I work with a lot of clients to help them understand and adopt cloud-native patterns and practices, as well as a platform that's optimized to run the software they produce. In particular, I work with and on the Cloud Foundry platform. I want to share an experience of one of my clients who adopted Cloud Foundry and deployed an existing application onto it.

Although that deployed software adhered to only a few of the cloud-native patterns covered in this book (the apps were stateless and were bound to backing services that held the needed state), my client realized immediate benefits from moving to a modern platform. After deploying onto Cloud Foundry, they found that the software was more stable than it had ever been. Initially, they attributed this to inadvertently improving quality during the light refactoring done for Cloud Foundry deployment.

But in reviewing the application logs, they found something surprising: the application was crashing just as frequently as it had before. They just hadn't noticed it. The cloud-native application platform was monitoring the health of the application, and when it failed, the platform automatically launched a replacement app. Under-the-covers problems remained, but the operator's, and more importantly the user's, experience was far better.

> **NOTE** The moral of the story is this: although cloud-native software prescribes many new patterns and practices, neither the developer nor the operator is responsible for providing all the functionality. Cloud-native platforms, those designed to support cloud-native software, provide a wealth of capabilities that support the development and operation of these modern digital solutions.

Now, let me be clear here: I'm not suggesting that such a platform should allow application quality to suffer. If a bug is causing a crash, it should be found and fixed. But such a crash needn't necessarily wake an operator in the middle of the night or leave the user with a subpar experience until the problem is fixed. The new platform provides a set of services designed to deliver on the requirements that I've described in the preceding chapters, requirements for software that are continuously deployed, extremely distributed, and running in a constantly changing environment.

In this chapter, I'll cover the key elements of cloud-native *platforms* to explain what capabilities you can look to them for. Having a solid understanding of these capabilities will not only help you focus on your business needs rather than on the plumbing to support it, but will also allow you to optimize your implementation for cloud-native deployment.

## 3.1 *The cloud(-native) platform evolution*

Using platforms to support the development and operation of software isn't new. The massively adopted Java 2 Platform, Enterprise Edition (J2EE) was first released nearly 20 years ago and has had seven major releases since then. JBoss, WebSphere, and Web-Logic are commercial offerings of this open source technology that have generated billions in revenue for RedHat, IBM, and Oracle, respectively. Many other proprietary platforms such those from TIBCO Software or Microsoft have been equally successful—and have brought benefit to their users.

But just as new architectures are needed to meet modern demands on software, new platforms are needed to support the new implementations and operational practices around them. Let's take a quick look at how we got to where we are today.

### 3.1.1 *It started with the cloud*

Arguably, cloud platforms began in earnest with Amazon Web Services (AWS). Its first offerings, made publicly available in releases throughout 2006, included compute (Elastic Compute Cloud, or EC2), storage (Simple Storage Service, or S3) and messaging (Simple Queue Service, or SQS) services. This was definitely a game changer in that developers and operations personnel no longer had to procure and manage their own hardware, but could instead obtain the resources they needed in a fraction of the time by using self-service provisioning interfaces.

Initially, this new platform represented the transference of existing client-server models into internet-accessible data centers. Software architectures didn't change dramatically, nor did the development and operational practices around them. In these early days, the *cloud* was more about *where* computing was happening.

Almost immediately, characteristics of the cloud began to put pressure on software that was built for precloud infrastructures. Instead of using "enterprise-grade" servers, network devices, and storage, AWS used commodity hardware in its data centers. Using less-expensive hardware was key to offering cloud services at a palatable price, but with that came a higher rate of failure. AWS compensated for the reduced level of hardware resilience within its software and offerings, and presented abstractions to its users, such as *availability zones* (AZs), that would allow for software running on AWS to remain stable even while the infrastructure wasn't.

What's significant here is that by exposing these new primitives, such as AZs or *regions*, to the user of the service, that user takes on a new responsibility of using those primitives appropriately. We may not have realized it at the time, but exposing these new abstractions in the application program interface (API) of the platform began influencing a new architecture for software. People began writing software that was designed to run well on such a platform.

AWS effectively created a new market, and it took competitors, such as Google and Microsoft, two years to have any response. When they did, each came with unique offerings.

Google first came to market with Google App Engine (GAE), a platform designed expressly for running web applications. The abstractions it exposed, the first-class entities in the API, were markedly different from those of AWS. The latter predominantly exposed compute, storage, and network primitives; AZs, for example, generally map to sets of servers, allowing the abstraction to give the user control over server pool affinity or anti-affinity. By contrast, the GAE interface didn't, and still doesn't, provide any access to the raw compute resources that are running those web apps; it doesn't expose infrastructure assets directly.

Microsoft came with its own flavor of cloud platform, including the capability to run *medium trust code*, for example. Similar to Google's approach, the Medium Trust offering provided little direct access to the compute, storage, and network resources, and instead took the onus to create the infrastructure in which the user's code would run. This allowed the platform to limit what the user's code could do in the

| | AWS | GCP | Azure |
|---|---|---|---|
| Compute | Elastic Compute Cloud (EC2) | Google Compute Engine | Azure virtual machines |
| Storage | Simple Storage Service (S3) | Google Cloud Storage | Azure Blob Storage |
| Network | Virtual private cloud (VPC) | Virtual private cloud (VPC) | Virtual private network (VPN) |

Figure 3.1   Infrastructure-as-a-service (IaaS) offerings from major cloud platform providers

infrastructure, thereby offering certain security and resilience guarantees. Looking back now, I see these offerings from Google and Microsoft as two of the earliest forays from cloud into cloud-native.

Google and Microsoft both eventually provided services that exposed infrastructure abstractions, as shown in figure 3.1, and, in reverse, AWS began offering cloud services with higher-level abstractions.

The different courses that these three vendors took in the latter half of the 2000s were hinting at the significant change that was coming in software architectures. As an industry, we were experimenting, seeing whether there might be ways of consuming and interacting with data center resources that would give us advantages in areas of productivity, agility, and resilience. These experiments eventually led to the formation of a new class of platform—the cloud-*native* platform—that's characterized by these higher-level abstractions, services tied to those, and the affordances they bring.

The cloud-native platform is what you'll study in this chapter. Let's start by talking more about the higher-level abstractions that the cloud-native platform provides.

### 3.1.2   *Cloud-native dial tone*

Developers and application operators care about whether the digital solutions they're running for their users function properly. In decades past, in order to provide the right service levels, they were required to correctly configure not only application deployments but also the infrastructure those applications ran on. This is because the primitives they had available to them were the same compute, storage, and network components they had always worked with.

As hinted at in the cloud platform evolution you just read about, this is changing. To clearly understand the difference, let's look at a concrete example. Say you have an application deployed. To make sure that it's running well, or to diagnose when things go wrong, you must have access to log and metric data.

As I've already established, cloud-native apps have multiple copies deployed, both for resilience and scale. If you're running those modern apps on an infrastructure-centric platform, one that exposes traditional infrastructure entities such as hosts, storage volumes, and networks, you must navigate through traditional data center abstractions to get or access those logs.

Figure 3.2 depicts the steps:

1 Determine which hosts are running the instances of your app; this is typically stored in a configuration management database (CMDB).

2 Determine which of those hosts are running the app instance you're trying to diagnose the behavior for. This sometimes comes down to checking one host at a time until the right one is found.

3 After you've found the right host, you must navigate to a specific directory to find the logs you seek.

The entities that the operator is interacting with to get the job done are CMDBs, hosts, and filesystem directories.

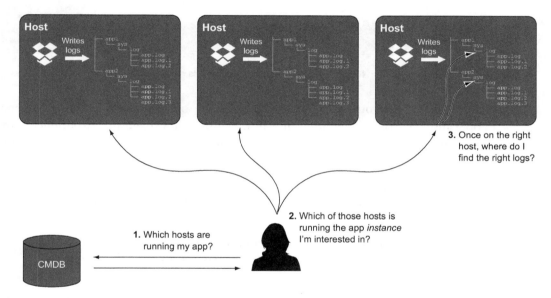

**Figure 3.2  Accessing application logs in an infrastructure-centric environment is tedious.**

By contrast, figure 3.3 shows the operator experience when the apps are running on a cloud-native platform. It's extremely simple: you ask for the logs for your application. You're making app-centric requests.

The cloud-native platform takes on a burden that was previously placed on the operator. This platform natively maintains an understanding of the application topology (previously stored in the CMDB), uses it to aggregate the logs for all application instances, and provides the operator the data needed for the entity they're interested in.

The key point is this: the entity that the operator is interested in is the *application*— not the hosts the app is running on, or the directories that hold the logs. The operator needs the logs for the application they're diagnosing.

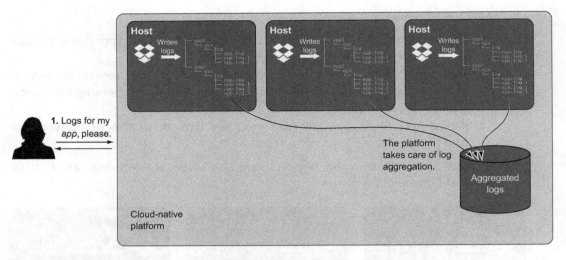

**Figure 3.3    Accessing application logs in an app-centric environment is simple.**

The contrast that you see in this example is one of infrastructure centricity versus application centricity. The difference in the application operator's experience is due to the difference in the abstractions they're working with. I like to call this a difference in *dial tone.*

> **DEFINITION**    Infrastructure-as-a-service (IaaS) platforms present *infrastructure dial tone*: an interface that provides access to hosts, storage, and networks—infrastructure primitives.

> **DEFINITION**    The cloud-native platform presents *application dial tone*: an interface that makes the application the first-class entity that the developer or operator interacts with.

You've surely seen the blocks that are stacked in figure 3.4, clearly separating the three layers that ultimately come together to provide a digital solution to consumers. Virtualized infrastructure enables easier consumption of compute, storage, and network abstractions, leaving the management of the underlying hardware to the IaaS provider. The cloud-native platform brings the level of abstraction up even further, allowing a consumer to consume OS and middleware resources more easily, and leaving the management of the underlying compute, storage, and network to the infrastructure provider.

The annotations on either side of the stack in figure 3.4 suggest differences in the operations performed against these abstractions. Instead of deploying an app onto one or more hosts via IaaS interfaces, on the cloud-native platform an operator deploys an application, and the platform takes care of distributing the requested instances against available resources. Instead of configuring the firewall rules to secure the boundary of the hosts that are running a particular application, the operator applies a policy to the

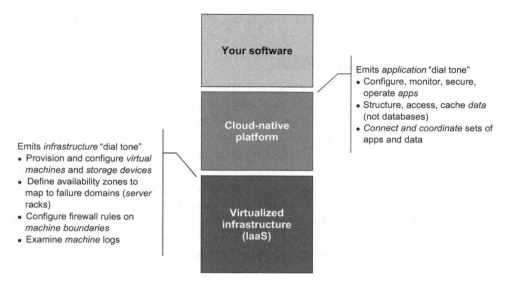

**Figure 3.4   The cloud-native platform abstracts infrastructure concerns, allowing teams to focus on their applications instead of these lower-level concerns.**

application, and the platform takes care of securing the application container. Instead of accessing hosts to get to logs for the app, the operator accesses the logs for the app. The experiential differences that a cloud-native platform offers over an IaaS platform are significant.

What I'll talk about in this chapter, and what I'm encouraging you to build your cloud-native software to, is a cloud-native platform—the one that emits application dial tone. Several of these platforms are available today. From the big cloud providers, we have Google App Engine, AWS Elastic Beanstalk, and Azure App Service (none of which are particularly widely adopted). Cloud Foundry is an open source cloud-native platform that has had remarkable penetration into large enterprises globally. Several vendors have commercial offerings (Pivotal, IBM, and SAP, to name only a few).[1] Although the details of these platforms vary, all have a common philosophical foundation and provide an application dial tone.

## 3.2   Core tenets of the cloud-native platform

Before I go deeper into some of the capabilities of and resultant benefits from adopting a cloud-native platform, it's important that you understand the philosophical underpinnings and the foundational patterns everything else is built on. It shouldn't surprise you that this foundation is really all about providing support for highly distributed apps that live in an environment that's constantly changing. But before I

---

[1] Full disclosure: at the time of this book's publication, I work for Pivotal on its Cloud Foundry, Kubernetes, and other emerging platforms.

present those two elements in more detail, let's talk about the technology that's essential to such platforms.

### 3.2.1  *First, let's talk about containers*

As it happens, containers are a great enabler of cloud-native software. Okay, that relationship isn't quite the coincidence that my somewhat flippant remark suggests, but it's a chicken-and-egg situation: the popularity of containers was without question driven by the need to support cloud-native applications, and the availability of containers has equally driven advances in cloud-native software.

If, when I use the term "container" you immediately think "Docker," that's cool—close enough. But I do want to cover key elements of containers in the abstract so that you can more easily connect those capabilities to the elements of cloud-native software.

Starting at the most basic level, a *container* is a computing context that uses functionality from a host that it's running on; for example, the base operating system. Generally, multiple containers are running on a single host, the latter of which is a server, either physical or virtual. These multiple containers are isolated from one another. At the highest level, they're a bit like virtual machines (VMs), an isolated computing environment running on a shared resource. Containers, however, are lighter weight than VMs, allowing them to be created in orders of magnitude less time, and they consume fewer resources.

I already mentioned that multiple containers running on a single host share the host's operating system, but that's all. The rest of the runtime environment needed by your app (and yes, your app will be running in a container) runs within the container.

Figure 3.5 shows the portions of the application and runtime environment that are running both on the host and inside your containers. Only the OS *kernel* is provided by the host. Inside the container you first have the OS root filesystem, including operating system functions such as `openssh` or `apt get`. The runtime needed by your application is also inside the container—the Java Runtime Environment (JRE) or the .NET Framework, for example. And then, finally, your application is also in the container, hopefully running there.

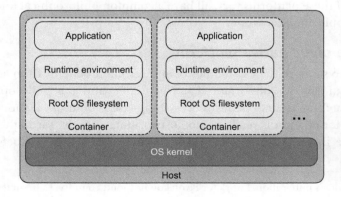

Figure 3.5  **A host usually has multiple containers running on it. These containers share the OS kernel from the host. But each container has its own root operating filesystem, runtime environment, and application code.**

When an application instance is to be run, a container is created on a host. All the bits necessary to run your app—the OS filesystem, application runtime, and the application itself—will be installed into that container and the appropriate processes started. The cloud-native platform, using containers at the core, provides a whole lot of functionality for your software, and creation of an app instance is but one. Others include the following:

- Monitoring the health of the application
- Appropriate distribution of app instances across the infrastructure
- Assignment of IP addresses to the containers
- Dynamic routing to app instances
- Injection of configuration
- And much more

The key points I want to you remember about the container as you begin to study what a cloud-native platform brings to bear is that (1) your infrastructure will have multiple hosts, (2) a host has multiple containers running on it, and (3) your app uses the OS and runtime environment installed into the container for its functionality. In many of the diagrams that follow, I depict the container with the icon shown in figure 3.6.

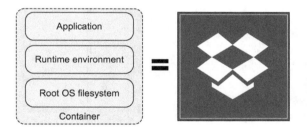

**Figure 3.6   When studying the capabilities of a cloud-native platform, at times we'll think of the container as a black box within which your application runs. A bit later, we'll drill into the details of what's running in the container.**

With this basic understanding of the container, let's now look at the key tenets of the cloud-native platform.

### 3.2.2   Support for "constantly changing"

I started this book with the story of an Amazon outage that demonstrated how an application can remain stable even as the platform it's running on is experiencing trouble. Although developers play a crucial role in achieving that resilience through the design of their software, they needn't be responsible for implementing every stability feature directly. The cloud-native platform provides a significant part of that service.

Take AZs, for example. To support reliability, Amazon provides its EC2 users with access to multiple AZs, giving them the option to deploy their apps into more than one so that the apps may survive an AZ failure. But when an AZ fails on AWS, some users still lose their entire online presence.

The exact reason surely varies, but in general, failing to deploy apps across AZs occurs because doing so is nontrivial. You must keep track of the AZs you use, launch machine instances into each AZ, configure networks across the AZs, and decide how to deploy app instances (containers) across the VMs that you have in each AZ. When you do any type of maintenance (an OS upgrade, for example), you must decide whether you'll do this one AZ at a time or via another pattern. Need to move workloads because AWS is decommissioning the host you're running on? You must think about your whole topology to see where, including which AZ, that workload should be moved to. It's definitely complicated.

Although the AZ is an abstraction that AWS exposes to the user of its EC2 service, it needn't be exposed to the user of the cloud-native platform. Instead, the platform can be configured to use multiple AZs, and all that orchestration of application instances across those AZs is then handled by the platform. An app team simply requests multiple instances of an app be deployed (say, four, as shown in figure 3.7), and the platform automatically distributes them evenly across all available zones. The platform implements all of the orchestration and management that humans would otherwise shoulder the burden for if they weren't using a cloud-native platform. Then when change happens (an AZ goes down, for example), the application continues to work.

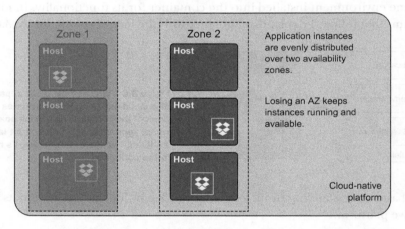

**Figure 3.7  Management of workloads across availability zones is handled by the cloud-native platform.**

Another concept that I've previously mentioned is *eventual consistency*, a key pattern in the cloud, where things are constantly changing. Deployments and management tasks, which we know must be automated, are designed with the expectation that they are never done. Instead, the management of the system comes through constant monitoring of the actual (constantly changing) state of the system, comparing it to a desired state, and remediating when necessary. This technique is easy to describe but difficult to implement, and realizing the capability through a cloud-native platform is essential.

Several cloud-native platforms implement this basic pattern, including Kubernetes and Cloud Foundry. Although the implementation details differ slightly, the basic

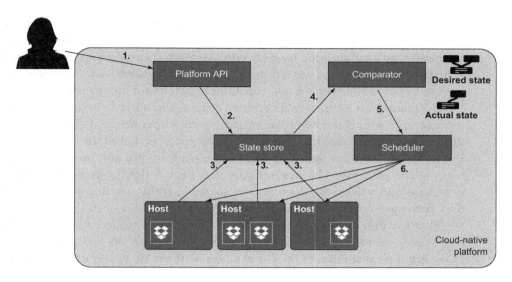

**Figure 3.8  The state of applications running on the platform is managed by continually comparing the desired state to the actual state and then executing corrective actions when necessary.**

approaches are the same. Figure 3.8 depicts the key actors and the basic flow among them:

1　The user expresses the desired state by interacting with the API for the platform. For example, the user may ask that four instances of a particular app be running.

2　The platform API continually broadcasts changes to the desired state into a fault-tolerant, distributed data store or messaging fabric.

3　Each host running workloads is responsible for broadcasting the state of what is running on them into a fault-tolerant, distributed data store or messaging fabric.

4　An actor, which I'm calling the *comparator* here, ingests information from the state store, maintains a model of both the desired state and the actual state, and compares the two.

5　If the desired and actual states don't match, the comparator informs another component in the system of the difference.

6　This component, which I'm calling the *scheduler*, determines where new workloads should be created or which workloads should be shut down, and communicates with the hosts to make this happen.

The complexity lies in the distributed nature of the system. Frankly, distributed systems are hard. The algorithms implemented in the platform must account for lost messages from the API or hosts, network partitions that may be brief but disrupt the flow nonetheless, and flapping state changes that are sometimes due to such flaky networks.

Components such as the state store must have ways of maintaining state when inputs to it are in conflict (Paxos and Raft protocols are two of the most widely used at the moment). Just as application teams needn't concern themselves with the complexity of managing workloads across AZs, they also needn't be burdened with implementation of eventually consistent systems; that capability is baked into the platform.

The platform is a complex distributed system, and it needs to be as resilient as distributed apps are. If the comparator goes down, either due to failure or even something planned such as an upgrade, the platform must be self-healing. The patterns I've described here for apps running on the platform are also used for the management of the platform. The desired state may include 100 hosts running application workloads and a five-node distributed state store. If the system topology differs from that, corrective actions will bring it back to the desired state.

What I've described throughout this section is sophisticated and goes well beyond the simple automation of steps that may have previously been performed manually. These are the capabilities of the cloud-native platform that support constant change.

### 3.2.3   Support for "highly distributed"

With all the talk about autonomy—team autonomy, which empowers the team to evolve and deploy its apps without high ceremony and heavily coordinated efforts, and app autonomy itself, which has individual microservices running within their own environment to both support independent development and reduce the risk of cascading failures—it feels like many problems are solved. And they are, but (yes, there's a "but") what comes from this approach is a system made up of distributed components that in prior architectures might have been singleton components or housed intraprocess; with that comes complexity where there once was none (or at least less).

The good news is that, as an industry, we've been working on solutions to these new problems for some time, and the patterns are fairly well established. When one component needs to communicate with another, it needs to know where to find that other component. When an app is horizontally scaled to hundreds of instances, you need a way to make a configuration change to all instances without requiring a massive, collective reboot. When an execution flow passes through a dozen microservices to fulfill a user request and it isn't performing well, you need to find where in the elaborate network of apps the problem lies. You need to keep retries—a foundational pattern in cloud-native software architectures in which a client service repeats requests to a providing service when responses aren't forthcoming—from DDoS[2]-ing your system as a whole.

But remember, the developer isn't responsible for implementing all the patterns required of cloud-native software; instead, the platform can give the assist. Let's take a brief look at some of the capabilities offered by cloud-native platforms in this regard.

---

[2]A distributed denial of service (DDoS) (http://mng.bz/4OGR) isn't always intentional or with malicious intent.

I want to use a concrete example to illustrate a handful of patterns; I'll use a recipe-sharing site. One of the services it provides is a list of recommended recipes, and in order to do this, the *recommendations service* calls a *favorites service* to obtain the list of recipes that the user previously starred. These favorites are then used to calculate the recommendations. You have several apps, each with multiple instances deployed, and the functionality of those apps and the interaction among them determines the behavior of your software. You have a distributed system. What are some of the things that a platform might provide to support this distributed system?

SERVICE DISCOVERY

Individual services are running in separate containers and on different hosts; in order for one service to call another, it must first be able to find the other service. One of the ways that can happen is via the well-known patterns of the World Wide Web: DNS and routing. The recommendations service calls the favorites service via its URL, the URL is resolved to an IP address through DNS lookup, and that IP address points to a router that then sends on the request to one of the instances of the favorites service (figure 3.9).

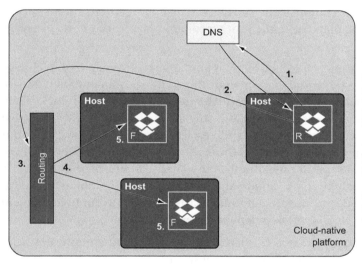

The (R) recommendations app needs to access the (F) favorites service and has a domain name URL configured in. It will **1.** use DNS to find an IP address for the favorites service and **2.** issue a request to that IP address.

That IP address resolves to a router **3.** that then **4.** routes the request to one of the instances of the favorites service.

**5.** Keeping the IP tables of the router up-to-date with changes to the app instance IPs is a function of the cloud-native platform.

**Figure 3.9   The recommendations service finds the favorites service via DNS lookup and routing.**

Another way is to have the recommendations service directly access instances of the favorites service via IP address, but because there are many instances of the latter, the requests must be load-balanced as before. Figure 3.10 depicts that this pulls the routing function into the calling service, thereby distributing the routing function itself.

Whether the routing function is logically centralized (figure 3.9) or highly distributed (figure 3.10), keeping what are effectively routing tables up-to-date is an important process. To fully automate this process, the platform implements patterns such as

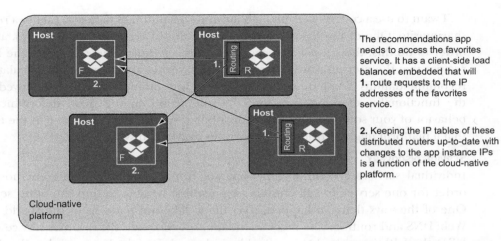

The recommendations app needs to access the favorites service. It has a client-side load balancer embedded that will **1.** route requests to the IP addresses of the favorites service.

**2.** Keeping the IP tables of these distributed routers up-to-date with changes to the app instance IPs is a function of the cloud-native platform.

**Figure 3.10   The recommendations service directly accesses the favorites service via IP address; the routing function is distributed.**

collecting IP address information from newly launched or recovered microservice instances, and distributing that data to the routing components, wherever they may be.

**SERVICE CONFIGURATION**

Our data scientists have done additional analysis and as a result would like to change some parameters for the recommendation algorithm. The recommendation service has hundreds of instances deployed, each of which must receive the new values. When the recommendation engine was deployed as a single process, you could go to that instance, supply a new configuration file, and restart the app. But now, with your highly distributed software architecture, no (human) individual knows where all the instances are running at any given time. But the cloud-native platform does.

To provide this capability in a cloud-native setting, a configuration service is required. This service works in concert with other parts of the platform to implement what's shown in figure 3.11. The process depicted there is as follows:

1  An operator will supply the new configuration values to a configuration service (likely via a commit to a source code control system).

2  Service instances know how to access a configuration service from which they obtain configuration values whenever necessary. Certainly, the service instances will do this at startup time, but they must also do this when the configuration values are changed or when certain lifecycle events occur.

3  When configuration values are changed, the trick is to have each service instance refresh itself; the platform knows about all the service instances. The actual state exists in the state store.

4  The platform notifies each of the service instances that new values are available, and the instances take on those new values.

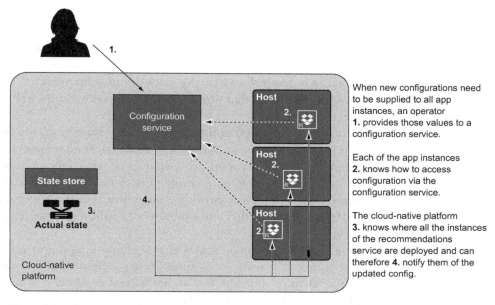

**Figure 3.11** **The configuration service of the cloud-native platform provides important configuration capabilities for microservice-based application deployments.**

Again, neither the developer nor the app operator is responsible for implementing this protocol; rather, it's automatically provided to apps deployed into the cloud-native platform.

Service discovery and service configuration are but two of the many capabilities offered by the cloud-native platform, but are exemplars of the runtime support needed for the modular and highly distributed nature of the cloud-native application. Other services include the following:

- A distributed tracing mechanism that allows you to diagnose issue requests that flow through many microservices by automatically embedding tracers into those requests
- Circuit breakers that prevent inadvertent, internal DDoS attacks when something like a network disruption produces a retry storm

These and many more services are table stakes for a cloud-native platform and greatly reduce the burden that would otherwise be placed on the developer and operator of the modern software we're now building. Adoption of such a platform is essential for a high-functioning IT organization.

## 3.3    *Who does what?*

The cloud-native platform can help with many more tasks—security and compliance, change control, multitenancy, and controlling the deployment process that I talked about in the previous chapter. But in order for you to fully appreciate the value, I first need to talk about humans. In particular, I want to map responsibilities against the structure of the cloud-native platform and data center.

Figure 3.12, a variant of figure 3.4, shows the same stack, but now I want to home in on the boundary between the cloud-native platform and your software. At that boundary is a contract that determines how the software must be provided (the platform API) and a set of service levels that provide guarantees around how well the software will run on the platform.

For example, to run a simple web application, you may supply, via the platform API, the JAR files and HTML files for a web app and some backend services as well as the deployment topology. You might want two instances of your web app, and three instances of the backend service, which are connecting to the customer database. In terms of service levels, the contract may provide a guarantee that the application will have five nines (99.999%) of availability and will have all application logs persisted in your Splunk instance.

Establishing these boundaries and contracts enables something powerful: it allows you to form separate teams. One team is responsible for configuring the cloud-native platform in such a way as to provide the service levels required by the organization. Members of this platform team have a particular skills profile; they know how to work with infrastructure resources, and they understand the inner workings of the cloud-native platform and the primitives that allow them to fine-tune the behavior of the platform (that application logs are sent to Splunk).

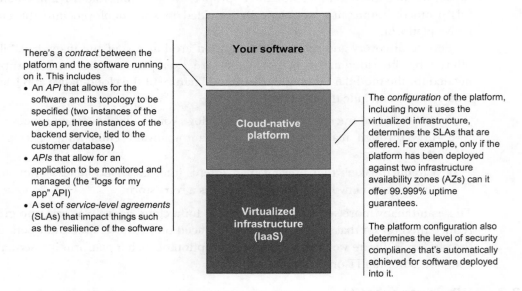

There's a *contract* between the platform and the software running on it. This includes
- An *API* that allows for the software and its topology to be specified (two instances of the web app, three instances of the backend service, tied to the customer database)
- *APIs* that allow for an application to be monitored and managed (the "logs for my app" API)
- A set of *service-level agreements* (SLAs) that impact things such as the resilience of the software

**Your software**

**Cloud-native platform**

**Virtualized infrastructure (IaaS)**

The *configuration* of the platform, including how it uses the virtualized infrastructure, determines the SLAs that are offered. For example, only if the platform has been deployed against two infrastructure availability zones (AZs) can it offer 99.999% uptime guarantees.

The platform configuration also determines the level of security compliance that's automatically achieved for software deployed into it.

**Figure 3.12  The cloud-native platform presents a contract that allows consumers to deploy and manage their software without being exposed to low-level infrastructure details. Nonfunctional requirements such as performance guarantees are realized via SLAs that are achieved via specific platform configurations.**

The other team, or shall I say *teams*, are the application teams whose members build and operate software for end consumers. They know how to use the platform APIs to deploy and manage the apps they're running there. Members of these teams have skills profiles that enable them to understand cloud-native software architectures and know how to monitor and configure them for optimal performance.

Figure 3.13 shows the part of the full stack that each team is responsible for. I want to draw your attention to two elements of this diagram:

- The parts of the stack that each team is responsible for don't overlap. This is extraordinarily empowering and one of the main reasons that application deployments can happen far more frequently when using such a platform. This lack of overlap, however, is achieved only if the contract at the boundary between layers is designed correctly.

- Each team "owns" a product that it's responsible for, and owns the entire lifecycle. The app team is responsible for building and operating the software; the platform gives those team members the contract that they need to do this. And the platform team is responsible for building (or configuring) and operating the product—the platform. The customers for this product are the app team members.

With the right contracts in place, the application team and the platform team are autonomous. Each can execute its responsibilities without extensive coordination with the others. Once again, it's interesting to note how similar their responsibilities are. Each team is responsible for deployment, configuration, monitoring, scaling, and upgrading its respective products. What differs are the products they're responsible for and the tools they use to perform those duties.

But achieving that autonomy, which is such an essential ingredient for delivering digital solutions in this era, depends not only on the definition of the contracts, but also on the inner workings of the cloud-native platform itself. The platform must support

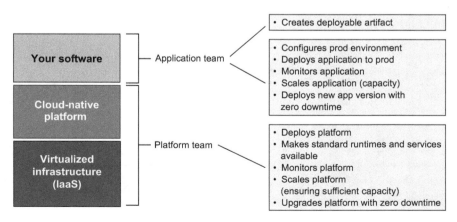

**Figure 3.13  The right abstractions support the formation of autonomous platform and application teams. Each is responsible for deployment, monitoring, scaling, and upgrading their respective products.**

the continuous delivery practices that are essential to achieving the agility we require. It must enable operational excellence by disallowing snowflakes and enabling app team autonomy, while concurrently implementing security, regulatory, and other controls. And it must provide services that lessen the burdens that are added when we create software composed of many highly distributed app components (microservices) running in a multitenant environment.

I already touched on some of these topics when talking about the core tenets of cloud-native platforms. Let's now dig a bit deeper.

## 3.4    More cloud-native platform capabilities

Now that you understand the basic support that platforms provide for highly distributed software running in an environment of constant change, as well as the workings of the application team and platform team, let's look at additional factors you should understand about the cloud-native platform.

### 3.4.1    The platform supports the entire SDLC

Continuous delivery can't be achieved by only automating deployments into production. Success begins early in the software development lifecycle. I've established that a single deployable artifact that carries through the SDLC is essential. What you need now are the environments into which that artifact will be deployed, and a way to have that artifact take on the appropriate configurations of those environments.

After you, as a developer, verify that the code is running on your own workstation, you check in the code. This kicks off a pipeline that builds the deployable artifact, installs it into an official dev environment, and runs the test suite. If the tests pass, you can move on to implementing the next feature, and the cycle continues. Figure 3.14 depicts these deployments into the dev environment. The dev environment contains lightweight versions of various services on which the app depends—databases, message queues, and so on. In the diagram, these are represented by the symbols on the right-hand side.

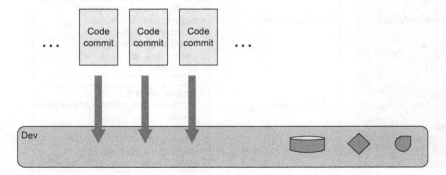

**Figure 3.14    Code commits generate deployable artifacts that are deployed into a dev environment that looks similar to production, but has development versions of services such as databases and message queues (depicted by the symbols on the right).**

Another, less-frequent, trigger, perhaps a time-based one that runs daily, will deploy the artifact into testing, where a more comprehensive (and likely longer-running) set of tests are executed in an environment that's a bit closer to production. You'll notice that in figure 3.15, the general shape of the test environment is the same as that of the dev environment, but the two are shaded differently, indicating variances. For example, the network topology in the dev environment might be flat, with all apps being deployed into the same subnet, whereas in the test environment, the network may be partitioned to provide security boundaries.

The instances of the services available in each environment also differ. Their general shapes are the same (if it's a relational database in dev, then it's relational in test), but the difference in shading again signifies that they differ. For example, in the test environment, the customer database to which the app is bound may be a version of the entire production customer database, cleansed of personally identifiable information (PII), whereas in the development environment, it's a small instance with some sample data.

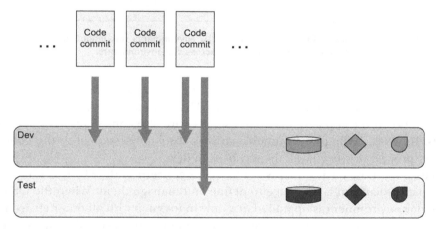

**Figure 3.15  The same deployable artifact is deployed into a staging environment, where it's bound to services (depicted by the symbols on the right) that more closely match those that exist in production.**

Finally, when the business decides it would like to release the software, the artifact is tagged with a release version and deployed into production; see figure 3.16. The production environment, including the service instances, again differs from that of testing. For example, here the app is bound to the live customer database.

Although differences exist in the dev, test, and production environments, I hinted at and want to emphasize that important similarities exist as well. For example, the API used to deploy into any of the environments is the same; managing the automation essential for a streamlined SDLC process with varying APIs would be an unnecessary burden and a barrier to efficiency. The base environment that includes elements such as the operating system, language runtimes, specific I/O libraries, and more

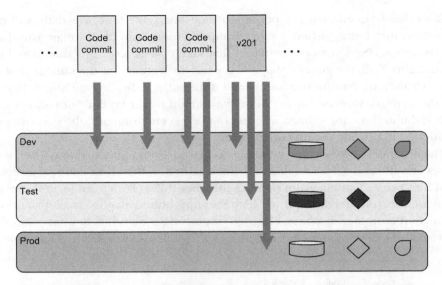

**Figure 3.16   The same artifact is deployed into similar environments throughout the SDLC and must absorb the unavoidable differences across the environments.**

must be the same across all environments (I'll come back to this when we talk about controlling the process in the next section). The contracts that govern the communication between the app and any bound services are also consistent across all environments. In short, having environment parity is absolutely essential to the continuous delivery process that begins all the way back in dev.

Managing those environments is a first-class concern of the IT organization, and a cloud-native platform is the place to define and manage them. When the OS version in the dev environment is upgraded, it's only in lockstep with all other environments. Similarly, when any of the services are revved (a new version of RabbitMQ or Postgres is made available, for example), it's simultaneously done in all environments.

But even more than ensuring that the runtime environments match, a platform must also provide contracts that allow deployed apps to absorb the differences that exist from one stage to the next. For example, environment variables, which are a ubiquitous way of supplying values needed by an app, must be served to the app the same way all through the SDLC. And the manner in which services are bound to apps, thereby supplying connection arguments, must also be uniform.

Figure 3.17 offers a visual depiction of this concept. The artifact deployed into each of the spaces is exactly the same. The contracts between the app and the environment config, and the app and services (in this case, the Loyalty Members database), are also uniform. Note that the arrows pointing from each of the deployable artifacts are exactly the same across all environments—what differs are the details behind the *env config* and *loyalty members* abstractions. Abstractions such as these are an essential part of a platform that's designed to support the entire SDLC.

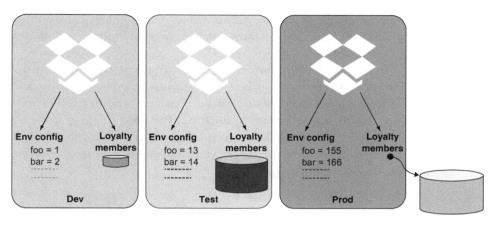

**Figure 3.17  The platform must include a mechanism that allows the contract between app and runtime environment and bound services to serve the needs of the SDLC.**

On occasion, I've had clients implement a platform only for preproduction environments or only for production. There's no question that having a cloud-native platform that offers capabilities such as automated health management or a means of controlling standardized machine images provides value, even if available only in production. But given the need for continuous delivery of digital solutions, the platform must be applied across the entire SDLC. When the platform offers environment parity with the right abstractions, and an API that can be used to automate all interactions with it, the process of developing software and bringing it all the way through to production can be turned into a predictable, efficient machine.

### 3.4.2  Security, change-control, compliance (the control functions)

I've found that many, if not most, developers aren't terribly fond of the chief security office, compliance, or change control. On the one hand, who can blame them? Developers want to get their app running in production, and these control functions require endless tickets to be filed and ultimately can stop a deployment from happening. On the other hand, if developers set their frustration aside for a moment, even they must admit the value that these organizations bring. We must protect our customer' personal data. We must keep changes from taking down critical business applications. We have to appreciate the safeguards in place to keep an oversight from turning into a full-blown production incident.

The trouble with the current process isn't the people, or even the organizations from which they come. The challenges arise because there are simply too many ways to make a mistake. A developer could, for example, specify a dependence on a particular version of the JRE that had been known to cause performance degradations for certain types of workloads and was therefore no longer permitted on production systems—so change control is needed to keep it from going to production. Do you have a control that says every user access to a particular database must be logged? The compliance office is going to verify that logging agents are correctly deployed and configured. An explicit and often manual check that the rules are being followed is sometimes the only point of control.

Those points of control are implemented in various places across the application lifecycle and all too often are pushed too late in the cycle. When a deficiency is detected only the day before a planned deployment, the schedule is then at great risk, deadlines are missed, and everyone is unhappy. The most sobering thing about this, illustrated in figure 3.18, is that these controls apply to every deployment: every version, of every app. The time from *ready to ship* to *deployed* is, at best, counted in days, and multiple deployments in weeks.

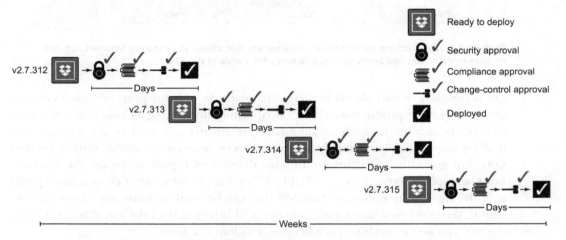

**Figure 3.18   Control functions that are on the critical path for every release of every app reduce the number of deployments that can be performed.**

Remember when I talked about Amazon performing tens of thousands of deployments per day? It's doing something fundamentally different. It isn't that Amazon is exempt from regulatory requirements, nor is it cavalier with customers' personal data. Instead, Amazon is satisfying the requirements that the controls are designed for in a different manner. It bakes the controls directly into its platform so that anything deployed there is guaranteed to meet the security and regulatory requirements.

In just a moment I'll talk about how baking those controls into the platform works, but first let's look at the outcome. If a deployment is guaranteed to meet the controls, you no longer have to go through a checklist before it happens. And if you no longer have a lengthy checklist, then the time from when you have your artifact ready to go to the time that it's deployed shrinks dramatically. A deployment that once took days now takes minutes. And whereas a sequence of deployments took weeks, you can now complete several cycles within a single day (figure 3.19). You can try things out and get feedback far more frequently than before, and you've already studied the many benefits of such a practice.

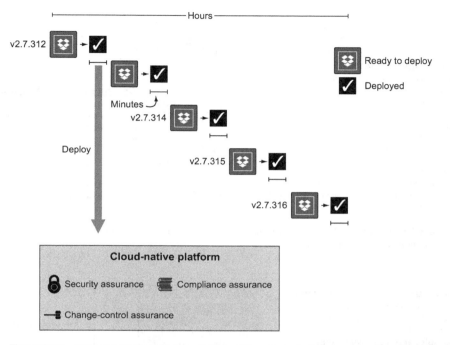

**Figure 3.19   By deploying to a platform that implements controls, you can reduce to mere minutes the time between having an app ready for deployment and performing that deployment.**

Next, let's dig into how such controls are built into the cloud-native platform. How do you get the security, compliance, and change-control assurances that are claimed in figure 3.19?

### 3.4.3 Controlling what goes into the container

In chapter 2, I talked about the need for repeatability and that you achieve it by controlling the runtime environment, controlling the deployable artifact, and controlling the deployment process itself. Using container technology, you have a way of baking that level of control directly into the platform and can therefore achieve the security, compliance, and change-control assurances you're after.

Figure 3.20 repeats figure 2.12 from chapter 2, which addressed the way the various parts of a running application are combined. Now that we've talked about containers, we can map each of the pieces in this diagram to the very entity that will be the running application.

Figure 3.21 shows a container running on a host. What I call the "base image" in figure 3.20 is now clearly shown as the root OS filesystem of the container. The runtime environment represents additional components that are installed into the root filesystem, such as the JRE or the .NET runtime. And then, finally, the deployable artifact also comes into the container. So then, how do you control each of these pieces?

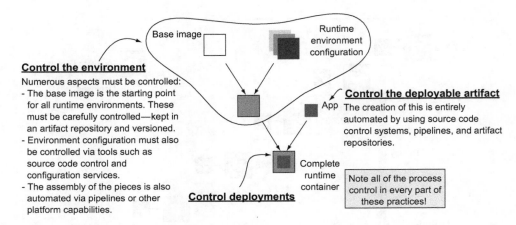

**Control the environment**
Numerous aspects must be controlled:
- The base image is the starting point
  for all runtime environments. These
  must be carefully controlled—kept in
  an artifact repository and versioned.
- Environment configuration must also
  be controlled via tools such as
  source code control and
  configuration services.
- The assembly of the pieces is also
  automated via pipelines or other
  platform capabilities.

**Control the deployable artifact**
The creation of this is entirely
automated by using source code
control systems, pipelines, and artifact
repositories.

Note all of the process
control in every part of
these practices!

**Control deployments**

**Figure 3.20    The assembly of standardized base images, controlled environment configurations, and single deployable artifacts is automated.**

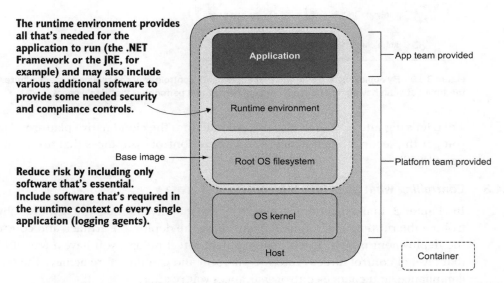

The runtime environment provides
all that's needed for the
application to run (the .NET
Framework or the JRE, for
example) and may also include
various additional software to
provide some needed security
and compliance controls.

Reduce risk by including only
software that's essential.
Include software that's required in
the runtime context of every single
application (logging agents).

**Figure 3.21    The structure of the container image clearly separates the concerns of the app team from those of the platform team.**

First, let's talk about the base image. Recall that the operating system kernel comes from that which is running on the host (and I'll come back to this in just a moment). In the root filesystem inside the container are additional things that are added to that kernel; you can think of them as the software packages installed into the OS. Because any software deployed into the operating system could bring with it a vulnerability, the best practice is to keep that base image as minimal as possible. For example, if you don't want to allow SSH access into the container (restricting SSH access is a *really* good idea), you wouldn't include OpenSSH in the base image. If you then control the set of base images, you have significant control over many security characteristics of your workloads.

Making the base image as small as possible is indeed a best practice, and making an attack surface smaller makes a system more secure. But security and compliance also come through ensuring that certain processes are guaranteed to run (logging agents, for example). Software packages that are required to run in every container should be included in the base image.

> **POINT 1**  The platform should allow only approved base images to be used.

That base image can be used as a foundation for a variety of specialized workloads. For example, some of your apps might be written in Java and therefore require the JRE, and other apps might be written in Python and therefore need the Python interpreter installed. This is the role of what is shown in figure 3.21 as the runtime environment. Of course, parts of that runtime environment, such as the JRE or the Python interpreter, may have themselves vulnerabilities, so the security office will have specific versions that are approved for use.

> **POINT 2**  The platform should control all runtime environments that may be included in a container.

Finally, the last piece that's in the container is the application itself, and practices for the careful creation of this deployable artifact are well understood.

> **POINT 3**  Build pipelines coupled with code scans to provide the automation to repeatably and safely create the artifact.

Let's now turn to the points of control. I've talked about having an architecture that separates the concerns of the app team from those of the platform team. The app team is responsible for delivering digital offerings that support the business, and the platform team is responsible for meeting security and compliance needs for the enterprise. The app team supplies only its app, and the platform team provides everything else.

Looking back at figure 3.21, you can see that the platform team supplies approved base images and approved runtime environments. You can also see that the platform team is responsible for the OS kernel that's running on the host. In short, the platform team is able to impose security and compliance controls through each of the layers you've just studied.

### 3.4.4  *Upgrading and patching vulnerabilities*

When any part of the application container depicted in figure 3.21 needs to be updated, running instances aren't modified. Instead, you deploy *new* containers with the new set of components. Because cloud-native apps always have multiple instances deployed, you can move from an old version to the new with zero downtime.

The basic pattern for such an upgrade is that (1) a subset of the app instances are shut down and disposed of, (2) an equal number of instances of the new container are launched, and (3) after they're up and running, you move on to replacing the next batch of old instances. The cloud-native platform handles this process for you; you need only provide the new version of the app.

Look at the first few words of this section's first paragraph: "When *any part* of the application container" needs to be updated—sometimes it's the app that's changing, and sometimes it's all the pieces supplied by the platform. That's right—the rolling upgrade is performed when you have a new version of your app, or whenever you have new versions of the operating system (kernel or root filesystem) or anything else in the runtime environment.

And it gets even better. The cloud-native platform, designed to serve both the platform and the app teams' needs, allows these teams to operate independently. This is extraordinarily powerful!

Figure 3.22 extends earlier diagrams that showed the app team doing deployments into the dev, test, and prod environments. Now you understand that with each deployment from the app team, a container is assembled with pieces supplied by the platform team and pieces supplied by the app team (recall figure 3.21).

It follows that when there are new versions of the parts of the container supplied by the platform team, a new container could also be assembled. If the app team has something new, a new container is assembled and deployed, and if the platform team has something new, a new container is assembled and deployed. This is shown in figure 3.22: from above, the app team is creating new containers; and from the side, on their own schedule, the platform team is revving the platform elements. The platform team is updating the platform-supplied portions of the container.

This autonomy is essential for patch management in the data center. When a new vulnerability (CVE) is found,[3] patches need to be applied quickly, without complex coordination across all apps running in the data center. This type of complex coordination was part of the reason that patches were often not applied as rapidly as they should have been in prior data center configurations.

Now, with the cloud-native platform—you guessed it—when the platform team rolls out a fix for the latest vulnerability, the platform automatically creates the new container image and then replaces the running instances in batches, always leaving a subset of the app instances running as others are being cycled. This is the rolling upgrade. Of course, you aren't going to be reckless; you'll first deploy the patch into the staging environment and run tests there, and only after those pass will you move on to deployments in production.

If you think about this for a moment from the perspective of Google Cloud Platform, Amazon Web Services, Azure, or any of the other cloud platform providers, this type of autonomy between the platform team and the users of the platform is essential. With

---

[3]CVE is an acronym for Common Vulnerabilities and Exposures; Wikipedia offers more details at http://mng.bz/QQr6.

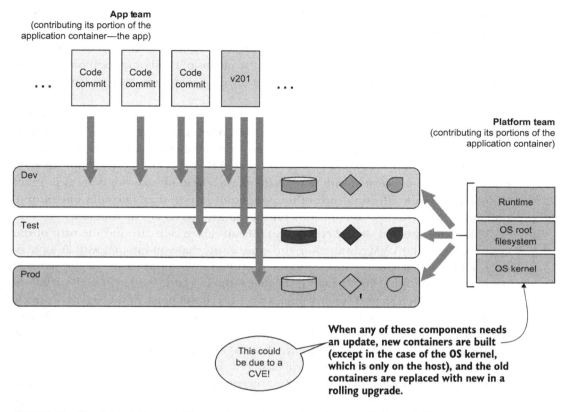

**Figure 3.22  The right platform enables app teams to operate independently from platform teams.**

over one million active users,[4] AWS couldn't manage its platform offering if it required coordination with individual members of that user base. You can absolutely apply the same practices in your data center, with the help of a cloud-native application platform.

### 3.4.5  Change control

The change-control function is the last defense against a change (an upgrade or a new app being deployed, for example) causing something bad to happen in production. This is quite a responsibility that's usually addressed by carefully looking at all the details of the planned deployment and evaluating how it might impact other systems running in the same environment. Impacts can include contention for computing resources, a broadening or restriction of access to various system components, or a dramatic increase in network traffic. What makes this job hard is that many things are

---

[4]See "Amazon's AWS Is Now a $7.3B Business as It Passes 1M Active Customers," by Ingrid Lunden (http://mng.bz/Xgm9) for more details.

used and deployed into the same IT environment, so a change in one area can have rippling effects in many others.

The cloud-native platform allows for a fundamentally different way of addressing the concerns of change control. It provides the means of insulating components from one another, so that problems in one part of the data center will be kept from impacting others.

It's helpful to have a name you can use to refer to the entities that need to be isolated from one another; the term I use is *tenant*. When I use that term in this context, I don't mean the proverbial Coke and Pepsi, two organizations that might be using the same environment but need to be so isolated that they don't even know of each other. I'm more concerned with tenants that have a level of isolation that keeps them from inadvertently affecting each other. Our conversation then becomes one of multitenancy: you have many tenants that are all using a shared IT environment.

VMware pioneered shared computing infrastructure right around the turn of the century. It created a VM abstraction, the same entity that you interact with as a physical resource—a machine—and software controlled doling out shares of the physical resources to multiple VMs. Arguably, the main concern addressed with such virtualization technologies is shared resource use, and many, if not most, of the digital products running in large and small enterprises are now running in virtual machines. Independent software deployments are tenants on a shared computing infrastructure, and this worked extraordinarily well for software that was architected to be run on machines.

But as you know, architectures have changed, and the smaller, individual parts that come together to form cloud-native software, coupled with the far more dynamic environments these apps are running in, have stressed the VM-based platforms. Although other attempts were previously made, container-based approaches have proven an outstanding solution. Based on the foundational concepts of control groups (cgroups), which control the use of shared resources, and namespaces, which control the visibility of shared resources, Linux containers have become the execution environments for the microservices collective that forms cloud-native software.[5]

Containers provide part of the isolation that stands to satisfy the concerns of the change-control office; an app that gobbles up all the memory or CPU available in one container won't affect other containers running on the same host. But, as I pointed out, other concerns remain. Who is allowed to deploy containers? How can you be sure to have monitoring data sufficient to assess whether an app is running amok? How can you allow routing changes for one app without allowing routing changes to be inadvertently made to another?

The answer is that the platform itself, which provides access control, monitoring, routing functions, and more, must be tenant aware. Figure 3.23 shows a set of hosts at the bottom, where Linux cgroups and namespaces are providing the compute isolation

---

[5]Container technology was initially innovated and used on Linux, and the majority of container-centric systems still run on this operating system. More recently, Windows has added container support, yet its embrace remains far behind that of Linux.

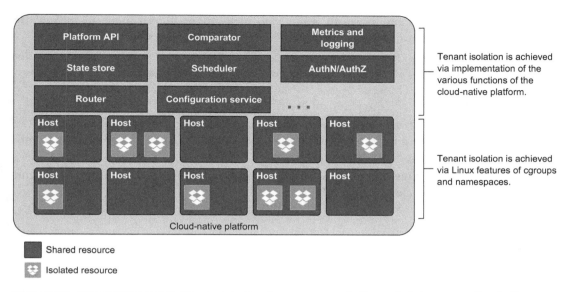

Figure 3.23  **True multitenancy in the compute tier shares resources in the control plane, as well as in the compute layer (the Linux host and kernel) while using containers to achieve resource isolation.**

you need. In the upper part of the diagram are a whole host of other platform components that govern its use. The platform API is the place that access control is enforced. The metrics and logging system needs to group collected data into buckets for individual tenants. The scheduler, which determines where containers will be run, must be aware of relationships within a tenant and across tenants. In short, the cloud-native application platform is multitenant.

And this multitenancy is what relieves the tension from the change-control function. Because deployment, upgrade, and configuration changes applied to one app/tenant are isolated from other apps/tenants, application teams are empowered to manage software on their own.

## Summary

- A cloud-native platform takes on a great deal of the burden of satisfying the requirements on modern software.
- The cloud-native platform is used throughout the entire software development lifecycle.
- A cloud-native platform projects higher-level abstraction than that of the infrastructure-centric platforms of the last decade.
- By baking control functions into the platform, deployments can be done far more frequently and are safer than when approvals are needed for every version of every app.

- App teams and platform teams can work independently, each managing the construction, deployment, and maintenance of their respective products.
- Eventual consistency is at the core of the platform as it constantly monitors the actual state of the system, compares it to the desired state, and remediates when necessary. This applies to both the software running on the platform and to the deployment of the platform itself.
- As software becomes more modular and distributed, the services that bring the components together into a whole do so as well. The platform must bake in support for these distributed systems.
- A cloud-native platform is absolutely essential for organizations building and operating cloud-native software.

# Part 2

# *Cloud-native patterns*

This is where the patterns are. Now, if you're expecting a *Gang of Four* style of patterns, I'm afraid you might be disappointed, though I hope not. The *Design Patterns* book by Erich Gamma, John Vlissides, Ralph Johnson, and Richard Helm is fantastic and is arguably the book most responsible for raising awareness of reusable patterns in a whole era of software developers. But instead of taking that reference-book-like approach, my coverage of patterns is all in the context of the problems they're designed to solve.

Virtually every chapter begins with a discussion of certain challenges, sometimes talking about design approaches that predate the cloud era, and then derives solutions—and those solutions are the patterns. It's not accidental that the solutions I present are some of the ones you've undoubtedly heard about— sidecars and event-driven architectures, for example—but again, I hope that presenting them in this way will deepen your understanding and help you learn when and how to best apply them.

I start this part by introducing *event-driven design* in chapter 4. Most of the patterns discussed in the context of cloud-native architectures implicitly assume a request/response approach at the core. Truth be told, that's how most of us naturally think about our software. I want to plant the seed of event-driven thinking right at the onset so that you at least have it in the back of your mind as you consume the rest of the chapters. And then I close this part of the book in chapter 12 with event-driven systems again, this time focusing on the important role that they play in enabling cloud-native data. It's an admittedly all-too-brief coverage of cloud-native data, but I hope enough to complete the cloud-native picture for you, at least at a high level.

Between these bookends of chapters 4 and 12, I cover a whole host of patterns. Chapters 5, 6, and 7 focus on the cloud-native app, covering statelessness, configuration, and the application lifecycle. Starting with chapter 8, I turn our focus more toward cloud-native interactions, first talking about service discovery and dynamic routing. Then in chapters 9 and 10, I focus on the patterns you'll apply to each side of an interaction after it's established—the client and service sides. I'll point out that chapter 4 on event-driven design is also fundamentally about cloud-native interactions. The highly distributed architecture that's constantly changing characterizes cloud-native software and poses new challenges for troubleshooting, and that's what I cover in chapter 11. It's also interesting that the solutions in this chapter themselves exercise many of the patterns covered in the earlier chapters. And, as I mentioned, the book closes out by introducing the fundamental patterns of cloud-native data.

# Event-driven microservices: It's not just request/response

**This chapter covers**

- Using the request/response programming model
- Using the event-driven programming model
- Considering both models for cloud-native software
- Understanding the models' similarities and differences
- Using Command Query Responsibility Segregation

One of the main pillars on which cloud-native software stands is microservices. Breaking what once was a large, monolithic application into a collection of independent components has shown many benefits, including increased developer productivity and more-resilient systems, provided the right patterns are applied to these microservice-based deployments. But an overall software solution is almost never made up of a single component; instead, microservices are brought together into a collection to form a rich digital offering.

But here's the risk: if you aren't careful, you could glue the components back together in such a way that the microservices you've created only give the illusion of loose coupling. You have to be careful not to re-create the monolith by coupling the individual pieces too tightly or too early. The patterns covered through the remainder of this book are designed to avoid this pitfall and to produce robust, agile software as a collection of independent components, brought together in a way that maximizes agility and resilience.

But before we jump deep into those topics, I need to cover one more umbrella topic—a cross-cutting concern against which all of the other cloud-native patterns will be applied: *the basic invocation style used in your software architecture.* Will the interaction between microservices be in a request/response or an event-driven style? With the former, a client makes a request and expects a response. Although the requestor may allow for that response to come asynchronously, the very expectation that a response will come establishes a direct dependence of one on the other. With the latter, the parties consuming events can be completely independent from those producing them. This autonomy gets to the heart of the difference between these two styles of interaction.

Large, complex software deployments employ both approaches—sometimes request/response, sometimes event-driven. But I suggest the factors that drive our choices are far more nuanced than we've likely given them credit for in the past. And once again, the highly distributed and constantly changing cloud context our software is now running in brings an added dimension that requires us to reexamine and challenge our previous understandings and assumptions.

In this chapter, I start with the style that seems to be the most natural for most developers and architects: request/response. It's so natural that you might not have even noticed that the basic model I presented in chapter 1 subtly favors it. I then challenge that bias and introduce the event-driven model in our cloud context. Event-driven thinking is fundamentally different from request/response, so the implications are great. You'll study these two models through code samples, and as a result will broaden your thinking about the interaction portion of our cloud-native software mental model.

## 4.1   We're (usually) taught imperative programming

The vast majority of students, whether learning to program in a classroom setting or via any of the many sources available online, learn imperative programming. They learn languages such as Python, Node.js, Java, C#, and Golang, most of which are designed to allow the programmer to provide a series of instructions that are executed from start to finish. Sure, control structures allow for branching and looping, and some instructions will be calls to procedures or functions, but even the logic within a loop or a function, for example, will execute from the top to the bottom.

You surely see where I'm going with this. This sequential programming model drives you to think in a request/response manner. As you're executing a set of instructions, you make a request of a function, anticipating a response. And in the context of a program that's executing in a single process, this works well. In fact, procedural programming has dominated the industry for nearly a half century.[1] As long as the programming process remains up and running, someone making a request of a function can reasonably expect a response from a function also running in that same process.

But our software as a whole is no longer executing in a single process. Much of the time, different pieces of our software aren't even running on the same computer. In the highly distributed, constantly changing environment of the cloud, a requestor can no longer depend on an immediate response when a request is made. Despite this, the request/response model has still dominated as the main programming paradigm for the web. True, with the availability of React.js and other similar frameworks, reactive programming is becoming more commonplace for code running in the browser, but server-side programming remains heavily dominated by request/response.

For example, figure 4.1 shows a significant fan-out of requests to dozens of microservices that occurs when a user accesses their Netflix homepage. This slide was taken from a presentation that Senior Software Engineer Scott Mansfield has given at numerous conferences, in which he talks about patterns Netflix uses to compensate for the cases when a response from a downstream request isn't immediately forthcoming.

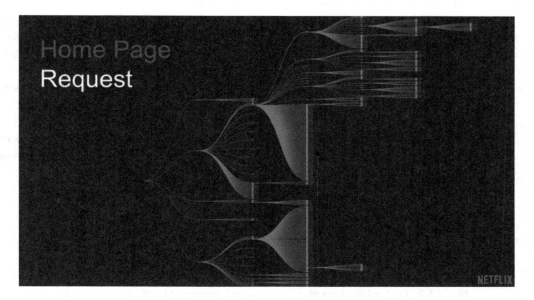

**Figure 4.1** Diagram appearing in a presentation from Scott Mansfield of Netflix shows a single request to retrieve the homepage for a user results in a significant fan-out of requests to downstream microservices.

[1]For more information on procedural programming, see Wikipedia at http://mng.bz/lp56.

I include this particular diagram because it does a great job illustrating the magnitude of the problem. If the homepage request were successful only when all of the cascading requests depicted in this tree were also successful, Netflix would have a great many frustrated customers. Even if each microservice could boast five nines of availability (99.999%), *and* the network was always up,[2] a single request with fewer than 100 downstream request/response dependencies loses two nines of availability, or approximately 99.9% at the root. I haven't seen estimates of the revenue loss to Netflix when its website is offline, but if we go back to the *Forbes* estimates of the economic impact to Amazon's bottom line, the resultant 500 minutes of downtime would cost Amazon $80 million yearly.

Of course, Netflix, and many other highly successful web properties, do far better than that by implementing patterns like automatic request retries when responses aren't received, and having multiple running instances of microservices that can fulfill requests. And as Scott Mansfield has expertly presented, caching can also help provide a bulkhead between clients and services.[3] These patterns and many more are built around the request/response invocation style, and although you can and will continue fortifying this basis with additional techniques, you should also consider a different foundation for building these resilience patterns.

## 4.2    *Reintroducing event-driven computing*

When you get into the details, you may find differing opinions on what makes up an event-driven system.[4] But even through this variability, one thing is common. The entity that triggers code execution in an event-driven system doesn't expect any type of response—*it's fire and forget.* The code execution has an effect (otherwise, why would you run it at all), and the outcome may cause other things to happen with the software solution, but the entity that triggered the execution doesn't expect a response.

This concept is easily understood with a simple diagram, particularly when you set it in contrast to the request/response pattern. The left side of figure 4.2 depicts a

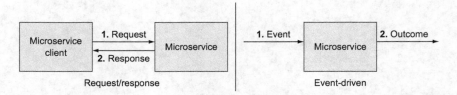

**Figure 4.2    Contrast the base primitive of request/response to event-driven invocation styles.**

---

[2]See #1 on the list of fallacies of distributed computing at Wikipedia (http://mng.bz/BD90).
[3]See "Caching at Netflix: The Hidden Microservice" on YouTube (http://mng.bz/dPvN).
[4]"What Do You Mean by Event-Driven?" by Martin Fowler (http://mng.bz/YPla) explores this topic further.

simple request and response: the code that's executed when a request is received is on the hook for providing some type of a response to the requestor. By contrast, the right-hand side of this figure shows an event-driven service: the outcome of the code execution has no direct relationship to the event that triggered it.

A couple of points are interesting to note in these two diagrams. First, on the left, two parties are involved in the dance: the microservice client and the microservice itself. Partners in the dance depend on each other to make things go smoothly. On the right-hand side, only one party is depicted, and this is significant. The microservice executes as a result of an event, but what triggered that event isn't of concern to the microservice at all. As a result, the service has fewer dependencies.

Second, notice that the event and the outcome are entirely disconnected. The lack of coupling between the former and the latter even allows me to draw the arrows on different sides of the microservice. That's something I couldn't do in the request/response style on the left.

The implications of these differences run fairly deep. The best way for you to start to wrap your head around them is with a concrete example. Let's jump into the first bit of code in the book.

## 4.3  *My global cookbook*

I love to cook, and I spend far more time browsing food-related blogs than I care to admit. I have my favorite bloggers (https://food52.com and https://smitten-kitchen.com, I'm looking at you) as well as my favorite "official" publications (www.bonappetit.com). What I want to do now is build a site that pulls together content from all of my favorite sites and allows me to organize that content. Yeah, basically I want a blog aggregator, but perhaps something that's specialized for my ~~addiction~~, er, hobby.

One of the content views I'm interested in is a list of the latest posts that come from my favorite sites: given a network of people or sites that I follow, what are their latest posts? I'm going to call this set of content the *Connections' Posts* content, and it'll be produced by a service I'm going to write. Two parts come together to form this content: a list of the people or sites that I follow and a list of content provided by those individuals. The content for each of these two parts is provided by two additional services.

Figure 4.3 depicts the relationship between these components. This diagram doesn't depict any particular protocol between the various microservices, but only the relationships between them. This is a perfect example for you to have a deeper look at the two protocols: request/response and event-driven.

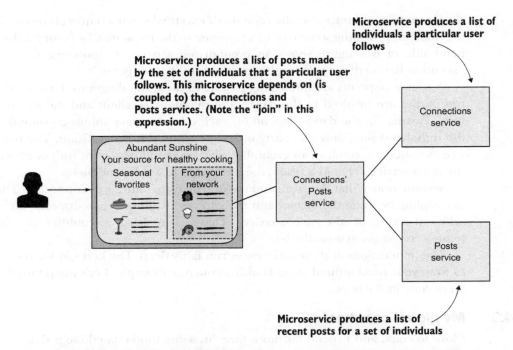

**Microservice produces a list of individuals a particular user follows**

**Microservice produces a list of posts made by the set of individuals that a particular user follows. This microservice depends on (is coupled to) the Connections and Posts services. (Note the "join" in this expression.)**

**Microservice produces a list of recent posts for a set of individuals**

**Figure 4.3    The Abundant Sunshine website will display a list of posts made by my favorite food bloggers. The aggregation is a composition of the network of people I follow and posts made by those individuals.**

### 4.3.1    *Request/response*

As I talked about earlier in the chapter, using the request/response protocol to concretely draw together the components depicted in figure 4.3 is, for most people, the most natural. When we think about generating a set of posts written by my favorite bloggers, it's easy to say, let's first get a list of the people I like, and then look up the posts that each of those individuals has made. Concretely, the flow progresses as follows (see figure 4.4):

1  JavaScript in the browser makes a request to the Connections' Posts service, providing an identifier for the individual who has requested the web page (let's say that's you), and waits for a response. Note that the response may be returned asynchronously, but the invocation protocol is still request/response in that a response is expected.

2  The Connections' Posts service makes a request to the Connections service with that identifier and waits for a response.

3  The Connections service responds with the list of bloggers that you follow.

4  The Connections' Posts service makes a request to the Posts service with that list of bloggers just returned from the Connections service, and awaits a response.

5   The Posts service responds with a list of posts for that set of bloggers.

6   The Connections' Posts service creates a composition of the data it has received in the responses and itself responds to the web page with that aggregation.

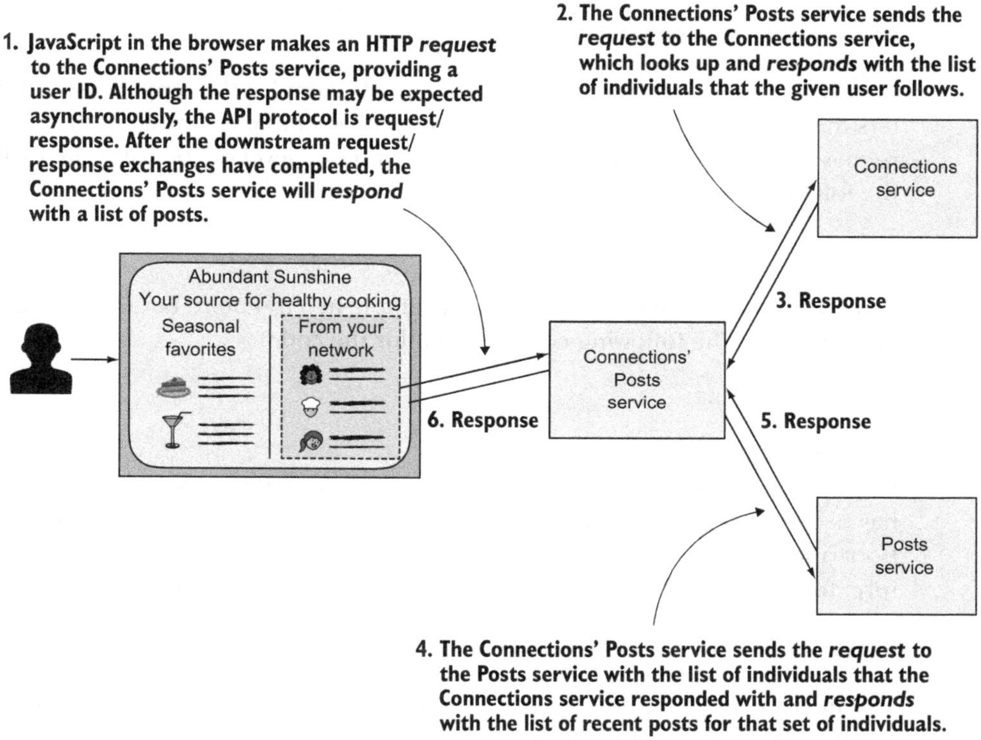

**1. JavaScript in the browser makes an HTTP *request* to the Connections' Posts service, providing a user ID. Although the response may be expected asynchronously, the API protocol is request/ response. After the downstream request/ response exchanges have completed, the Connections' Posts service will *respond* with a list of posts.**

**2. The Connections' Posts service sends the *request* to the Connections service, which looks up and *responds* with the list of individuals that the given user follows.**

**3. Response**

**6. Response**

**5. Response**

**4. The Connections' Posts service sends the *request* to the Posts service with the list of individuals that the Connections service responded with and *responds* with the list of recent posts for that set of individuals.**

**Figure 4.4   Rendering a portion of the web page depends on a series of coordinated requests and responses.**

Let's have a look at the code that implements the steps I've depicted in figure 4.4.

**SETTING UP**

This and most of the examples throughout the book require you to have the following tools installed:

- Maven
- Git
- Java 1.8

I won't require you to write any code. You need only check it out of GitHub and execute a few commands to build and run the applications. Although this isn't a programming book, I use code throughout to demonstrate the architectural principles that I cover.

**OBTAINING AND BUILDING THE MICROSERVICES**

You'll begin by cloning the cloudnative-abundantsunshine repository with the following command and then changing into that directory:

```
git clone https://github.com/cdavisafc/cloudnative-abundantsunshine.git
cd cloudnative-abundantsunshine
```

Here you'll see subdirectories containing code samples that appear in various chapters throughout this text. The code for this first example is located in the cloudnative-requestresponse directory, so I'll have you step one level deeper into the project with the following:

```
cd cloudnative-requestresponse
```

You'll drill into the source code of the example in a moment, but first let's get you up and running. The following command builds the code:

```
mvn clean install
```

**RUNNING THE MICROSERVICES**

You'll now see that a new JAR file, cloudnative-requestresponse-0.0.1-SNAPSHOT.jar, has been created in the target subdirectory. This is what we call a *fat jar*—the Spring Boot application is completely self-contained, including a Tomcat container. Therefore, to run the application, you need only run Java, pointing to the JAR:

```
java -jar target/cloudnative-requestresponse-0.0.1-SNAPSHOT.jar
```

The microservices are now up and running. In a separate command-line window, you can curl the Connections' Posts service:

```
curl localhost:8080/connectionsposts/cdavisafc
```

To obtain a response:

```
[
  {
    "date": "2019-01-22T01:06:19.895+0000",
    "title": "Chicken Pho",
    "usersName": "Max"
  },
  {
    "date": "2019-01-22T01:06:19.985+0000",
    "title": "French Press Lattes",
    "usersName": "Glen"
  }
]
```

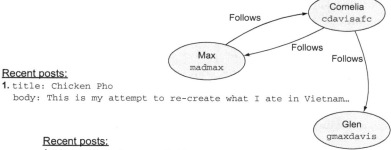

<u>Recent posts:</u>
**1.** `title: Whole orange cake`
    `body: That's right, you blend up whole oranges, rind and all...`
**2.** `title: German dumplings (kloesse),`
    `body: Russet potatoes, flour (gluten free!) and more...`

<u>Recent posts:</u>
**1.** `title: Chicken Pho`
  `body: This is my attempt to re-create what I ate in Vietnam…`

<u>Recent posts:</u>
**1.** `title: French press lattes`
    `body: We've figured out how to make these dairy free, but just as good!...`

**Figure 4.5**   **Users, the connections between them, and the posts each has recently made**

As part of starting this application, I've prepopulated several databases with sample content. This response represents a list of posts by individuals that I, `cdavisafc`, follow. In this case, one post is titled "Chicken Pho," written by someone whose name is Max; and a second post is titled "French Press Lattes," written by someone whose name is Glen. Figure 4.5 shows how the three sample users are connected as well as the posts that each user has recently made.

Indeed, you can see this data reflected by invoking the Connections' Posts service for each of the users:

```
curl localhost:8080/connectionsposts/madmax
curl localhost:8080/connectionsposts/gmaxdavis
```

### A note on the project structure

I've bundled the implementations of each of the three services into the same JAR, but let me be clear: in any real setting, this would be completely discouraged. One of the advantages of a microservices-based architecture is the existence of bulkheads between the services, so that failures in one don't cascade to others. The implementation here has none of those bulkheads. If the Connections service crashes, it will take the other two services with it.

I start the implementation with this antipattern in place for two reasons. First, it allows you to get the code sample running with a minimum number of steps; I've taken a shortcut for simplicity. This approach also will allow you to clearly see the benefits as you refactor the implementation by applying patterns that serve cloud-native architectures well.

### STUDYING THE CODE

The Java program that you're running implements all three of the microservices depicted in figure 4.4. I've organized the code for the implementation into four packages, each a subpackage of the com.corneliadavis.cloudnative package:

- The *config* package contains the Spring Boot application and configuration, as well as a bit of code that fills the databases with sample data.
- The *connections* package contains the code for the Connections microservice, including domain objects, data repositories, and controllers.
- The *posts* package contains the code for the Posts microservice, including domain objects, data repositories, and controllers.
- The *connectionsposts* package contains the code for the Connections' Posts microservice, including domain objects and controllers (note, no data repository).

One package draws all the pieces together into a single Spring Boot application and contains some utility implementations. Then you have one package for each of the three microservices that make up the digital solution.

The Connections and Posts microservices are similar in structure. Each contains classes that define the domain objects for the service, as well as interfaces used by Spring's Java Persistence API (JPA) implementation to generate databases that store the content for objects of each type. Each package also contains the controller that implements the service and the core functionality of the microservice. These two microservices are basic CRUD services: they allow objects to be created, read, updated, and deleted, and data is persisted in a database.

The microservice of most interest in this first implementation is Connections' Posts because it doesn't only store data into and retrieve data from a database, but it also calculates a composite result. Looking at the contents of the package, you can see there are only two classes: a domain object called PostSummary and a controller.

The PostSummary class defines an object containing fields for the data that the Connections' Posts service will return: for each post, it returns the title and date, and the name of the individual who made the post. There's no JPA repository for this domain object because the microservice only uses it in memory to hold the results of its computation.

The ConnectionsPosts controller implements a single public method—the one that's executed when a request is made to the service with an HTTP GET. Accepting a username, the implementation requests from the Connections service the list of users being followed by this individual, and when it receives that response, makes another HTTP request to the Posts service with that set of user IDs. When the response from the request to Posts is received, the composite result is produced. Figure 4.6 presents the code for that microservice, annotated with the steps detailed in figure 4.4.

For steps 2 and 3 and for steps 4 and 5, the Connections' Posts microservice is acting as a client to the Connections and Posts microservices, respectively. Clearly, you have instances of the protocol depicted on the left-hand side of figure 4.2—the

```
1  @RequestMapping(method = RequestMethod.GET, value="/connectionsposts/{username}")
   public Iterable<PostSummary> getByUsername(
                                  @PathVariable("username") String username,
                                  HttpServletResponse response) {

       ArrayList<PostSummary> postSummaries = new ArrayList<~>();
       logger.info("getting posts for user network " + username);

       String ids = "";
       RestTemplate restTemplate = new RestTemplate();

       // get connections
3      ResponseEntity<Connection[]> respConns
               = restTemplate.getForEntity( url: connectionsUrl+username,   2
                                        Connection[].class);
       Connection[] connections = respConns.getBody();
       for (int i=0; i<connections.length; i++) {
           if (i > 0) ids += ",";
           ids += connections[i].getFollowed().toString();
       }
       logger.info("connections = " + ids);

       // get posts for those connections
5      ResponseEntity<Post[]> respPosts
               = restTemplate.getForEntity( url: postsUrl+ids, Post[].class);   4
       Post[] posts = respPosts.getBody();

       for (int i=0; i<posts.length; i++)
           postSummaries.add(new PostSummary(getUsersname(posts[i].getUserId()),
                                        posts[i].getTitle(),
                                        posts[i].getDate())));
6      return postSummaries;
   }
```

**Figure 4.6   The composite result generated by the Connections' Posts microservice is produced by making calls to the Connections and Posts microservices and aggregating results.**

request/response. If you look closely, however, you'll see that there's one more instance of this pattern. The composite result includes the name of the user who made the post, but this data is returned neither from the request to Connections, nor from the request to Posts; each response includes only user IDs. Admittedly naïve, at the moment the implementation retrieves the name for each user of each post by making a set of additional HTTP requests to the Connections service. In a moment, when you move to an event-driven approach, you'll see that these extra calls will go away on their own.

Okay, so this basic implementation works reasonably well, even if it could use some optimizations for efficiency. But it's rather fragile. To generate the result, the Connections microservice needs to be up and running, as does the Posts microservice. And the network must also be stable enough for all of the requests and responses to execute without any hiccups. Proper functioning of the Connections' Posts microservice is heavily dependent on many other things functioning correctly; it's not truly in control of its own destiny.

Event-driven architectures, to a large extent, are designed to address the problem of systems that are too tightly coupled. Let's now look at an implementation that satisfies the same requirements on the Connections' Posts microservice but with a different architecture and level of resilience.

### 4.3.2   Event-driven

Instead of code being executed only when someone or some entity makes a request, in an event-driven system, code is executed when something happens. What that "something" is can vary wildly, and could even be a user request, but the main idea with event-driven systems is that events cause code to be executed that may, in turn, generate events that further flow through the system. The best way to understand the fundamentals is with a concrete example, so let's take the same problem we've just solved in the request/response style and refactor it to be event-driven.

Our end goal is still to have a list of posts made by the people I follow. In that context, what are the events that could affect that result? Certainly, if one of the individuals I follow publishes a new post, that new post would need to be included in my list. But changes in my network will also affect the result. If I add to or remove from the list of individuals I am following, or if one of those individuals changes their username, that could also result in changes to the data produced by the Connections' Posts service.

Of course, we have microservices that are responsible for posts and for user connections; they keep track of the state of these objects. In the request/response approach you just looked at, those microservices manage the state of these objects, and when requested, serve up that state. In our new model, those microservices are still managing the state of these objects, but are more proactive and generate events when any of that state changes. Then, based on the software topology, those events affect the Connections' Posts microservice. This relationship is depicted in figure 4.7.

Of course, you've already seen relationships between Connections' Posts, Connections, and Posts in figures 4.3 and 4.4, but of significance here is the direction of the arrows. As I said, the Connections and Posts microservices are *proactively* sending out

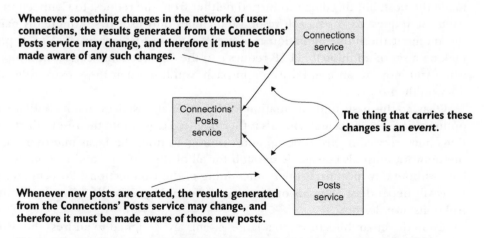

**Figure 4.7   Events are the means through which related microservices are connected.**

change notifications rather than waiting to be asked. When the Connections' Posts service is asked for data, it *already knows the answer*. No downstream requests are needed.

I want to dig into these implications in more detail, but first, let's look at the code that implements this pattern. Doing so will help you make your way to this fundamentally different way of thinking.

### SETTING UP

As with all the samples in this book, you'll need the following tools installed on your workstation:

- Maven
- Git
- Java 1.8

### OBTAINING AND BUILDING THE MICROSERVICES

If you haven't already done so, you must clone the cloudnative-abundantsunshine repository with the following command:

```
git clone https://github.com/cdavisafc/cloudnative-abundantsunshine.git
cd cloudnative-abundantsunshine
```

The code for this example is housed in the cloudnative-eventdriven subdirectory, so you'll need to move to that directory:

```
cd cloudnative-eventdriven
```

You'll drill into the source code of the example in a moment, but first let's get you up and running. The following command builds the code:

```
mvn clean install
```

### RUNNING THE MICROSERVICES

Just as before, you'll see that a new JAR file, cloudnative-eventdriven-0.0.1-SNAPSHOT.jar, has been created in the target subdirectory. This is a fat jar—the Spring Boot application is completely self-contained, including a Tomcat container. Therefore, to run the application, you need only run Java, pointing to the JAR:

```
java -jar target/cloudnative-eventdriven-0.0.1-SNAPSHOT.jar
```

The microservices are now up and running. As before, I've loaded sample data during startup so that you can, in a separate command-line window, `curl` the Connections' Posts service:

```
curl localhost:8080/connectionsposts/cdavisafc
```

You should see exactly the same output that you did when running the request/response version of the application:

```
[
    {
        "date": "2019-01-22T01:06:19.895+0000",
        "title": "Chicken Pho",
        "usersName": "Max"
    },
    {
        "date": "2019-01-22T01:06:19.985+0000",
        "title": "French Press Lattes",
        "usersName": "Glen"
    }
]
```

If you didn't go through the exercise before, please look at section 4.3.1 for a description of the sample data and the other API endpoints that are available for you to send requests to in exploring the sample data. Each of the three microservices implements the same interface as before; they vary only in implementation.

I now want to demonstrate how the events we just identified (the creation of new posts and the creation of new connections) will change what is produced by the Connections' Posts microservice. To add a new post, execute the following command:

```
curl -X POST localhost:8080/posts \
-d '{"userId":2,
     "title":"Tuna Onigiri",
     "body":"Sushi rice, seaweed and tuna. Yum..."}' \
--header "Content-Type: application/json"
```

Execute the original command again:

```
curl localhost:8080/connectionsposts/cdavisafc
```

This yields the following:

```
[
    {
        "date": "2019-01-22T05:36:44.546+0000",
        "usersName": "Max",
        "title": "Chicken Pho"
    },
    {
        "date": "2019-01-22T05:41:01.766+0000",
        "usersName": "Max",
        "title": "Tuna Onigiri"
    },
    {
        "date": "2019-01-22T05:36:44.648+0000",
        "usersName": "Glen",
        "title": "French Press Lattes"
    }
]
```

### STUDYING THE CODE

This is exactly what you'd expect, and the same steps executed against the request/ response implementation would yield just this. In that prior implementation, shown in figure 4.6, you can clearly see how the new result is generated with calls first to obtain the list of followed individuals and then to obtain the posts for those individuals.

To see how things work in the event-driven implementation, you have to look in several places. Let's first look at the implementation of the aggregating service—Connections' Posts:

#### Listing 4.1 Method from ConnectionsPostsController.java

```
@RequestMapping(method = RequestMethod.GET,
               value="/connectionsposts/{username}")
public Iterable<PostSummary> getByUsername(
                    @PathVariable("username") String username,
                    HttpServletResponse response) {

    Iterable<PostSummary> postSummaries;
    logger.info("getting posts for user network " + username);

    postSummaries = mPostRepository.findForUsersConnections(username);

    return postSummaries;
}
```

Yes, that's it. That's the entire implementation. To generate the result for the Connections' Posts microservice, the only thing that the getByUsername method does is a database query. What makes this possible is that changes that have an effect on the output of the Connections' Posts service are known to that service before a request to it is made. Rather than waiting for a request to Connections' Posts to learn about any new posts that have been created, our software is designed to proactively make such changes known to the Connections' Posts service through the delivery of an event.

I don't want to get into the details of the database that the getByUsername method is querying right now. I cover it in detail in chapter 12, when I talk about cloud-native data. For the moment, just know that the Connections' Posts service has a database that stores the state that's the result of propagated events. Summarizing, the getByUsername method *returns* a result when a *request* has come in from the Abundant Sunshine single-page app, as shown in figure 4.8; you'll recognize this as the pattern you see on the

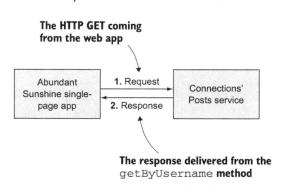

Figure 4.8 When a request is received, the Connections' Posts service can generate a result without depending on other services in the system.

left-hand side of figure 4.2. What is important is to note that the Connections' Posts service can generate its response without depending on any other services.

Let's now turn to that event that the Connections' Posts service benefitted from, starting with the endpoint on the Posts service that allows for new posts to be created. You'll find the newPost method in the com.corneliadavis.cloudnative.posts.write package:

---

**Listing 4.2    Method from PostsWriteController.java**

```
@RequestMapping(method = RequestMethod.POST, value="/posts")
public void newPost(@RequestBody Post newPost,
                    HttpServletResponse response) {

    logger.info("Have a new post with title " + newPost.getTitle());

    if (newPost.getDate() == null)
        newPost.setDate(new Date());
    postRepository.save(newPost);

    //event
    RestTemplate restTemplate = new RestTemplate();
    ResponseEntity<String> resp =
restTemplate.postForEntity("http://localhost:8080/connectionsposts/posts",
                        newPost, String.class);
    logger.info("[Post] resp " + resp.getStatusCode());

}
```

---

The Posts service is first taking the HTTP POST event and storing the data for that post in the Posts repository; this is the primary job of the Posts service, to implement the create and read operations for blog posts. But because it's part of an event-driven system, it also generates an event so that it may be picked up by any other services for which it's relevant. In this particular example, that event is represented as an HTTP POST to a party that's interested in that event—namely, the Connections' Posts service. This bit of code implements the pattern shown in figure 4.9, which you'll recognize as an instance of the right-hand side of figure 4.2.

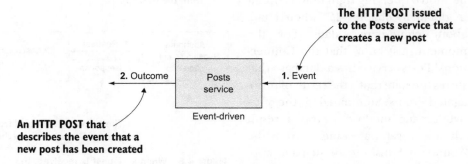

**Figure 4.9   The Posts service not only persists the new post that was created, but also delivers an event reporting that this post has been created.**

Turning now to the recipient of that event, let's look at the `newPost` method in the Connections' Posts service; you'll find this in the com.corneliadavis.cloudnative.new-postsfromconnections.eventhandlers package:

**Listing 4.3    Method from EventsController.java of Connections' Posts service**

```
@RequestMapping(method = RequestMethod.POST, value="/posts")
public void newPost(@RequestBody Post newPost, HttpServletResponse
response) {

    logger.info("[NewFromConnections] Have a new post with title "
                + newPost.getTitle());
    MPost mPost = new MPost(newPost.getId(),
                           newPost.getDate(),
                           newPost.getUserId(),
                           newPost.getTitle());
    MUser mUser;
    mUser = mUserRepository.findOne(newPost.getUserId());
    mPost.setmUser(mUser);
    mPostRepository.save(mPost);

}
```

As you can see, that method simply takes the event as the body of an HTTP POST and stores the result of that event for future use. Remember that when requested, the Connections' Posts service need only do a database query to generate the result. This is the code that allows that to happen. You'll notice that the Connections' Posts service is interested in only a few of the fields from the message it receives, the ID, date, user ID, and title, storing those in a locally defined post object. It also establishes the right foreign-key relation between this post and the given user.

Wow—there's a lot in there. Most of the elements of this solution are covered in great depth later in the book. For example, the fact that each microservice in this solution has its own data stores, and the point about Connections' Posts needing only a subset of the content in the post event—these are topics in their own right. But don't worry about those details right now.

What I do want to draw your attention to at this juncture is the independence of the three microservices. When the Connections' Posts service is invoked, it doesn't reach out to the Connections or Posts services. Instead, it operates on its own; it's autonomous. It will function even if a network partition cuts Connections and Posts off in the very moment of the request to Connections' Posts.

I also want to point out that the Connections' Posts service is handling both requests and events. When you issued the `curl` for the list of posts from individuals a given user follows, the service generated a response. But when the new post event was generated, the service handled that event without a response. Instead, it generated only a specific outcome of storing the new post in its local repository. It generated no further event. Figure 4.10 composes the patterns depicted in figure 4.2 to diagram what I've just laid out here.

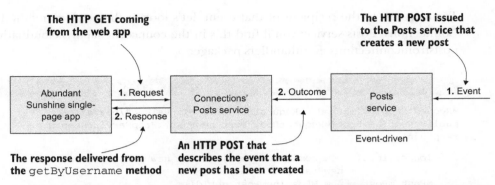

Figure 4.10   Microservices can implement both request/response and event-driven patterns. Events are primarily used to loosely couple microservices.

You'll notice in this diagram that the two services are loosely coupled. Each executes autonomously. The Posts microservice does its thing anytime it receives a new post, generating a subsequent event. The Connections' Posts microservice processes requests by simply querying its local data stores.

## You got me!

You might be thinking that my claims of loose coupling are a bit exaggerated, and with the current implementation you're absolutely correct. The far-too-tight binding exists with the implementation of the arrow labeled "Outcome" in figure 4.10. In the current implementation, I've implemented that "event" from the Posts microservice as an HTTP POST that makes a call directly to the Connections' Posts microservice. This is brittle; if the latter is unavailable when the former issues that POST, our event will be lost and our system is broken.

Ensuring that this event-driven pattern works in a distributed system requires more sophistication than this, and those are exactly the techniques that are covered in the remainder of this book. For now, I've implemented the example in this manner only for simplicity.

Putting all of the pieces together, figure 4.11 shows the event-driven architecture of our sample application. You can see that each microservice is operating independently. Notice the many "1" annotations; there's little sequencing. Just as you saw in the Posts example, when events affecting users and connections occur, the Connections service does its work, storing data and generating an event for the Connections' Posts service. When events affecting the outcome of the Connections' Posts service occur, the event handler does the work of drawing those changes into its local data stores.

What's particularly interesting is that the work of aggregating data from the two sources has shifted. With the request/response model, it's implemented in the NewFromConnectionsController class. With the event-driven approach, it's implemented through the generation of events and through the implementation of event handlers.

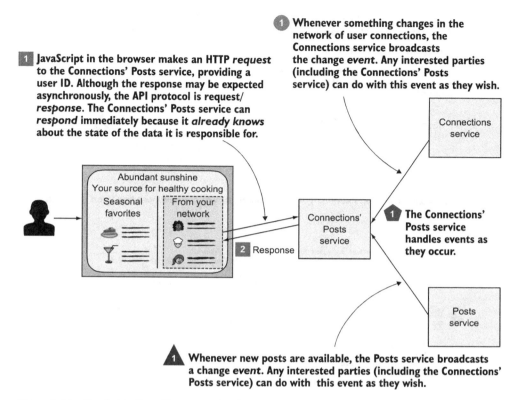

**1** JavaScript in the browser makes an HTTP *request* to the Connections' Posts service, providing a user ID. Although the response may be expected asynchronously, the API protocol is request/*response*. The Connections' Posts service can *respond* immediately because it *already knows* about the state of the data it is responsible for.

**1** Whenever something changes in the network of user connections, the Connections service broadcasts the change *event*. Any interested parties (including the Connections' Posts service) can do with this event as they wish.

**1** The Connections' Posts service handles events as they occur.

**1** Whenever new posts are available, the Posts service broadcasts a change *event*. Any interested parties (including the Connections' Posts service) can do with this event as they wish.

**Figure 4.11** Rendering the web page now only requires execution of the Connections' Posts microservice. Through event handling, it already has all of the data it needs to satisfy the request, so no downstream requests and responses are required.

The code corresponding to the annotations on the microservices shown in figure 4.11 appear in the three figures that follow. Figure 4.12, from the Connections service, shows the ConnectionsWriteController. Figure 4.13, from the Posts service, shows the PostsWriteController. And figure 4.14, from the Connections' Posts service, shows the EventsController (event handler).

```
@RequestMapping(method = RequestMethod.POST, value="/connections")
public void newConnection(@RequestBody Connection newConnection, HttpServletResponse response) {

    logger.info("Have a new connection: " + newConnection.getFollower() +
                " is following " + newConnection.getFollowed());
    connectionRepository.save(newConnection);

    //event
    RestTemplate restTemplate = new RestTemplate();
    ResponseEntity<String> resp = restTemplate.postForEntity(           1
            url: "http://localhost:8080/connectionsposts/connections", newConnection, String.class);
    logger.info("resp " + resp.getStatusCode());
}
```

**Figure 4.12** The Connections service generates an event when a new connection has been recorded.

```
@RequestMapping(method = RequestMethod.POST, value="/posts")
public void newPost(@RequestBody Post newPost, HttpServletResponse response) {

    logger.info("Have a new post with title " + newPost.getTitle());

    if (newPost.getDate() == null)
        newPost.setDate(new Date());
    postRepository.save(newPost);

    //event
    RestTemplate restTemplate = new RestTemplate();
    ResponseEntity<String> resp = restTemplate.postForEntity(          ①
            url: "http://localhost:8080/connectionsposts/posts", newPost, String.class);
    logger.info("[Post] resp " + resp.getStatusCode());

}
```

**Figure 4.13   The Posts service generates an event when a new post has been recorded.**

```
①  @RequestMapping(method = RequestMethod.POST, value="/users")
    public void newUser(@RequestBody User newUser, HttpServletResponse response) {

        logger.info("[NewPosts] Creating new user with username " + newUser.getUsername());
        mUserRepository.save(new MUser(newUser.getId(), newUser.getName(), newUser.getUsername()));

    }

①  @RequestMapping(method = RequestMethod.PUT, value="/users/{id}")
    public void updateUser(@PathVariable("id") Long userId,
                           @RequestBody User newUser, HttpServletResponse response) {

        logger.info("Updating user with id " + userId);
        MUser mUser = mUserRepository.findById(userId).get();
        mUserRepository.save(mUser);

    }

①  @RequestMapping(method = RequestMethod.POST, value="/connections")
    public void newConnection(@RequestBody Connection newConnection, HttpServletResponse response) {

        logger.info("Have a new connection: " + newConnection.getFollower() +
                    " is following " + newConnection.getFollowed());
        MConnection mConnection = new MConnection(newConnection.getId(), newConnection.getFollower(),
                                        newConnection.getFollowed());
        // add connection to the users
        MUser mUser;
        mUser = mUserRepository.findById(newConnection.getFollower()).get();
        mConnection.setFollowerUser(mUser);
        mUser = mUserRepository.findById(newConnection.getFollowed()).get();
        mConnection.setFollowedUser(mUser);
        mConnectionRepository.save(mConnection);

    }

①  @RequestMapping(method = RequestMethod.DELETE, value="/connections/{id}")
    public void deleteConnection(@PathVariable("id") Long connectionId, HttpServletResponse response) {

        MConnection mConnection = mConnectionRepository.findById(connectionId).get();

        logger.info("deleting connection: " + mConnection.getFollower() +
                    " is no longer following " + mConnection.getFollowed());
        mConnectionRepository.delete(mConnection);

    }

①  @RequestMapping(method = RequestMethod.POST, value="/posts")
    public void newPost(@RequestBody Post newPost, HttpServletResponse response) {

        logger.info("Have a new post with title " + newPost.getTitle());
        MPost mPost = new MPost(newPost.getId(), newPost.getDate(), newPost.getUserId(), newPost.getTitle());
        MUser mUser;
        mUser = mUserRepository.findById(newPost.getUserId()).get();
        mPost.setmUser(mUser);
        mPostRepository.save(mPost);

    }
```

**Figure 4.14   The event handler for the Connections' Posts service processes events as they occur.**

```
@RequestMapping(method = RequestMethod.GET, value="/connectionsposts/{username}")
public Iterable<PostSummary> getByUsername(@PathVariable("username") String username,
                                           HttpServletResponse response) {

    Iterable<PostSummary> postSummaries;
    logger.info("getting posts for user network " + username);

    postSummaries = mPostRepository.findForUsersConnections(username);

    return postSummaries;
}
```

**Figure 4.15** The Connections' Posts service generates and delivers a response when a request is received. This is completely independent from the operations of the other microservices in our solution.

And finally, in figure 4.15, the Connections' Posts service responds to requests, in the `ConnectionsPostsController`.

Although it's interesting to see how the processing that ultimately generates the Connections' Posts result is distributed across the microservices, even more significant are the temporal aspects. With the request/response style, the aggregation occurs when the user makes a request. With the event-driven approach, it's whenever the data in the system changes; it's asynchronous. As you'll see, asynchronicity is valuable in distributed systems.

## 4.4 *Introducing Command Query Responsibility Segregation*

I want to look at another aspect of the code for this example, starting with the Posts and Connections services. These are essentially CRUD services; they allow for posts, users, and connections to be *created*, *updated*, and *deleted*, and, of course, they allow values to be *read*. A database stores the state for the service, and the RESTful service implementation supports HTTP GET, PUT, POST, and DELETE operations that essentially interact with that data store.

In the request/response implementation, all of this functionality is found in a single controller; for example, for the Posts service in the `PostsController`. But in the event-driven implementation, you can see that there's now a read controller in the com .corneliadavis.cloudnative.posts package and a write controller in the com.corneliadavis .cloudnative.posts.write package. For the most part, these two controllers have methods that implement what was previously in that single Posts controller, except that I've added the delivery of events for any state-changing operations. But you might be wondering why I've gone through the trouble of breaking that single body of code into two.

Truth be told, in this simple example—the Posts and Connections services—that separation has little value. But for even only slightly more sophisticated services, the separation of read from write allows us greater control over our service design. If you're familiar with the Model, View, Controller (MVC) pattern that has been in widespread use over the past several decades, you know that the controller, which is the business logic for a service (that's why you find ...Controller classes throughout my implementations), operates against a model. When you have a single controller, the model for both read and write operations is the same, but when you separate the business logic into two separate controllers, each can have its own model. This can be powerful.

Our services don't even need to be complex in order for you to see this power. Consider a connected car scenario in which sensors on a vehicle are collecting data every second. That data will include a timestamp and GPS coordinates—lat and long—and a service allows for those values to be stored. The model for that service includes these data fields and more: a timestamp, the latitude, and the longitude. One of the things that you want to support is the ability to access trip data speeds; for example, you may want to analyze segments of a car trip in which the speed was greater than 50 miles per hour. That velocity data isn't directly provided via the write controller, yet obviously it can be computed from the data that was provided; part of the business logic for that service is to generate this derived data.

It's clear that the models on the read and the write sides are different. Although some fields exist in both, others are meaningful on only one side or the other (figure 4.16). This is one of the first benefits of having two separate models; it allows you to write code that's easier to understand and maintain, and greatly reduces the surface area in which bugs can creep in.

In summary, what you're doing is separating write logic (commands) from read logic (queries). This is the root of the *Command Query Responsibility Segregation* (CQRS) pattern. At its core, CQRS is just about separating those two concerns. Numerous advantages can come from CQRS. The preceding example of more-elegant code is just one. Another is beginning to show itself in the event-driven implementation of our sample.

With the Posts service, for example, the code that was distributed across the read and the write controllers in the event-driven implementation was, for the most part, in the single controller of the request/response solution. But if you turn to the implementation of the Connections' Posts service, there are greater differences.

In the event-driven solution, the query implementation is found in the com .corneliadavis.cloudnative.connectionsposts package, and the code for the command implementation is found in the com.corneliadavis.cloudnative.connectionsposts .eventhandlers package. Comparing that to the request/response implementation, the first thing to note is that in the request/response solution, there's no command code.

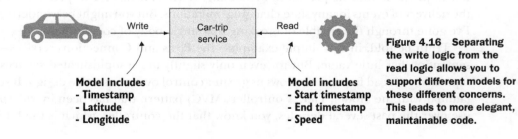

**Write** → **Car-trip service** ← **Read**

Model includes
- Timestamp
- Latitude
- Longitude

Model includes
- Start timestamp
- End timestamp
- Speed

**Figure 4.16** Separating the write logic from the read logic allows you to support different models for these different concerns. This leads to more elegant, maintainable code.

Because the Connections' Posts service was completely stateless, with its result being an aggregation of data from two other services, no command implementation was needed. As you saw, in the event-driven solution, the query implementation is greatly simplified; all of the aggregation logic disappeared. The aggregation now appears, albeit in a fairly different form, in the command controller. Whereas in request/response you saw calls to downstream resources, users, connections, and posts, in the event-driven command controller you now see event handlers that deal with changes to those same objects.

Those commands are changing state, and although I won't talk in detail about that data store here (that will come in chapter 12), it's interesting to note other CQRS implications. Although my current implementation of the event processors that make up the command side of the Connections' Posts service are implemented as HTTP endpoints, as is the query side, separating out the query from the command processing will ultimately allow us to use different protocols for the two sides. On the query side in this case, implementing a REST over HTTP protocol is ideal for the web apps that will access the service. On the command side, however, an asynchronous or even function-as-a-service (FaaS) implementation might be better.[5] The separation of command from query implementations offers this flexibility. (For those of you who are inclined to jump ahead, look at the implementation of the event handler for the Connections' Posts service in the cloudnative-eventlog module of our code repository. You'll see that a different approach has replaced the HTTP-based one you see here.)

I'd like to share one final observation on this topic. I've found that CQRS is often conflated with event-driven systems. If the software is using an event-driven approach, then CQRS patterns may be employed, but otherwise CQRS isn't really considered. I encourage you to consider CQRS independently from event-driven systems. Yes, they complement one another and used together are powerful, but the separation of command logic from query logic is also applicable in designs that are not event-driven.

## 4.5 Different styles, similar challenges

These two implementations yield exactly the same outcome—on the happy path. The choice of using a request/response or event-driven invocation style is arbitrary if all of the following conditions are true:

- No network partitions are cutting off one microservice from another.
- No unexpected latency occurs in producing the list of individuals that I follow.
- All the containers my services are running in maintain stable IP addresses.
- I never have to rotate credentials or certificates.

But these conditions, and many more, are exactly the things that characterize the cloud. Cloud-native software is designed to yield the needed outcomes even when the network is unstable, some components suddenly take longer to produce results, hosts

---

[5]FaaS is an approach that spins up compute for a bit of logic, such as updating a record in a database, on demand and is well suited for event-driven designs.

and availability zones disappear, and request volumes suddenly increase by an order of magnitude.

In this context, the request/response and event-driven approaches can yield very different outcomes. But I'm not suggesting that one is always more suitable than the other. Both are valid and applicable approaches. What you must do, however, is apply the right patterns at the right times, to compensate for the unique challenges the cloud brings.

For example, to be ready for spikes and valleys in request volume, you design so that you can scale capacity by creating or deleting instances of your services. Having those multiple instances also lends a certain level of resilience, especially when they're distributed across failure domains (availability zones). But when you then need to apply new configuration to what could be hundreds of instances of a microservice, you need some type of a configuration service that accounts for their highly distributed deployment. These patterns and many more apply equally to microservices, regardless of whether they're implementing a request/response or an event-driven protocol.

But some concerns may be handled differently depending on that protocol. For example, what type of compensating mechanisms must you put in place to account for a momentary (could be subsecond or might be last-minute) network partition that cuts related microservices off from one another? The current implementation of the Connections' Posts service will outright fail if it can't reach the Connections or the Posts microservices. A key pattern used in this type of scenario is a *retry*: a client making a request to a service over the network will try again if a request they've made fails to yield any results. A retry is a way of smoothing out hiccups in the network, allowing the invocation protocol to remain synchronous.

On the other hand, given that the event-driven protocol is inherently asynchronous, the compensating mechanisms to address the same hazards can be quite different. In this architecture, you'll use a messaging system, such as RabbitMQ or Apache Kafka, to hold onto events through network partitions. Your services will implement the protocols to support this architecture, such as having a control loop that continuously checks for new events of interest in the event store. Recall the HTTP POST from the Posts microservice directly to the event handler of the Connections' Posts service: you'd use a messaging system to replace that tight coupling. Figure 4.17 depicts the differences in the patterns used to handle this characteristic of distributed systems.

The remainder of the book dives into these various patterns, always with a focus on the problems that the cloud context brings. Choosing one of the invocation styles over the other isn't, on its own, a solution. That choice, along with the patterns that complement them, is. I'll be teaching you how to select the right protocol and apply the additional patterns that support them.

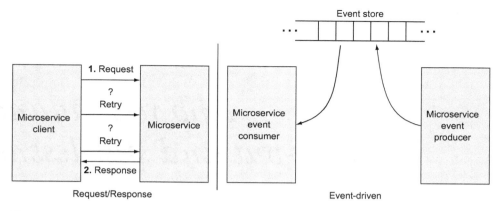

**Figure 4.17** **The retry is a key pattern used in request/response microservice architectures to compensate for network partitions. In event-driven systems, the use of an event store is a key technique that compensates for network instability.**

## Summary

- Both request/response and event-driven approaches are used to connect components that make up cloud-native software.
- A microservice can implement both request/response and event-handling protocols.
- Under ideal, stable circumstances, software implemented using one approach can yield exactly the same outcomes as software implemented using the other approach.
- But in a cloud setting, where the solution is a distributed system and the environment is constantly changing, the outcomes can vary wildly.
- Some architectural patterns are applied equally to cloud-native software following request/response and event-driven styles.
- But other patterns specifically serve one invocation protocol or the other.
- CQRS plays an important role in event-driven systems.

# App redundancy: Scale-out and statelessness

5

**This chapter covers**

- Scale-out as a central tenet of cloud-native apps
- Pitfalls of stateful apps in cloud-native software
- What it means for an app to be stateless
- Stateful services and how they're used by stateless apps
- Why sticky sessions shouldn't be used

The title says "Scale-out," but really, it's not just a matter of scaling. There are many reasons for what is probably the core tenet of cloud-native software: redundancy. Whether your application components are micro or macro, whether they can be configured via environment variables or have config baked into property files, whether they fully implement fallback behaviors or not, a key to change tolerance is that there is no single point of failure. Apps always have multiple instances deployed.

But then because any one of those multiple instances of the app can satisfy a request (and you'll see shortly why *that* is essential), you need those multiple instances to behave as a single logical entity. Figure 5.1 depicts this clearly.

Although this seems simple enough, it can be a bit tricky, because the context in which each app instance is running will vary. The input coming in with an invocation of the app (I'm not implying any particular invocation pattern here—could be request/response or event-driven) isn't the only thing that affects the result. Each app instance will be running in its own container—which could be a JVM, a host (virtual or physical), or a Docker (or similar) container—and environment values in that context can influence the execution of the app. Application configuration values will be supplied to each app instance as well. And, of primary interest to us in this chapter, the user's history of interaction with the app also has a marked effect.

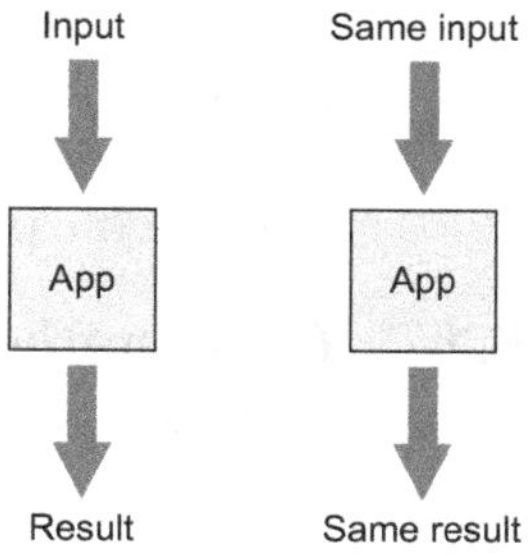

Figure 5.2 wraps context around the app instances and shows the challenges to achieving parity across the external influences on the app.

Chapter 6 addresses the system environment and app configuration influencers. In this chapter, I cover the request history.

I begin by covering the benefits of deploying multiple instances of an app, and you'll immediately see what happens when this intersects with stateful apps. I do this in the context of the cookbook example we started with in the previous chapter, breaking that monolith into individual microservices that are then independently deployed and managed. I introduce local state into one of those microservices, specifically storing authentication tokens. Yes, sticky sessions are a common pattern for

**Figure 5.1  Given the same input, the result produced by an app instance must be the same, regardless of whether there are one, two, or one hundred instances of the app.**

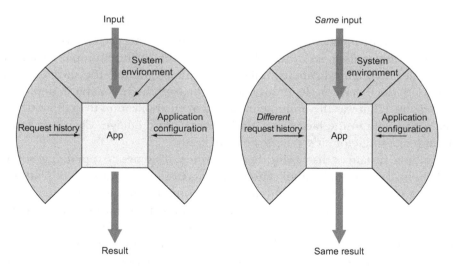

**Figure 5.2  The cloud-native app must ensure consistent results in spite of possible differences in other contextual influencers.**

addressing this type of session state, but it's a bad idea in the cloud, and I'll cover why. I also introduce the notion of a *stateful service*, a special type of service that's carefully designed to handle the complexities of state. And finally, I'll show you how to keep separate the parts of your software that are stateful from the parts that are stateless.

## 5.1  Cloud-native apps have many instances deployed

In the cloud, the prevailing model for increasing or decreasing application capacity to handle changing request volumes is to scale horizontally. Rather than adding or reducing capacity to a single application instance (vertical scaling), increased or decreased request volumes are handled by adding or removing app instances.

That isn't to say that app instances can't be allocated with substantial compute resources; Google Cloud Platform (GCP) is now offering a machine type with 1.5 TB of memory, and AWS is offering one with nearly 2 TB. But changing the specs of the machine that an app is running on is a substantial event. Say, for example, you've estimated that 16 GB of memory is ample for your application, and for some time things are working fine. But then your request volume picks up, and you'd now like to add to that capacity. There's no way in cloud environments such as AWS, Azure, or GCP to change the machine type for a running host. Instead, you'd have to create a new machine with 32 GB of memory (even if you need only around 20 GB, because there's no machine type with 20 GB of memory), deploy your app there, and then figure out how to move your users over to the new instances with as little disruption as possible.

Contrast that with the scale-out model. Instead of provisioning your app with 16 GB of memory, you provision four instances with 4 GB each. When you need more capacity, you simply request a fifth instance of the app, make that instance available by, for example, registering it with a dynamic router, and now you're running with a collective 20 GB of memory. Not only are you given finer-grained control over the consumption of resources, but the mechanics of achieving the greater scale are far easier.

But flexible scaling isn't the only motivation for having multiple instances of an app. So too are high availability, reliability, and operational efficiency. Going all the way back to the first example in this book, in the hypothetical scenario depicted in figures 1.2 and 1.3, it was the multiple instances of an application that allowed Netflix to remain operable in the face of an AWS infrastructure outage. Clearly, if you deploy your app as a singleton, it's a single point of failure.

Multiple instances also bring benefits when it comes to operating software in production. For example, applications are increasingly being run on platforms that provide a set of services over and above raw compute, storage, and networking. No longer must application teams (dev and ops) supply their own operating system, for example. Instead, they can simply send their code to the platform, and it will establish the runtime environment and deploy the app. If the platform (which from an app perspective is part of the infrastructure) needs to upgrade the OS, ideally the app should remain running throughout that upgrade. While a host is having its OS upgraded, the workloads running thereon must be stopped, but if you have other app instances running on other hosts (recall the discussion in chapter 3 around app instance distribution), you can roll through your hosts one at a time. While one app instance is taken offline, other app instances are still serving traffic.

Finally, when you bring together app scale-out and a decomposed, microservices-based software architecture, you gain a great deal of flexibility in the overall resource consumption of the system. As demonstrated by the cooking community software that I introduced in the previous chapter, having separate app components allows you to scale the Posts API, which is being invoked by many more clients than those depicted in our scenario to date, to handle large volumes of traffic, while other apps such as the Connections API have fewer instances handling much smaller volumes. See figure 5.3.

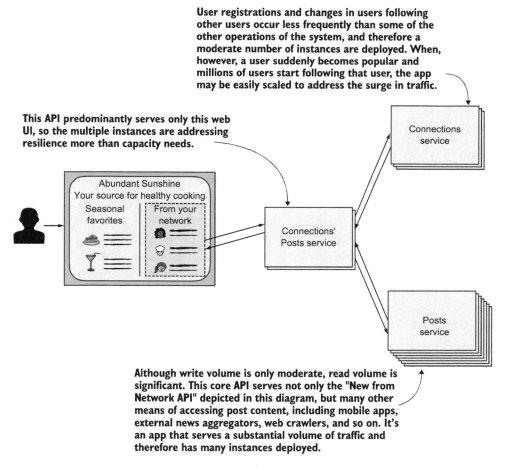

Figure 5.3  Architecting apps for multi-instance deployments affords significant gains in the efficiency of resource use as well as resilience and other operational benefits.

## 5.2    *Stateful apps in the cloud*

As you can see, the need for things such as flexible scaling, resilience, and operational efficiencies leads to having multiple instances of an app running as a part of your software solutions. These same goals, as well as the multi-instance architecture I've just described, all have a strong relationship to the statefulness or statelessness of your apps. But rather than discuss these elements only in the abstract, let's turn to a concrete example to start.

I'm going to begin with the application from the previous chapter, in particular, the one that was written in the request/response style. This implementation is heavily stateful in that it even stores all of the app data, users, connections, and posts in an in-memory database. It's also a monolithic application. The Connections' Posts, Connections, and Posts services are all part of the same project and ultimately compiled into the same JAR file (Java archive). To start, you'll fix both of these things.

You'll find the source code for this example in the cloud-native repository, in particular in the cloudnative-statelessness directory/module. You'll begin with an implementation that first demonstrates the downsides of carrying state in your apps and you'll later implement a solution. After cloning the repository, please check out a specific tag and move into the cloudnative-statelessness directory:

```
git clone https://github.com/cdavisafc/cloudnative-abundantsunshine.git
git checkout statelessness/0.0.1
cd cloudnative-statelessness
```

### 5.2.1    *Decomposing the monolith and binding to the database*

Let's first look at how I've broken the previously monolithic application into three separate services. The cloudnative-statelessness directory now holds only a pom.xml file and a subdirectory/submodule for each of the three microservices. Two of the microservices, cloudnative-posts and cloudnative-connections, are completely standalone. Each has no dependency on any of the other microservices.

The third microservice, the cloudnative-connectionsposts app, is also mostly disconnected from the other two, with the only real indication of any dependency seen in the application.properties file:

```
management.endpoints.web.exposure.include=*
connectionpostscontroller.connectionsUrl=http://localhost:8082/connections/
connectionpostscontroller.postsUrl=http://localhost:8081/posts?userIds=
connectionpostscontroller.usersUrl=http://localhost:8082/users/
INSTANCE_IP=127.0.0.1
INSTANCE_PORT=8080
```

Recall that this app makes a request to the *Connections* service to obtain the list of individuals a particular user follows, and then makes a request to the *Posts* service to obtain the posts from any of those individuals. URLs are configured into this app to facilitate reaching those services over HTTP. (Note that configuring these URLs into the application.properties file is a cloud antipattern and will be corrected in the next chapter.)

Turning now to the storage of the user, connections, and posts data, whether you're running this app in the cloud or not, it almost certainly requires that the data for the app isn't just held in memory but is also stored on persistent disk somewhere. That I previously stored it only in an in-memory H2 database was purely out of convenience; the persistent storage of the data wasn't germane to our conversation in the previous chapter. Ultimately, we also have to concern ourselves with the resilience of this persisted data, and I'll soon talk about this in more depth. I've added a dependence on a MySQL database in the pom.xml files of the Connections and Posts apps. The POM file now includes both of the following dependencies:

```
<dependency>
    <groupId>com.h2database</groupId>
    <artifactId>h2</artifactId>
</dependency>
<dependency>
    <groupId>mysql</groupId>
    <artifactId>mysql-connector-java</artifactId>
</dependency>
```

The H2 dependency was previously present; the MySQL dependency is new. I've kept the H2 dependency primarily to allow it to be used in testing. If a MySQL URL is provided on startup, Spring Boot JPA will instantiate and configure the MySQL client. Otherwise, it will use H2.

Let's get this code up and running.

### SETTING UP

Just as with the examples of the previous chapter, in order to run the samples, you must have standard tools installed; the last two on this list are new:

- Maven
- Git
- Java 1.8
- Docker
- Some type of a MySQL client, such as the `mysql` command-line interface (CLI)
- Some type of a Redis client, such as `redis-cli`

### BUILDING THE MICROSERVICES

From the cloudnative-statelessness directory, type the following command:

```
mvn clean install
```

Running this command builds each of the three apps, producing a JAR file in the target directory of each module.

**RUNNING THE APPS**

Before running any of the microservices, you need to start a MySQL service and create the cookbook database. To start the MySQL service, you'll use Docker. Assuming you have Docker installed, you can do so with the following command:

```
docker run --name mysql -p 3306:3306 -e MYSQL_ROOT_PASSWORD=password \
 -d mysql:5.7.22
```

To create the database, you can connect to your MySQL server via a client tool of your choice. Using the `mysql` CLI, you can type the following:

```
mysql -h 127.0.0.1 -P 3306 -u root -p
```

Then type in the password, `password`. At the MySQL command prompt, you can execute the following command:

```
mysql> create database cookbook;
```

Now you're ready to run the apps—plural. That, right there, is the first point: because you've separated out the software into three independent microservices, you need to run three different JAR files. You'll be running each app locally, so each Spring Boot app server (which is Tomcat by default) must start on a different port. You'll supply this, and for the Posts and Connections services, the URL to the MySQL service on the command line. So in three terminal windows, execute the following three commands:

```
java -Dserver.port=8081 \
-Dspring.datasource.url=jdbc:mysql://localhost:3306/cookbook \
-jar cloudnative-posts/target/cloudnative-posts-0.0.1-SNAPSHOT.jar

java -Dserver.port=8082 \
-Dspring.datasource.url=jdbc:mysql://localhost:3306/cookbook \
-jar cloudnative-connections/target/
➥ cloudnative-connections-0.0.1-SNAPSHOT.jar

java -jar cloudnative-connectionposts/target/
➥ cloudnative-connectionposts-0.0.1-SNAPSHOT.jar
```

I like to set up my terminal as shown in figure 5.4: I'm in the cloudnative-statelessness directory in all windows. This arrangement allows me to look in on the database on the far right, watch the log output for each of the three microservices across the top (I run the Java commands I've just given you in each of these three windows), and execute `curl` commands to test my services in the larger window in the lower left.

Next, you can execute the following `curl` commands to exercise each microservice:

```
curl localhost:8081/posts
curl localhost:8082/users
curl localhost:8082/connections
curl localhost:8080/connectionsposts/cdavisafc
```

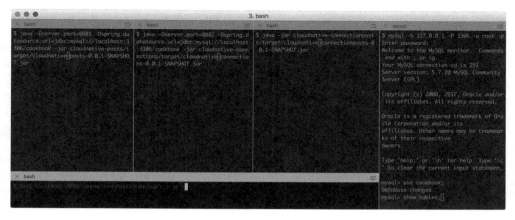

**Figure 5.4  My terminal configuration allows me to send requests to the microservices while watching the results in the other windows.**

In particular, watch all three of the upper windows when you execute the final `curl` command. You'll see how that single request ultimately touches all three microservices.

With this version of the software, you're now able to realize a deployment topology such as that depicted in figure 5.3; the different apps are independently scaled. Your current deployment is, however, rather noncloud: everything is running locally, you have only single instances of each app, and your configuration is embedded within the JAR files with the inclusion of values in the application.properties files. The apps, however, are stateless. You could stop and start any of the app instances without data loss.

Without explicitly focusing on it, I've just snuck in an implementation of the pattern that allows you to make your apps stateless; I've moved the state into an external store. The reason I haven't focused on that so far, however, is that connecting to an external database is something that's so familiar to most of you that the points I want to make around statelessness might be lost. So to study statelessness, I want to reintroduce state into one of the microservices—a type of state that can easily creep into your designs if you don't focus on keeping it out.

**NOTE**   A common way for state to creep in is through session state.

### 5.2.2  Poorly handling session state

Up until now, a client of the Connections' Posts service could simply provide a username on the query string and retrieve the posts written by people followed by that individual. You could request that set of posts for any user in the system, unencumbered. What you want to do, however, is allow Max to retrieve only the posts of people he follows, and Glen to retrieve only the posts of the people he follows. To facilitate this, you'll ask a client of the Connections' Posts service to authenticate before serving any content.

To follow along, please check out the following tag for the same repository you've been working with:

```
Git checkout statelessness/0.0.2
```

I've added a login controller to the implementation of the Connections' Posts service. Invoking the login functionality, which for simplicity takes only a username as input, will generate a token that's then passed to subsequent invocations of the Connections' Posts service. If the passed-in token is found to be valid, the set of posts is returned; if the token is invalid, an HTTP 1.1/401 Unauthorized response is returned.

The login controller is part of the Connections' Posts service and is found in the LoginController.java file. As you can see in the following code, after the login token is created, it's stored in an in-memory hash map that associates a token to a username.

**Listing 5.1   LoginController.java**

```
package com.corneliadavis.cloudnative.connectionsposts;

import ...

@RestController
public class LoginController {

    @RequestMapping(value="/login", method = RequestMethod.POST)
    public void whoareyou(
        @RequestParam(value="username", required=false) String username,
        HttpServletResponse response) {

        if (username == null)
            response.setStatus(400);
        else {
        UUID uuid = UUID.randomUUID();
        String userToken = uuid.toString();

            CloudnativeApplication.validTokens.put(userToken, username);
            response.addCookie(new Cookie("userToken", userToken));
        }
    }
}
```

That in-memory hash map is declared in the CloudnativeApplication.java file, as shown next.

**Listing 5.2   CloudnativeApplication.java**

```
public class CloudnativeApplication {

    public static Map<String, String> validTokens
        = new HashMap<String, String>();

    public static void main(String[] args) {
        SpringApplication.run(CloudnativeApplication.class, args);
    }
}
```

I've made one other relevant change to the method that serves posts from a user's connections, as shown in the following code, an excerpt of code found in the ConnectionsPosts.java file. Rather than providing a username as a part of the service URL, the service takes no usernames, but instead looks for a token in the cookie that is passed to the service.

**Listing 5.3 ConnectionsPostsController.java**

```java
@RequestMapping(method = RequestMethod.GET, value="/connectionsposts")
public Iterable<PostSummary> getByUsername(
    @CookieValue(value = "userToken", required=false) String token,
    HttpServletResponse response) {

    if (token == null)
        response.setStatus(401);
    else {
        String username =
            CloudnativeApplication.validTokens.get(token);
        if (username == null)
            response.setStatus(401);
        else {

            // code to obtain connections and relevant posts

            return postSummaries;
        }
    }
    return null;
}
```

You can rebuild the application and redeploy the Connections' Posts service to test this functionality. From the cloudnative-statelessness directory, run the following command to build the project:

```
mvn clean install
```

Now, just as you've done previously, run the microservices in three terminal windows with the following commands:

```
java -Dserver.port=8081 \
-Dspring.datasource.url=jdbc:mysql://localhost:3306/cookbook \
-jar cloudnative-posts/target/cloudnative-posts-0.0.1-SNAPSHOT.jar

java -Dserver.port=8082 \
-Dspring.datasource.url=jdbc:mysql://localhost:3306/cookbook \
-jar cloudnative-connections/target/
➥ cloudnative-connections-0.0.1-SNAPSHOT.jar

java -jar cloudnative-connectionposts/target/
➥ cloudnative-connectionposts-0.0.1-SNAPSHOT.jar
```

The Connections' Posts service is no longer invoked with a username as a part of the URL. Calls to the new endpoint prior to performing any login will result in an HTTP error. To see this, include the -i switch in your curl command as follows:

```
$ curl -i localhost:8080/connectionsposts
HTTP/1.1 401
X-Application-Context: application
Content-Length: 0
Date: Mon, 27 Nov 2018 03:42:07 GMT
```

You'll log in with the following command; use one of the usernames preloaded in the sample data:

```
$ curl -X POST -i -c cookie localhost:8080/login?username=cdavisafc
HTTP/1.1 200
X-Application-Context: application
Set-Cookie: userToken=f8dfd8e2-9e8b-4a77-98e9-49aaed30c218
Content-Length: 0
Date: Mon, 27 Nov 2018 03:44:42 GMT
```

And now when you invoke the Connections' Posts service, passing the cookie with the -b command line switch, you'll receive this response:

```
$ curl -b cookie localhost:8080/connectionsposts | jp -

[
  {
    "date": "2019-02-01T19:09:41.000+0000",
    "usersname": "Max",
    "title": "Chicken Pho"
  },
  {
    "date": "2019-02-01T19:09:41.000+0000",
    "usersname": "Glen",
    "title": "French Press Lattes"
  }
]
```

I haven't called it out explicitly yet, but you might have noticed that our implementation is no longer stateless. The valid tokens are stored in memory. Lest you think this example is contrived—a hash map in my main Spring Boot app—I assure you it's quite representative of a pattern commonly found in apps today. As part of my work at Pivotal, I recently brought a new caching product to market (Pivotal Cloud Cache) and had many conversations with developers and architects who were looking for effective ways of handling the HTTP session state that many of their apps were using. Although I'm not expressly using any of the HTTP interfaces here, to keep the code as simple as possible, the basic structure is the same.

Despite this supposed limitation in the implementation, if you rerun that last curl repeatedly, you'll consistently receive the expected response. If it's all working fine, then what's the problem? The issue is that at this point, you're still running the app in a noncloud and non-cloud-native setting. You have only a single instance of each app, and provided they remain functional and the Connections' Posts service remains running, your software functions as expected.

But you know that things are always changing in a cloud setting, and from the previous section, you also know that apps almost always have multiple instances deployed, so let's run a few experiments.

First, let's simulate the cycling of the Connections' Posts service. In a real setting, this could happen if the app itself crashed, but even more likely it happens because a new version of the app is being deployed or the infrastructure is going through a change that causes the app to be re-created in a refreshed infrastructure context. To simulate this, stop the app by pressing Ctrl-C in the right window and rerunning the java command:

```
java -jar cloudnative-connectionposts/target/
➥ cloudnative-connectionposts-0.0.1-SNAPSHOT.jar
```

When you now attempt the curl command and pass in the valid authentication token, you'll receive the HTTP 1.1/401 Unauthorized response:

```
$ curl -i -b cookie localhost:8080/connectionsposts
HTTP/1.1 401
X-Application-Context: application
Content-Length: 0
Date: Mon, 27 Nov 2018 04:12:07 GMT
```

I'm certain this doesn't surprise you. You're well aware that the tokens are stored in memory, and when you stopped and restarted the application, you lost everything that was in memory. The main realization that I hope you have, however, is that you no longer can count on this type of application cycling not happening. Change is the rule, not the exception.

Let's now look at a second scenario: deploying multiple instances of the app. As soon as you have those multiple instances, you'll need a load balancer to route traffic among them. You could establish this yourself, running something like nginx and configuring all of your instances into it, but this is exactly what cloud platforms do for you, so I will take this as an opportunity to introduce you to one. As it happens, Kubernetes has an easy-to-use, locally deployable version that makes it a perfect option for what I want to demonstrate. It has a vibrant community around it that can offer support when needed, and I have to tell you, Kubernetes is an awesome piece of technology that I love working with. If you have familiarity with and access to another cloud platform such as Cloud Foundry, Heroku, Docker, OpenShift, or others, by all means, run these experiments there.

**INTRODUCING A CLOUD-NATIVE PLATFORM**

Kubernetes is a platform for running applications. It includes capabilities that allow you to deploy, monitor, and scale your apps. It brings the type of health monitoring and automatic remediation that I've talked about in earlier chapters of this book and will allow you to test various examples and patterns in a compelling way. For example, when app instances are lost for any reason, Kubernetes will launch new instances to replace them. As I've already mentioned several times (and will continue to do so), a cloud-native platform will provide support for, and even implementations of, many of the patterns I cover in this book.

To run an application in Kubernetes, it must be containerized. You must have a Docker image (or similar) that contains your app. I won't cover containerization in detail, but will give you the steps to perform so that your app can be bundled into a Docker image and made available to Kubernetes.

The distribution of the open source Kubernetes project that you'll be using here is called Minikube (https://github.com/kubernetes/minikube). Whereas in production Kubernetes would always be deployed as a multinode distributed system (probably across availability zones, as we've talked about in preceding chapters), Minikube gives you a single-node deployment that allows you to get up and running quickly on your own workstation. The installation instructions for Minikube are included in the README file of the GitHub repository and provide steps for running on Linux, Windows, and macOS. Prior to installing Minikube, you should also install the Kubernetes CLI, `kubectl` (https://kubernetes.io/docs/tasks/tools/install-kubectl/). After you've addressed the prerequisites (for example, having VirtualBox installed on your machine) and installed Minikube, you'll be ready to deploy our sample app on Kubernetes.

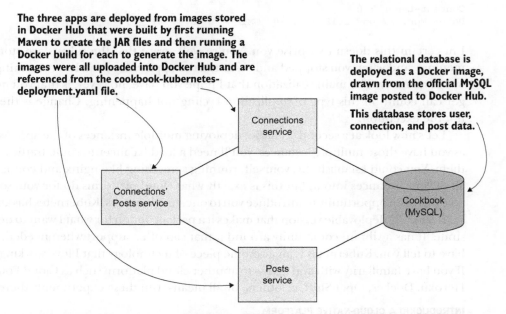

Figure 5.5   The deployment topology of the cookbook software, refactored into separate components and deployed into a cloud setting. At the moment, each app has only a single instance deployed.

I've provided you deployment manifests for all the components that make up our software example. At this stage, you have the four components you previously ran locally: the MySQL database and each of the three microservices (Connections, Posts, and Connections' Posts). To deploy the software in the topology shown in figure 5.5, proceed as follows.

#### DEPLOYING AND CONFIGURING THE DATABASE

You'll run the exact same Docker image in Kubernetes as you did when running our example locally. The deployment manifest you'll use is mysql-deployment.yaml. You instruct Kubernetes to launch and manage this component with the following command:

```
kubectl create -f mysql-deployment.yaml
```

You can watch the status of this deployment as follows:

```
$ kubectl get all
NAME                            READY    STATUS     RESTARTS   AGE
pod/mysql-75d7b44cd6-dbnvp      1/1      Running    0          30s

NAME                  TYPE        CLUSTER-IP     EXTERNAL-IP   PORT(S)          AGE
service/kubernetes    ClusterIP   10.96.0.1      <none>        443/TCP          14d
service/mysql-svc     NodePort    10.97.144.19   <none>        3306:32591/TCP   6h14m

NAME                        READY   UP-TO-DATE   AVAILABLE   AGE
deployment.apps/mysql       1/1     1            1           30s

NAME                                   DESIRED   CURRENT   READY   AGE
replicaset.apps/mysql-75d7b44cd6       1         1         1       30s
```

You'll notice that the output displays numerous entities that have a MySQL association. Here's a brief overview: you have a *deployment* of MySQL that's running the app in a *pod* (Docker images run in pods) and can be accessed via the MySQL *service*. *Replica sets* indicate the number of copies of a particular workload that are to be running.

To create the cookbook database, you'll use the same mechanism you did when running locally. You need only know the connection string to pass to your MySQL client. This is something that you can obtain from Minikube with the following command:

```
minikube service mysql -url
```

If you're using the mysql CLI for access, you can execute the following command to access the database and then the next command to create the database:

```
$ mysql -h $(minikube service mysql-svc --format "{{.IP}}") \
    -P $(minikube service mysql-svc --format "{{.Port}}") -u root -p
mysql> create database cookbook;
Query OK, 1 row affected (0.00 sec)
```

Your database server is now running, and the database your app will use is created.

**CONFIGURING AND DEPLOYING THE CONNECTIONS AND POSTS SERVICES**

The ways in which the Connections and Posts services are configured and deployed are virtually identical. Each must know the connection string and credentials for the MySQL database you've just deployed, and each will be run in its own container (and Kubernetes pod). There's a deployment manifest for each service, and you must edit each to insert the MySQL connection string. To obtain the URL that will be inserted into each file, execute the following command:

```
minikube service mysql-svc --format "jdbc:mysql://{{.IP}}:{{.Port}}/cookbook"
```

The response when you run this command is as follows:

```
jdbc:mysql://192.168.99.100:32713/cookbook
```

Now edit the cookbook-deployment-connections.yaml and cookbook-deployment-posts.yaml files, replacing the string <insert jdbc url here> with the jdbc URL returned from the preceding minikube command. For example, the final lines of cookbook-deployment-kubernetes-connections.yaml will look something like this:

```
- name: SPRING_APPLICATION_JSON
  value: '{"spring":{"datasource":{"url":
➥ "jdbc:mysql://192.168.99.100:32713/cookbook"}}}'
```

You can then deploy both services by executing the following two commands:

```
kubectl create -f cookbook-deployment-connections.yaml
kubectl create -f cookbook-deployment-posts.yaml
```

Running kubectl get all again will show that you now have two microservices running in addition to the MySQL database:

```
$ kubectl get all
NAME                             READY   STATUS    RESTARTS   AGE
pod/connections-7dffdc87c4-p8fc8 1/1     Running   0          12s
pod/mysql-75d7b44cd6-dbnvp       1/1     Running   0          13m
pod/posts-6b7486dc6d-wmvmv       1/1     Running   0          12s

NAME                    TYPE        CLUSTER-IP     EXTERNAL-IP   PORT(S)
service/connections-svc NodePort   10.106.214.25  <none>        80:30967/TCP
service/kubernetes      ClusterIP   10.96.0.1      <none>        443/TCP
service/mysql-svc       NodePort    10.97.144.19   <none>        3306:32591/TCP
service/posts-svc       NodePort    10.99.106.23   <none>        80:32145/TCP

NAME                         READY   UP-TO-DATE   AVAILABLE   AGE
deployment.apps/connections  1/1     1            1           12s
deployment.apps/mysql        1/1     1            1           13m
deployment.apps/posts        1/1     1            1           12s

NAME                                     DESIRED   CURRENT   READY   AGE
replicaset.apps/connections-7dffdc87c4   1         1         1       12s
replicaset.apps/mysql-75d7b44cd6         1         1         1       13m
replicaset.apps/posts-6b7486dc6d         1         1         1       12s
```

To test that each service is running correctly, use the following two commands to retrieve the sample connections and posts that have been loaded into your database:

```
$ curl $(minikube service --url connections-svc)/connections
[
  {
    "id": 4,
    "follower": 2,
    "followed": 1
  },
  {
    "id": 5,
    "follower": 1,
    "followed": 2
  },
  {
    "id": 6,
    "follower": 1,
    "followed": 3
  }
]
$ curl $(minikube service --url posts-svc)/posts
[
  {
    "id": 7,
    "date": "2019-02-03T04:36:28.000+0000",
    "userId": 2,
    "title": "Chicken Pho",
    "body": "This is my attempt to re-create what I ate in Vietnam..."
  },
  {
    "id": 8,
    "date": "2019-02-03T04:36:28.000+0000",
    "userId": 1,
    "title": "Whole Orange Cake",
    "body": "That's right, you blend up whole oranges, rind and all..."
  },
  {
    "id": 9,
    "date": "2019-02-03T04:36:28.000+0000",
    "userId": 1,
    "title": "German Dumplings (Kloesse)",
    "body": "Russet potatoes, flour (gluten free!) and more..."
  },
  {
    "id": 10,
    "date": "2019-02-03T04:36:28.000+0000",
    "userId": 3,
    "title": "French Press Lattes",
    "body": "We've figured out how to make these dairy free, but just as
     good!..."
  }
]
```

### CONFIGURING AND DEPLOYING THE CONNECTIONS' POSTS SERVICE

Finally, let's deploy the service that collects and returns the set of posts made by the folks that a particular individual follows. This service doesn't access the database directly; instead, it makes service calls to both the Connections and Posts services. With the deployments you've just executed in the immediately preceding section, these services are now running at the URLs you've just tested, and you need only configure those URLs into the Connections' Posts service. You'll do this by editing the deployment manifest, cookbook-deployment-connectionsposts-stateful.yaml. There are placeholders for three URLs, and they should be filled in with values obtained by issuing the following commands:

| Posts URL | `minikube service posts-svc --format`<br>`"http://{{.IP}}:{{.Port}}/posts?userIds=" --url` |
|---|---|
| Connections URL | `minikube service connections-svc --format`<br>`"http://{{.IP}}:{{.Port}}/connections/" --url` |
| Users URL | `minikube service connections-svc --format`<br>`"http://{{.IP}}:{{.Port}}/users/" --url` |

The final lines of your deployment manifest will look something like the following:

```
- name: CONNECTIONPOSTSCONTROLLER_POSTSURL
  value: "http://192.168.99.100:31040/posts?userIds="
- name: CONNECTIONPOSTSCONTROLLER_CONNECTIONSURL
  value: "http://192.168.99.100:30494/connections/"
- name: CONNECTIONPOSTSCONTROLLER_USERSURL
  value: "http://192.168.99.100:30494/users/"
```

Finally, you'll deploy the service with the following command:

```
kubectl create \
-f cookbook-deployment-connectionsposts-stateful.yaml
```

You can now test this service just as you have before, by executing the following commands:

```
curl -i $(minikube service --url connectionsposts-svc)/connectionsposts
curl -X POST -i -c cookie \
$(minikube service --url connectionsposts-svc)/login?username=cdavisafc
curl -i -b cookie \
$(minikube service --url connectionsposts-svc)/connectionsposts
```

> **I PROMISE THIS WILL GET BETTER SOON.** I know that all of this manual configuration is frustrating you, but fear not. The next chapter covers application configuration, and with the use of proper practices, some of this tedium will be eliminated.

To set up for the next demonstration, I'm going to have you stream the logs for this Connections' Posts service. In a new terminal window, execute the following command, providing the name of the `connectionsposts` pod (you can see this from running the `kubectl get pods` command):

```
kubectl logs -f pod/<name of your connectionsposts pod>
```

You can now repeat the final `curl` command shown previously and see the resultant activity in those `connectionsposts` logs. You're up and running. And provided you don't cycle the Connections' Posts service, this deployment will continue serving your users quite well. But what happens when you scale the service to multiple instances? To do so, execute the following command:

```
kubectl scale --replicas=2 deploy/connectionsposts
```

Executing the `kubectl get all` command again shows several interesting things:

```
NAME                                    READY   STATUS    RESTARTS   AGE
pod/connections-7dffdc87c4-cp7z7        1/1     Running   0          10m
pod/connectionsposts-5dc77f8bf9-8kg1d   1/1     Running   0          5m4s
pod/connectionsposts-5dc77f8bf9-mvt89   1/1     Running   0          81s
pod/mysql-75d7b44cd6-dbnvp              1/1     Running   0          36m
pod/posts-6b7486dc6d-kg8cp              1/1     Running   0          10m

NAME                         TYPE        CLUSTER-IP      EXTERNAL-IP   PORT(S)
service/connections-svc      NodePort    10.106.214.25   <none>        80:30967/TCP
service/connectionsposts-svc NodePort    10.100.25.18    <none>        80:32237/TCP
service/kubernetes           ClusterIP   10.96.0.1       <none>        443/TCP
service/mysql-svc            NodePort    10.97.144.19    <none>        3306:32591/TCP
service/posts-svc            NodePort    10.99.106.23    <none>        80:32145/TCP

NAME                               READY   UP-TO-DATE   AVAILABLE   AGE
deployment.apps/connections        1/1     1            1           10m
deployment.apps/connectionsposts   2/2     2            2           5m4s
deployment.apps/mysql              1/1     1            1           36m
deployment.apps/posts              1/1     1            1           10m

NAME                                           DESIRED   CURRENT   READY   AGE
replicaset.apps/connections-7dffdc87c4         1         1         1       10m
replicaset.apps/connectionsposts-5dc77f8bf9    2         2         2       5m4s
replicaset.apps/mysql-75d7b44cd6               1         1         1       36m
replicaset.apps/posts-6b7486dc6d               1         1         1       10m
```

You can see that a second pod running an instance of the Connections' Posts service has been created. But there remains only a single `connectionsposts-svc` service. This single service will now load-balance requests across both instances of the app. You can also see that both the deployment and the replication controllers are showing a desire to have two instances of the app running at any point.

### Don't do this in production!

I can't help but point out that issuing a command to provision a second instance of the Connections' Posts app *at the command line* should *never be done in production*. As soon as you've done so, you've created a snowflake, a software topology that isn't recorded anywhere.

> *(continued)*
>
> The deployment manifest that you used to initially deploy the software captures the initial topology, and likely what you expect is running in production, but reality has diverged from that which is recorded. When individuals manually apply changes to a running system, that system is no longer reproducible from the artifacts that are recorded and controlled as a part of your operational practices.
>
> The right practice for achieving this scale-out is to modify the deployment manifest, check it into a control system, and apply it to the cloud environment. Kubernetes supports this, updating a running system rather than producing a new one with a command such as `kubectl apply`. I take the shortcut here only for simplicity.

Before testing your application functionality in the new deployment topology, please stream the logs for the new app instance. In another terminal window, execute the `kubectl logs -f` command with the name of the new pod, as you can see in the `kubectl get all` output:

```
kubectl logs -f po/<name of your new pod>
```

Now, let's test the application functionality again by issuing your final `curl` command a few more times:

```
curl -i -b cookie \
$(minikube service --url connectionsposts-svc)/connectionsposts
```

Keep an eye on the two windows in which you're streaming the application logs. If the load balancer routes traffic to the first instance, you'll see activity in that log stream and results will be returned as expected. If, however, traffic is routed to the second instance, that log will show there was an attempt to access the app with an invalid token, and a `401` will be returned. But of course, the token *is* valid; the trouble is that the second instance doesn't know about that valid token.

I'm sure we'd all agree this is a terrible user experience. Sometimes the `curl` command returns the requested information, and sometimes it reports that the user is unauthenticated. When the user then scratches his head and thinks, "Aren't I already logged in?" and refreshes the page, he might get a valid response, but then the next request again reports `unauthenticated`.

### Using Kubernetes requires you to build Docker images

You might notice that I haven't asked you to build the application as with previous examples. I've skipped the steps here because in order to deploy apps to Kubernetes, they must be containerized, and the build process is somewhat involved. You must create JAR files, run a `docker build` command to create the Docker images, upload those images into an image repository, update the deployment manifest to point to those images, and then do the deployment.

I've included the Dockerfile that I used to create each of the container images. But for brevity, the deployment manifests I provide point to the Docker images I've already produced and uploaded into my own Docker Hub repository. The commands I've executed to do all of this are as follows:

Build source:

```
mvn clean install
```

Create Docker images:

```
docker build --build-arg \
jar_file=cloudnative-connectionposts/target\
/cloudnative-connectionsposts-0.0.1-SNAPSHOT.jar \
-t cdavisafc/cloudnative-statelessness-connectionposts-stateful .

docker build --build-arg \
jar_file=cloudnative-connections/target\
/cloudnative-connections-0.0.1-SNAPSHOT.jar \
-t cdavisafc/cloudnative-statelessness-connections .

docker build --build-arg \
jar_file=cloudnative-posts/target/cloudnative-posts-0.0.1-SNAPSHOT.jar \
-t cdavisafc/cloudnative-statelessness-posts .
```

Upload to Docker hub:

```
docker push cdavisafc/cloudnative-statelessness-connectionposts-stateful
docker push cdavisafc/cloudnative-statelessness-connections
docker push cdavisafc/cloudnative-statelessness-posts
```

Although in this simple example it's easy to see why this occurs, let's look at what's going on from an architectural perspective. Figure 5.6 depicts the desired behavior of our app. I'm showing a single entity for the Connections' Posts app to designate that *logically* you have only a single app. As I pointed out at the beginning of the chapter, the same input should yield the same result, regardless of the number of instances of the app and which app a particular request is routed to.

But you haven't achieved this in this current implementation because your app isn't stateless. As a simple way to visualize what is happening, figure 5.7 separates your single logical app into two instances and distributes the sequence of requests across those instances. In this diagram, I haven't changed the sequencing of the requests but only distributed them across different application instances. It's now easy to see that if

**Figure 5.6   Logically, you have a single app that serves a series of requests. Because each user logs in before trying any Get Data calls, you expect each of those will succeed.**

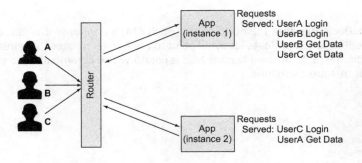

**Figure 5.7   When a single logical entity is deployed as multiple instances, care must be taken to ensure that the distributed set of events continues to be treated as a whole.**

your app considers only the local requests, in many cases your application functionality will be compromised.

Turning back to our cookbook example, figure 5.8 summarizes the behavior that your current implementation presents.

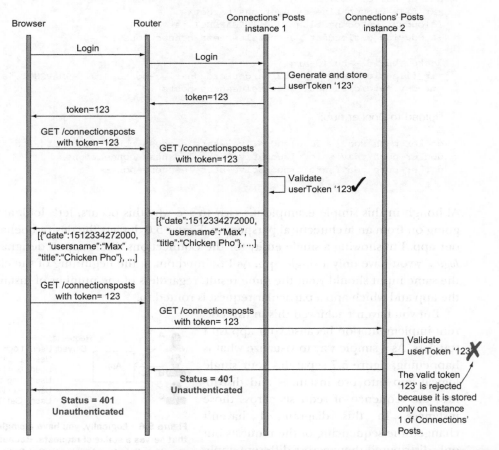

**Figure 5.8   When you add a second instance of the Connections' Posts app, its local list of valid tokens differs from that of the first. This is exactly the problem with stateful apps in cloud-native software.**

How do you then solve this problem? Let's consider one "solution" that's in relatively widespread use today, but isn't appropriate in the cloud setting—sticky sessions. (I'll then present the cloud-native solution.)

## 5.3 *HTTP sessions and sticky sessions*

What about sticky sessions? For almost as long as we've been using load balancers to distribute requests across multiple instances of applications—and this is far longer than those apps have been designed in a cloud-native manner—we've been using sticky sessions. Why can't we continue to use those to deal with stateful services?

First, let me briefly explain the technique. *Sticky sessions* are an implementation pattern in which an app includes a session ID in the response to a first request from a user—a fingerprint for that user, if you will. That session ID is then included, usually via a cookie, in all subsequent requests. This effectively allows the load balancer to keep track of individual users who are interacting with an app. That load balancer, which is responsible for deciding where to send a specific request, will remember which instance was first accessed and will then do its best to route all requests carrying that session ID to the same app instance. If that app instance has a local state, requests consistently routed to that instance will have that local state available.

Figure 5.9 shows that sequence: when a session ID is present in the request, the router looks up the instance to which that ID corresponds and sends the request to that app instance.

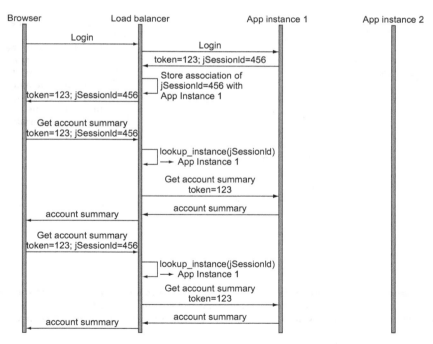

**Figure 5.9  Sticky sessions are implemented by the load balancer and are used to tie a specific user to a specific instance of an app.**

Isn't that an easier solution than ensuring that each and every one of your apps is completely stateless?

Did you catch the part about "do its best"? Despite its best efforts, the router may not be able to send the request to the "right" instance. That instance may have vanished or may be unreachable because of network anomalies. In figure 5.10, for

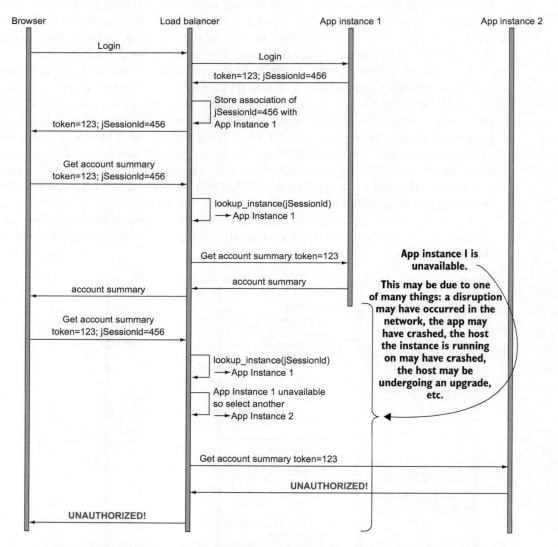

**Figure 5.10    A load balancer supporting sticky sessions will attempt to stick specific users to specific app instances, but may be forced to send a request to a different instance. In cloud-native software, you must assume that instances come and go with some regularity. If you don't, the user experience suffers.**

example, app instance 1 is unavailable, so the router will send the user request to another app instance. Because that instance doesn't have the local state that app instance 1 had, the user will once again experience the negative behavior that I demonstrated previously.

Developers have, for some time, justified the use of sticky sessions, arguing that anomalies such as disappearing instances or network outages are rare, and that when they do occur, subpar user experiences, while undesirable, are acceptable. This is a poor argument for two reasons. First, the recycling of app instances is increasingly common because of either unanticipated or deliberate changes to the infrastructure. Second, it isn't difficult to implement something better—namely, persisting session state in a connected backing-store, and this is an approach that brings with it many other advantages. Let's have a look at that now.

## 5.4 Stateful services and stateless apps

The right approach to solving this problem is suggested in the title to this chapter: make apps stateless. To first demonstrate the antipattern—stateful services—and now show the good pattern, I've chosen the specific example of user authentication because it's an area where I've so often seen subpar solutions implemented. To excuse the use of sticky sessions, people often make the argument that we can't have users providing their credentials with every request. Although that argument is sound, it doesn't mean the app instances need to hold that state.

### 5.4.1 Stateful services are special services

Of course, there has to be state somewhere. As a whole, an application must carry state somewhere in order to be of any use. Your banking website wouldn't provide much value if you couldn't see your account balances, for example. So when I suggest that apps be stateless, what I'm really saying is that we needn't have state everywhere in our architecture.

> **NOTE** Cloud-native applications have places where state lives, and just as important, places where it doesn't.

The app is stateless. State lives in data services. This is the narrative that we hear a lot these days. I confess that I'm not the type of person to follow any guidance unless I understand why the advice is sound, so let's do a proof by briefly studying what we'd have to do to keep our software running well if we carried a lot of state in our apps. Remember, one of the primary things we have to anticipate is constant change.

In this case, anytime that the internal state of an app changes, and that state is either in memory or on local disk, that state needs to be preserved, just in case the app instance is lost. Several approaches for preserving state exist, but all involve replication. One option, which is completely independent of any knowledge of the application logic, is to take snapshots; simply make copies of memory and disk at a certain interval.

But as soon as we start talking about snapshots, we have a host of decisions to make around how to produce and manage those snapshots. How often do you do them? How do you ensure that the snapshots are consistent (that is, capture a state that isn't inadvertently transitory because changes occurred in the middle of taking a snapshot)? How long will it take to recover them? Trade-offs of recovery time objectives (RTOs) against recovery point objectives (RPOs) are inherently complex. Even if you aren't familiar with the details of snapshotting, RTO, and RPO (I spent more than a decade working for a major storage system vendor ☺), this description alone has probably been sufficient to raise your stress level a bit.

Another approach to making copies of data for resilience is to make the replication step a part of the data storage. Here the application events trigger both the storage of a primary copy of data as well as one or more replicas. To ensure that replicas are available when the primary vanishes for any reason, the copies are distributed across failure boundaries: copies are stored on different hosts, in different availability zones, or on different storage devices. But then, as soon as these processes cross such boundaries, you have a distributed system dealing with data, and frankly, these are hard problems to solve.

You've surely heard of the CAP theorem, which states that only two of the three attributes of *consistency, availability,* and *partition* tolerance can be maintained in any system. Because a distributed system will always suffer from occasional network partitions, distributed data systems can only be *either* consistent *or* available. Detailed study of the CAP theorem and the challenges of distributed stateful services is beyond the scope of the discussion at hand, but the following note makes my point.

**NOTE**   Handling state in cloud-based systems, which by definition are highly distributed, requires special care and complex algorithms. Rather than solving those problems in each and every app that makes up our software, we'll concentrate the solutions in only specific parts of our cloud-native architecture. Those parts are the *stateful services.*

So, you put the state in specially designed stateful services and remove the state from your apps. In a moment, you'll do that in the context of our cookbook application. But first I want to point out a few other advantages of stateless apps, those beyond avoiding the complexity of distributed data resilience. When your apps are stateless, a cloud-native application platform can easily create new instances of an app when older instances are lost. It need only start a new instance from the same base state that it started the original, and it's good to go. The routing tier can evenly distribute the load across multiple instances, the number of which can be adjusted based on the volume of requests that need to be handled; no operations beyond registering the coordinates of the new instances are necessary. Instances can be moved around with ease. Need to upgrade a host that your instances are running on? No problem, just start a new instance and route traffic.

You can reasonably manage multiple *versions* of an app all deployed and running side by side (recall the importance of parallel deploys in our earlier conversations on continuous delivery). You can have some of your traffic routing to the newest version and other traffic reaching prior versions, and despite the variability in the app components, state continues to be handled consistently in the stateful services.

Now, to be clear, there's absolutely nothing wrong with having an app store data in memory and even on local disk. But that data can be counted on to be there only for the duration of the single app invocation that generated it in the first place. A concrete example comes with an app that will load an image, process it in some way, and return a new rendering thereof. The processing could be multistep and store interim results on disk, but that local storage is ephemeral, existing only until the final image has been generated and is returned to the caller. At the risk of beating a dead horse, you can't count on any of that data being available when the next request comes into that same app instance.

The job of developers, then, is to be explicit about which state is important to preserve and which is not, and to design their apps so that any data that's needed across invocations is placed in the stateful services. With careful consideration of this design element, you have the best of both worlds. A portion of your overall implementation can be managed to handle the scale and fluidity of the system it's running on (the stateless app), and a portion can be designed to handle the trickier task of managing data (state).

### 5.4.2   *Making apps stateless*

Let's now turn back to our cookbook example. When you left off, you had implemented some simple user authentication. But because you stored valid tokens in memory, if a request was routed to an instance that wasn't storing a user's token, they'd be asked to log in, even if they already had.

The solution is simple: you'll introduce a key/value store that will be used to persist valid login tokens, and you'll bind your app to that stateful service. Every instance of the app will include that binding (how the binding is recorded foreshadows the next chapter on app configuration), so any request can be routed to any app instance, and the valid tokens will be accessible. Figure 5.11 reflects this topology, updating figure 5.8, which contained the prior flow.

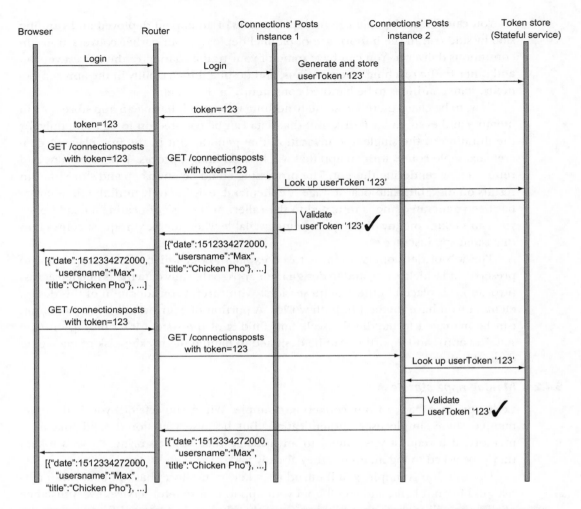

**Figure 5.11   Storing valid tokens in a stateful service that's bound to all instances of the Connections' Posts service allows apps to be stateless but our overall software solution to be stateful.**

I've implemented this solution within the cloudnative-statelessness directory/module of the cloud-native repository. The deployment topology that you'll achieve with the following instructions is shown in figure 5.12. The solution is in the master branch of your repository, so if you had previously cloned and checked out an earlier tag, you can switch to the master branch with the following:

```
git checkout master
```

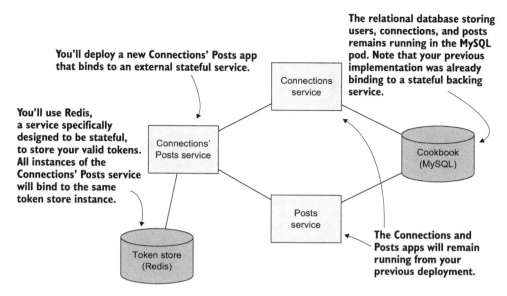

**Figure 5.12** Your new deployment replaces the Connections' Posts service with a stateless version and adds a Redis server to store authentication tokens.

The implementation uses Redis as the stateful service. You'll run that service via another deployment to your Minikube environment. Execute the following command to start the Redis server:

```
kubectl create -f redis-deployment.yaml
```

After the container is running, you can connect to it by using the Redis CLI (or another client if you prefer) with the following command, and you can view the keys stored in Redis as well:

```
redis-cli -h $(minikube service redis-svc --format "{{.IP}}") \
-p $(minikube service redis-svc --format "{{.Port}}")
> keys *
```

You'll now replace the prior Connections' Posts service with a new one. The code changes to the app are minimal.

First, in the CloudnativeApplication Spring Boot configuration and main class, delete the local storage for tokens and add configuration for the Redis client that will be used to connect to your token store.

**Listing 5.4  CloudnativeApplication.java**

```
public class CloudnativeApplication {

@Value("${redis.hostname}")
```

```
        private String redisHostName;
        @Value("${redis.port}")
        private int redisPort;

        @Bean
        public RedisConnectionFactory redisConnectionFactory() {

            return new LettuceConnectionFactory
                (new RedisStandaloneConfiguration(redisHostName, redisPort));
        }

        public static void main(String[] args) {
            SpringApplication.run(CloudnativeApplication.class, args);
        }
    }
```

Next, instead of storing tokens in the now deleted local storage, in the LoginController.java code you use the Redis client to store the token to the username pair in your external stateful store.

### Listing 5.5   LoginController.java

```
...
CloudnativeApplication.validTokens.put(userToken, username);   ⟵── We've removed this

ValueOperations<String, String> ops = this.template.opsForValue();
ops.set(userToken, username);
```

Then, instead of retrieving tokens from the now deleted local storage, in the `ConnectionsPostsController` you use the Redis client to retrieve a username via the token that was supplied via the cookie.

### Listing 5.6   ConnectionsPostsController.java

```
...
String username
    = CloudnativeApplication.validTokens.get(token);   ⟵── We've removed this

ValueOperations<String, String> ops = this.template.opsForValue();
String username = ops.get(token);
```

To make clear what you're doing here, I will have you delete the old version of the Connections' Posts app with the following command:

```
kubectl delete deploy connectionsposts
```

Before you deploy the new version of the Connections' Posts app, you must configure the Redis connection information into the deployment manifest. Edit the cookbook-deployment-connectionsposts-stateless.yaml file, inserting the Redis hostname and port into the appropriate locations. You can obtain the hostname and port values with the following two commands:

```
minikube service redis --format "{{.IP}}"
minikube service redis --format "{{.Port}}"
```

When completed, this YAML file will appear similar to this:

```
    - name: CONNECTIONPOSTSCONTROLLER_POSTSURL
      value: "http://192.168.99.100:31040/posts?userIds="
    - name: CONNECTIONPOSTSCONTROLLER_CONNECTIONSURL
      value: "http://192.168.99.100:30494/connections/"
    - name: CONNECTIONPOSTSCONTROLLER_USERSURL
      value: "http://192.168.99.100:30494/users/"
    - name: REDIS_HOSTNAME
      value: "192.168.99.100"
    - name: REDIS_PORT
      value: "32410"
```

You can now deploy the new app with the following command:

```
kubectl create \
-f cookbook-deployment-connectionsposts-stateless.yaml
```

And test your software with the usual series of commands:

```
curl -i $(minikube service --url connectionsposts-svc)/connectionsposts
curl -X POST -i -c cookie \
$(minikube service --url connectionsposts-svc)/login?username=cdavisafc
curl -i -b cookie \
$(minikube service --url connectionsposts-svc)/connectionsposts
```

The POST curl command will have created a new key in the Redis store, something you can see by executing the keys * command, run via the Redis CLI. And now let's get the topology back to what you had when you saw the problems with the stateful app. Scale your Connections' Posts app to two instances with the following:

```
kubectl scale --replicas=2 deploy/connectionsposts
```

You can now stream the logs for both instances (using the kubectl logs -f <podname> command as you've done previously) and repeat the final curl command to see that both instances are now able to see all valid tokens and correctly serve responses:

```
curl -i -b cookie \
 $(minikube service --url connectionsposts-svc)/connectionsposts
```

Yes, it really is that simple. Sure, you'll have to be deliberate about making your apps stateless, perhaps breaking old habits, but the pattern is straightforward, and the resultant benefits immense. A limited few of you will be working on the more difficult problems of managing distributed, stateful services, but the majority of us (myself included) can easily make our apps stateless and simply take advantage of the hard work and innovation happening in the realm of cloud-native stateful services.

But our application topology is now more complex, and with the greater distribution comes several challenges. What happens when you need to move your stateful service to new coordinates? Say it gets a new URL, or you need to update the credentials you're using to connect to it (something we haven't even touched upon yet). What happens when access to the stateful service is disrupted, even for a moment? We'll address these challenges and more as we move further through the material in the book. Next up, you'll learn how to handle application configuration in such a way that you can easily adapt to the changing nature of your cloud and application requirements.

## Summary

- Stateful applications don't work well in a cloud-native context.
- A sequence of interactions with a user, thought of logically as captured in session state, is a common way for state to creep into your applications.
- Stateful services are a special type of service that must address the significant challenges of data resilience in a distributed, cloud-based setting.
- Most apps should be stateless and should offload the handling of state to these stateful services.
- Making apps stateless is simple and, when done, realizes significant advantages in a cloud setting.

# Application configuration: Not just environment variables

## This chapter covers

- Application configuration requirements
- Difference between system and app configuration values
- Proper use of property files
- Proper use of environment variables
- Configuration servers

At the start of the preceding chapter, I presented the illustration repeated here in figure 6.1. This diagram shows that although it seems simple that the same inputs to any of a number of application instances would yield the same results, other factors are also influencing those results—namely, the request history, the system environment, and any application configuration. In chapter 5, you studied techniques for eliminating the impact of the first of these by ensuring that any state resulting from a sequence of requests would be stored in a shared backing service, and this allowed the app instances to be stateless.

This chapter addresses the remaining two influencers: the system environment and app configuration. Neither of these is entirely new in cloud-native software; app functionality has always been influenced by the context it's running in and the configuration applied. But the new architectures I'm talking about in this book bring new challenges. I start the chapter by presenting some of those. Next, I talk about what I call the app's *config layer*—the mechanism for having both the system environment and application configuration make their way into the app. Then I drill into the specifics of bringing in system environment values; you've probably heard the phrase "store the config in env variables," and I explain that. And finally, I focus on app configuration with an eye on the antisnowflaking that I talked about in earlier chapters. I also explain the parenthetical "eventually" you see in figure 6.1.

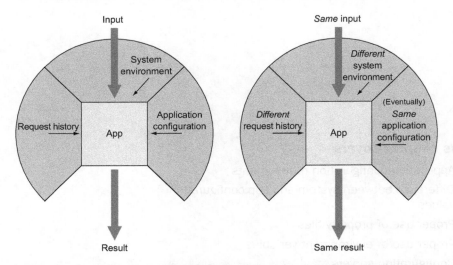

**Figure 6.1  The cloud-native app must ensure consistent outcomes despite differences in contextual influencers such as request history (different app instances have processed a different set of requests) and system environment values (such as IP addresses). Application configuration should be the same across instances but may differ at times.**

## 6.1   *Why are we even talking about config?*

Why am I even talking about application configuration? Developers know better than to hardcode config into their software (right?). Property files exist in virtually every programming framework, and we've had best practices for ages. Application configuration is nothing new.

But the cloud-native context *is* new—sufficiently new that even seasoned developers will need to evolve the patterns and practices they employ to properly handle app config. Cloud-native applications are inherently more distributed than they were before. We adapt to increasing workloads by launching additional instances of an app instead of allocating more resources to a single one, for example. The cloud infrastructure itself is also constantly changing, far more than the infrastructures on which we deployed apps in the last several decades. These core differences in the platform bring new ways in which the contextual influencers present themselves to the app and therefore require new ways for apps to handle them. Let's take a quick look at some of those differences.

### 6.1.1 Dynamic scaling—increasing and decreasing the number of app instances

The preceding chapter introduced the concept of multiple app instances and should already have given you a good sense of how this impacts your designs. Here I want to draw your attention to two nuances that affect application configuration.

First, although in the past you might have had multiple instances of an app deployed, it was likely a relatively small number. When configuration needed to be applied to those app instances, doing so through "hand" delivery of configuration was tractable (even if less than ideal). Sure, you might have used scripts and other tooling to apply config changes, but you could get away with not using industrialized automation. Now, when apps are scaled to hundreds or thousands of instances, and those instances are constantly being moved around, a semiautomated approach will no longer work. Your software designs, and the operational practices around them, must ensure that *all* app instances are running with the same configuration values, and you must be able to update those values with zero app downtime.

The second factor is even more interesting. Until now, I've addressed app configuration from the viewpoint of the results generated by the app; I've focused on the need for any of the instances of an app to produce the same output, given the same input. But the configuration of an app can also markedly impact how consumers of that app find and connect with it. To be direct, if the IP address and/or port of an app instance changes, and by some measure we'd consider this (system) configuration data, does the app bear any responsibility for making sure those changes are known to all possible consumers of the app? The short answer is yes, and I will cover this, though not fully until chapters 8 and 9 (this is the essence of service discovery). For the time being, please simply appreciate that app configurations have a network effect.

### 6.1.2 Infrastructure changes causing configuration changes

We've all heard this narrative: the cloud brought with it the use of lower-end, commodity servers, and because of their internal architectures and the robustness (or lack thereof) of some embedded components, a higher percentage of your infrastructure may fail at any given time. All this is true, but hardware failure is still only one cause of infrastructure change, and likely a small part of it.

A much more frequent and necessary infrastructure change comes from upgrades. For example, applications are increasingly being run on platforms that provide a set of services over and above raw compute, storage, and networking. No longer must application teams (dev and ops) supply their own operating system, for example. Instead, they can simply send their code to a platform that will establish the runtime environment, and then deploy and run the app. If the platform, which from an app perspective is part of the infrastructure, needs an upgrade to the version of the operating system (because of an OS vulnerability, for example), then that represents a change in the infrastructure.

Let's stay with this example of upgrading the OS, which is illustrative of many types of infrastructure changes in that it requires an app to be stopped and restarted. That's one of the advantages of cloud-native, apps: you have multiple instances that keep the system from incurring downtime as a whole. Before taking down an instance still running on an old OS, a new instance of the app will first be started on a node that already has the new version of the OS. That new instance will be running on a different node and clearly in a different context from the old, and your app and the software as a whole will need to adapt. Figure 6.2 depicts the various stages in this process; note that the IP address and port differ for the application before and after the upgrade.

An upgrade isn't the only deliberate cause of infrastructure changes. An interesting security technique gaining widespread acceptance calls for application instances to be frequently redeployed because a constantly changing attack surface is harder to penetrate than a long-lived one.[1]

### 6.1.3   *Updating application configuration with zero downtime*

So far, I've given examples of changes that are, if you will, inflicted on the application from an external source. Scaling the number of instances of an app isn't directly applying a change to that instance. Instead, the existence of multiple instances imposes contextual variability across the set.

But sometimes an app running in production simply needs to have new configuration values applied. For example, a web application may display a copyright at the bottom of each and every page, and when the calendar turns from December to January, you want to update the date without redeploying the entire app.

Credential rotation, whereby the passwords used by one system component to gain access to another are periodically updated, serves as another example, one that's commonly required by the security practices of an organization. This should be as simple as having the team that's operating the application in production (which hopefully is the same team that built it!) provide new secrets, while the system as a whole continues to operate normally.

These types of contextual changes represent changes in the application configuration data and, in contrast to things like infrastructure changes, are generally under the control of the app team itself. This distinction may tempt you to handle this type of variability in a manner that might be a bit more "manual." But as you'll see shortly,

---

[1]See "The Three Rs of Enterprise Security: Rotate, Repave, and Repair," by Justin Smith at http://mng.bz/gNKe for more information.

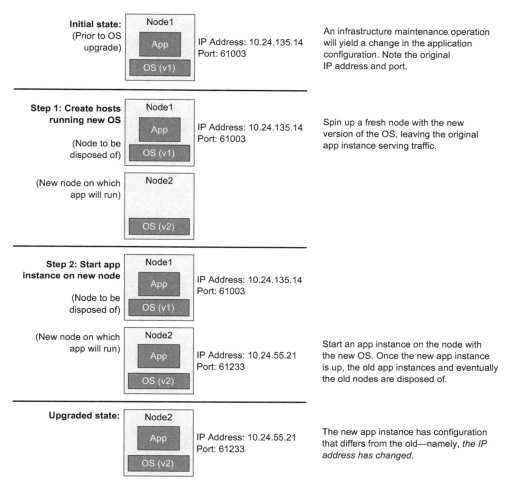

Figure 6.2 **Application configuration changes are often brought about from changes in the infrastructure, which are either anticipated (as depicted here, a rolling upgrade) or unexpected.**

from the app perspective, handling intentional changes and imposed changes by using similar approaches isn't only possible, but highly desirable.

That's the trick in all these scenarios: to create the proper abstractions, parameterizing the app deployment so that the elements that will vary across different contexts can be injected into the app in a sensible way and at the right time. Just as with any pattern, your aim is to have a tried, tested, and repeatable way to design for these requirements.

The place to start with this repeatable pattern is at the application itself—creating a technique to clearly define the precise configuration data for an application that will allow for values to be inserted as needed.

## 6.2    *The app's configuration layer*

If you're reading a book about cloud-native software, you've almost assuredly heard of the Twelve-Factor App (https://12factor.net), a set of patterns and practices that are recommended for microservices-based applications. One of the most frequently cited factors is #3: "Store config in the environment." Reading the admittedly brief description at https://12factor.net/config, you can see that it advises that configuration data for an app be stored in environment variables.

Part of the valid argument for this approach is that virtually all operating systems support the concept of environment variables, and all programming languages offer a way to access them. This not only lends to application portability but also can form the basis of consistent operating practices, regardless of the types of systems your app is running on. Following this guidance in Java, for example, you could have code such as the following to access and use the configuration data stored in those environmental variables:

```
public Iterable<Post> getPostsByUserId(
    @RequestParam(value="userIds", required=false) String userIds,
    HttpServletResponse response) {
    String ip;
    ip = System.getenv("INSTANCE_IP");
    ...
}
```

Although this approach will certainly allow your code to be used in different environments, a couple of flaws arise from this simple advice, or at least the preceding implementation of it. First, environment variables aren't the best approach for all types of config data. You'll see shortly that they work well for system config, but less so for application config. And second, having System.getenv calls (or similar in other languages) spread throughout your codebase makes keeping track of your app configuration difficult.

A better approach is to have a specific configuration layer in your application—one place that you can go to see the configuration options for an app. As you progress through this chapter, you'll see that there are differences in the way system environment configuration and app configuration are handled, but this app config layer is common to both (figure 6.3). In Java, this comes through the use of property files, and most languages provide a similar construct.

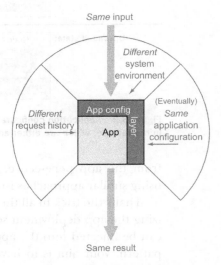

Figure 6.3    **Apps have a specific configuration layer that supports both system environment and application configuration. This layer allows the implementation to use values regardless of how their values are provided.**

Although you're almost certainly familiar with the use of property files, I have a way of looking at them that I want to share—one that will set you up well when we get into the differences between system and app configuration later in the chapter.

The biggest advantage of the approach I describe here may be that property files are a single logical place for all configuration parameters to be defined. (You may have several property files, but they're generally all placed in the same location in a project structure.) This allows a developer or application operator to easily review and understand the configuration parameters of an application. Remember my earlier remark about the System.getenv calls being scattered throughout a body of code? Imagine that you're a developer taking over an existing codebase and you have to "spelunk" through dozens of source code files to even see what data is acting as input to the app. Ugh. Property files are good.

The biggest disadvantage with the way property files are used today is that they're usually bundled into the deployable artifact (with Java, into the JAR file), and the property files often carry actual configuration values. Recall from chapter 2 that one of the keys to optimizing an application's development-to-operations lifecycle is that you have a single deployable artifact that's used throughout the entire SDLC. Because the context will be different in the various development, test, and production environments, you might be tempted to have different property files for each, but then you'd have different builds and different deployable artifacts. Do this, and you're back to providing ample opportunity for the proverbial "it works on my machine" to creep back in.

> **TIP** The good news is that you have an alternative to having different property files for different deployments.

And this is where my tweak comes in. I've come to think of the property file first as a specification of the configuration data for the application, and second as a gateway to the application context. The property file defines variables that can be used throughout the code, and the values are bound to those variables from the most appropriate sources (system env or app config) and at the right times. All languages provide a means for accessing the variables defined in these property files throughout the code. I've already been using this technique in the code samples.

Let's look at the application.properties file for the Posts service.

---

**Listing 6.1   application.properties**

```
management.security.enabled=false
spring.jpa.hibernate.ddl-auto=update
spring.datasource.username=root
spring.datasource.password=password
ipaddress=127.0.0.1
```

To trace the thread from property files to code, let's have a closer look at the ipaddress property. I haven't drawn your attention to it yet, but I've been printing the IP address that an app instance is serving traffic on within the log output. When you run this software locally, the value of 127.0.0.1 will be printed. But you might have noticed that when you deployed the services to Kubernetes, the log files were reporting that same IP, incorrectly. This is because I've been doing the very thing I just said isn't so good: binding values to those variables directly in the property file. I'll start fixing that shortly; I'll talk about how our properties get their values in the next two sections. Right now, I want to focus on the property file as an abstraction for the app implementation. In the PostsController.java file, you find the following code.

> **Listing 6.2    PostsController.java**

```
public class PostsController {

    private static final Logger logger
        = LoggerFactory.getLogger(PostsController.class);
    private PostRepository postRepository;

    @Value("${ipaddress}")
    private String ip;

    @Autowired
    public PostsController(PostRepository postRepository) {
        this.postRepository = postRepository;
    }
...
}
```

The local variable, ip, is drawing its value from the ipaddress environment variable. Spring provides the @Value annotation to make this simple. Putting the pieces together: the application source defines data members that may have their values injected, and it draws those values from the defined properties. The property file lists all of the configuration parameters, not only to facilitate the entry of those values into the application, but also to provide the developer or operator a specification of the configuration data for the app.

But, again, it's not at all good that you have the 127.0.0.1 value hardcoded in the property file. Some languages, like Java, provide an answer to this by allowing you to override property values when you launch an app. For example, you could start your Posts service with the following command, providing a new value for ipaddress:

```
java -Dipaddress=192.168.3.42 \
     -jar cloudnative-posts/target/cloudnative-posts-0.0.1-SNAPSHOT.jar
```

But I want to draw you back to factor #3, "Store config in the environment." This advice points to something important. It's true that moving value bindings out of property files and into the command line eliminates the need for different builds for different environments, but the different start commands now offer a new way for config errors to creep into your operational practices. If, instead, you store the IP address in an env variable, then you can use the following command to launch the app in any of the environments. The app will simply absorb the context that it's running in:

```
java -jar cloudnative-posts/target/cloudnative-posts-0.0.1-SNAPSHOT.jar
```

Some language frameworks support mapping env variables to application properties. For example, with the Spring Framework, setting the env variable IPADDRESS will cause that value to be injected into the ipaddress property. We're getting there, but I'm going to add one more abstraction to give you even more flexibility and code clarity. I want to update the ipaddress line in the property file to this:

```
ipaddress=${INSTANCE_IP:127.0.0.1}
```

This line now states that the value for ipaddress will be specifically drawn from the env variable INSTANCE_IP, and if that env variable isn't defined, ipaddress will be set to the *default* value of 127.0.0.1. You see, it's okay to have values in the property file as long as they represent sensible defaults, and you're intentional about how the values will be overridden when the default isn't correct.

Let's put all of this together in a diagram—figure 6.4. The application source references properties that are defined in the property file. The property file acts as a

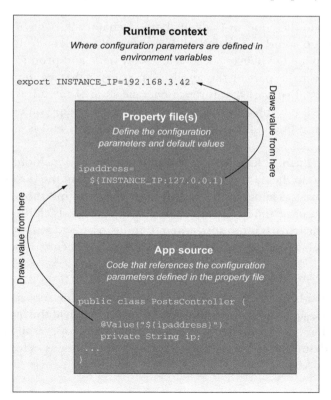

Figure 6.4   The application source references properties that are defined in the property file. The property file acts as a specification of the configuration parameters for the app, and can indicate that values should come from env variables (INSTANCE_IP).

specification of the configuration parameters for the app and will clearly indicate which values may come from env variables.

Property files written in this way are compiled into a single deployable artifact that can now be instantiated into any environment; the artifact is expressly designed to absorb the context of that environment. This is goodness—and a key pattern for properly configuring your applications in a cloud context!

But I haven't given you the whole story. Everything I've said is 100% true, but through omission, I've implied that the property files always source values from environment variables (though I did hint that this might not always be the case). That is but one place from which configuration data can come; there are alternatives. And the differences are generally drawn along the lines of whether you have system config or application config data. Let's look at each of those now.

## 6.3   *Injecting system/environment values*

What I mean by *system values* are those that the application developer or operator aren't in direct control of. Whoa—what? In the world I've spent most of my career in, this is an absolutely crazy concept. Computers and computer programs are deterministic, and if you supply all the inputs in the same way, you can totally control the output. A suggestion to cede some of that control would make many software professionals uncomfortable. But moving to the cloud necessitates exactly that. It takes us all the way back to the concept I talked about in chapter 2: *change is the rule, not the exception.* Giving up some control also allows systems to operate more independently, ultimately making the delivery of software more agile and productive.

System variables reflect the part of the application context that's generally supplied by the infrastructure. I suggest that it represents the state of the infrastructure. As we've already discussed, our job as developers is to ensure that app outcomes are consistent, despite running in a context that's not known a priori and is constantly changing.

To explore this a bit further, let's look at a concrete example: including the IP address in logging output. In the past, you might not have thought of the IP address as something that was constantly changing, but in the cloud it is. App instances are constantly being created and each time will receive a new IP address. Including the IP address in log output is particularly interesting when running in a cloud setting because it allows you to track which specific instance of an app served a particular request.

### 6.3.1   *Let's see this in action: Using ENV variables for configuration*

To get started, I invite you back to the cloudnative-abundantsunshine repository, specifically to the cloudnative-appconfig directory and module. Looking at the implementation for the Connections' Posts service, you can see that the property file already reflects the `ipaddress` definition shown in the previous section. It reads as follows:

```
ipaddress=${INSTANCE_IP:127.0.0.1}
```

The app needs the `ipaddress` value, and the infrastructure has such a value. How, then, do you connect the two? This is where factor #3 nailed it: environment variables are the constant in virtually all environments; the infrastructure and platforms know how to supply them, and application frameworks know how to consume them. Using this ubiquity is important. It allows you to establish best practices, regardless of whether your app is running on Linux (any of the flavors!), macOS, or Windows.

To see all of this in action, I want to deploy the latest version of the app into Kubernetes.

### SETTING UP

Just as with the examples of the previous chapters, in order to run the samples, you must have these standard tools installed:

- Maven
- Git
- Java 1.8
- Docker
- Some type of a MySQL client, such as the `mysql` CLI
- Some type of a Redis client, such as `redis-cli`
- Minikube

### BUILDING THE MICROSERVICES (OPTIONAL)

I will have you deploy the apps into Kubernetes. To do so, Docker images are required, so I've prebuilt those images and made them available in Docker Hub. Therefore, building the microservices from source isn't necessary. That said, studying the code is illustrative, so I invite you to follow some of these steps, even if you don't build the code yourself.

From the cloudnative-abundantsunshine directory, check out the following tag and then change into the cloudnative-appconfig directory:

```
git checkout appconfig/0.0.1
cd cloudnative-appconfig
```

Then, to build the code (optional), type the following command:

```
mvn clean install
```

Running this command builds each of the three apps, producing a JAR file in the target directory of each module. If you want to deploy these JAR files into Kubernetes, you must also run the `docker build` and `docker push` commands as described in the "Using Kubernetes requires you to build Docker images" sidebar in chapter 5. If you do this, you must also update the Kubernetes deployment YAML files to point to your images instead of mine. I won't repeat those steps here. Instead, the deployment manifests I provide point to images stored in my Docker Hub repository.

If you don't already have it running, start Minikube as described in section 5.2.2 of chapter 5. To start with a clean slate, delete any deployments and services that might be left over from your previous work. I've provided you a script to do that: `delete-DeploymentComplete.sh`. This simple bash script allows you to keep the MySQL and Redis services running. Calling the script with no options deletes only the three microservice deployments; calling the script with `all` as an argument deletes MySQL and Redis as well. Verify that your environment is clean with the following command:

```
$kubectl get all
NAME                            READY   STATUS      RESTARTS   AGE
pod/mysql-75d7b44cd6-jzgsk      1/1     Completed   0          2d3h
pod/redis-6bb75866cd-tzfms      1/1     Completed   0          2d3h

NAME                 TYPE        CLUSTER-IP     EXTERNAL-IP   PORT(S)          AGE
service/kubernetes   ClusterIP   10.96.0.1      <none>        443/TCP          2d5h
service/mysql-svc    NodePort    10.107.78.72   <none>        3306:30917/TCP   2d3h
service/redis-svc    NodePort    10.108.83.115  <none>        6379:31537/TCP   2d3h

NAME                        READY   UP-TO-DATE   AVAILABLE   AGE
deployment.apps/mysql       1/1     1            1           2d3h
deployment.apps/redis       1/1     1            1           2d3h

NAME                                   DESIRED   CURRENT   READY   AGE
replicaset.apps/mysql-75d7b44cd6          1         1         1      2d3h
replicaset.apps/redis-6bb75866cd        1    1     1    2d3hNAME
```

Note that you've left MySQL and Redis running.

If you've cleared out Redis and MySQL, deploy each with the following commands:

```
kubectl create -f mysql-deployment.yaml
kubectl create -f redis-deployment.yaml
```

Once completed, the deployment will be as depicted in figure 6.5. You'll have one each of the Connections and Posts services, and two instances of the Connections' Posts service. To achieve this topology, for now, you may still have to edit deployment manifests. These steps, summarized next, are detailed in chapter 5:

1  Configure the Connections service to point to the MySQL database. Look up the URL with this command and insert into the appropriate position in the deployment manifest:

```
minikube service mysql-svc  \
   --format "jdbc:mysql://{{.IP}}:{{.Port}}/cookbook"
```

2  Deploy the Connections service with the following:

```
kubectl create -f cookbook-deployment-connections.yaml
```

3  Configure the Posts service to point to the MySQL database. Use the same URL that you obtained with the command in step 1 and insert it into the appropriate position in the deployment manifest.

4  Deploy the Posts service:

```
kubectl create -f cookbook-deployment-posts.yaml
```

5  Configure the Connections' Posts service to point to the Posts, Connections, and Users services, as well as the Redis service. These values can be found with the following commands, respectively:

| | |
|---|---|
| Posts URL | `minikube service posts-svc --format "http://{{.IP}}:{{.Port}}/posts?userIds=" --url` |
| Connections URL | `minikube service connections-svc --format "http://{{.IP}}:{{.Port}}/connections/" --url` |
| Users URL | `minikube service connections-svc --format "http://{{.IP}}:{{.Port}}/users/" --url` |
| Redis IP | `minikube service redis-svc --format "{{.IP}}"` |
| Redis port | `minikube service redis-svc --format "{{.Port}}"` |

6  Deploy the Connections' Posts service:

```
kubectl create -f cookbook-deployment-connectionsposts.yaml
```

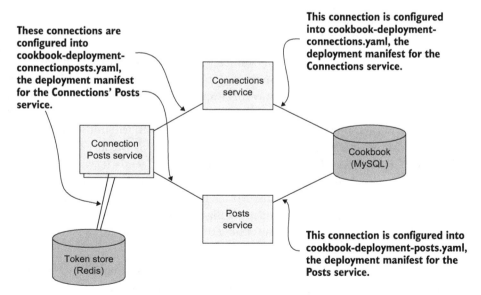

**Figure 6.5  This software deployment topology currently requires a great deal of hand edits of connections between the services. These manual configurations will be progressively eliminated as you proceed through more cloud-native patterns.**

Your deployment is now complete, but I'd like to draw your attention to the lines in the deployment manifests that get to the topic at hand: configuration of system values. The following shows a portion of the deployment manifest for the Connections' Posts service:

Listing 6.3    cookbook-deployment-connectionsposts.yaml

```
apiVersion: apps/v1
kind: Deployment
metadata:
  name: connectionsposts
  labels:
    app: connectionsposts
spec:
  replicas: 2
  selector:
    matchLabels:
      app: connectionsposts
  template:
    metadata:
      labels:
        app: connectionsposts
    spec:
      containers:
      - name: connectionsposts
        image: cdavisafc/cloudnative-appconfig-connectionposts:0.0.1
        env:
          - name: INSTANCE_IP
            valueFrom:
              fieldRef:
                fieldPath: status.podIP
```

As part of the specification for the service, you see a section labeled env. Yep, that's exactly where you define environment variables for the context in which your app will run. Kubernetes supports several ways of supplying a value. In the case of INSTANCE_IP, it draws the value from attributes supplied by the Kubernetes platform itself. Only Kubernetes knows the IP address of the pod (the entity in which the app will run), and that value can be accessed in the deployment manifest via the attribute status.podIP. When Kubernetes establishes the runtime context, it seeds it with the INSTANCE_IP value that, in turn, is drawn into the application through the property file.

Figure 6.6 summarizes all of this. Notice that the box labeled "Linux Container" is exactly that of figure 6.4. What you're seeing here is the app config layer running in a Kubernetes context. Figure 6.6 shows how that context interfaces with the app config layer. The diagram shows a lot of sophistication:

- Kubernetes has an API that allows for a deployment manifest to be supplied.
- That deployment manifest allows for env variables to be defined.
- When the deployment is created, Kubernetes creates a pod and containers within the pod, and seeds each of those with a host of values.

But despite this relative complexity, what's in the Linux container remains simple; the app will draw values from env variables. The app is shielded from all of the Kubernetes complexity by using env variables as the abstraction. This is why factor #3 of the Twelve-Factor App is so spot on; it drives simplicity and elegance.

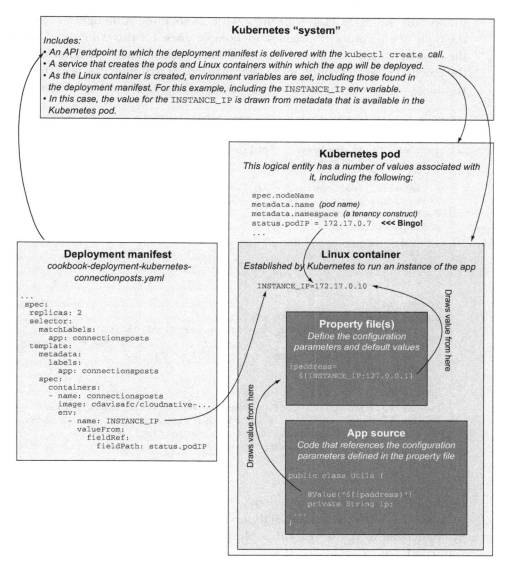

**Figure 6.6　Responsible for the deployment and management of the app instances, Kubernetes establishes the environment variables defined in the deployment manifest, drawing values from the infrastructure entities it has established for the app.**

If you look at the code in listing 6.3, you'll see that a Utils Java class is used to generate a tag that concatenates the IP address and port that the app is running on. This tag is then included in the log output. When an instance of this class is created, the Linux container has already been initialized, including having the INSTANCE_IP environment variable set. This has the result of initializing the ipaddress property that's then drawn into the Utils class with the @Value annotation. Although it's not related to the topic of environment variables, for completeness I'll also point out that I've made the class ApplicationContextAware and have implemented a listener that waits for the embedded servlet container to be initialized. At that time, the port that the app is running on has been set and can be looked up through EmbeddedServletContainer.

---

**Listing 6.4   Utils.java**

```
public class Utils implements ApplicationContextAware,
                    ApplicationListener<ServletWebServerInitializedEvent> {

    private ApplicationContext applicationContext;
    private int port;
    @Value("${ipaddress}")
    private String ip;

    public String ipTag() {
        return "[" + ip + ":" + port +"] ";
    }

    @Override
    public void setApplicationContext(
                        ApplicationContext applicationContext)
                                            throws BeansException {
        this.applicationContext = applicationContext;
    }

    @Override
    public void onApplicationEvent(ServletWebServerInitializedEvent
                            embeddedServletContainerInitializedEvent) {
        this.port = embeddedServletContainerInitializedEvent
                        .getApplicationContext().getWebServer().getPort();
    }
}
```

Okay, time to see all of this in action.

If you've re-created your MySQL service, be sure to create the cookbook database by connecting to the server with a MySQL client and issuing the create database command. For example:

```
$mysql -h $(minikube service mysql-svc --format "{{.IP}}") \
 -P $(minikube service mysql-svc --format "{{.Port}}") -u root -p
mysql> create database cookbook;
Query OK, 1 row affected (0.00 sec)
```

In addition to what I detail here, you're welcome to stream the logs from both the Connections and Posts services, but what I really want to home in on is the log output for the Connections' Posts service. Let's invoke this service a few times. Recall that the first step is to authenticate, and then you can access the posts for your connections with a simple `curl` command:

```
# authenticate
curl -X POST -i -c cookie \
   $(minikube service --url connectionsposts-svc)/login?username=cdavisafc
# get the posts - repeat this command 4 or 5 times
curl -i -b cookie \
   $(minikube service --url connectionsposts-svc)/connectionsposts
```

Kubernetes doesn't support aggregated log streaming, which is why I've had you invoke the service several times before looking at the logs. You can now, however, look at the logs from both instances with a single command:

```
$ kubectl logs -lapp=connectionsposts
...
... : Tomcat started on port(s): 8080 (http) with context path ''
... : Started CloudnativeApplication in 16.502 seconds
... : Initializing Spring FrameworkServlet 'dispatcherServlet'
... : FrameworkServlet 'dispatcherServlet': initialization started
... : FrameworkServlet 'dispatcherServlet': initialization completed
... : Starting without optional epoll library
... : Starting without optional kqueue library
... : [172.17.0.7:8080] getting posts for user network cdavisafc
... : [172.17.0.7:8080] connections = 2,3
... : [172.17.0.7:8080] getting posts for user network cdavisafc
... : [172.17.0.7:8080] connections = 2,3
...
... : Started CloudnativeApplication in 15.501 seconds
... : Initializing Spring FrameworkServlet 'dispatcherServlet'
... : FrameworkServlet 'dispatcherServlet': initialization started
... : FrameworkServlet 'dispatcherServlet': initialization completed
... : Starting without optional epoll library
... : Starting without optional kqueue library
... : [172.17.0.4:8080] getting posts for user network cdavisafc
... : [172.17.0.4:8080] connections = 2,3
... : [172.17.0.4:8080] getting posts for user network cdavisafc
... : [172.17.0.4:8080] connections = 2,3
```

Looking through this example, you can see that you have output from both instances of the Connections' Posts service. The logs aren't interleaved. This command simply accesses the logs from one instance and dumps them out, and then does the same for the next instance. You can, however, see where the output has come from two different instances, because the IP addresses for each have been reported; one instance has IP address 172.17.0.7, and the other has 172.17.0.4. Here you can see that two requests went to the instance serving traffic on 172.17.0.4, and two requests went to the instance at 172.17.0.7. Kubernetes has instantiated values into the environment variables present in the context of each instance, and the app has drawn the value in through the property files that were crafted to access environmental variables. It's a good design.

Let's take a look at the environment variables in the running containers. You may do this by executing the following command, replacing the pod name with your own:

```
$ kubectl exec connectionsposts-6c69d66bb6-f9bjn -- env
PATH=/usr/local/sbin:/usr/local/bin:/usr/sbin:/usr/bin:/sbin:/bin...
CONNECTIONPOSTSCONTROLLER_POSTSURL=http://192.168.99.100:32119/posts?userIds=
CONNECTIONPOSTSCONTROLLER_CONNECTIONSURL=http://192.168.99.100:30955/
➥ connections/
CONNECTIONPOSTSCONTROLLER_USERSURL=http://192.168.99.100:30955/users/
REDIS_HOSTNAME=192.168.99.100
REDIS_PORT=31537
INSTANCE_IP=172.17.0.7
KUBERNETES_PORT_443_TCP_PROTO=tcp
...
```

Among the long list of values printed out, you'll see INSTANCE_IP. At your direction (recall the lines in the deployment YAML for the Connections' Posts service), Kubernetes set that value to the IP address of the pod. This is an application configuration value that's set by the system in which your app is running.

Hopefully, this exercise has helped make things clear. But even so, I want to offer one other insightful tool. I haven't told you yet that I have something running as a part of each of the services. Through the magic of Spring Boot, the application automatically implements an endpoint where you can view the environment in which your apps are running. Run the following command to see the output:

```
curl $(minikube service --url connectionsposts-svc)/actuator/env
```

The JSON output is lengthy, but you'll see that it includes some of the following:

```
...
  "systemEnvironment": {
    "PATH": "/usr/local/sbin:/usr/local/bin:...",
    "INSTANCE_IP": "172.17.0.7",
    "PWD": "/",
    "JAVA_HOME": "/usr/lib/jvm/java-1.8-openjdk",
    ...
  },
  "applicationConfig: [classpath:/application.properties]": {
    ...
    "ipaddress": "172.17.0.7"
  },
...
```

Among the available data is the IP address you've been manipulating. Under the systemEnvironment key, you see a map that includes the INSTANCE_IP key with the value 172.17.0.7. You can also see under the applicationConfiguration key a map that includes the same address associated with the key ipaddress. The connection was established just as you intended.

Looking through other values in this output, there appear to be many environment variables, and indeed there are. But you can see that many other contextual values are also reported. You see, for example, the process ID (PID), the operating system version (os.version), and many other values that aren't stored in env variables. This drives home the point that environment variables aren't the only contextual values for your app. The /actuator/env endpoint reports on the broader superset. I'd now like to move on to another part of that application context and a different way of bringing in values.

## 6.4 Injecting application configuration

For the type of configuration data that you just looked at, with values that are part of the runtime environment and managed by the runtime platform, using environment variables is natural and effective. But when I first started working with cloud-native systems, I struggled with rationalizing factor #3 (store config in the environment) with some of the other things we need for managing application configuration. Ultimately, the answer is that there are better ways to manage application configuration data. That's what I want to take you through now.

When it comes to getting an application running in production, I'd argue that the configuration data is just as important as the implementation itself, for without the proper configuration, the software just won't work. This calls for applying the same level of rigor to managing app config data as you apply to managing code. In particular:

- The data must be persisted and access controlled. This is so similar to the way you handle source code that one of the most common tools used for this is a source code-control (SCC) system, like Git.
- You'll never set config data by hand. If you need to change a configuration, you'll make a change to the source code-controlled (Git) repository and invoke some action to apply that config to the running system.
- Configurations must be versioned so that you can consistently re-create deployments based solely on a specific version of the app, tied together with a specific version of the configuration. It's also essential to know what properties were being used at what times so that operational behaviors (good and bad) can be correlated to the configuration that was applied.
- Some configuration data is sensitive, such as credentials used for intercomponent communication in a distributed system. This brings added requirements that are addressed by special-purpose configuration repositories such as Vault from HashiCorp.

The first part of the answer for managing application configuration data is that it's managed in what I refer to as a *configuration data store*. (I'm avoiding the use of *configuration management database* because that term comes with a bit of baggage. It implies particular patterns that aren't the ones that apply in the cloud-native world.) The configuration store will simply house key/value pairs, maintain a version history, and have various access control mechanisms applied.

And the second part of the answer for managing application configuration is that a service facilitates the delivery of this versioned, access-controlled data to the application. This service is provided by a config server. Let's begin adding this to our running example.

### 6.4.1 Introducing the configuration server

At the moment, our implementation offers some level of control at the Connections' Posts service. A user must authenticate before the service will deliver results. But the two services that ultimately provide the data, the Connections and Posts services, remain wide open. Let's secure these services with secrets. We'll use secrets instead of user authentication and authorization because these services won't be called by a specific logged-in user, but rather will be called by another software module (in our case, the Connections' Posts service). For example, you use the Posts service here to get the posts for the set of users being followed by the logged-in user, but in another setting, you might use the same service to get the posts for any bloggers who are currently trending.

I've implemented secrets in the example by configuring a secret into both service being secured (the Connections and the Posts services), and by configuring the same secret into the client (the Connections' Posts service). Before looking at the implementation in detail, let's first look at how to manage these values.

First, you want to create a source-code repository to hold the secrets. You can create a repo from scratch, or to make things easier, you can fork a super-simple repo that I have at https://github.com/cdavisafc/cloud-native-config.git. You'll need to fork it so you can commit changes as you go through the exercise. In there, you'll see something that looks suspiciously close to a properties file: mycookbook.properties. This file contains two values—the secret that will protect the Posts service and another that will protect the Connections service:

```
com.corneliadavis.cloudnative.posts.secret=123456
com.corneliadavis.cloudnative.connections.secret=456789
```

Now you'll establish the service that will manage access to these configuration values, and for that you'll use Spring Cloud Configuration (https://github.com/spring-cloud/spring-cloud-config). The Spring Cloud Configuration Server (SCCS) is an open source implementation that's well suited to managing data for distributed systems (cloud-native software). It runs as an HTTP-based web service and provides support for organizing data around your complete software delivery lifecycle. I refer you to the README in the repository for further details, but demonstrate a few key capabilities here.

Let's start putting the pieces together. First, check out the following repository tag:

```
git checkout appconfig/0.0.2
```

Next, let's get SCCS up and running. Fortunately, there's already a Docker image for the server, and I've provided you a Kubernetes deployment manifest. Before creating the pod with the usual command, fork the https://github.com/cdavisafc/cloud-native-config.git repository, and then replace the URL in the following snippet of the deployment manifest with the URL to your repository:

```
env:
  - name: SPRING_CLOUD_CONFIG_SERVER_GIT_URI
    value: "https://github.com/cdavisafc/cloud-native-config.git"
```

Then create the service with the following command:

```
kubectl create -f spring-cloud-config-server-deployment.yaml
```

After the server is up and running, you can access the configurations with the following command:

```
$ curl $(minikube service --url sccs-svc)/mycookbook/dev | jq
{
  "name": "mycookbook",
  "profiles": [
    "dev"
  ],
  "label": null,
  "version": "67d9531747e46b679cc580406e3b48b3f7024fc8",
  "state": null,
  "propertySources": [
    {
      "name": "https://github.com/cdavisafc/cloud-native-
      ⮡ config.git/mycookbook.properties",
      "source": {
        "com.corneliadavis.cloudnative.connections.secret": "456789",
        "com.corneliadavis.cloudnative.posts.secret": "123456"
      }
    }
  ]
}
```

SCCS supports tagging configurations with both Git labels and application profiles. My sample config repository includes two configuration files for the mycookbook application—one for dev and one for prod. Executing the preceding curl command and replacing /dev with /prod will show the values for the production profile. What you've now established is shown in figure 6.7: a GitHub repository that stores configs, and a configuration service that manages access.

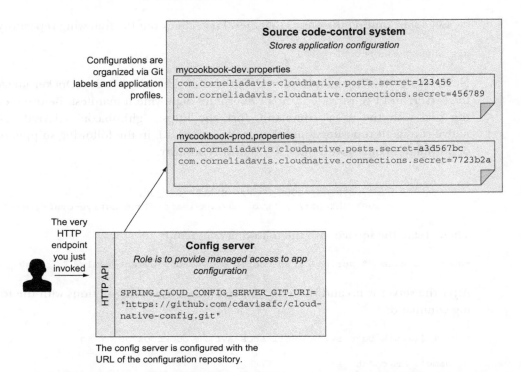

**Figure 6.7   Application configuration is facilitated through the use of a source code-control system that will persist configuration values, and a configuration service that provides managed access to that data.**

Let's look at both ends of the relationship that you're securing with your secrets. In the following listing, the Posts (and in the same way, the Connections) service will now check that the passed secret matches what has been configured in, and the Connections' Posts service will pass the secret that has been configured into it.

---

**Listing 6.5   PostsController.java**

```
public class PostsController {
    ...

    @Value("${com.corneliadavis.cloudnative.posts.secret}")
    private String configuredSecret;
    ...

    @RequestMapping(method = RequestMethod.GET, value="/posts")
    public Iterable<Post> getPostsByUserId(
        @RequestParam(value="userIds", required=false) String userIds,
        @RequestParam(value="secret", required=true) String secret,
        HttpServletResponse response) {
```

```
        Iterable<Post> posts;

    if (secret.equals(configuredSecret)) {

            logger.info(utils.ipTag() +
                "Accessing posts using secret " + secret);

            // look up the posts in the db and return
            ...
        } else {
            logger.info(utils.ipTag() +
                "Attempt to access Post service with secret " + secret
                + " (expecting " + password + ")");
            response.setStatus(401);
            return null;
        }

    }
    ...
}
```

In the Connections' Posts service, the secret that's configured in will be passed in the request to the Connections or Posts services, as shown in the following listing.

**Listing 6.6    ConnectionsPostsController.java**

```
public class ConnectionsPostsController {
    ...

    @Value("${connectionpostscontroller.connectionsUrl}")
    private String connectionsUrl;
    @Value("${connectionpostscontroller.postsUrl}")
    private String postsUrl;
    @Value("${connectionpostscontroller.usersUrl}")
    private String usersUrl;
    @Value("${com.corneliadavis.cloudnative.posts.secret}")
    private String postsSecret;
    @Value("${com.corneliadavis.cloudnative.connections.secret}")
    private String connectionsSecret;

    @RequestMapping(method = RequestMethod.GET, value="/connectionsposts")
    public Iterable<PostSummary> getByUsername(
        @CookieValue(value = "userToken", required=false) String token,
        HttpServletResponse response) {

        if (token == null) {
            logger.info(utils.ipTag() + ...);
            response.setStatus(401);
        } else {
            ValueOperations<String, String> ops =
                this.template.opsForValue();
```

```
        String username = ops.get(token);
        if (username == null) {
            logger.info(utils.ipTag() + ...);
            response.setStatus(401);
        } else {
            ArrayList<PostSummary> postSummaries
                = new ArrayList<PostSummary>();
            logger.info(utils.ipTag() + ...);

            String ids = "";
            RestTemplate restTemplate = new RestTemplate();

            // get connections
            String secretQueryParam = "?secret=" + connectionsSecret;
            ResponseEntity<ConnectionResult[]> respConns
                = restTemplate.getForEntity(
                    connectionsUrl + username + secretQueryParam,
                    ConnectionResult[].class);
            ConnectionResult[] connections = respConns.getBody();
            for (int i = 0; i < connections.length; i++) {
                if (i > 0) ids += ",";
                ids += connections[i].getFollowed().toString();
            }
            logger.info(utils.ipTag() + ...);

            secretQueryParam = "&secret=" + postsSecret;
            // get posts for those connections
            ResponseEntity<PostResult[]> respPosts
                = restTemplate.getForEntity(
                    postsUrl + ids + secretQueryParam,
                    PostResult[].class);
            PostResult[] posts = respPosts.getBody();

            for (int i = 0; i < posts.length; i++)
                postSummaries.add(
                    new PostSummary(
                        getUsersname(posts[i].getUserId()),
                        posts[i].getTitle(),
                        posts[i].getDate()));

            return postSummaries;
        }
    }
    return null;
}
    ...
}
```

Aside from certain things you'd never do in a real implementation, and I'll come back
to those in a moment, none of this is causing you any surprise. But look at the way that
the configuration value is brought into the app. The property file for the Connections' Posts service is as follows.

**Listing 6.7   Connections' Posts application.properties**

```
management.endpoints.web.exposure.include=*
connectionpostscontroller.connectionsUrl=http://localhost:8082/connections/
connectionpostscontroller.postsUrl=http://localhost:8081/posts?userIds=
connectionpostscontroller.usersUrl=http://localhost:8082/users/
ipaddress=${INSTANCE_IP:127.0.0.1}
redis.hostname=localhost
redis.port=6379
com.corneliadavis.cloudnative.posts.secret=drawFromConfigServer
com.corneliadavis.cloudnative.connections.secret=drawFromConfigServer
```

As I've already talked about, the properties defined here may simply be acting as placeholders. Both the secrets have values that read `drawFromConfigServer`. (This isn't an instruction, but rather is arbitrary. It could equally have been set to `foobar`.) And then the Connections' Posts controller has lines that read like this:

```
@Value("${com.corneliadavis.cloudnative.posts.secret}")
private String postsSecret;
@Value("${com.corneliadavis.cloudnative.connections.secret}")
private String connectionsSecret;
```

This looks familiar, because it's exactly the same technique that was used to draw in the `INSTANCE_IP` system config value. And that's exactly the point. The application config layer takes exactly the same form, whether the values are system/environment values or application configuration values being injected.

Figure 6.8 shows how application config data makes its way into the running application. Notice that the application configuration layer, with the property file at the center, remains as simple as shown in figure 6.4. The only thing that has changed is that the configuration server is supplying the bindings to the variables defined in the property file.

Now let's put both the application and system configuration together in one diagram; see figure 6.9. This is exactly what's implemented in our sample application. Again, note that the patterns used in the application configuration layer are the same for both types of config data. What differs is the way the values are injected into that application configuration layer. For system data, it's handled by the platform (in this case, Kubernetes) and is well served through the use of env variables. For application configuration data, you're using Spring (there are other options—look for future blog posts from me on the subject), which makes calls to the HTTP interface for the Spring Cloud Configuration Server; this approach allows you to version the app config data.

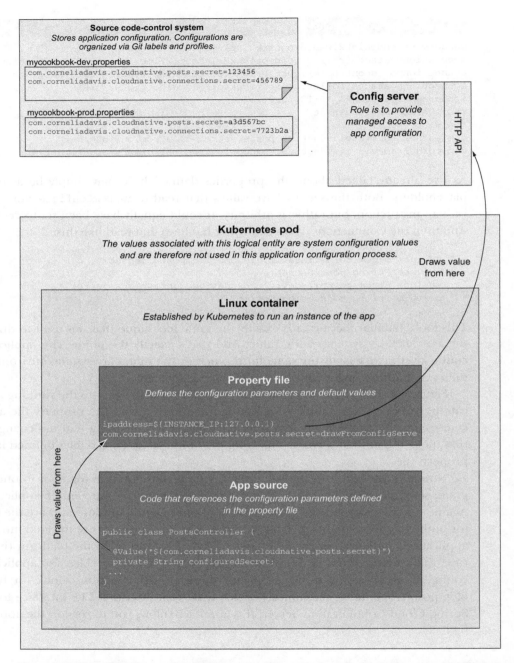

**Figure 6.8   The application configuration layer depends on the property file as the means for injecting values; those values come in through the use of a config server.**

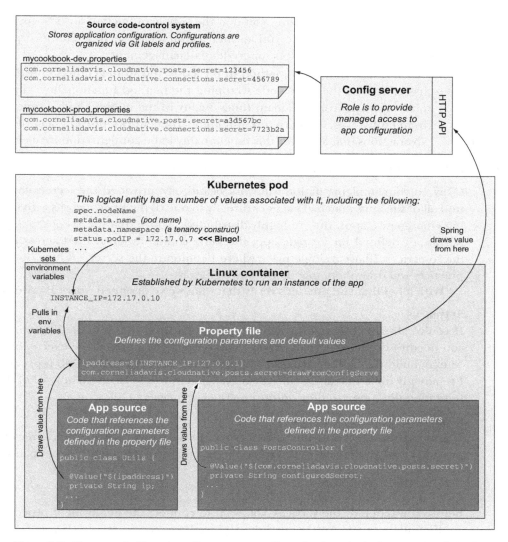

**Figure 6.9** The property file acts as the common configuration layer for both system config and application config. System config data is injected via env variables, and app config data is injected via a configuration service.

### 6.4.2 Security adds more requirements

I've created the implementation this way to make it easy to reason about the main design patterns for configuring cloud-native applications. But there are several things that you wouldn't do as I have here:

- You would never pass secrets on the query string; they'd instead be passed in an HTTP header or in the body.
- You definitely wouldn't print the values of secrets in log files.

- In the configuration store, you'd at the very least encrypt any sensitive values. SCCS does support encryption, and technologies such as HashiCorp's Vault provide additional services for credential management.
- You'll notice that every method in the Posts and Connections controllers now has effectively the same code wrapping the method functionality. This boilerplate distracts from the main functionality of the method and is repeated too frequently. Most modern programming frameworks provide security-related abstractions that allow for this functionality to be configured more elegantly.

### 6.4.3   Let's see this in action: Application configuration using a config server

Okay, so your implementation will work beautifully, provided the secrets configured into all of the apps match. That goes directly to one of the key concerns with configuring cloud-native apps: they're highly distributed! Notice that the mycookbook properties aren't defined for a single app; the same configuration is used across different microservices. I have a single place where I configure the secret, and my operational practices will draw them together in the right way.

With all of that laid out, let's verify that what we've designed works as advertised.

#### SETTING UP

If you've already followed the setup instructions from the example in section 6.3.1, you needn't do more here. As always, you're welcome to build the executables from source, build the Docker images, and push them to your Docker Hub repository. But I've already done that and made them available to you in Docker Hub. All of the configuration files point to the appropriate Docker images.

#### RUNNING THE APPS

First, clean up the set of microservices you've deployed to Kubernetes; recall that I provided a script that allows you to do this in one shot by typing this command:

```
./deleteDeploymentComplete.sh
```

Before you redeploy the services, you want to connect the deployment process to the configuration server. You've already deployed the config server (if you haven't yet done this as described previously, please do so now). Now you must inject the coordinates of that config server into the implementation so that the Spring Framework can use that connection to find and inject the configuration values. In the Kubernetes deployment manifests for each of the services, you'll find the definition of, what else, an environment variable that has the URL for SCCS. You need to provide your specific URL in all three places—the Posts, Connections, and Connections' Posts deployment manifests. You can obtain the correct value with the following command:

```
minikube service --url sccs-svc
```

Assuming you've left the Redis and MySQL services running, those URLs don't need to be updated. You can deploy the Posts and Connections services with the following two commands:

```
kubectl create -f cookbook-deployment-connections.yaml
kubectl create -f cookbook-deployment-posts.yaml
```

Again, you must now update the deployment manifest for the Connections' Posts service to point to the property URLs for the Posts and Connections services. Recall that you can obtain these values as follows:

| | |
|---|---|
| Posts URL | `minikube service posts-svc --format "http://{{.IP}}:{{.Port}}/posts?userIds=" --url` |
| Connections URL | `minikube service connections-svc --format "http://{{.IP}}:{{.Port}}/connections/" --url` |
| Users URL | `minikube service connections-svc --format "http://{{.IP}}:{{.Port}}/users/" --url` |

Now deploy the Connections' Posts service with the following:

```
kubectl create -f cookbook-deployment-connectionsposts.yaml
```

Invoke the Connections' Posts service just as you previously have, by first authenticating and then fetching the posts:

```
# authenticate
curl -X POST -i -c cookie \
    $(minikube service --url connectionsposts-svc)/login?username=cdavisafc
# get the posts
curl -i -b cookie \
    $(minikube service --url connectionsposts-svc)/connectionsposts
```

Nothing has changed, huh? Just as you should expect, but let's take a quick peek under the covers by looking into the log files for the Posts service:

```
... : [172.17.0.4:8080] Accessing posts using secret 123456
... : [172.17.0.4:8080] getting posts for userId 2
... : [172.17.0.4:8080] getting posts for userId 3
```

You can see that the Posts service has been accessed using the secret 123456. Obviously, the secrets were properly configured into both the caller (Connections' Posts) and the callee (Posts) services.

Now, what happens when you need to update application configuration? You want new values injected equally in all application instances for a single service, and of course, when values are to be inserted into different services, that must be coordinated as well. Let's try this out. The first thing I'll ask you to do is update the secret values for the dev profile of mycookbook; you can change the values to anything you like. You must then commit those changes to your repo and push to GitHub. From the cloud-native-config directory:

```
git add .
git commit -m "Update dev secrets."
git push
```

If you now issue the final curl that accesses the Connections' Posts data, it all works as expected. But if you look at the Posts log file again, you'll see that the Posts access still uses, and successfully, the secret 123456. And here we come to the topic of the next chapter—application lifecycle. You must be deliberate about when configuration changes are applied. From the example so far, you can see that the new credentials haven't yet been applied.

But they will be on startup, so I'll have you restart the Posts service by deleting the pod. Because you've instantiated a Kubernetes deployment that specifies that one instance of the Posts service should always be running, Kubernetes will immediately create a new pod for a new instance of the Posts service:

```
kubectl delete pod/posts-66bcfcbbf7-jvcqb
```

Now curl the Connections' Posts service again. You'll see two things:

- First, the service invocation will fail.
- And second, looking at the log file for the Posts service shows you why:

```
... : [172.17.0.7:8080] Attempt to access Post service with secret
      123456 (expecting abcdef)
```

When you deleted and re-created the Posts service, it picked up the new configuration values. However, the Connections' Posts service still has the old ones configured in. The old are sent; the new are expected. Clearly, you need to coordinate the update of configuration across instances and sometimes across services, but before you can go there, you must study application lifecycle concerns and patterns. That is the topic of the next chapter.

## *Summary*

- Cloud-native software architecture requires a reevaluation of the techniques you use for app configuration. Some existing practices remain, and some new approaches are useful.
- Cloud-native application configuration is not as simple as just storing config in environment variables.
- Property files remain an important part of proper handling of software configuration.

- Using environment variables for configuration is ideally suited to system config data.
- You can use cloud-native platforms such as Kubernetes to deliver environment values into your apps.
- App config should be treated just as source code is: managed in a source code repository, versioned, and access controlled.
- Configuration servers, such as Spring Cloud Configuration Server, are used to deliver configuration values into your apps.
- You now have to think about when config is applied, which is inherently related to the cloud-native application lifecycle.

# The application lifecycle: Accounting for constant change

The application lifecycle seems pretty basic: an app gets deployed, is started, is running for a bit, and is eventually shut down. Aside from the chaos that ensues when that "shutting down" part happens unexpectedly, this lifecycle is generally boring (or so we hope). Why, then, have an entire chapter dedicated to the topic?

Before I answer that question, let me first be clear on my definition of *application lifecycle*. The application lifecycle I cover here is distinctly different from the software development lifecycle (SDLC) that I've already talked about a great deal. The latter is about the phases your software goes through in the *development* and *delivery* of software—from design, to being under development, to first passing unit tests and then integration tests, to delivering it to production.

The application lifecycle, on the other hand, is all about the stages an application goes through after it's ready for production deployment. The central concern isn't the work going into the development or management of the software, but the state of the application itself. Is it deployed? Running? Stopped (either via crash or intentional stop)? Although it's natural to consider an app being deployed as a part of the SDLC, the focus here is on the running state of an application.

To help you understand the content of this chapter as well as provide a basis for later explanations, figure 7.1 depicts a fairly vanilla sequence of stages an app goes through in its lifetime. You'll notice that I've excluded the creation of the deployable artifact from the app lifecycle; that's part of the SDLC. On the other hand, you might find it curious that I've included having a provisioned environment and, later, a disposed-of environment, within the app lifecycle. I'll ask for your patience; I promise this will become clear soon.

So apps are started and stopped. What makes this interesting in our cloud-native setting? As it happens, both of the factors that characterize cloud-native apps: that they're highly distributed and constantly changing.

Let's start with the former. You've already learned that even when multiple instances of an app are deployed, collectively they need to behave as a single logical entity. How, then, do you properly handle something like applying new configuration to an app, or deploying a new version? Do you do this for all the apps in lockstep, or is there another approach? (Look back at figure 6.1, which indicates that "eventually" all instances must have the same configuration; this was a foreshadowing of material I cover in this chapter.)

As for constant change, recall that apps will regularly be moved around, because of either a failure or a management event such as addressing a vulnerability in the operating system. Aside from this leading to many starts and stops, there are cascading effects we need to account for. For example, when another microservice depends on an app that has just been started, information about the newly running app might need to be made available to those dependent apps.

Application lifecycles for the cloud-native app are different from those of apps running in decades past, and this places new requirements on app design. This is why I've focused this entire chapter on the app lifecycle.

After briefly reviewing some operational concerns that intersect with the app lifecycle, I will talk about the application lifecycle for multiple instances of an app (which is

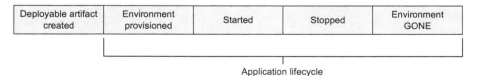

Figure 7.1 A simple depiction of the stages in an app's lifecycle

what you'll have pretty much always). As is already abundantly clear, your software consists of many apps working together, so I'll talk about the need to be aware of the ways that application lifecycle events for one app affect another. Then I'll cover the ephemeral context in which our apps now live and what that means for your app designs. In an environment that's constantly changing, it becomes paramount that app health can be accurately assessed, and if necessary, acted upon, so you'll see a section on that. And finally, I'll talk briefly about the serverless, or rather, function-as-a-service programming paradigm from the lens of the app lifecycle.

## 7.1   *Having empathy for operations*

The app lifecycle is more about ops than development, but as a developer, you need to deliver software that can be effectively managed in production. Having empathy for the application operator is a theme that runs through this text. Heck, these days you're likely to be doing ops as well as dev, so attention placed here is self-serving. Let's have a brief look at some of the main operational concerns, with an eye on the impact of the cloud-native lifecycle:

- *Manageability*—One of the first concerns for operations is the sustainability of managing application deployments. Wherever possible, management functions should be automatable, and when any management tasks are necessary, they should be done efficiently and reliably. The way you design your software can have a marked impact. For example, as you'll see, a change in app configuration almost always necessitates a restart of the app, so you should carefully decide whether to make something configuration or input data.

- *Resilience*—By the end of this book, you'll have a solid appreciation for platforms that keep apps running on your behalf, even while a constant stream of changes are happening around them. I sometimes like to think of these platforms as robots—robots that are handling a whole host of operational tasks that humans used to do. But here's the thing: robots don't read release notes. I make this statement with a wink, and definitely metaphorically, but the intent holds as true for the app lifecycle as it does for many other aspects of your cloud-native software. For example, if a system like Kubernetes will stand up a new instance of an app when one has failed, it must have a nonsubjective way of detecting that an app has failed or is failing. It's up to you, the application developer, to ensure that the platform has a fail-safe way of detecting when an app has failed.

- *Responsiveness*—Users of your software must receive outputs in a timely manner, and what is considered timely depends on the use case. For example, if a user is uploading a PowerPoint deck to SlideShare, it's okay if that deck isn't available to others for several minutes, allowing time for any format conversions to take place. On the other hand, if a user is trying out a news aggregation website for the first time and sees that pages are taking tens of seconds to render, it will likely be their last visit. Many factors will affect the responsiveness of your app, and the way the app lifecycle relates to user actions is one. For example, if an app is started up only after a user request has been made, the user will feel the cost of that startup. In the former example, they probably won't notice. In the latter, that cost could mean the difference between a retained or lost customer.

- *Cost management*—One of the great promises of the cloud is that of cost efficiency. Instead of provisioning, configuring, and managing infrastructure for peak loads, or, inevitably, an overestimation of peak loads, you're able to use only the resources you need at the moment. Being able to scale application capacity out or in depending on the traffic load, even being able to optimize away any idle computing time, is a powerful lever in IT cost management. These scaling operations mean new apps are started and old ones are stopped. Handling these app lifecycle events gracefully is essential.

In the remainder of this chapter, I'll cover many of the patterns that well serve the preceding list of concerns.

## 7.2 Single-app lifecycle, multiple-instance lifecycles

Let's start with a concrete example: our Posts service. In chapter 6, you added some configuration to this service, a secret used for authorization. Let's assume you have more than one instance of the app, each of which is running with the same configuration (the same secret). Everything is humming along just fine, the app is functioning exactly as you want, and then, oops, you inadvertently check your mycookbook.properties file that contains the secret into a public GitHub repository.

Although you quickly realize your mistake and pull the file, your secret may have been compromised, so you need to rotate this credential. To do so, you're going to change your configuration source file and, via the config server, deliver that configuration to all of the running apps. And here's where you need to think about the application lifecycle.

> **WARNING** Yes, I realize that in the running code sample, I've had you do exactly the thing that I've now characterized as a problem: storing credentials in a public GitHub repository. I'll direct your attention to the comments in chapter 6, which I'm repeating here: secrets should be stored in a repository expressly designed for handling sensitive information—something like HashiCorp's Vault or Pivotal's CredHub. I'm using GitHub in our samples only to keep things simple.

I say, "deliver that configuration to the running apps," but that statement is a bit disingenuous. What I mean is that I want you to roll the application—to restart it with the new configuration applied. That's exactly what I had you do at the end of chapter 6; I had you delete the Posts pod, causing Kubernetes to create a new one. This is lesson number one when it comes to application configuration and the app lifecycle.

> **NOTE** When new configuration is being applied to your running app, the app should be re-created, and hence restarted, with the new configuration applied.

Some of you might feel uncomfortable with this guidance. It might seem wasteful to restart the app when a cost is associated with that; it takes time to start an app. And re-creating the runtime environment goes even further and costs even more. And if you know Spring well, you might already be thinking of the easily enabled /refresh endpoint that, when invoked, will refresh the application context without completely restarting the app. I suggest that use of /refresh is a hack that can easily lead to unmanageable application deployment.

To explain why, let's consider the following scenario. Say you have two instances of the Posts service deployed. As I've already covered, one of the tricks with cloud-native application architectures when you're running more than one instance of an app is to have those multiple instances serving results as a single logical application. When a request is made to the Posts service, it will result in the same outcome regardless of which instance is reached. Figure 7.2 shows two instances of the Posts service fronted by a load balancer.

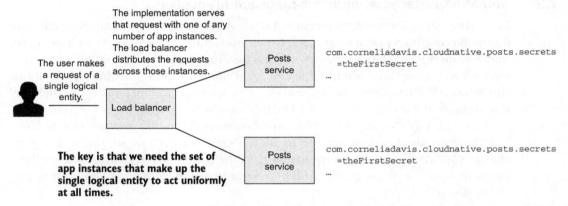

**Figure 7.2   Both instances of the Posts service are running with the same configuration and act as a single logical application.**

Now let's consider what would happen if you curled the /refresh endpoint. That curl command would reach only one instance, effectively updating the secret only for that instance. Now, as seen in figure 7.3, one instance is running with theFirstSecret, and the other is running with theSecondSecret configured in. It's now easy to see that when a request such as the following is issued, if the load balancer directs the request to the first instance, the request will succeed, but if it reaches the second, it will fail. Our two instances are definitely not acting as a single logical app:

```
$ curl http://myapp.example.com /posts?secret=theFirstSecret
```

Okay, so you might think the answer is simple: just roll through all the instances and update the configuration. Ultimately, you'd be right, but rolling through the instances in such a way that things stay running throughout is a bit tricky. You must consider

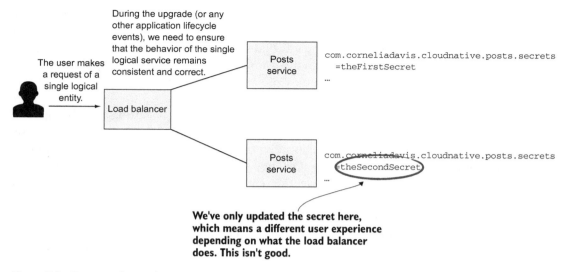

During the upgrade (or any other application lifecycle events), we need to ensure that the behavior of the single logical service remains consistent and correct.

The user makes a request of a single logical entity.

Load balancer

Posts service

com.corneliadavis.cloudnative.posts.secrets
=theFirstSecret
...

Posts service

com.corneliadavis.cloudnative.posts.secrets
=theSecondSecret
...

We've only updated the secret here, which means a different user experience depending on what the load balancer does. This isn't good.

**Figure 7.3  Because the two instances of the Posts service have different configurations applied, the outcome of issuing a request will differ greatly depending on whether a request is routed to the first instance of the app or the second. This must be avoided, even during a zero-downtime upgrade.**

factors including the way all app instances are cycled through and the state of the system as a whole during the upgrade process.

To hit all the instances, you might be tempted to just issue another /refresh curl command, but there's no guarantee that this command will reach the other app instance. This is why using the /refresh URL is a hack. You're trying to use a user's interface to perform a management function. Upgrading the configuration of all app instances is absolutely a management function, and you need to use a tool that will operate on each and every instance, and you need to be in control of this. You can't be at the mercy of a load balancer. The management function of upgrading the configuration of all the instances must sit behind the load balancer, not in front of it.

I will show you one of those control tools (spoiler alert: it's in Kubernetes) when you look at a concrete example in section 7.3, but for now let's continue the discussion assuming such a control plane function exists. Although the mechanism of using the /refresh URL isn't right, the intent is to refresh the application configuration, and you want to apply this new configuration all with zero downtime. Let's consider three options:

- Change the configuration while the app is running.
- Stand up a second set of instances, all of which will have the new configuration applied, and then switch all traffic from the first set to the second in one fell swoop. This is a *blue/green deployment*.
- Roll through the application instances, replacing a subset of them with the new, and then moving on to the next subset. This is a *rolling upgrade*.

I'd like to immediately rule out the first option for a couple of reasons. First, many applications and application frameworks apply configuration changes only at app startup time. For example, with the way that we've used .property files in our samples, a good practice for sure, config changes won't be applied until the application context is refreshed, and this is pretty close to an app restart (and exactly what the /refresh endpoint does).

In addition, applying configuration changes without restarting may bring your application into a state that can't be reproduced. Let's say, for example, an app loads reference data on startup, and the location from which that data is loaded is supplied in a configuration parameter. If you change that configuration parameter and trigger a load of data from the new location, the reference data loaded in memory would be a combination of the first load and the second, and the functionality of the app will reflect that state. Now suppose the app crashes and you want to troubleshoot. There's no way for you to obtain an instance that has the same state that the crashed app did. As you've already seen repeatedly, reproducible app deployments are absolutely essential in a cloud context in which app instances are frequently being created.

NOTE   Applying application configuration at startup time (figure 7.4) greatly simplifies operational practices and is therefore strongly recommended.

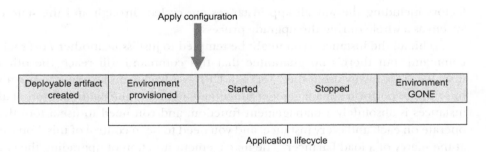

Figure 7.4   **Application configuration is best applied when the application is started. Most application frameworks naturally function this way.**

The second and third options are both valuable in the context of cloud-native apps. Let's look more deeply at each of them.

### 7.2.1   *Blue/green upgrades*

Used to update the configuration or version of your running app, the blue/green deployment is, particularly from a developer perspective, the simplest approach. It starts when you have one version of the app running, the "blue" version, and wish to deploy a new version, the "green" one.

Figure 7.5, which assumes that multiple instances of your cloud-native app are deployed, depicts the process. To start, you have a load balancer serving traffic to all blue instances of the app. In the next step, you deploy a complete set of instances of the

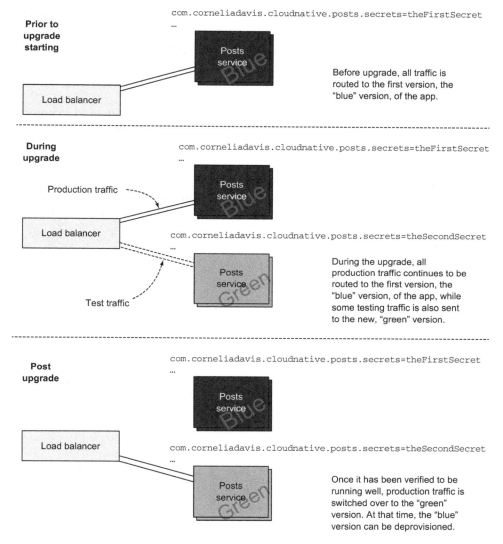

**Figure 7.5** The blue/green deployment is used when an app can't tolerate having multiple versions running side by side (when the multiple versions can't be made to act as a single logical instance).

new, green version but leave all production traffic routed to the blue. Now you can check to see that the green instances are operating correctly by sending traffic to them, and after that's verified, you cut all traffic over from the blue version to the green.

> **NOTE** What makes blue/green deployments simpler than rolling upgrades from the viewpoint of your application design is that with the former, you have only one version of the app running at a time.

This preceding NOTE is interesting indeed. The idea that you have in production only a single version of an app at a time is what you're used to, but when you eliminate this assumption, it affords you a great deal of power. The rolling upgrade is one of those things.

### 7.2.2   *Rolling upgrades*

A *rolling upgrade* is also used to perform a zero-downtime update to a running application, and just as with blue/green deployments, when completed, all traffic to the app will be routed to the new version of an app. During the upgrade process, however, things are markedly different.

Figure 7.6 depicts the process. At the onset, all traffic is being load-balanced across the multiple instances of the current version of the app. During the upgrade, you'll incrementally take a subset of the current version instances offline and bring a number

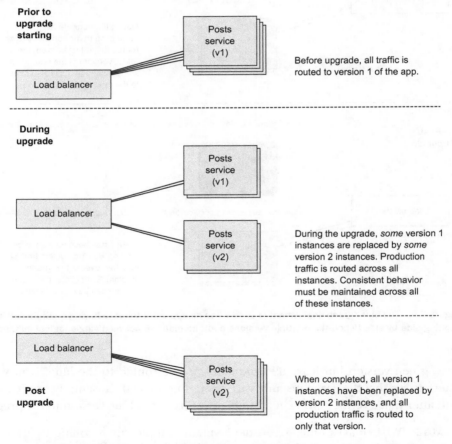

**Figure 7.6   During rolling upgrades, production traffic is routed to more than one version of the app. The app must be able to function as a single logical whole, even as requests are being distributed over different versions.**

of instances of the new version of the app online to replace them. As you do so, traffic is load-balanced across instances of the original version of the app *and* instances of the new version of the app. Traffic is being served to more than one version of the app! After the first batch is running well, you upgrade the next batch, and so on. The rolling upgrade is complete when all old versions of the app have been replaced by new.

I once again draw your attention back to figure 6.1, which indicates that eventually all instances of an app will be running with the same configuration. Now you can see concretely what I mean.

> **NOTE** During a rolling upgrade, application traffic will be handled by different versions of the same app.

The point in the above NOTE is interesting indeed. Recall one of our fundamental premises: the set of independent application instances should all operate collectively, as a whole. The outcome of invoking an app should be the same regardless of which app instance responds to the invocation request. Think about this for a moment. This means that you, the application architect/developer, are responsible for making sure that your app design supports this deployment pattern. Now, let me be clear here: this may not always be possible, but if you can realize this characteristic in your design, then and only then will a rolling upgrade deployment pattern be available.

### 7.2.3   *Parallel deployments*

No question, it takes more care to create software that allows for rolling upgrades (and shortly I'll take you through a code-based, concrete example of this). Therefore, you might wonder what you get from this added effort, if in the end a blue/green and a rolling upgrade yield the same result—all instances have been switched to the new version. The short answer is, "a lot," but let me draw your attention to two points in particular.

First, a blue/green deployment requires more resources than the rolling. During the upgrade, in order to keep the application capacity stable, you'll need as many instances of the green as you do of the blue. Only after the switch is flipped and all the traffic is routed to the new version may the resources being used by the old be freed. With the rolling upgrade, you choose the batch size—the number of instances that will be replaced per cycle—and with that, you're able to control the resources required of the upgrade process. You can see this contrast in figure 7.7.

Second, an app design that allows for multiple versions to be running at once offers more benefits than the rolling upgrade. One of those is agility.

Your cloud-native software is made up of many apps, with multiple instances of each app running at any given time, and a major goal in this modern era is the frequent evolution of that software. You know from our prior conversations that requiring all of the different microservices that make up the software to upgrade in lockstep effectively thwarts that speed. Approaches such as these yielded the nightmarish Gantt charts of the past that tracked dozens or hundreds of dependencies across various

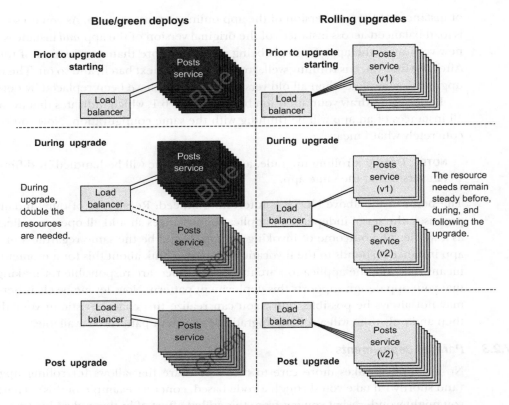

**Figure 7.7   One consideration when deciding between blue/green and rolling upgrades is the resource requirement. Note that during a blue/green deployment, double the resources are needed for the Posts API, whereas the rolling upgrade has only a slight increase in the resource requirements.**

components and teams, and forced alignment before production changes could be made.[1]

Now consider that your app may be used from many other components of the software. When you want to upgrade your app, do you want all of your consumers to have to adjust to the new at the same time? Of course, the answer is no, and if you've built your app in such a way that multiple versions can be running side by side, you can have some consumers using the old, while other consumers are using the new. We call this *parallel deploys*.

Another use case for parallel deploys is to support experimentation. The example I always use to explain this concept is that of an e-commerce recommendation engine. Although I don't have direct knowledge of this, I'd be willing to bet that Amazon has multiple versions of its recommendation engine running at once. The algorithms that suggest related items to a shopper are complex, almost certainly driven by models produced through machine learning. Slight tweaks to an algorithm, or even only

---

[1]Wikipedia's entry on Gantt charts (http://mng.bz/O2za) provides more information.

different configurations to a model, can produce different click-through rates and purchase volumes. To optimize results, a retailer can have these multiple versions running side by side for a time, analyze the results, and then keep the better-performing version.

Parallel deployments are powerful, but they do place an increased importance on the versioning of your software. When traffic is being routed to more than one version of an app, the version must be identifiable, and the version of running software is ultimately made up of the version of the deployable artifact and the version of the configuration applied to the running instances.

> **NOTE** Running App Version = Version of Deployable Artifact + Version of the App Config

Controlling the version of your deployable artifact should be handled by your build pipelines. Application configuration versioning is handled through source code control. If you're using Git, for example, the app operator can use the commit SHA (Secure Hash Algorithm) as the version.

To summarize the main points of this section:

- You need to have multiple app instances act collectively even during an upgrade application lifecycle event.
- Building apps in a way that allows multiple versions to run side by side allows for rolling upgrades to be used (and provides other benefits as well).
- Rolling upgrades have benefits over blue/green deploys.

Finally, it's worth pointing out that any app that allows for rolling upgrades can also be deployed in a blue/green fashion. However, the opposite isn't true. To use a rolling upgrade, your app must be designed to allow different instance versions and configurations to be running at the same time; with a blue/green deploy, only one version/configuration is serving traffic at once, so this special handling isn't required.

Proper behavior of an app across multiple instances during an app lifecycle event such as an upgrade is only half of the picture. It's also important to consider how an app upgrade affects the clients of that app. How does the application lifecycle of one app affect those of another? Let's cover that now.

## 7.3  Coordinating across different app lifecycles

Coming back to our Posts service, in figure 7.3 it was clear that the two app instances wouldn't provide consistent behavior, an obvious problem. And now that you've just digested the content of the previous section, you can see that this app can't be upgraded in a rolling fashion. Let's say that you've updated the app by using a blue/green deployment. The Posts service now has a new secret configured in.

This brings us to another problem: application lifecycle events affect not only the app to which they're being applied, but also affect other, dependent apps. For example, because the Connections' Post service is a client of the Posts service, you see how application lifecycle events of one app affect a dependent app. In this specific scenario, when you rotate the credential in the Posts service, you also need to rotate it in the Connections' Posts service. This dependency is depicted in figure 7.8.

The question, then, is how to coordinate these updates. Clearly, it's not in any type of a "transaction."[2] Your software is a distributed system, and as has been made abundantly clear, maintaining autonomy is an important characteristic for the apps that make up your cloud-native software. If you can update clients and services only in lockstep, you've lost a great deal of that autonomy.

Instead, you'll design your apps so that application lifecycle events across different apps can proceed independently, all while keeping the software fully functional with zero downtime. No single pattern provides the solution for all cases. As the application architect/developer, it's your job to design the right algorithm.

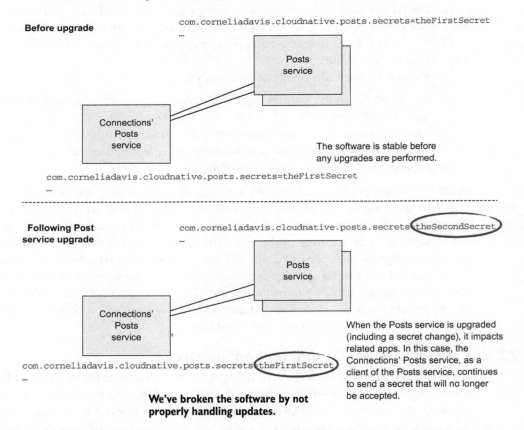

Figure 7.8  **Application lifecycle events must be coordinated across different components of your software.**

---

[2]Incurring downtime for your software while you update all of the dependent pieces is one type of transaction, one that clearly isn't zero downtime.

**NOTE** You must design your apps and document the API so that any lifecycle events that have an impact on dependent services are eliminated, are minimized, or can be adapted to by those clients.

Okay, I concede, this is all a bit abstract. Let's turn back to our sample app to make this more understandable. Recall that earlier you had compromised the secret for your Posts service and as a result needed to update the configuration of your running app. You do so by restarting all app instances with the new configuration applied. For the moment, don't concern yourself with whether you do so using a blue/green deployment or a rolling update. The first, naïve approach poses the following challenge:

- If you first update the Posts service, requests coming from the Connections' Post service, which are sending over the old secret, will fail.
- If you first update the Connections' Posts service, it will start sending the new credential, and requests to the Posts service, which still has the old, will fail.
- We've already established that you can't update them at the same time without incurring downtime.

So you have to be cleverer with your application design. For credential rotation, there's a commonly used pattern. The key to this technique is that you'll implement a phased approach to updating the secret; in one stage, the client service accepts more than one secret. Figure 7.9 depicts the following flow:

- Before you start the update, you have the same secret configured into both the client and the server.
- You update the Posts service app, *adding* a new credential to a *list* of accepted credentials. The authorization semantics are that any of the credentials in the list will allow access (in most cases, the list is limited to two credentials). Notice that the client is still using the old, but because that secret is still in the service list, the requests will succeed.
- You then update the Connections' Posts app, replacing the old credential with the new. Because the new secret has already been configured into the Posts app, which now supports a list of credentials, requests from the new client instances will succeed.
- Finally, after the upgrade of the client is complete, the Posts service app can be updated to remove the old secret.

If you, like I, have been in the software business for some time, you might initially have a negative reaction to this operational flow. It involves a whole lot of redeploys, each of which comes through a disposal and creation of new app instances. But those old instincts need to be unlearned. Cloud-native apps are designed for this kind of ephemerality—remember, change is the rule, not the exception—and allow us to use this to make our software more robust and manageable.

Finally, I want to point out that this design also allows you to perform upgrades of each of the apps in a rolling style. In the first phase of your upgrade, the Connections'

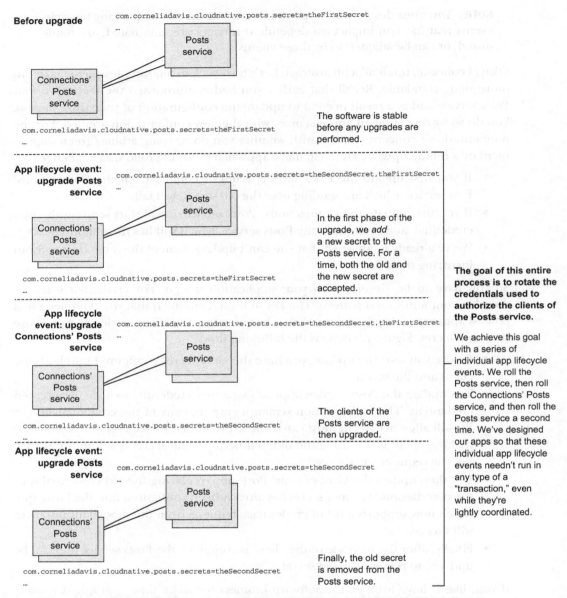

**Figure 7.9   This credential rotation pattern is an exemplar of the consideration that the software architect/developer must pay mind to. The goal is to ensure that the software has zero downtime during application lifecycle events that affect numerous apps.**

Posts service is using the old secret, and both the old and new instances of the Posts service accept that credential even while the new instances already have added the updated secret. In the next phase, some instances of the Connections' Posts service will be sending over the old secret while others will be sending the new; again, the

Posts service accepts both. After the Connections' Posts service is fully updated, it will be sending only the new credential, so during the second update of the Posts service, both old and new versions will succeed. This is depicted in figure 7.10.

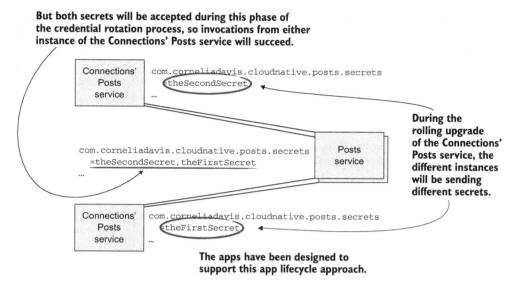

Figure 7.10 During the rolling upgrade of the Connections' Posts service, the different instances will be sending different secrets. The apps have been designed to support this app lifecycle approach.

Having had the architectural discussions, let's now get some practical experience with rolling upgrades as well as the coordination of lifecycle events across apps. We'll do so with proper credential rotation in our sample application—fixing the gotcha from the end of chapter 6.

## 7.4 Let's see this in action: Credential rotation and app lifecycle

To follow along with the code (I'll have you run things in a moment), make sure you have the master branch checked out of our sample repository and change into the application lifecycle directory:

```
git checkout master
cd cloudnative-applifecycle
```

In this example, you'll implement the credential rotation pattern depicted in figure 7.9. You'll update the Posts service in a rolling fashion, then the Connections' Posts service in a rolling fashion, and then finally the Posts service, again in a rolling fashion. Notice that each app has two instances deployed; in the starting state, the credentials configured in match across the instances of an app, and they're coordinated across the Connections' Posts service and the Connections and Posts services. I'll remind you that each of the three apps is drawing its configuration, via the config server, from the single mycookbook.properties file that's checked into GitHub. Note that this is a configuration file for the composition of the three apps that collectively form the My Cookbook software.

To follow the credential rotation pattern described in section 7.3, you need to update the Posts and the Connections implementations so that they can hold a list of valid secrets, any of which may be used to invoke the service. The storage of the credentials occurs within the singleton instance of the `Utils` class, the key parts of which are shown in the following code.

**Listing 7.1    Utils.java**

```java
public class Utils implements
        ApplicationContextAware, ApplicationListener<ApplicationEvent> {

    // <lines omitted for brevity>
    @Value("${com.corneliadavis.cloudnative.posts.secrets}")
    private String configuredSecretsIn;
    private Set<String> configSecrets;

    // <lines omitted for brevity>

    @Override
    public void onApplicationEvent(ApplicationEvent applicationEvent) {

        if (applicationEvent instanceof ServletWebServerInitializedEvent) {
            ServletWebServerInitializedEvent
                servletWebServerInitializedEvent
                    = (ServletWebServerInitializedEvent) applicationEvent;
            this.port = servletWebServerInitializedEvent…
        } else if (applicationEvent instanceof ApplicationPreparedEvent) {
            configSecrets = new HashSet<>();
            String secrets[] = configuredSecretsIn.split(",");
            for (int i=0; i<secrets.length; i++)
                configSecrets.add(secrets[i].trim());
            logger.info(ipTag()
                    + "Posts Service initialized with secret(s): "
                    + configuredSecretsIn);
        }
    }

    public String ipTag() { return "[" + ip + ":" + port +"] "; }

    public boolean isValidSecret(String secret) {
        return configSecrets.contains(secret);
    }

    // The following method is included only to facilitate some
    // logging that wouldn't exist in production.
    public String validSecrets() {
        String result = "";
        for (String s : configSecrets)
```

```
            result += s + ",";
        return result;
    }
}
```

First, I draw your attention to the onApplicationEvent method, specifically the case where you handle the ApplicationPreparedEvent. Without going into the details of the rich set of application lifecycle events implemented through the Spring Framework, know that the ApplicationPreparedEvent is triggered when the application has been fully initialized. The configuredSecretsIn string has been initialized, via the config server, from the com.corneliadavis.cloudnative.posts.secrets property. What you're doing here is parsing it and loading the values in a Set so that the test for validity is trivial, as seen in the definition of the isValidSecret method.

Now, looking at the implementation of the Posts controller in the following listing, you can see that you simply need to check whether the secret passed in is valid before proceeding with processing. When the secret is invalid, you print out both the secret that was passed in as well as the valid one or ones that are configured into the app. In a real application, you wouldn't print these values in the log, but doing so here is helpful for experimenting with these concepts.

**Listing 7.2  Method from PostsController.java**

```java
@RequestMapping(method = RequestMethod.GET, value="/posts")
public Iterable<Post> getPostsByUserId(
    @RequestParam(value="userIds", required=false) String userIds,
    @RequestParam(value="secret", required=true) String secret,
    HttpServletResponse response) {

    Iterable<Post> posts;

    if (utils.isValidSecret(secret)) {

        logger.info(utils.ipTag()
            + "Accessing posts using secret " + secret);

        if (userIds == null) {
            logger.info(utils.ipTag() + "getting all posts");
            posts = postRepository.findAll();
            return posts;
        } else {
            ArrayList<Post> postsForUsers = new ArrayList<Post>();
            String userId[] = userIds.split(",");
            for (int i = 0; i < userId.length; i++) {
                logger.info(utils.ipTag()
                    + "getting posts for userId " + userId[i]);
                posts = postRepository.findByUserId(
                                Long.parseLong(userId[i]));
                posts.forEach(post -> postsForUsers.add(post));
            }
            return postsForUsers;
        }
    }
}
```

```
        }
    } else {
        logger.info(utils.ipTag()
            + "Attempt to access Post service with secret " + secret
            + " (expecting one of " + utils.validSecrets() + ")");
        response.setStatus(401);
        return null;
    }

}
```

This covers the two key parts of the service side of the pattern: (1) secrets are configured on application startup, and (2) to support the zero-downtime credential rotation pattern, the service allows more than one valid secret at a time. I've presented only the code from the Posts service here, but the structure is identical in the Connections service.

Let's now look at the client side, in the implementation of the Connections' Posts app in listing 7.3. The basic structure is similar to that of the Posts and Connections apps. You use the Utils class to process the secrets configuration. Then in the app controller, in which the calls are made to the Posts and Connections services, you access the values through the singleton utils object. Looking first at the controller code, you can see that it's straightforward. You access the posts or connections secret that's configured into the app by asking for the value from the utils object, and send it on the query string.

**Listing 7.3   Method from ConnectionsPostsController.java**

```
@RequestMapping(method = RequestMethod.GET, value="/Connections' Posts")
public Iterable<PostSummary> getByUsername(
    @CookieValue(value = "userToken", required=false) String token,
    HttpServletResponse response) {

    // <lines omitted for brevity>                      Accesses the connections
                                                        secret configured into
        // get connections                              the app
        String secretQueryParam
            = "?secret=" + utils.getConnectionsSecret();
        ResponseEntity<ConnectionResult[]> respConns
            = restTemplate.getForEntity(
                connectionsUrl + username + secretQueryParam,
                ConnectionResult[].class);
        // <lines omitted for brevity>

        secretQueryParam = "&secret=" + utils.getPostsSecret();
        // get posts for those connections
        ResponseEntity<PostResult[]> respPosts
            = restTemplate.getForEntity(
                postsUrl + ids + secretQueryParam,
                PostResult[].class);
        // <lines omitted for brevity>

}
```

Accesses the posts secret configured into the app

Although most of the `Utils.class` here is similar to the same class in the Posts app, it has one nuance. Notice that although the `com.corneliadavis.cloudnative` `.connections.secrets` and `com.corneliadavis.cloudnative.posts.secrets` properties are drawn from the mycookbook.properties file and may each contain a list of secrets, in the Connections' Posts service, you need only the most recent one. You'll establish an operational practice, and this must be covered in the documentation for the Connections' Posts service, where the newest secret is always in the first position in the list. As you can see, you store in the state of the singleton `utils` object only one secret for each of the Posts and Connections services. To make that clear, the property that's configured into the app is the single secret, even though the property file is carrying more than one. Again, the following code includes logging output that isn't suitable for a production system but is a valuable teaching tool.

**Listing 7.4    Method from the `Utils` class of the ConnectionsPosts service**

```
@Override
public void onApplicationEvent(ApplicationEvent applicationEvent) {
    if (applicationEvent instanceof ServletWebServerInitializedEvent) {
            ServletWebServerInitializedEvent
                servletWebServerInitializedEvent
                    = (ServletWebServerInitializedEvent) applicationEvent;
            this.port = servletWebServerInitializedEvent...;
    } else if (applicationEvent instanceof ApplicationPreparedEvent) {
        connectionsSecret = connectionsSecretsIn.split(",")[0];
        postsSecret = postsSecretsIn.split(",")[0];
        logger.info(ipTag()
            + "Connection Posts Service initialized with Post secret: "
            + postsSecret + " and Connections secret: "
            + connectionsSecret);
    }
}
```

Okay, so let's put this to work.

**SETTING UP**

Just as with the examples of the previous chapters, you must have the following standard tools installed in order to run the samples:

- Maven
- Git
- Java 1.8 (optional—needed only if you plan to build the container images yourself)
- Docker (optional—needed only if you plan to build the container images yourself)
- Some type of a MySQL client, such as the `mysql` CLI
- Some type of a Redis client, such as `redis-cli`
- Minikube

#### BUILDING THE MICROSERVICES (OPTIONAL)

Because I will have you deploy the apps into Kubernetes, and in order to do so Docker images are required, I've prebuilt those images and made them available in Docker Hub. Therefore, building the microservices from source isn't necessary.

If you haven't already done so, check out the master branch; and from the cloudnative-abundantsunshine directory, change into the cloudnative-applifecycle directory:

```
git checkout master
cd cloudnative-applifecycle
```

Then, to build the code (optional), type the following command:

```
mvn clean install
```

Running this command builds each of the three apps, producing a JAR file in the target directory of each module. If you want to deploy these JAR files into Kubernetes, you must also run the `docker build` and `docker push` commands as described in the "Using Kubernetes requires you to build Docker images" sidebar in chapter 5. If you do this, you must also update the Kubernetes deployment YAML files to point to your images instead of mine. I don't repeat those steps here; instead, the deployment manifests I provide point to images stored in my Docker Hub repository.

#### RUNNING THE APPS

If you don't already have it running, start Minikube as described in section 5.2.2 of chapter 5. To start with a clean slate, delete any deployments that might be left over from your previous work. I've provided you a script to do that: `deleteDeploymentComplete.sh`. This simple bash script allows you to keep the MySQL and Redis services running.

Calling the script with no options deletes only the three microservice deployments; calling the script with `all` as an argument deletes MySQL and Redis as well. No Kubernetes services are deleted—something that will likely save you the step of configuring URLs into each of the app deployment manifests.

Verify that your environment is clean with the following command:

```
$ kubectl get all
NAME                           READY    STATUS     RESTARTS    AGE
pod/mysql-75d7b44cd6-s8zcr     1/1      Running    0           70m
pod/redis-6bb75866cd-kf99k     1/1      Running    0           72m
pod/sccs-787888bfc-x9p2m       1/1      Running    0           73m

NAME                           TYPE        CLUSTER-IP      EXTERNAL-IP  PORT(S)
service/connections-svc        NodePort    10.103.148.230  <none> 80:30955/TCP
service/connectionsposts-svc   NodePort    10.104.253.33   <none> 80:31742/TCP
service/kubernetes             ClusterIP   10.96.0.1       <none> 443/TCP
service/mysql-svc              NodePort    10.107.78.72    <none> 3306:30917/TCP
service/posts-svc              NodePort    10.110.192.11   <none> 80:32119/TCP
service/redis-svc              NodePort    10.108.83.115   <none> 6379:31537/TCP
service/sccs-svc               NodePort    10.107.16.107   <none> 8888:30455/TCP
```

```
NAME                              READY    UP-TO-DATE    AVAILABLE    AGE
deployment.apps/mysql             1/1      1             1            70m
deployment.apps/redis             1/1      1             1            72m
deployment.apps/sccs              1/1      1             1            73m

NAME                                       DESIRED    CURRENT    READY    AGE
replicaset.apps/mysql-75d7b44cd6           1          1          1        70m
replicaset.apps/redis-6bb75866cd           1          1          1        72m
replicaset.apps/sccs-787888bfc             1          1          1        73m
```

Note that this leaves MySQL and Redis running. If you've cleared out Redis and MySQL, deploy each of these with the following commands, and create the cookbook database with the next two commands:

```
kubectl create -f mysql-deployment.yaml
kubectl create -f redis-deployment.yaml
mysql -h $(minikube service mysql-svc --format "{{.IP}}") \
    -P $(minikube service mysql-svc --format "{{.Port}}") -u root -p
mysql> create database cookbook;
```

After the following steps are completed, the deployment will be as depicted in the first stage of figure 7.9. You'll have two each of the Connections and Posts services, and two instances of the Connections' Posts service. To achieve this topology, for now, you still have to edit deployment manifests. These steps, summarized here, are detailed in chapter 5:

1  Configure the Connections and Posts services with the following values:

| MySQL URL | `minikube service mysql-svc --format`<br>`"jdbc:mysql://{{.IP}}:{{.Port}}/cookbook"` |
|---|---|
| SCCS URL | `Minikube service sccs-svc --format`<br>`"http://{{.IP}}:{{.Port}}"` |

2  Deploy the Connections service:

```
kubectl apply -f cookbook-deployment-connections.yaml
```

3  Deploy the Posts service:

```
kubectl apply -f cookbook-deployment-posts.yaml
```

4  Configure the Connections' Posts service to point to the Posts, Connections, and Users services as well as the Redis service. These values can be found with the following commands, respectively:

| Posts URL | `minikube service posts-svc --format`<br>`"http://{{.IP}}:{{.Port}}/posts?userIds=" --url` |
|---|---|
| Connections URL | `minikube service connections-svc --format`<br>`"http://{{.IP}}:{{.Port}}/connections/" --url` |

*(continued)*

| Users URL | `minikube service connections-svc --format`<br>`"http://{{.IP}}:{{.Port}}/users/" --url` |
|---|---|
| Redis IP | `minikube service redis-svc --format "{{.IP}}"` |
| Redis port | `minikube service redis-svc --format "{{.Port}}"` |
| SCCS URL | `Minikube service sccs-svc --format`<br>`"http://{{.IP}}:{{.Port}}"` |

5  Deploy the Connections' Posts service:

```
kubectl apply -f cookbook-deployment-connectionsposts.yaml
```

You can test out your deployment by issuing `curl` commands against any of the microservices. The Posts and Connections services require that the secret be passed in the query string, and the Connections' Posts service requires login before content will be served. The commands are as follows:

```
curl -i $(minikube service --url connections-svc)/connections?secret=anyval
curl -i $(minikube service --url connections-svc)/users?secret=anyvalue
curl -i $(minikube service --url posts-svc)/posts?secret=foobar
curl -X POST -i -c cookie \
    $(minikube service --url connectionsposts-svc)/login?username=cdavisafc
curl -b cookie \
    $(minikube service --url connectionsposts-svc)/connectionsposts
```

> **TIP**  A simple way to look up the secrets configured into the software is to `curl` the Posts and Connections services with `?secret=anyvalue`, and look at the logs; recall that you're printing the accepted value to the log.

Let's now perform the first part of the upgrade process. You'll do this by updating the config file for the software deployment and then rolling the Posts service. Recall that you're storing the config in GitHub and are using SCCS (Spring Cloud Config Server) to deliver that configuration to the application instances. Edit the mycookbook.properties file in the cloud-native-config repo by updating the following line:

```
com.corneliadavis.cloudnative.posts.secrets=originalSecret
```

Add a new secret to the front of the list:

```
com.corneliadavis.cloudnative.posts.secrets=newSecret,originalSecret
```

You must commit and push these changes to your GitHub repository. You now want to perform a rolling upgrade on the Posts service, and you'll use the `kubectl apply` command to do so. Because this configuration change is done via SCCS, and that property change is therefore not seen by Kubernetes, you must do something to cause

Kubernetes to cycle the application instances. The trick I'm using is having an env variable in the deployment YAML that you can bump when you want Kubernetes to roll through your app instances. You simply must change the value of `VERSIONING_TRIGGER` to something new. This is done in the cookbook-deployment-posts.yaml file:

```
- name: VERSIONING_TRIGGER
  value: "1"
```
**Updates the value to something new— I typically just increment the number**

Before running the command to initiate the rolling upgrade, in a terminal window, set a watch on the pods currently running in your environment:

```
watch kubectl get pods
```

Now start the rolling upgrade with the following command:

```
kubectl apply -f cookbook-deployment-posts.yaml
```

In the watch window, you'll see new instances of the Posts service being created and old ones being terminated and then eventually discarded. This is performing the upgrade process that's depicted in figure 7.6. (I don't know about you, but watching this type of application lifecycle automation the first time was pretty darn cool for me!) Now let's `curl` the Posts service, experimenting with various secrets, starting with a bad secret:

```
curl -i $(minikube service --url posts-svc)/posts?secret=aBadSecret
```

Have a look into the logs for the two pod instances. In one, you'll find a message that reads something like the following:

```
Attempt to access Post service with secret aBadSecret (expecting one of
    newSecret,oldSecret,)
```

I'll once again remind you that you should never send secrets out to log files, but you're doing so here because it's helpful in exercising our examples. This message shows you that the new configuration has been applied to the Posts service. You can now invoke the Posts service with either of the secrets and receive a response.

The Connections' Posts service is still using the `oldSecret`, so let's update it now.

You've already updated the configuration in GitHub, so you must have Kubernetes do only a rolling upgrade. You'll do so by editing the cookbook-deployment-connectionsposts.yaml file, bumping the `VERSIONING_TRIGGER` just as you'd done with the Posts service:

```
- name: VERSIONING_TRIGGER
  value: "1"
```
**Updates the value to something new—I typically just increment the number.**

Now issue the following command to initiate the rolling upgrade:

```
kubectl apply -f cookbook-deployment-connectionsposts.yaml
```

Both after and throughout the upgrade, you can invoke the Connections' Posts service. Depending on which instance is routed to, either the old or the new secret will be sent to the Posts service. Again, because of the pattern you've implemented, everything will function as expected.

Finally, after the Connections' Posts service has been fully upgraded, you can remove the old secret from the configuration (don't forget to commit and push to GitHub), update the deployment YAML to bump the VERSIONING_TRIGGER, and execute the following command:

```
kubectl apply -f cookbook-deployment-posts.yaml
```

After Kubernetes has completed the rolling upgrade for the Posts service, the credential rotation will be complete. You just upgraded your software with *absolutely no downtime* and were able to use a rolling upgrade (application lifecycle automation built into Kubernetes) because your software was specifically designed to support it.

## 7.5    *Dealing with ephemeral runtime environments*

It should be clear by now that one of the main characteristics of cloud-native apps is that they're constantly disposed of and created anew. You just experienced that in the credential rotation example, in which you rolled through all instances of both the Posts and the Connections apps twice, first to add a new secret and then later to remove the old. Again, I understand your possible aversion to this practice; it goes against the deeply held belief that stable is good and change is bad, but in the cloud, change is inevitable and can even bring a new type of stability.

Like many other cloud-native patterns and practices, however, embracing this new paradigm brings cascading effects—new concerns for you, the application developer/architect. The main one that I want to talk about right now is the impact that the ephemerality of these runtime contexts has on the manageability of our apps. Under that heading, I want to talk about two topics: (1) troubleshooting and (2) repeatability.

Let me talk about the latter first, only briefly because this is a point I've made several times already. The main point is that an application deployment (the specific bits that are deployed, the way that it's running, and the context it's running in) should be 100% reproducible. Cloud-native application platforms provide many features that support this goal, so learning the best practices for using such platforms is important. But, because I'm about to say a bit more about troubleshooting, let me point out that the best of these platforms, when properly configured, will not allow you to ssh into the runtime environment. Why? Simply put, to make sure that you can't create a running instance of your app that's not reproducible.

Let's suppose you were allowed to ssh into the container in which your app was running. While there, you do a few things that you think are only for troubleshooting, things that aren't part of the production configuration of the app; for example, you might open ports to allow monitoring tools in, or you might install additional packages. You fix the problem, and because you're a responsible engineer, you go back into the source or configuration and reflect the changes there. You leave that container running—why not; it's working fine. But the container is now a snowflake; although you think you've reflected all of the "fixes" back in the app and config source, it's possible that only this unique container has just the right config to make it work. Later, when the instance is replaced (for any number of reasons), the new app instance may (or may not) bring back old problems. Restricting operations that allow for snowflakes to be created greatly enhances manageability of software deployments.

Which brings me to my second point. If you can't ssh into an instance, how will you figure out what's going on when your apps aren't working as expected? Short answer: logging and metrics. As a software developer, you play a crucial role in ensuring that the logs and metrics feeds contain information sufficient to diagnose problems. And here comes another twist in this plot, one that's specifically related to application lifecycle: it's possible that by the time you're troubleshooting, the app instance with which the trouble arose is no longer in existence. If the app crashed, the container is likely to have been discarded, a new instance taking its place.

The practice of disposing of problematic app instances is so common in cloud-native platforms that the Twelve-Factor App guidance includes factor #11, "Treat logs as event streams." The point of this particular bit of advice is to establish a contract, or API, for the "publication" of log data so that platforms running the cloud-native apps can take care of making that data available, even while *it* maintains control of the application lifecycle. In a story that rings familiar, because you've seen similar arguments when I described using env variables for configuration data, stdout and stderr streams exist in pretty much every runtime environment, and every programming language/ framework supports writing to those streams. And it's a simple standard; there's no need for locating log files stored in bespoke directories or even doing log file rotations. All of the log data is streamed out and can then be handled by the platform itself.

**TIP** So this brings us to the punch line: write your logs to stdout and stderr.

This doesn't mean that you should simply have System.out calls throughout your code. There's a reason that logging frameworks such as Apache Log4j or Logback were invented. But these may be configured, and often by default are, to direct any logging output to stdout and stderr.

The metrics story isn't as straightforward, mainly because metrics data is inherently more structured than log data and varies widely across different applications and platforms. There isn't one set of metrics data that platforms and tooling can be built around to provide all of the needed insight. That said, the topic is important, and some de facto standard practices and tools have begun to emerge; chapter 11 covers some of these.

Hopefully, by now it's clear that although I have a whole chapter on the topic, I briefly include troubleshooting here because of the impact that the application lifecycle has on it. Just as it is with core application logic, how you handle observability data must also account for the inherently more dynamic nature of the application lifecycle. I emphasized a word a few paragraphs ago ("it") that stresses the point: in the cloud-native world, humans don't control the application lifecycle; systems do (and in the best cases, intelligent systems such as Kubernetes or Cloud Foundry). Systems demand much stronger contracts or APIs, and you're responsible for ensuring that your applications meet those contracts.

## 7.6    *Visibility of app lifecycle state*

In section 7.3, I talked about application lifecycle concerns across different but related apps. Specifically, you looked at how an operational need is addressed through a series of lifecycle events. There's another element to that cross-app relationship that I want to talk about now, and it arises when one app needs to know about app lifecycle events of another.

For example, as you well know (and by this time are completely irritated by), when the Posts service is re-created for any reason (and I do mean the Kubernetes *service*, not the pods), you need to redeploy the Connections' Posts service with a configuration that includes the new URL to that service. If instead you could have the latter app automatically updated upon such a change in the former, your experience would be far better. (Bear with me just a bit longer; you're only a few pages away from fixing this!)

From an application lifecycle perspective, this means that the Connections' Posts service depends on knowing when lifecycle events happen to the Posts service. In the simplest sense, the Posts service is responsible for making its lifecycle state available. For example, figure 7.11 shows an application lifecycle event being broadcast when an app is started.

Taking this one step further, figure 7.12 shows a dependency on this lifecycle event. In this diagram, initially the Connections' Posts service was reaching the Posts

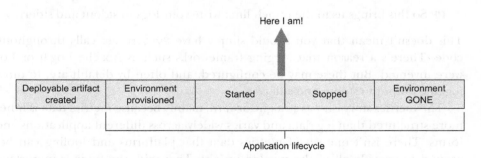

**Figure 7.11   Application startup is an important event that many other components in the cloud-native software will be interested in.**

service at IP address 10.24.1.35, but when a new Posts service is started at IP address 10.24.1.128, it's responsible for broadcasting that information, and the Connections' Posts service needs to be updated with that IP address.

The exact mechanics of how this broadcast from Posts is handled, where it's published, and how interested parties can pick up the pertinent information isn't germane at this point in our discussion. That's represented in figure 7.12 with a nebulous "magic" blob, and we'll come back to that later. Until now, you've been implementing that entire protocol—looking up the new IP and port with the `minikube service list` command and editing YAML files. But this needs to be automated, and the main point should be clear: app lifecycle events on Posts affect other parts of your software, and you must specifically account for this.

When talking about the responsibilities on either side of the relationship, I've been a bit vague. I admit that I've implied that you, the developer, are responsible for broadcasting or consuming the events. Although the full answer is a bit complicated, and you'll study this in more detail as you progress through the text, the short one is this: if you're using a cloud-native application platform, it will generally take care of these concerns for you. For the moment, I just want you to have an appreciation for this dependency.

Although you may understand the problem, I hope that you're reading what I've written thus far with a healthy dose of skepticism. In figure 7.12, you're looking at a bunch

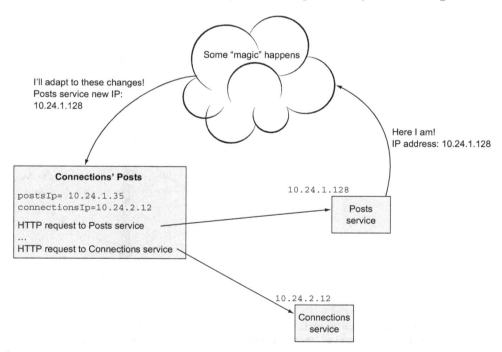

**Figure 7.12** Apps have the responsibility for broadcasting lifecycle events because other components will be affected. Those other components likewise have the responsibility for adapting to those changes.

of coordination across many components that are highly distributed over an unreliable network, yet I've suggested that proper operations are dependent on broadcasted life-cycle events reaching all interested parties.

Here's the truth: the broadcasted event as I've described it here should be thought of as an optimization. The reason I started with an optimization is that it illustrates the challenge beautifully. You have a whole bunch of pieces that need to act in concert to make modern software work. In an abstract sense, it's simple: an app lifecycle event needs to be received by those that will be affected by the state change. But the reality is more complicated: all this needs to happen in the face of a multitude of failure scenarios. App lifecycle events won't always be generated; when they are, they'll sometimes be lost; and even when not lost, they sometimes won't be recognized or operated on by the components that should do so.

To understand this, let me present in figure 7.13 a far less trivialized application lifecycle than the one shown in figures 7.1 and 7.11. In addition to modeling possible failure scenarios, figure 7.13 also shows a richer set of possible transitions between the application lifecycle states. After an app is deployed, the startup may succeed (Started and Responsive), or it may fail—the app might be running but not running well (Started and Unresponsive), or it may outright crash. An app that started successfully

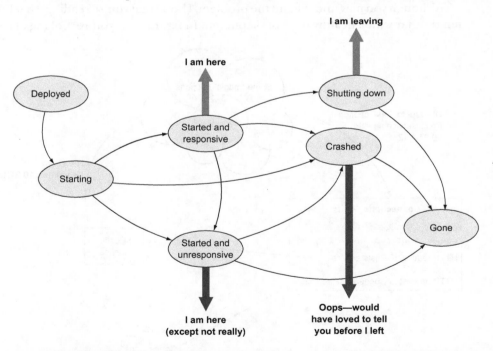

**Figure 7.13   Application lifecycle states and transitions between them. In the happy path, when apps are started and stopped, there's an opportunity to broadcast app lifecycle change events. But when something goes awry, state-change broadcasts will be incorrect or may never even be generated.**

and was operable for some time may also crash or, worse, may stay running but be unresponsive. Whether gracefully shut down or not so gracefully, at some point the app and its environment will be gone.

Expanding our scenario a bit, realize that the Connections' Posts service needs to know not only when new Posts services are started, but also when they go away. This diagram allows you to study both cases. Note that I've added a few thick arrows with annotations. These are equivalent to the single arrow from figure 7.11 but updated to the more complex lifecycle model. The annotations at the top show the broadcast of "happy path" events: when the app successfully starts, it announces its existence, and when it's being gracefully shut down, it can first let the world know it's going away. But what happens when, as shown in the downward-facing arrows, the startup isn't so great, or when the app crashes without warning, robbing it of the opportunity to let the world know of its impending doom?

Without getting overly dramatic, this is part of the magic of cloud-native. Apps are built not only to work in the happy path, but also to continue working, or self-heal when things go awry. To handle this particular circumstance, the answer is health endpoints combined with health checks/responders, and you, as the developer, play a critical role in the coordination among these things. The concept is simple: a health endpoint presents data representing the state of an app, and health checks/responders implement some type of control loop that interrogates, and acts upon that status. This addresses the aforementioned deficiencies of lost lifecycle events with redundancy. The interrogating control loop does so continuously (say, every 10 seconds), so if one or even a couple of communication attempts are unsuccessful because of momentary lapses, the next will succeed and the system continues functioning. This is another example of what I've already referred to as *eventual consistency*.

Figure 7.14 presents two sequence diagrams depicting this basic pattern. Whenever asked, the app responds with its current lifecycle state, and the control loop regularly asks and responds appropriately. The first sequence diagram shows what happens when the system is functioning properly: the control loop checks the app health endpoint, and upon getting a response indicating that everything is fine, simply waits for the next interval and asks again. The second sequence diagram shows what happens when the app is running but unresponsive, or the health endpoint returns an error. One failure won't necessarily trigger remediation actions, but repeated ones will (you'll see this in action in a moment).

I've made the point that as the developer, you play a critical role in making this whole thing work, but I want to be clear here that I don't consider you responsible for both sides of that protocol. The control loop will come from the cloud-native platform—Kubernetes, Cloud Foundry, or similar.[3] You're responsible for the app health endpoints, and for building apps that can be fixed—by creating new instances—when they're experiencing problems. Right now, we'll focus on the endpoint. The

---

[3]If your application platform doesn't have these types of control loops, it isn't a cloud-native platform.

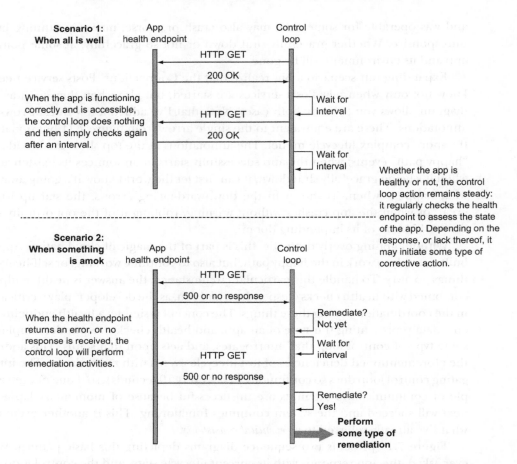

**Figure 7.14    Control loops play an important role in cloud-native systems, providing redundancy that compensates for "glitches" in the system.**

remediation stuff—well, that's what this book is all about. What you're responsible for is implementing a health endpoint that accurately reflects the state of the app. You may want to ensure that any connectivity to persistent services such as databases are functioning, for example.

The system as a whole is built to be resilient to glitches—network outages, app failures, and more—and the control loop provides needed redundancy. And now it's clear why the earlier broadcast-based design should be thought of as an optimization. Rather than waiting for the next control loop cycle to broadcast the status, the lifecycle state-change event immediately initiates the broadcast. If, for any reason, that broadcast event is lost, the next time the control loop fires, there will be another.

### 7.6.1   *Let's see this in action: Health endpoints and probes*

Okay, enough abstract. Let's make this real with an example. If you ran the samples from earlier in the chapter, you're already set up. The code you've been running already includes what I want to demonstrate here.

Implementing the polling approach I described previously, you'll add a /healthz endpoint into each of the services. The code, slightly contrived, simply checks a Boolean class member. When it's set to true (the default), it returns a success status code, and when it's set to false, the application sleeps for a long time, effectively rendering it unresponsive. You have an app that's in the Started and Unresponsive state, as follows.

---
**Listing 7.5   Method from Posts_Controller.java**

```
@RequestMapping(method = RequestMethod.GET, value="/healthz")
public void healthCheck(HttpServletResponse response)
                                        throws InterruptedException {

    if (this.isHealthy) response.setStatus(200);
    else Thread.sleep(400000);

}
```

The other half of the demonstration, the control loop that continuously polls the health endpoint retrieving the data and acting upon it as appropriate, comes from Kubernetes. There are some new lines in the Kubernetes deployment manifest, as follows.

---
**Listing 7.6   Excerpt from cookbook-deployment-posts.yaml**

```
livenessProbe:
  httpGet:
    path: /healthz
    port: 8080
  initialDelaySeconds: 60
  periodSeconds: 5
```

These lines configure that control loop, the liveness probe, so that every 5 seconds, Kubernetes will send an HTTP GET request to the /healthz endpoint of this pod (Kubernetes also supports TCP liveness probes). When a new pod is started, Kubernetes will wait 60 seconds before the control loop is initiated, offering time for the service to initialize before it expects the health endpoint to accurately reflect the app status. If at any time Kubernetes receives an error status code, or no response, it will restart the container. Let's see this in action.

#### SEEING THIS IN ACTION

If you don't have the software running, follow the steps in the "Running the apps" portion of section 7.5. Please stream the logs from each of your two Posts service pods in two side-by-side terminal windows. With my two current pods, I'd use the following commands in those two separate windows:

```
$ kubectl logs -f posts-439493379-0w7hx
$ kubectl logs -f posts-439493379-hfzt1
```

To verify that all is well, you can `curl` any of the Posts endpoints, including the `/healthz` endpoint. You will, of course, see activity in the logs:

```
$ curl $(minikube service --url posts-svc)/posts?secret=newSecret
[
  {
    "id": 7,
    "date": "2019-02-17T05:42:51.000+0000",
    "userId": 2,
    "title": "Chicken Pho",
    "body": "This is my attempt to re-create what I ate in Vietnam..."
  },
  {
    "id": 9,
    "date": "2019-02-17T05:42:51.000+0000",
    "userId": 1,
    "title": "Whole Orange Cake",
    "body": "That's right, you blend up whole oranges, rind and all..."
  },
  {
    "id": 10,
    "date": "2019-02-17T05:42:51.000+0000",
    "userId": 1,
    "title": "German Dumplings (Kloesse)",
    "body": "Russet potatoes, flour (gluten free!) and more..."
  },
  {
    "id": 11,
    "date": "2019-02-17T05:42:51.000+0000",
    "userId": 3,
    "title": "French Press Lattes",
    "body": "We've figured out how to make these dairy free, but just as
➥ good!..."
  }
]
$ curl -i $(minikube service --url posts-svc)/healthz
HTTP/1.1 200
X-Application-Context: mycookbook
Content-Length: 0
Date: S un, 17 Feb 2019 06:13:34 GMT
```

Now, to place one of your Posts service instances into the Started and Unresponsive state, issue the following `curl` command:

```
$ curl -i -X POST $(minikube service --url posts-svc)/infect
```

Keep an eye on your log streams. Within 5 to 10 seconds, you'll see lines such as the following emitted to one of your two log streams, and the log-streaming session will terminate; the log streaming terminates when the container to which it is connected goes away. That infect endpoint simply flips the isHealthy Boolean in the Posts service:

```
... ConfigServletWebServerApplicationContext : Closing
➥ org.springframework.boot.web.servlet.context.AnnotationConfigServletWeb
➥ ServerApplicationContext@27c20538: startup date [Sun Feb 17 06:03:15 GMT
➥ 2019]; parent: org.springframework.context.annotation.AnnotationConfig
➥ ApplicationContext@2fc14f68
... o.s.j.e.a.AnnotationMBeanExporter : Unregistering JMX-exposed beans on
➥ shutdown
... o.s.j.e.a.AnnotationMBeanExporter : Unregistering JMX-exposed beans
... j.LocalContainerEntityManagerFactoryBean : Closing JPA
➥ EntityManagerFactory for persistence unit 'default'
```

But discarding the old container isn't all that the control loop in Kubernetes did. The loop also started a new instance of the app in a new container. If you start streaming the logs from that new container, which you can do by issuing the kubectl logs command again (note that because Kubernetes restarts only the container and not the pod, the pod name will be unchanged), you'll see that the app once again is up and running:

```
$ kubectl logs -f posts-5876ffd568-gr5bf
... s.c.a.AnnotationConfigApplicationContext : Refreshing org.
➥ springframework.context.annotation.AnnotationConfigApplicationContext
➥ @2fc14f68: startup date [Sun Feb 17 06:15:30 GMT 2019]; root of context
➥ hierarchy
... trationDelegate$BeanPostProcessorChecker : Bean 'configuration
➥ PropertiesRebinderAutoConfiguration' of type [org.springframework
➥ .cloud.autoconfigure.ConfigurationPropertiesRebinderAutoConfiguration
➥ $$EnhancerBySpringCGLIB$$3cd10333] is not eligible for getting
➥ processed by all BeanPostProcessors (for example: not eligible for
➥ auto-proxying)

  .   ____          _            __ _ _
 /\\ / ___'_ __ _ _(_)_ __  __ _ \ \ \ \
( ( )\___ | '_ | '_| | '_ \/ _` | \ \ \ \
 \\/  ___)| |_)| | | | | || (_| |  ) ) ) )
  '  |____| .__|_| |_|_| |_\__, | / / / /
 =========|_|==============|___/=/_/_/_/
 :: Spring Boot ::        (v2.0.6.RELEASE)
...
... o.s.b.w.embedded.tomcat.TomcatWebServer  : Tomcat started on port(s):
➥ 8080 (http) with context path ''
... c.c.c.config.CloudnativeApplication     : Started
➥ CloudnativeApplication in 15.74 seconds (JVM running for 16.605)
```

This example demonstrates that making the state of an app available allows a system such as Kubernetes to appropriately respond when the inevitable changes happen to an app. As a developer of cloud-native applications, it's your responsibility to produce the appropriate implementation for the model being used in your cloud-native application runtime.

What I've described in this section is a polling approach, but I'd like to point out that control loops that broadcast heartbeats are another way of implementing this pattern. Using this technique, components are continually broadcasting their lifecycle state with one control loop, and entities that have an interest in this app's status will be listening for these events and responding appropriately. I'll remind you of the discussion of chapter 4: what I'm describing here is an event-driven pattern. As the architect/developer, you must understand the architectural patterns of the software as a whole and design/implement appropriately. The key with either approach is that control loops provide the redundancy that compensates for the uncertainty inherent in distributed systems.

## 7.7    *Serverless*

This isn't a book, or even a chapter, on serverless computing. But especially here in this chapter on the application lifecycle, having a brief look allows you to understand certain elements of cloud-native software more deeply. As is usually pointed out within the first few moments of a discussion on serverless, the name is a bit of a misnomer because the functions being executed in this style are absolutely running on servers. It's just that the developer is completely unconcerned with these details. Instead, the serverless system takes care of it all.

Developer productivity is certainly one of the goals of this computing style, but so is operational efficiency and economics, because most serverless systems charge for use only for the time that a function is executing. Regardless of the specific goals, the thing that I want to focus on is the serverless platform; that platform is very much a cloud-native platform. Let's start by looking at the model in the most basic way.

At the most basic level, serverless computing has an application running only when it's actively processing to produce a response to an event. If you view that from an application lifecycle perspective, it's only when a request comes in that a runtime environment is provisioned, the app is deployed and started, and the request processing is done. And after it has run, the runtime environment is disposed of; see figure 7.15.

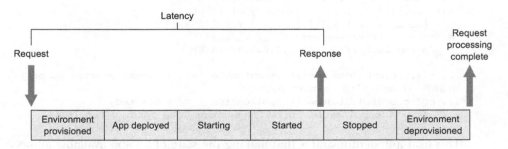

**Figure 7.15    All lifecycle stages are passed through for a single-function invocation.**

This application lifecycle isn't unfamiliar. What is unconventional is that all the stages, from provisioning through disposal, happen with each invocation. What I like best about serverless computing is that this extreme serves to amplify the patterns for cloud-native software. For example, if the runtime environment is entirely re-created for each invocation, the apps can never, ever depend on internal state from previous invocations. Buh-bye, sticky sessions, for example.

But there's more that I want to draw your attention to that's specific to cloud-native apps running in a serverless setting. This has to do with efficiency and latency. Looking at figure 7.15, it's obvious that a lot needs to happen between a request for processing and the completion thereof. How can all of this happen while meeting requirements for responsiveness? The short of it is through optimizations, some of which you're responsible for.

Figure 7.16 again shows our serverless lifecycle stages, but this time with a few notations overlaid. The early stages of the app lifecycle are entirely handled by the system, and indeed serverless platforms specifically focus on, among other things, making environment provisioning and app deployment fast. Most are built on containers and use formats for the deployable artifacts that allow for rapid deployment. As a developer, you're responsible for, and have control over, only the application startup and its actual execution. You must focus on making that happen as quickly as is necessary.

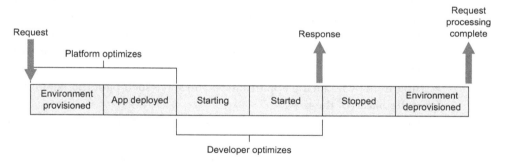

**Figure 7.16** Serverless computing requires a platform that optimizes the early stages, and the developer is responsible for optimizing the starting and execution of the app.

Let me be blunt: not all of your processing is best accomplished in a serverless setting. If you have a workload that takes little time to run and is constantly being requested, particularly if the startup "cost" is greater than that of executing the function, you're likely better off starting up one or more instances of the app and having requests served from those already running instances. If, on the other hand, you have processing that's less frequently run and takes far more time to run than it takes to provision, deploy the app, and start it up, then the serverless paradigm might be ideal.

If you're building an app that will run in a serverless context, you must pay special attention to the startup costs and ensure that they don't dwarf those of the function execution. You have several levers to control that. First, the programming language you use has a direct impact. Starting a JVM can take tens of seconds, which would be awful if the code execution time was in the milliseconds. And second, even after you choose a language, be sure to minimize what you need to load into the runtime to support your app functionality. For example, don't include dependencies in your code that are never used; you'll pay the price of slow startup for no reason.

Now, I do want to point out that most of the serverless platforms in the market today implement optimizations to lessen the impact of the app lifecycle in its purest form. For example, app environments are often preserved and reused for requests that come in relatively close in time to one another, but it's clearer here than in other platforms that no app should use such features. Again, that's one of the things I like most about serverless: that it makes clear the need for cloud-native patterns.

## Summary

- In a cloud-native setting, you must think about an app's lifecycle and treat it as a single logical entity even while each app instance has its own independent lifecycle.
- You must also pay careful attention to how app lifecycle events affect other apps that form the broader piece of software.
- Only if multiple instances of an app can tolerate different configurations running at the same time can a rolling upgrade be used. Otherwise, a blue/green deployment must be used. Both can be done with zero downtime.
- A carefully constructed credential rotation pattern can be done with rolling upgrades.
- Intentionally replacing app instances can serve such patterns, so do that. Let go of the biases of the past.
- Application logs should be sent to stdout and stderr, where most cloud-native platforms will process them.
- Application state must be made available so that system health can be maintained and dependent apps can appropriately adapt to changes.
- Serverless is an extreme form of cloud-native processing that uses most of the patterns covered in this text.

# 8

*Accessing apps:*
*Services, routing,*
*and service discovery*

**This chapter covers**

- Single services representing multiple app instances
- Server-side load balancing
- Client-side load balancing
- Dynamic routing to service instances
- Service discovery

I've already been going on a bit about apps being deployed as multiple instances but needing to behave as a single logical entity. You learned that you must keep your apps stateless so that one request to an app isn't dependent on previous requests having hit the same instance. You saw how configurations need to be carefully managed across all instances so as to ensure the same outcome regardless of which instance ends up serving a particular request, even during application lifecycle events. At this point, I want to formalize this *single logical entity,* and in doing so you'll be able to get rid of the brittle connectivity between the three microservices in our sample application.

Bear with me a moment while I start with first principles. They're important. You know your apps will be deployed as multiple instances, thereby affording you an effective way to scale deployments to meet demand, and to create a more resilient system. Figure 8.1 shows multiple instances for each of the three apps that make up our running example.

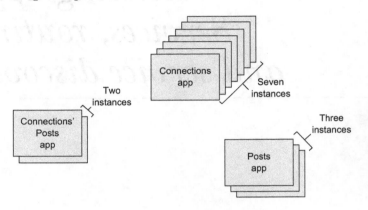

Figure 8.1    In cloud-native software, apps are deployed as multiple instances. For the software to function predictably, you want each set of app instances to operate as a single logical entity.

In previous chapters, you've been connecting these apps to each other without looking at the details of how it's done. Turning to that now, for each set of instances, let's introduce a box that represents the *single logical app* abstraction. As a part of that, as shown in figure 8.2, I've more precisely labeled each piece; I've labeled the logical entities with the app name and more accurately labeled the instances as, well, instances.

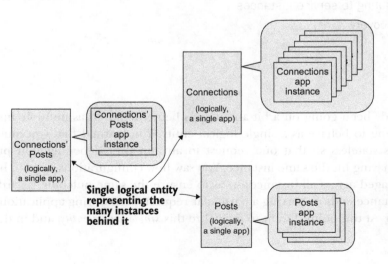

Figure 8.2    Each set of app instances is represented by a logical entity that defines the behavior of the app. That behavior is expected from all instances.

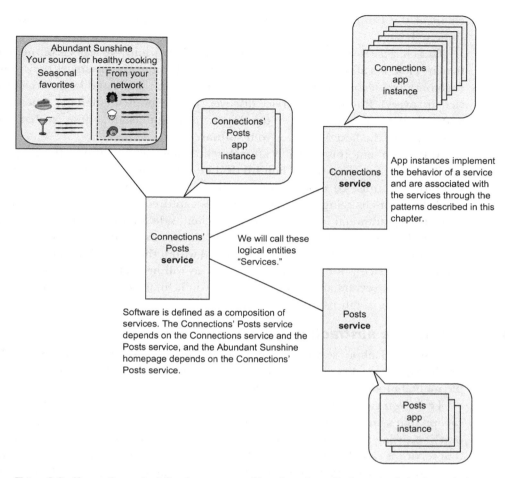

**Figure 8.3   Your software is defined as a composition of services. Each service is implemented as a set of service instances.**

You can then push the implementation details of each app into the background, as I've done in figure 8.3 (just for a moment—don't worry, we'll come back to the details shortly). Another thing I've done in this diagram is label the logical entities as "Services." I've already used this term in a different context, but the way I use it here is totally consistent with the way I've used it before. Previously, I referred to a "service" as a component that was used by your app code (a database or a message bus, for example). But recall that apps are most often software components used by other apps; thus they are, in fact, services.

If you now focus on the (logical apps)/services, you can define your software as the set of connected services. As you know, the Connections' Posts service depends on both the Connections service and the Posts service, as shown in figure 8.3. The client of the Connections' Posts service is, in this deployment, the Abundant Sunshine web page.

This chapter is fundamentally about these services, and two aspects of them in particular. First, it's about how these services are tied to the app instances they represent (routing) and second, how the services are found and addressed by their clients (service discovery). Routing and service discovery may be implemented in numerous ways, and you, the software architect/developer, must understand these so that you can come up with the best design for your software.

At the moment, this probably all feels a little abstract, so I'll start the chapter with familiar, concrete examples. Then I'll drill into the topic of routing. For cloud-native software, this must be *dynamic* routing, the means by which incoming requests will reach the ever-changing set of app instances captured in the service abstraction. I'll cover both traditional load balancing and client-side load balancing. In the former, client calls pass through a centralized load balancer that routes requests to instances, and in the latter, load balancing is embedded within the client. I'll then turn to how a client of a service will find and address it. This will naturally lead us into a conversation on name servers and DNS. And then you'll finally do it—fix the brittle service configurations in our running example.

## 8.1   *The service abstraction*

It's easy to talk about services at a high level. I've been doing so for more than half of this book, but I've been a bit vague and want to fix that now. I want to start with a simple mental model, shown in figure 8.4.

There you can see four *app instances* and the service that represents the single logical app that's implemented by those instances. On the left side of the service is a client that's accessing the service via the service address. The means by which the client finds that service is called *service discovery*. When a request comes into the service, it's routed to one of the instances. As you know, the service instances are going to be changing all the time—sometimes there'll be two, sometimes ten. Their IP addresses are also changing. In order for an instance to accurately represent the implementation at any given moment, the service must be kept up to date with the list of instances it will route to. This is what I refer to as *dynamic routing*. I refer to this diagram repeatedly throughout the chapter, so you might want to bookmark this page.

> **NOTE**  Some design decisions around service addressing, routing, and service discovery will be made at the time of software deployment, and others will be made at software development time.

Like virtually everything we've talked about so far, the patterns for handling cloud-native services are implemented both in the software you'll be building and in the platforms your software will run on. Ultimately, your job as a software architect or developer is to ensure that your implementation enables different deployment options, or, if you build a pattern into the implementation itself, you need to clearly

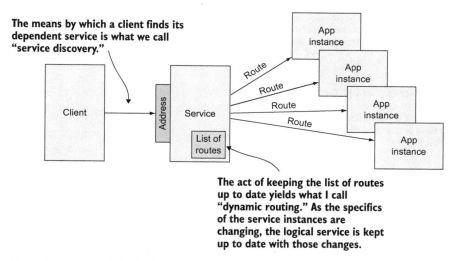

**The means by which a client finds its dependent service is what we call "service discovery."**

**The act of keeping the list of routes up to date yields what I call "dynamic routing." As the specifics of the service instances are changing, the logical service is kept up to date with those changes.**

**Figure 8.4   The single logical app represented by a set of app instances is a *service*. The protocol that allows a client to find and access its dependent services is *service discovery*. The means for distributing incoming requests across the set of app instances is *dynamic routing*.**

understand the implications of those choices. This chapter is designed to help you understand the techniques and trade-offs so you can make the right choices around service handling.

To start on the journey of understanding these design choices, let's look at a couple of examples.

### 8.1.1   *Service example: Googling*

Let's begin with something you're completely familiar with, though you probably haven't thought of it in the context of services and services discovery. Let's look at what happens when you Google something. When you type www.google.com into a browser, the service client in this case, you're addressing the Google search service by name. The request for the Google homepage, however, is sent to a specific IP address, and the means of translating the name into that address is via Domain Name System (DNS) resolution.

The details of the DNS that powers the internet are complex, and the implementation is a highly distributed, hierarchical system with rules for how data is propagated through it. For simplicity, let's use `ping` to obtain an IP address for the name www.google.com:

```
$ ping www.google.com
PING www.google.com (216.58.193.68): 56 data bytes
64 bytes from 216.58.193.68: icmp_seq=0 ttl=53 time=19.189 ms
```

In reality, this name can resolve to many different IP addresses, but we need only one to make the point here. Figure 8.5, which is a more detailed version of figure 8.4, now shows this search service IP address. When the client refers to the service via name,

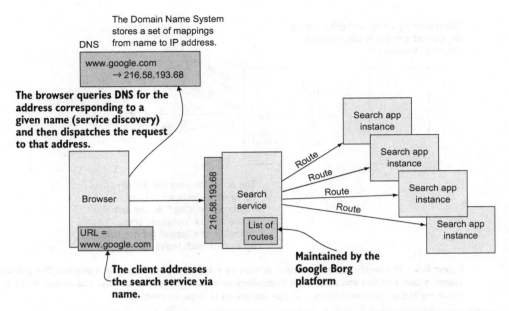

**Figure 8.5    The Google search service is addressed via the name www.google.com, and that name is mapped to a concrete IP address via DNS. The Google platform keeps the list of routes to search service instances up to date, and load-balances requests among them.**

the service discovery process consults DNS for the name → IP address mapping, and the service is then addressed via this IP address.

On the right-hand side of the service abstraction are the routes used to direct traffic to the instances that implement the service. Although I've never been part of the Google Site Reliability Engineering (SRE) team, it's a reasonable assumption that at this IP address sits a load balancer that distributes incoming traffic over a set of instances of the Google homepage app. The instances of this app are constantly changing, so the list of routes that the service contains must be kept up to date, and this is done by the Google platform itself.[1] Figure 8.5 makes note of the role that Borg plays in the process of dynamic routing.

The basic services pattern comes into play for a simple operation that you likely do many times a day. You use a name, www.google.com, to address a service. DNS is used as a part of the service discovery process, mapping this name to an IP address. A load balancer, whose list of routes is kept up to date by the Google platform itself, routes traffic to app instances that implement the service.

Let's look at a second example that illustrates two things. First, it shows what happens when no service discovery process is being used, and second, it offers more insight into the task of maintaining dynamic routing tables.

---

[1]Google has written about this platform in the 2015 paper "Large-Scale Cluster Management at Google with Borg," which is available at http://mng.bz/pgv5.

### 8.1.2   *Service example: Our blog aggregator*

Let's look at our running example of the blog aggregator. In particular, you'll look at the Posts service because you're running multiple instances of the app and therefore need dynamic routing. You can also look at a client of the service, specifically the Connections' Posts app. Just as with the Google example, you'll look at both the right-hand side (dynamic routing) and the left (service addressing and service discovery) of the service abstraction; figure 8.6 again provides a more detailed version of figure 8.4.

The Connections' Posts service, which is the Posts service client, is configured with an IP address to the Posts service; looking at the env variables defined in the cookbook-deployment-connectionposts.yaml file, you can see that the Posts URL is set to something like `http://192.168.99.100:31930/posts?userIds=`. You might recall that anytime you re-created the Posts *service*, you were forced to reconfigure the Connection' Posts app, providing a new IP address/port combination in this URL. You were forced to do this because you weren't using service discovery. At the end of this chapter, you'll fix this. In figure 8.6, you can see that the service is assigned this IP address, and that value is also hardcoded into the service client.

On the right-hand side of the service are the routes. Kubernetes has a simple and elegant way of designating which app instances a service fronts: tags and selectors. Each instance of the Posts service is tagged with the key/value pair `app:posts`. The service is defined via a selector, designating that this service represents the list of app instances with the `app:posts` tag. This is depicted on the right-hand side of figure 8.6.

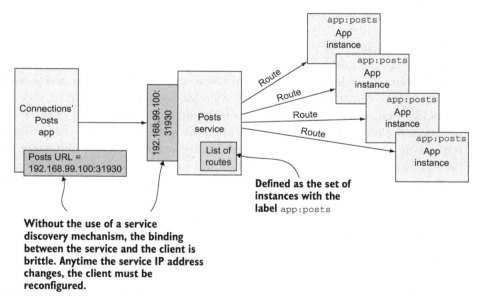

Without the use of a service discovery mechanism, the binding between the service and the client is brittle. Anytime the service IP address changes, the client must be reconfigured.

**Figure 8.6   Until now, the configuration of your blog aggregation software lacked the use of any type of service discovery protocol and bound the Connections' Posts service to the Posts service via IP address. This results in a brittle deployment.**

Kubernetes itself implements processes that continually keep the list of routes up to date so that anytime the service is accessed, the request will be routed to one of the current instances.

Although I hope that these two examples have helped explain the key parts of your mental model for services, I also hope that you're left looking for more. I haven't yet covered any concrete implementations, nor have I said much about the trade-offs I've alluded to. Let's dig deeper now, starting with the right-hand side of your service abstraction.

## 8.2    Dynamic routing

We need to talk about two elements on the right-hand side of the service abstraction: the means by which the list of app instances is kept up to date, and the routing of traffic to those service instances. I refer to the latter as *load balancing*, and I want to cover two approaches: server-side load balancing and client-side load balancing.

### 8.2.1    Server-side load balancing

Surely because it's the most commonly implemented, server-side load balancing is likely familiar to you. In a deployment that implements this pattern, there's a component that performs the operation of accepting incoming requests and sends those requests on to one of the corresponding instances. In my customer base, I typically see both hardware-based and software-based load balancers (including F5, nginx, and offerings from entrenched networking companies like Cisco and Citrix) as well as load-balancing services from all of the major cloud providers (such as Google, Amazon, and Microsoft).

Load balancing is generally done at the TCP/UDP protocol level, or at the HTTP level. The way the load balancer chooses an instance to route to will vary; for example, round-robin or random. The details of these selection algorithms aren't something you should concern yourself with. I will intentionally omit the details here because for your cloud-native software, you absolutely shouldn't depend on any of these specifics. Just as your cloud-native apps shouldn't be built so as to have the processing for one request depend on a previous request having reached exactly the same instance before, so too should you not depend on the instances being cycled through in any particular order. And because load balancers often allow you to turn on session affinity, otherwise known as *sticky sessions*, I must reiterate that you shouldn't do so. Apps that depend on sticky sessions aren't cloud-native.

Centralized load balancing has several advantages:

- The technology is mature. The load balancer implementations I've mentioned here have been evolving for several decades and as a result are robust.
- A centralized implementation is often easier to reason about than a highly distributed one.
- Configuration of a single, centralized entity is often easier than a highly distributed one.

On the other hand, a single entity can represent a single point of failure in a system, but in actuality, server-side load balancers are almost always deployed as a cluster, both for scale and resilience. Figure 8.7 shows a client request passing through a server-side load balancer (depicted as a cluster) that distributes the load across all of the service instances.

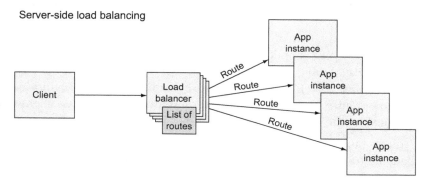

**Figure 8.7   With centralized, or server-side, load balancing, a client request is handled by a cluster of load balancers that has a list of routes to service instances. The load balancer distributes the client requests across different app instances.**

### 8.2.2   Client-side load balancing

If you take the idea of a cluster of load-balancers to an extreme, you can distribute the load-balancing components so widely that they're included in the clients themselves, as shown in figure 8.8. Note that each instance of the client has its own load-balancing capability built in.

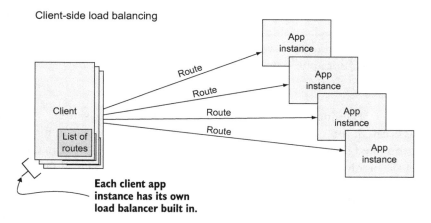

**Figure 8.8   With client-side load balancing, the client sends requests directly to the service instances and performs the task of distributing requests across all instances. The list of routes to service instances is maintained within the client itself.**

Client-side load balancing has gained in popularity because the number of microservices making up our software implementations has increased dramatically, and commensurate with that, so has the number of network requests flowing through the system. Pulling the load balancer into the client effectively eliminates one hop across the network, and at scale, this can make a noticeable difference in performance. Compare figure 8.7 to figure 8.8, and you can see that the client accesses service instances directly in the latter.

For client-side load balancing, you almost always use a framework that will either pull libraries into your application binary (as with Netflix Ribbon, https://github.com/Netflix/ribbon), or will employ other techniques such as sidecars (as with Istio, https://istio.io/). Either way, before you jump to the conclusion that you always want to optimize for performance and therefore will always use client-side load balancing, consider the following ramifications:

- If you're bundling libraries into your code, updates to the client-side load-balancing framework will require that you rebuild your applications.
- Configuration of the load-balancing functionality may be more difficult.
- You'll need to learn the details of how to use the particular client-side load-balancing capability that you choose. You're likely already well versed in making TCP or HTTP requests from your client by using libraries that are well tested and ubiquitous. You're now learning a new protocol.
- Most important, you'll be limiting the deployment options for your apps. By choosing to use Ribbon, for example, you make it far more difficult to use a server-side load balancer in which corporate policies may be enforced.

Whether your software will use client-side or server-side load balancing is likely a decision that's influenced by corporate standards, and will certainly be heavily influenced by the architectural principles agreed upon within your development teams. Regardless of whether you use client-side load balancing, or server-side, you need to understand one more pattern, even if your platform implements it for you: how the list of service instances is kept up to date for the routing function.

### 8.2.3   *Route freshness*

On the surface, keeping this list of routes up to date seems simple: when a new instance is created, you need to add its address to the list, and when an instance is disposed of, you need to remove it from the list. But something so simple in concept gets complex in a highly distributed, constantly changing environment. Looking back at the previous chapter's discussion around application lifecycle, recall that you already considered some edge cases—for example, one in which an application is denied the opportunity to announce its impending departure before a sudden crash. If accuracy of the routing table depended on such edge cases never happening, your system wouldn't work well.

At the core of a properly functioning system is a control loop (yes, another control loop!) whose job it is to constantly assess the actual state of the deployment and ensure that this reality is reflected in the routing tables. Your cloud-native platform will provide the core capabilities on which this depends, and your job is to ensure that your app presents the information needed for the platform to properly do its job. For route freshness, this means two things: (1) providing information so that the platform can build an accurate model of the actual state of the system, and (2) providing a means by which the instances implementing a service are identified.

The first portion of this has already been covered in chapter 7. You're responsible for implementing endpoints that the platform can use to assess the health of the app. Recall that you configured Kubernetes, your cloud-native platform, to implement probes of these health endpoints, and these are used to build that model of the state of the system.

The second part to keeping the routes fresh is a means by which the set of app instances that should be on the list can be identified. Again, the way this is accomplished depends on the platform, and in Kubernetes this is done with tags and selectors. Although I haven't previously presented the details, this has been included in the deployment of our software all along. Figure 8.9 shows a portion of the deployment manifest for Posts, cookbook-deployment-posts.yaml.

Here you can see that Kubernetes appropriately calls the service abstraction a `Service`, and part of the definition is a selector with the tag `app:posts`. Further down, in the definition of the app instance, you see that instances will be tagged with

```
kind: Service
apiVersion: v1
metadata:
  name: posts-svc
spec:
  selector:
    app: posts
  ports:
  - protocol: "TCP"
    port: 80
    targetPort: 8080
  type: NodePort
---
apiVersion: apps/v1beta1
kind: Deployment
metadata:
  name: posts
  labels:
    app: posts
spec:
  replicas: 2
  selector:
    matchLabels:
      app: posts
  template:
    metadata:
      labels:
        app: posts
    spec:
      containers:
      - name: posts
        image: cdavisafc/cloudnative-applifecycle-posts
```

**Defines the (abstract) service —an entity that represents the single logical Posts service**

**The list of instances that this service represents is given with a selector. That selector designates all app instances with the tag** app:posts.

**The app instances are labeled with the tag** app:posts. **When Kubernetes launches an app instance, it attaches this metadata to it.**

**Figure 8.9 The manifest for the Posts (abstract) service and the service instances that implement it. The list of service instance routes is kept up to date via a control loop that uses the service selector to find all app instances that meet certain criteria (in this case, the label** app: posts**).**

metadata, including the app:posts tag. The control loop that keeps the list of routes up to date will issue the appropriate query against the model of the actual state of the system and will update the routing tables accordingly.

Okay, you now have enough information about dynamic routing and load balancing that I can present to you our concrete implementation of the right-hand side of the Posts service. What I present here is specific to the Minikube-based deployment that we've been using throughout the text.

If you go all the way back to figure 8.6, it's tempting to think of the service depicted there as the load balancer, but it's just an abstraction. In our Minikube-based deployment, the load balancer is implemented with a single instance of a Kubernetes component called the Kube Proxy (Minikube is a nonproduction Kubernetes deployment, so single points of failure are acceptable). As the name indicates, Kube Proxy is just that: a proxy that takes incoming requests and routes them to the appropriate backends. In Kubernetes, each app instance is assigned its own IP address and, as you saw just a moment ago, a control loop is continuously querying the set of instances for those with the app:posts tag. The resultant system is shown in figure 8.10. To be clear, this is an implementation of server-side load balancing.

Having covered the right-hand side of the service abstraction depicted in figure 8.4 (and many of the figures following), let's now turn to the left side, which shows how the service is accessed. When you created the Posts service, Minikube dynamically assigned a port on which the Kube proxy is listening—the IP address of the Minikube virtual machine, along with this port, is what you've been using to access the service. But this is brittle. When the service address changes, the client must be reconfigured; this is because you haven't been using any service discovery process in your sample. A client can refer to a service in a better way through that service discovery process we'll dig into now.

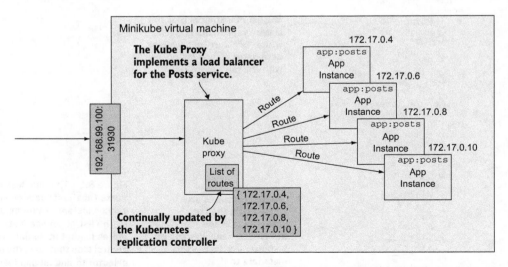

**Figure 8.10   Concrete implementation of the Posts service running in Minikube. The Kube Proxy is a load-balancer implementation and includes the list of IP addresses to all instances of the Posts service.**

## 8.3 Service discovery

At the core, what you need is a simple abstraction that loosely couples a client from the (changing) address of the service it depends on. It's not complex. You just need a naming service. Figure 8.11 depicts a simple protocol that allows the client to refer to a service by name; an address lookup on that name is performed, and connectivity is established.

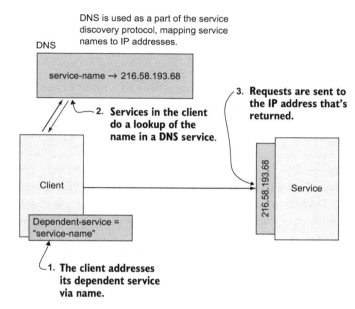

DNS is used as a part of the service discovery protocol, mapping service names to IP addresses.

DNS

service-name → 216.58.193.68

2. **Services in the client do a lookup of the name in a DNS service.**

3. **Requests are sent to the IP address that's returned.**

Client

216.58.193.68

Service

Dependent-service = "service-name"

1. **The client addresses its dependent service via name.**

**Figure 8.11 At the time of service access, the service discovery protocol allows a client to refer to a service by name, resulting in a more resilient binding between them.**

There are two parts to making this pattern work. First, there needs to be a way for entries to be placed into the name service. Second, there must be a way for an address to be fetched, given a name. Once again this sounds simple; it sounds like a simple map. But as soon as you do this in the context of a distributed system, it gets trickier. The good news is that you don't have to solve this yourself. Naming systems abound, and your job is simply to use them effectively.

But before moving on to how you'll use them, let me talk about the characteristics of a naming system in the context of your cloud-native apps. You already have a pretty solid appreciation for the fact that in a highly distributed software topology, having replicated pieces that operate independently is crucial. Your name service is itself a replicated, distributed system. Without getting into the details of the CAP Theorem,[2] naming services are generally configured to favor availability over consistency, a choice that suits this particular use case. To see why, let's consider what happens when a client accesses a service.

---

[2]The CAP theorem, proven by computer scientist Eric Brewer, states that of the three—Consistency, Availability, and Partition-tolerance (CAP)—only two can be realized in a distributed data store. See http://mng.bz/DVlV.

Favoring availability over consistency means that when the client asks the naming service for an address, it will always get an answer, but that answer may be stale. Incorrect answers will only be given when a service is available at a new address or is no longer available at an old address, but that latest information hasn't yet propagated throughout the entire system; the naming-service node that's answering the question for the client is a bit out of date. But a well-constructed naming system will minimize the windows in which this inconsistency may occur. Because a client can do nothing to reach a service without name resolution, and because most of the time the answer given by the naming service will be accurate, favoring availability over consistency is good. But, because inconsistencies may happen, albeit rarely, the client of the name resolution system must account for this possibility.

As the developer of the client app, you're responsible for implementing necessary compensating behaviors. This isn't the only case where you have to create an implementation that adapts to certain inconsistencies, but the good news is that some basic patterns, such as retries, which you'll be studying in detail in the next chapter, serve to help out in many cases. So let's add some basic retries to your service discovery protocol.

Suppose you have a service that recently experienced some lifecycle events that have disposed of an instance and have created a new one. When a client goes to access that service, it consults DNS to obtain the IP address where it can be reached, but, because it favors availability over consistency, the DNS responds with the IP address of the now disposed-of service instance. The client attempts to access that service and, of course, receives no response. It may retry the request another time or two (and I cover retries in far more detail in the next chapter), but eventually it will fail. This behavior is shown in the upper part of figure 8.12.

Knowing that DNS is eventually consistent, if you adjust this behavior just a bit, you get far better results. After failing a couple of retries, you can ask DNS for an IP address again, and because in the meantime DNS was updated and is now consistent, you get a new IP address. Your attempt to access the service at the new address is successful, and your client can now complete its job. The lower part of figure 8.12 shows this protocol. Depending on the framework that you're using within your client code, you may or may not be explicitly responsible for this implementation; the framework may transparently implement this protocol for you. It's, of course, important that you clearly understand whether you're personally responsible for the implementation.

But what happens if there is, in fact, a service on the old IP address, but it's a different service? This is a far more dangerous proposition. The short answer to this conundrum is that naming services should never, ever be used as a security implementation. The service implementation and/or deployment must implement access control mechanisms so that unauthorized access isn't permitted. With such an implementation in place, client access to a stale IP address will be met with an error message indicating that access was denied, and the client can respond appropriately. Knowing that the access control issue may be a result of a stale IP address means that, as a client developer, you could check back with the naming service to see if an updated IP address is available, and if so, perform a retry.

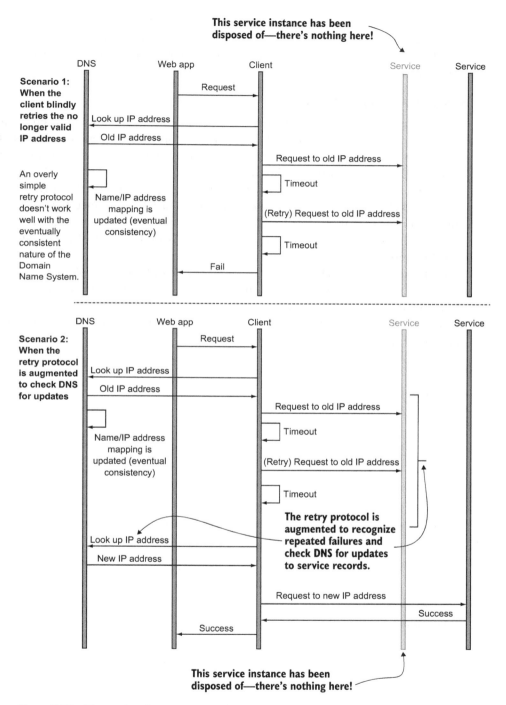

**Figure 8.12 The service discovery protocol must account for the eventually consistent nature of the Domain Name System.**

This discussion into the edge cases surrounding service discovery foreshadows a deeper discussion on compensating mechanisms that's coming in chapters 9 and 10. Let's leave this discussion for now and look at concrete implementations of the core service discovery pattern.

### 8.3.1    Service discovery on the web

You already looked at this scenario earlier in the chapter: what happens when you access www.google.com by using your web browser? The browser implements the client-side protocol of accessing the naming service (in this case, DNS) and then dispatches the request to that address. But how did the appropriate entries make it into DNS in the first place? You know that this is done by explicitly putting entries into the registry.

Figure 8.13 shows the console for Cloud DNS, a DNS interface that Google provides within its Google Cloud Platform (GCP). There you can see records mapping names to IP addresses. In this case, these were created as part of an installation of Cloud Foundry onto GCP.

In this scenario, the DNS service of the web is providing the implementation of the naming service, entries were placed into DNS via a software deployment process, and when you access the URL pcf.kerman.cf-app.com, your web browser interrogates DNS to obtain the IP address 35.184.74.187 and fetch your Cloud Foundry Operations Manager application.

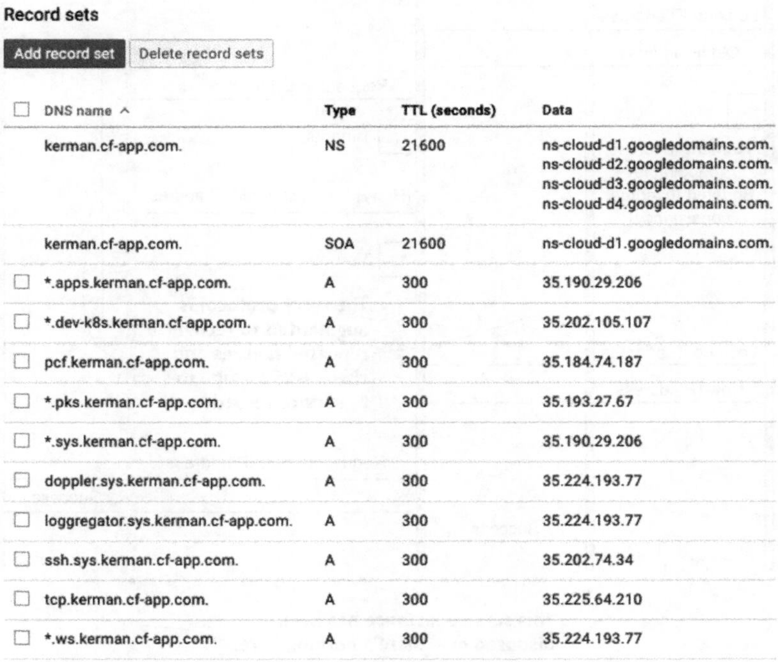

**Record sets**

`Add record set`  `Delete record sets`

| DNS name ^ | Type | TTL (seconds) | Data |
|---|---|---|---|
| kerman.cf-app.com. | NS | 21600 | ns-cloud-d1.googledomains.com.<br>ns-cloud-d2.googledomains.com.<br>ns-cloud-d3.googledomains.com.<br>ns-cloud-d4.googledomains.com. |
| kerman.cf-app.com. | SOA | 21600 | ns-cloud-d1.googledomains.com. |
| *.apps.kerman.cf-app.com. | A | 300 | 35.190.29.206 |
| *.dev-k8s.kerman.cf-app.com. | A | 300 | 35.202.105.107 |
| pcf.kerman.cf-app.com. | A | 300 | 35.184.74.187 |
| *.pks.kerman.cf-app.com. | A | 300 | 35.193.27.67 |
| *.sys.kerman.cf-app.com. | A | 300 | 35.190.29.206 |
| doppler.sys.kerman.cf-app.com. | A | 300 | 35.224.193.77 |
| loggregator.sys.kerman.cf-app.com. | A | 300 | 35.224.193.77 |
| ssh.sys.kerman.cf-app.com. | A | 300 | 35.202.74.34 |
| tcp.kerman.cf-app.com. | A | 300 | 35.225.64.210 |
| *.ws.kerman.cf-app.com. | A | 300 | 35.224.193.77 |

**Figure 8.13   DNS entries that map domain names to IP addresses**

### 8.3.2 *Service discovery with client-side load balancing*

As you've seen, service discovery is all about allowing a service to be found at a particular address without tightly coupling that address into the client implementation. The protocol is used both when load balancing is implemented server-side and when it's implemented client-side, but some differences exist. Figure 8.14 makes this clear. The difference is, if you will, temporal.

With server-side load balancing, the name resolution is usually done as part of the invocation of the service—after consulting DNS, a request is dispatched to the service. On the other hand, with client-side load balancing, the service discovery protocol is used to update the list of routes that are part of the client-side load balancer. To some

**Server-side load balancing**

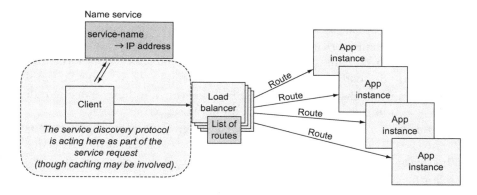

**Client-side load balancing**

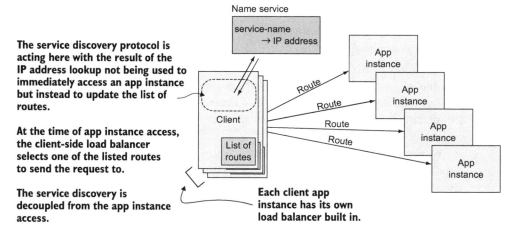

**Figure 8.14** Service discovery differs depending on whether client-side load balancing or server-side load balancing is used.

extent, you've blended load balancing and service discovery, so it bears us looking at the details for a moment.

I already mentioned Netflix Ribbon and implementation of a client-side load balancer. This framework supports a programming model in which the client code can refer to its dependent service via name. Using the Spring Framework, this may be done with a class annotation such as the following:

```
@RibbonClient(name = "posts-service")
```

Later in the code, you can then use that name, via `restTemplate`, for example, to contact the service:

```
String posts
  = restTemplate.getForObject("http://posts-service/posts", String.class);
```

The lookup of the address and request dispatch is implemented with a combination of the Spring Framework and the Ribbon client. But service discovery also depends on the registration of name/address pairs into the name service. Here, where you're using client-side load balancing, you need a special service to facilitate this. Netflix Ribbon is almost always used in combination with another service, Netflix Eureka (https://github.com/Netflix/eureka), the service discovery service.

In this case, a Eureka service must be running; it's the naming service that resolves IP addresses from a given name. The simplest way of registering a service instance with Eureka is to once again use the Spring Framework. Any application that includes the Spring Boot starter for Eureka in the class path and has the coordinates of the Eureka service configured in will automatically be registered with Eureka by the Spring Framework. It's part of the application lifecycle that the Spring Framework is managing for you.

### 8.3.3   *Service discovery in Kubernetes*

The last example that I want to cover sets the stage for adding service discovery into our running sample implementation, thereby eliminating the brittle configuration that has plagued us through the early chapters of the book. The pattern, of course, is the same as for the last two examples: there's some type of a name service, a process for placing entries into that name service, and another protocol for obtaining IP addresses from a name.

Kubernetes provides an implementation of a DNS service called—wait for it—*CoreDNS*. (Okay, saying it that way was a bit more fun when the included DNS was called *Kube-DNS*. In late 2018, Kube-DNS was effectively replaced with the next-generation CoreDNS.) Although it's an optional component, I have yet to find a Kubernetes deployment that fails to install it by default. It's deployed as an app (in a pod) into your running Kubernetes cluster. Other portions of the Kubernetes platform, as well as elements within your app code, will interface with it to perform the registration and lookup actions that make up the service discovery protocol. You can see that CoreDNS is running by executing the following command:

```
$ kubectl get pods --namespace=kube-system
NAME                                    READY   STATUS    RESTARTS   AGE
coredns-86c58d9df4-8mfq8                1/1     Running   0          6d19h
coredns-86c58d9df4-sfqjm                1/1     Running   0          6d19h
etcd-minikube                           1/1     Running   0          6d19h
kube-addon-manager-minikube             1/1     Running   0          6d19h
kube-apiserver-minikube                 1/1     Running   0          6d19h
kube-controller-manager-minikube        1/1     Running   0          6d19h
kube-proxy-jwcmg                        1/1     Running   0          16h
kube-scheduler-minikube                 1/1     Running   0          6d19h
storage-provisioner                     1/1     Running   0          6d19h
```

In this output, you might notice that CoreDNS is running as a cluster of two pods. Naming services are a critical component in the system that makes up your software and must therefore be deployed in a highly resilient manner. Multiple instances contribute to that resilience.

Starting with one part of the service discovery protocol, DNS registration is done automatically by Kubernetes when services are created. The names that Kubernetes registers for a specific service may be set explicitly in the deployment manifest, or defaults may be derived from standard service fields such as the service name.

For the other part of the protocol, the lookup, the approach is simple. CoreDNS acts just like any other DNS. Any processing that would normally interface with a DNS service—using `restTemplate` to make an HTTP request, for example—will do those lookups against CoreDNS. Kubernetes ensures that the address for CoreDNS is configured into the running pods.

Figure 8.15 puts it all together:

1 The Kubernetes cluster houses a DNS service called CoreDNS.
2 On startup, a service's name and address are added to the CoreDNS service.
3 All pods (apps) running in the Kubernetes environment have the address of the CoreDNS service configured in.
4 Any DNS-accessing operations, such as making an HTTP request to a URL that contains a name, access the CoreDNS service to resolve the address.

You're now ready to apply all this newfound knowledge to our blog aggregation example.

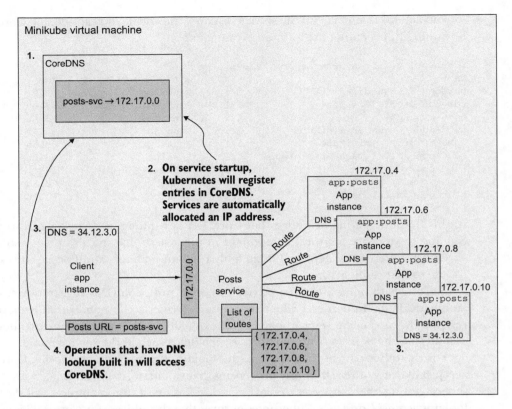

**Figure 8.15   Kubernetes provides an implementation of the service discovery protocol with the inclusion of a domain name service and processes that automatically create and access entries in that registry.**

### 8.3.4   *Let's see this in action: Using service discovery*

The time has come! You will now get rid of the brittle configuration between the various services that make up our sample application. When you're done here, no longer will one service address another via IP address, and no longer will that previously brittle configuration need updating when the IP address for a service changes. Instead, you will use a DNS service to implement a service discovery protocol. Or better put, the platform you deploy the apps to, in this case, Kubernetes, will implement that protocol for you.

#### SETTING UP

At this point, I refer you to the setup instructions for running the samples in earlier chapters in this text; there are no new requirements for running the sample in this chapter.

You'll be accessing files in the cloudnative-servicediscovery directory, so in your terminal window change into that directory.

### RUNNING THE APPS

Because I've made changes to the deployment manifests, and because there are no longer any brittle steps in configuring components of the deployment, I suggest that you delete the entire deployment of your sample app, including the databases and config server components, as well as all of the Kubernetes services. This will allow you to see clearly how much simpler your deployment is with the addition of automated service discovery (instead of you having implemented the service discovery protocol by hand). You may do this by running the script I've provided as follows:

```
$ ./ deleteDeploymentComplete.sh all
```

Looking at what I've provided here, I'll first point out that this directory is sparse. It contains only a couple of utility scripts and the deployment manifests for our sample application. There's no source code whatsoever, and this is telling. Remember the point that I made early on in the chapter? I said design decisions are just as likely to be a deployment time concern as a development one. Because the code that made calls to dependent services, from the Connections' Posts app to the Posts service, for example, was already using techniques that used DNS services, replacing the brittle IP addresses with names in the app deployment manifests required no code changes. The deployment manifests point to the Docker images I created for chapter 7.

Let's start by deploying the two database services and the Spring Cloud Configuration Server; this is done with the following three commands:

```
kubectl apply -f mysql-deployment.yaml
kubectl apply -f redis-deployment.yaml
kubectl apply -f spring-cloud-config-server-deployment-kubernetes.yaml
```

Don't forget to re-create the cookbook database:

```
$ mysql -h $(minikube service mysql-svc --format "{{.IP}}") \
    -P $(minikube service mysql-svc --format "{{.Port}}") -u root -p
mysql> create database cookbook;
```

By issuing the well-worn command, `kubectl get all`, you can see the deployment, service, and pods that are created as a result.

Now let's look at changes I've made in the deployment manifests for the Connections service:

- I've updated the URI to the MySQL service to reference it by name; the definition of the relevant environment variable now reads as follows:

```
- name: SPRING_APPLICATION_JSON
  value: '{"spring":{"datasource":{"url":
  ➥ "jdbc:mysql://mysql-svc/cookbook"}}}'
```

- You can also see that referring to the SCCS is also by name:

```
- name: SPRING_CLOUD_CONFIG_URI
  value: "http://sccs-svc:8888"
```

You're now ready to launch the Connections service with the following command:

```
kubectl apply -f cookbook-deployment-connections.yaml
```

You can see the same configurations for the Posts service, which you can now launch with the following command:

```
kubectl apply -f cookbook-deployment-posts.yaml
```

Finally, in the following listing, you can see that in the Connections' Posts deployment manifest, you now refer to Redis, SCCS, and each of the Posts and Connections services by name.

**Listing 8.1    Excerpt from cookbook-deployment-connectionsposts.yaml**

```
- name: CONNECTIONPOSTSCONTROLLER_POSTSURL
  value: "http://posts-svc/posts?userIds="
- name: CONNECTIONPOSTSCONTROLLER_CONNECTIONSURL
  value: "http://connections-svc/connections/"
- name: CONNECTIONPOSTSCONTROLLER_USERSURL
  value: "http://connections-svc/users/"
- name: REDIS_HOSTNAME
  value: "redis-svc"
- name: REDIS_PORT
  value: "6379"
- name: SPRING_APPLICATION_NAME
  value: "mycookbook"
- name: SPRING_CLOUD_CONFIG_URI
  value: "http://sccs-svc:8888"
```

You can launch this service with the following command:

```
kubectl apply -f cookbook-deployment-connectionsposts.yaml
```

Did you notice that you didn't have to edit a single one of the deployment manifests? Ah, the beauty of loose coupling through service discovery.

I want to draw your attention to two additional things in the configuration of the Connections' Posts service.

First, the names used to refer to the Posts and Connections services aren't followed by any port number. You might have noticed that the former configurations showed that both services were listening at the same IP address (the address of your Minikube virtual machine) but on different ports. When you replaced the URI (Universal Resource Identifier) with the service name, you not only eliminated a brittle binding to an IP address, but also changed something about the way in which traffic was routed. When the IP address was used, you routed to the Posts or Connections services through a north/south avenue. Your request traveled outside the Kubernetes environment and reentered it via the IP address of your Minikube VM. In replacing the IP address and port with the service name, the routing from Connections' Posts to Posts stayed within the Kubernetes environment, using an east/west avenue. Also, when Kubernetes creates a service object, it assigns an internal IP address to that object, and that's the IP address associated with the name in CoreDNS.

The second thing I want to draw your attention to is related to this first point. Notice that the port number for the Redis service is now set to 6379. In the prior configurations, you accessed the Redis service through north/south avenues, just as you did for the Posts and Connections services. But in changing the Redis hostname to the DNS-registered redis-svc, east/west routing is used, and traffic will be sent directly to redis-svc. Looking at the definition of the Redis service, you can see that it's configured to listen on port 6379, and requests coming into that port will be passed on to the targetPort on which the pod that's running the actual Redis service is listening.

**Listing 8.2 Excerpt from redis-deployment.yam**

```
kind: Service
apiVersion: v1
metadata:
  name: redis-svc
spec:
  selector:
    app: redis
  ports:
  - protocol: "TCP"
    port: 6379
    targetPort: 6379
  type: NodePort
```

You now have the sample application fully functional, and with one important difference from before: you can delete the Posts or Connections services and re-create them, and the client of those services, the Connections' Posts service, needn't be reconfigured or even redeployed. Because access to the dependent services is facilitated with the service discovery protocol, your cloud-native software deployment is tolerant of such changes.

Adapting to the constant changes in cloud-native software deployments would be intractable without the help of a platform that provides things like health checks and route freshness. Service discovery is an equally essential protocol to use. Your job is to build your app code and deployments in a manner that allows these platforms to provide such services to your software.

## Summary

- A simple abstraction can be used to more loosely couple clients from dependent services.
- Two main load-balancing approaches are available—centralized (or server-side) and client-side. Each has advantages and disadvantages.
- Configuration of load balancers must be dynamic and highly automated because in a cloud-native setting, the instances to which traffic is routed are changing far more frequently than they have in the past.
- Naming services such as DNS are central to the service discovery protocol that allows clients to find dependent services even in a topology that's constantly changing.
- When using a domain name service, as a developer you must account for the fact that the name-to-IP-address tables are eventually consistent. You must account for entries potentially being out of date.
- Using a service discovery protocol yields far more resilient software deployments.

# Interaction redundancy: Retries and other control loops

*9*

**This chapter covers**

- Retries: repeating access attempts on timeouts
- Retry storms
- Safe and idempotent services
- Fallbacks
- Control loops

While surfing the web, what do you do when a web page you're trying to access fails to load? You hit the refresh button, right? I've talked a lot about redundant service instances, but now want to turn to another place where redundancy is used in cloud-native software: when making requests. Just as depending on a single instance of an app to always be up is untenable, so too is depending on each and every request to never experience any trouble. Instead, your software will repeat requests, just as you do. Well, maybe not *just as*. Let's explore this a bit.

The case that I started with is the simplest: you're loading a page to read it. For example, you might be looking at the Hacker News homepage (https://news.ycombinator.com/), the headline "Monks Who Play Punk (2007)" catches your fancy, and you click the link to read the full article. The article doesn't load, or it only partially loads, so you hit the refresh button and all is fine.

But if you experience a failure to load right after clicking the Place Your Order button on your favorite e-commerce site, you're unlikely to just click that button again. You'll first check to see whether the purchase went through, perhaps by checking the shopping cart, accessing your list of open orders, or maybe even checking to see whether you got an order confirmation email. If you find evidence that the order was placed, you're good to go—no need to repeat the partially failed request. If, on the other hand, you're reasonably confident that the order wasn't placed, you'll go back and repeat the request for purchase.

Let me also draw your attention to another feature you've likely run across in some of the websites you visit: the I Am Not a Robot check box or captcha. This type of a widget is generally used to put a governor on certain website interactions, to keep bots from creating (large numbers of) accounts, or to keep them from hacking passwords, for example. This feature is fundamentally about retries and highlights another aspect of request redundancy that I'll cover here: when you move from human users to machine clients, you need to be cognizant of the orders-of-magnitude increases in both volume and frequency of requests.

These familiar scenarios are a good place to begin our exploration of redundant interactions, yet it's important to understand that both the actors and the context are different. In our cloud-native software architectures, the client and the service of the interaction are programs. The software-based client has to make decisions similar to what you do as a human—how long should it wait before giving up on a request, for example. It also needs to understand when retries shouldn't be made, and it needs to be aware of its own power.

You might have noticed that I'm using the word "interaction," and hopefully this takes you back to the mental model for cloud-native software that I established in the first chapter. The interaction is one of the primary entities I introduced there. And although chapter 8 approached the topic, it was primarily about what is needed before an interaction is established—how the client finds a dependent service, for example. Now I begin to address the interaction in earnest (see figure 9.1), first with this chapter's focus on the client side of that interaction. Chapter 10 covers the service end of the interaction.

I start the chapter by adding a naïve retry implementation to our sample application, and we'll run some experiments to demonstrate the value of this pattern. Then I take those experiments to an extreme, so you can see what happens when large volumes of retries have negative consequences that ripple through the entire system. We'll then explore techniques to guard against these retry storms. Finally, request retries are but one example of repeat actions, and I close the chapter by talking about the general pattern of control loops and their valuable role in cloud-native software.

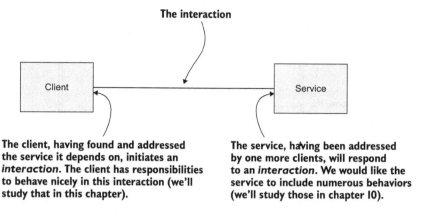

**The interaction**

**The client, having found and addressed the service it depends on, initiates an** *interaction.* **The client has responsibilities to behave nicely in this interaction (we'll study that in this chapter).**

**The service, having been addressed by one more clients, will respond to an** *interaction.* **We would like the service to include numerous behaviors (we'll study those in chapter 10).**

**Figure 9.1   Certain design patterns applied on both sides of an interaction will yield far more robust and reliable systems. We'll cover client-side patterns in this chapter, and service-side patterns in the next.**

## 9.1   Request retries

Cloud-native software is, almost by definition, a distributed system. In the past, invocation of a functionality from another part of your code was just a method call, and everything was running within the same process. Today, your implementations are filled with requests that go over the network—a network that isn't always reliable. And even when the network is fine, there are no guarantees that while your process is up and running, the service you're calling is equally healthy. It's these attributes of distributed systems that drive the need for addressing request resilience.

Let me clarify one thing right at the onset. There are a number of ways we might define or realize *request resilience.* A more traditional approach might focus on *request durability*—coming up with ways to ensure that requests are never lost. But this is analogous to the traditional approach of hardening servers and storage devices: make them stronger and stronger so they don't fail. Instead, the more modern paradigm, which is the undercurrent of everything in this book, accepts that components *will* fail and that we achieve resilience by adapting to that inevitable disruption. That's what this chapter does with requests. It explores achieving resilience with a redundancy of requests instead of treating each request as something that simply can't be lost. All of that said, upcoming chapters present approaches that store requests, but with a twist; but I'll leave all of that for later.

### 9.1.1   The basic request retry

The basic pattern is simple: your app is going to make a request to a remote service, and if it doesn't hear back within a reasonable time, it's going to try again. By now you're familiar with our running example—the blog aggregator—in which the Connections' Posts service makes calls to both the Connections service and the Posts service and then returns an aggregated result.

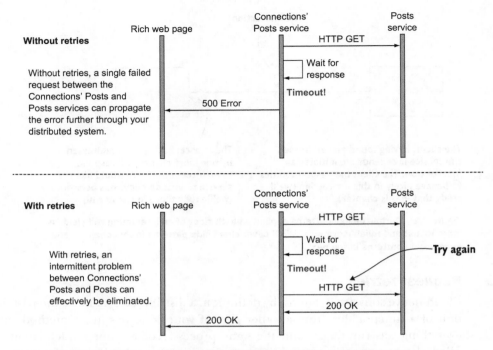

**Figure 9.2   Retries can insulate parts of your distributed system from errors in other parts.**

The demonstration that you'll be looking at in a moment focuses on the Connections' Posts service as a client that makes an HTTP request to the Posts service (it's still making requests to the Connections service, but for the purposes of this exercise, you'll focus on the interaction between Connections' Posts and Posts). In this example, you've implemented a retry around this request (figure 9.2), so that now, when the Connections' Posts service makes a call to the Posts service and doesn't receive a response, it will simply try the request again.

This simple retry will make your overall system more tolerant to failures, returning results in cases where, otherwise, the Connections' Posts service might have failed to produce the aggregated set of blog posts.

### 9.1.2   *Let's see this in action: Simple retries*

In this chapter and the next, I'm going to have you run a series of experiments that explore the impact of applying various cloud-native patterns to the interaction between services. This first example lays the foundation, with each subsequent implementation building on the last. You'll start by implementing a simple retry.

#### SETTING UP
At this point, I refer you to the setup instructions for running the samples in earlier chapters. There are no new requirements for running the sample in this chapter.

You'll be accessing files in the cloudnative-requestresilience directory, so in your terminal window change into that directory.

As I've described in previous chapters, I've already prebuilt Docker images and made them available in Docker Hub. If you want to build the Java source and Docker images and push them to your own image repository, I refer you to earlier chapters (the most detailed instructions are in chapter 5).

### RUNNING THE APPS

As you progress through the chapter, you'll use different versions of the retry pattern, so to start, you'll need to check out the right tag on the GitHub repo:

```
git checkout requestretries/0.0.1
```

You'll need a Kubernetes cluster, and for this initial example you may use Minikube. See section 5.2.2 in chapter 5 for instructions on how get Minikube up and running. To start with a clean slate, delete any deployments that might be left over from your previous work. I've provided you a script to do that: `deleteDeploymentComplete.sh`. This simple bash script allows you to keep the MySQL, Redis, and Spring Cloud services running. Calling it with no options deletes only the three microservice deployments; calling the script with `all` as an argument deletes MySQL, Redis, and SCSS services as well. Verify that your environment is clean with the following command:

```
$ kubectl get all
NAME                          READY   STATUS          RESTARTS   AGE
pod/mysql-6585c56bff-hfwn5    1/1     Running         0          2m
pod/redis-846b8c56fb-wr6zx    1/1     Running         0          2m
pod/sccs-84cc988f57-d2mgm     1/1     Running         0          2m

NAME                           CLUSTER-IP       EXTERNAL-IP   PORT(S)          AGE
service/connectionsposts-svc   10.101.76.173    <none>        80:31224/TCP     44s
service/connections-svc        10.105.144.139   <none>        80:32290/TCP     44s
service/kubernetes             10.96.0.1        <none>        443/TCP          4m
service/mysql-svc              10.109.9.155     <none>        3306:32260/TCP   2m
service/posts-svc              10.98.202.179    <none>        80:32746/TCP     45s
service/redis-svc              10.109.19.150    <none>        6379:30270/TCP   2m
service/sccs-svc               10.98.94.67      <none>        8888:32640/TCP   2m

NAME                      DESIRED   CURRENT   UP-TO-DATE   AVAILABLE   AGE
deployment.apps/mysql     1         1         1            1           2m
deployment.apps/redis     1         1         1            1           2m
deployment.apps/sccs      1         1         1            1           2m

NAME                                 DESIRED   CURRENT   READY   AGE
replicaset.apps/mysql-6585c56bff     1         1         1       2m
replicaset.apps/redis-846b8c56fb     1         1         1       2m
replicaset.apps/sccs-84cc988f57      1         1         1       2m
```

Note that you've left `mysql`, `redis`, and `sccs` running, as well as the services for your three microservices. If you've cleared out `redis`, `mysql`, and `sccs`, deploy each by running the `deployServices.sh` bash script. If you've created the MySQL service anew, don't forget to create the cookbook database with the following commands:

```
$ mysql -h $(minikube service mysql-svc --format "{{.IP}}") \
     -P $(minikube service mysql-svc --format "{{.Port}}") -u root -p
mysql> create database cookbook;
```

You can now deploy the three microservices by running three `kubectl apply` commands pointing to the Connections' Posts, Connections, and Posts YAML files. I've created a script that encapsulates all three, so you can simply run this:

```
./deployApps.sh
```

As you've done in the past, invoke the Connections' Posts microservice, by first logging in and then accessing the list of posts for your connections:

```
curl -i -X POST -c cookie \
    $(minikube service --url connectionsposts-svc)/login?username=cdavisafc
curl -i -b cookie \
    $(minikube service --url connectionsposts-svc)/connectionsposts
```

At this point, you should be able to execute that last command repeatedly with consistent results.

Now let's cause some trouble. Recall that in an earlier chapter you added an endpoint to the Posts service to break it. By issuing an HTTP post against the `/infect` endpoint, responses to subsequent requests to the service will be delayed by 400 seconds. That's pretty broken. Notice that in the deployment manifest, I've removed the liveness probe that I added at the end of chapter 8; for our experiments here, I want to keep these services broken. You currently have two instances of the Posts service running, so let's break one of them by making that POST request:

```
curl -i -X POST $(minikube service --url posts-svc)/infect
```

Before invoking the Connections' Posts service again, let's start streaming the logs for that service by running the following command in another terminal window:

```
kubectl logs -f <name of your Connections' Posts pod>
```

Now access the Connections' Posts service a few more times. I'd like you to notice two things. First, on each `curl`, you receive a response—the aggregation service is working just fine. But second, looking at the logs, you can see entries such as this one:

```
... : [172.17.0.10:8080] getting posts for user network cdavisafc
... : [172.17.0.10:8080] connections = 2,3
... : [172.17.0.10:8080] On (0) request to unhealthy posts service I/O
➥ error on GET request for "http://posts-svc/posts": Read timed out;
➥ nested exception is java.net.SocketTimeoutException: Read timed out
... : [172.17.0.10:8080] On (1) request to unhealthy posts service I/O
➥ error on GET request for "http://posts-svc/posts": Read timed out;
➥ nested exception is java.net.SocketTimeoutException: Read timed out
```

```
... : [172.17.0.10:8080] On (2) request to unhealthy posts service  I/O
➡ error on GET request for "http://posts-svc/posts": Read timed out;
➡ nested exception is java.net.SocketTimeoutException: Read timed out
... : [172.17.0.10:8080] Retrieved results from database
```

This shows that requests were made to the Posts service that timed out, but instead of that failure propagating all the way back to you, the client, the Connections' Posts service automatically recovered by retrying the request. Even if it took a few retries (in the preceding example, it took three retries), eventually the non-infected Posts service was reached, and the result was returned.

Let's look at the implementation from the ConnectionsPostsController.java file.

**Listing 9.1  Excerpt from ConnectionsPostsController.java**

```java
int retryCount = 0;
while (implementRetries || retryCount == 0) {
  try {
    RestTemplate restTemp = restTemplateBuilder
                              .setConnectTimeout(connectTimeout)
                              .setReadTimeout(readTimeout)
                              .build();
    ResponseEntity<PostResult[]> respPosts
      = restTemp.getForEntity(postsUrl + ids + secretQueryParam,
                              PostResult[].class);
    if (respPosts.getStatusCode().is5xxServerError()) {
      response.setStatus(500);
      return null;
    } else {
      logger.info(utils.ipTag() + "Retrieved results from database");
      PostResult[] posts = respPosts.getBody();
      for (int i = 0; i < posts.length; i++)
        postSummaries.add(
          new PostSummary(getUsersname(posts[i].getUserId()),
          posts[i].getTitle(), posts[i].getDate()));
      return postSummaries;
    }
  } catch (Exception e) {
    // Will occur when a connection times out.
    // For this naive implementation, we will simply
    // try again.
    logger.info(utils.ipTag() +
      "On (" + retryCount + ") request to unhealthy posts service  " +
      e.getMessage());
    if (implementRetries)
      retryCount++;
    else {
      logger.info(utils.ipTag() +
        "Not implementing retries - returning with a 500");
      response.setStatus(500);
      return null;
    }
  }
}
```

As you can see, the implementation is simple. If you're implementing retries, which are controlled through a new application property, you'll make a request to the Posts service. If it times out, you stay in the `while` loop and try again. You can see the lines that generate the very log messages you looked at when running the sample.

Although this is indeed simple, here you're already getting to the first nuance: how long will your implementation wait before a timeout exception is thrown? (Ultimately, this is something that the application operator is likely to decide—and that could be you.) Too long, and your upstream clients (the web page invoking the Connections' Posts service) may be left waiting for an extended period of time and may themselves time out. Too short, and Connections' Posts may be forfeiting perfectly valid results (and causing some of the downstream ramifications covered in the next section). In the current implementation, I've set the connect timeout to ¼ of a second and the read timeout to ½ of a second, as you can see in these lines:

```
RestTemplate restTemplate = restTemplateBuilder
                                    .setConnectTimeout(250)
                                    .setReadTimeout(500)
                                    .build();
```

I want to draw your attention to something: in everything you've done here, both in the case where a human refreshed a web page and in our implementation, never did you concern yourself with *why* you didn't get a response from the downstream service. It could have been a network problem, or a bug in the application (arguably what I've demonstrated here), or any number of other problems. When the problem is intermittent, the reason is most often immaterial. Only when you start to see persistent problems will you care, and even then, it's not a concern of your apps, but rather a general monitoring concern. We'll cover troubleshooting in a later chapter.

Okay, this looks pretty good; it's easy and it seems to work. What of these downstream ramifications and persistent problems I keep alluding to? Let's jump in.

### 9.1.3   Retries: what could go wrong?

In the preceding example, the software operates just fine with the limited load that you're placing on the system with your command-line `curl`s. But it can be a different story when something goes wrong in a system that is otherwise well tuned for a particular load. It's a bit like highway traffic.

Consider a freeway that has enough lanes to allow 14,000 cars traveling at 60 mph to pass through it in an hour (by my back-of-the-envelope calculations, that's a four-lane highway). As long as no accidents occur, all is well. But when two lanes are made impassable by a fender-bender, things change quickly. Not only will the same volume of traffic now traveling in half the lanes have to slow down to maintain safe driving distance, but the cars approaching the constrained stretch of highway, at the same volume as before, will fairly quickly generate quite a traffic jam. And, as we've all likely experienced, even when the accident site is cleared, it takes some

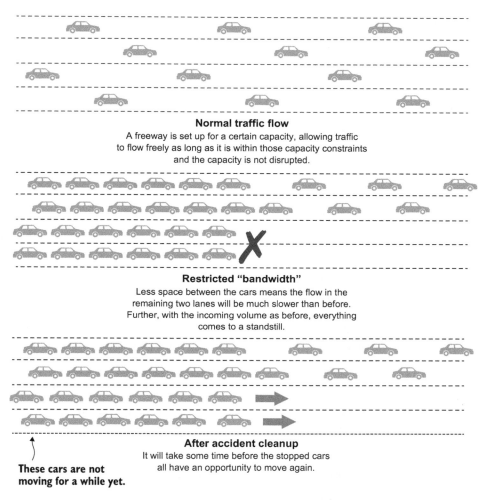

**Normal traffic flow**
A freeway is set up for a certain capacity, allowing traffic to flow freely as long as it is within those capacity constraints and the capacity is not disrupted.

**Restricted "bandwidth"**
Less space between the cars means the flow in the remaining two lanes will be much slower than before. Further, with the incoming volume as before, everything comes to a standstill.

**After accident cleanup**
It will take some time before the stopped cars all have an opportunity to move again.

**These cars are not moving for a while yet.**

**Figure 9.3   Restricted networks act like restricted highways, backing up requests that keep coming in the same volumes as before. Even when the restrictions are lifted, it can take some time before all of the queued-up traffic is moving again.**

time before all the queued-up traffic is flowing again. This scenario is depicted in figure 9.3.

The situation is exactly the same with the request flow through your network of app instances. Even though your site reliability engineer has no doubt designed a deployment topology that leaves a bit of room for fluctuations in request volume and minor hiccups, when a sizeable portion of your load gets backed up, the effects can ripple through the system. Let's see this in action.

### 9.1.4    *Creating a retry storm*

In the previous section, I presented a basic pattern: the Connections' Posts service will retry calls to the Posts service in the event that it doesn't initially receive a response. At a high level, this makes complete sense, and the current implementation will handle minor glitches just fine. But when something more significant occurs (the metaphorical highway accident), retries may not be as helpful and may even hurt the overall health of the system. What I want to do here is experiment with the naïve implementation that I presented in the previous section.

By way of reminder, you're focusing on the interaction between the Connections' Posts service (the client) and the Posts service. As you saw in the first example, you've

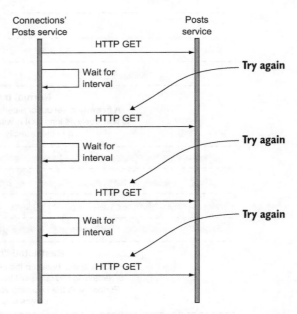

**Figure 9.4    The client, the Connections' Posts service, will retry on connection or read timeouts to the Posts service. It will continue trying until it receives a success status code from the HTTP request to the Posts service.**

implemented a retry around this request. Figure 9.4 shows repeated retries, just as you saw previously and will see even more of in this coming example. Let's get you set up so you can follow along.

### 9.1.5    *Let's see this in action: Creating a retry storm*

This experiment makes no changes to the code of the previous one, but you will send a sizeable load of traffic to the system, simulate a short disruption, and observe the results (spoiler alert: they're rather unpleasant).

#### SETTING UP

You'll need everything that I listed in the first example of this chapter with one adjustment:

- Access to a larger Kubernetes cluster.
- That Kubernetes cluster must allow privileged containers to be run.

You'll be placing your software under load and then introducing failures into the system. I want to have you explore, for example, what happens when you lose all lanes on our metaphorical highway and, just as important, what happens when those lanes are restored. To be able to place a significant load on the system, you'll create a larger deployment of our sample app; hence, you'll need a larger environment to run this in.

Without getting into the details of a fairly complex topic, I'll say this: privileged containers allow for more commands to be executed within them than nonprivileged containers do, and you'll need this when you begin to restrict network traffic. The good news is that most of the cloud providers will serve Kubernetes clusters with privileged containers enabled by default.

At the time of writing, I find that Google Kubernetes Engine (GKE) provides the easiest public cloud experience in creating Kubernetes clusters. You'll need a cluster with approximately 25–30 GB of memory across all of the nodes. GKE also enables privileged containers by default, something you'll need.

To run the simulations in this section, please check out the following tag from your Git repo:

```
git checkout requestretries/0.0.2
```

#### RUNNING THE APPS
There are three parts to executing the experiments:

1 Deploying the application
2 Placing load against the application
3 Simulating various failure scenarios and observing the results

Unless you've already been running the examples on a larger Kubernetes cluster, or one that you can resize to have sufficient capacity, you'll likely have to deploy all the components that make up our sample anew. I won't go over the installation in detail here, instead referring you to earlier chapters, but in summary, after creating that new Kubernetes cluster and connecting to it with `kubectl`, you need to do the following:

1 Edit the deployment manifest for the Spring Cloud Configuration Server (SCCS), spring-cloud-config-server-deployment-kubernetes.yaml, to point to the Git repo that houses your app configs. You may, of course, keep it pointing at my repo.
2 Deploy MySQL, Redis, and SCCS. I've provided a script, so you can simply run the `deployServices.sh` bash script.
3 Create the cookbook database by connecting to MySQL with a command-line client and executing the command `create database cookbook;`. Notice that the MySQL deployment manifest specifies `LoadBalancer` for the service type that should have allocated a public IP address for your MySQL database. You can use that to connect with your `mysql` CLI.
4 Deploy all three microservices by executing the `deployApps.sh` bash script.

This should result in a deployment that looks something like this:

```
$ kubectl get pods
NAME                                  READY   STATUS    RESTARTS   AGE
connection-posts-685c669f7b-4qvx7     1/1     Running   0          6d
connection-posts-685c669f7b-61gmf     1/1     Running   0          6d
```

```
connection-posts-685c669f7b-6pt9p      1/1         Running    0         6d
connection-posts-685c669f7b-d8q8h      1/1         Running    0         6d
connection-posts-685c669f7b-z7gsw      1/1         Running    0         6d
connections-7cf9b5ccf9-cjnhs           1/1         Running    0         6d
connections-7cf9b5ccf9-cw4s9           1/1         Running    0         6d
connections-7cf9b5ccf9-kskqm           1/1         Running    0         6d
connections-7cf9b5ccf9-mfj8b           1/1         Running    0         6d
connections-7cf9b5ccf9-nd4nw           1/1         Running    0         6d
connections-7cf9b5ccf9-nnl8r           1/1         Running    0         6d
connections-7cf9b5ccf9-xjq8j           1/1         Running    0         6d
mysql-64bd6d89d8-96vb6                 1/1         Running    0         27d
posts-7785bcf45-9tfj4                  1/1         Running    0         6d
posts-7785bcf45-bsn8g                  1/1         Running    0         6d
posts-7785bcf45-w5xzs                  1/1         Running    0         6d
posts-7785bcf45-wtbv8                  1/1         Running    0         6d
redis-846b8c56fb-bm5z9                 1/1         Running    0         27d
sccs-84cc988f57-hp2z2                  1/1         Running    0         27d
```

To place load against the application, you'll be using Apache JMeter. I've created both a Kubernetes deployment of JMeter, as well as the config file containing the specifications for our load test. The first step in getting this running is to upload the config file, which you'll do with the creation of a Kubernetes config map. Execute the following command:

```
kubectl create configmap jmeter-config \
  --from-file=jmeter_run.jmx=loadTesting/ConnectionsPostsLoad.jmx
```

When you want to run the load tests, you can now simply create the JMeter deployment; to stop the load test, you'll delete the deployment. Let's try that now. Execute the following command:

```
kubectl create -f loadTesting/jmeter-deployment.yaml
```

To see the JMeter output, stream the logs for the JMeter pod with a command such as the following (inserting the name of your JMeter pod):

```
kubectl logs -f <name of your jmeter pod>
```

You'll see log output such as the following:

```
$ kubectl logs -f jmeter-deployment-7d747c985-kjxct
START Running Jmeter on Mon Feb 18 19:42:17 UTC 2019
JVM_ARGS=-Xmn506m -Xms2024m -Xmx2024m
jmeter args=-n -t /etc/jmeter/jmeter_run.jmx
Feb 18, 2019 7:42:19 PM java.util.prefs.FileSystemPreferences$1 run
INFO: Created user preferences directory.
Creating summariser <summary>
Created the tree successfully using /etc/jmeter/jmeter_run.jmx
Starting the test @ Mon Feb 18 19:42:19 UTC 2019 (1550518939413)
Waiting for possible Shutdown/StopTestNow/Heapdump message on port 4445
summary +    530 in 00:00:30 =   17.7/s Err:     0 (0.00%) Active: 328
```

```
summary  =    612 in 00:00:40 =  15.3/s Err:    0 (0.00%)
summary  +   1027 in 00:00:30 =  34.3/s Err:    0 (0.00%) Active: 576
summary  =   1639 in 00:01:10 =  23.4/s Err:    0 (0.00%)
summary  +   1521 in 00:00:30 =  50.7/s Err:    0 (0.00%) Active: 823
summary  =   3160 in 00:01:40 =  31.6/s Err:    0 (0.00%)
summary  +   2014 in 00:00:30 =  66.6/s Err:    0 (0.00%) Active: 1073
summary  =   5174 in 00:02:10 =  39.7/s Err:    0 (0.00%)
summary  +   2512 in 00:00:30 =  84.4/s Err:    0 (0.00%) Active: 1319
summary  =   7686 in 00:02:40 =  48.0/s Err:    0 (0.00%)
summary  +   2939 in 00:00:30 =  98.0/s Err:    0 (0.00%) Active: 1500
summary  =  10625 in 00:03:10 =  55.9/s Err:    0 (0.00%)
```

This shows that the Connections' Posts app was serving close to 100 requests per second after the load reached full capacity (I've set up the tests to ramp slowly) with 0.0% error (you'll be watching that error number as you progress). To stop the load test, execute the following command:

```
kubectl delete deploy jmeter-deployment
```

Now that you've established your deployment and verified that load testing is functioning properly, let's begin our experiments.

You'll be simulating network outages between the Posts service and the MySQL service. In the real world, such network outages can be caused by hardware failures (the loss of a physical switch, for example) or by a configuration error (the incorrect modification of a firewall rule, for example). To create the same effect here, you'll be changing the routing rules in the MySQL service to either disallow or, later when you fix the network, allow for requests from specific instances of the Posts service.

Figure 9.5 shows the five instances of the Connections' Posts service, the four instances of the Posts service, and the single instance of the MySQL service that you've deployed. The lines between each of the instances represent the different ways that these services can communicate. Notice that each Posts service is annotated with an IP address and that the MySQL service is annotated with a pod name. To disallow traffic to flow on one of those connections, you'll create a routing rule in the MySQL instance that rejects traffic from a specific IP address. To do this, you'll run a `route` command in the MySQL container; and this is done with a `kubectl exec` command. To break the network connection between the Posts service running at IP address 10.36.1.13 and the Posts instance running in the pod named mysql-57bdb878f5-dhlck, you'll execute the following command:

```
kubectl exec mysql-57bdb878f5-dhlck -- route add -host 10.36.1.13 reject
```

This is indicated in figure 9.5 with the X through the connectivity line. When the Posts service running at IP address 10.36.1.13 tries to connect to the MySQL service, it will time out. That timeout will propagate up to the Connections' Posts service, and the result will be a retry. If you're lucky, that retry will reach a different Posts instance and will be able to access the database, and the Connections' Posts request will succeed.

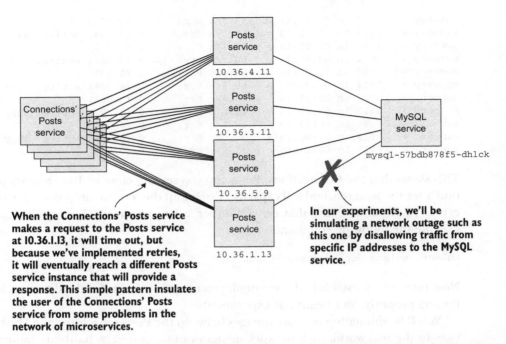

When the Connections' Posts service makes a request to the Posts service at 10.36.1.13, it will time out, but because we've implemented retries, it will eventually reach a different Posts service instance that will provide a response. This simple pattern insulates the user of the Connections' Posts service from some problems in the network of microservices.

In our experiments, we'll be simulating a network outage such as this one by disallowing traffic from specific IP addresses to the MySQL service.

Figure 9.5   A deployment containing five instances of the Connections' Posts service and four of the Posts service results in 20 ways that an instance of the former may connect to an instance of the latter. There are four connections between instances of the Posts service and the single instance of the MySQL service. Retries are an effective way of finding a healthy path through the network of microservices.

Reestablishing the connection is done with a similar `kubectl exec` command that removes the reject-routing rule from the container running the MySQL service:

```
kubectl exec mysql-57bdb878f5-dhlck -- route delete -host 10.36.1.13 reject
```

With those mechanics established, let's now run two experiments:

1   Completely disconnect, via the `route` commands shown previously, all instances of Posts from the MySQL service, with the *retry logic enabled.* This is done by setting the `CONNECTIONPOSTCONTROLLER_IMPLEMENTRETRIES` env variable in the deployment manifest for the Connections' Posts app to `true`.

2   Completely disconnect, via the `route` commands shown previously, all instances of Posts from the MySQL service, with the *retry logic disabled.* This is done by setting the `CONNECTIONPOSTCONTROLLER_IMPLEMENTRETRIES` env variable in the deployment manifest for the Connections' Posts app to `false`. When the attempted connections to the Posts service time out, the Connections' Posts service will return with an error status and no result.

To save you the trouble of executing the preceding `kubectl exec` command four times by hand, I've provided you a script, `alternetwork-db.sh`. You'll need to edit that script, however, to reflect your MySQL pod name and the IP addresses of your Posts instances. You can get the name of your MySQL service with the usual `kubectl` command:

```
kubectl get pods
```

And to get the IP addresses for the Posts instances, use this:

```
kubectl get pods -l app=posts -o wide
```

Now you can deny connections from all Posts instances to the MySQL instance by running this command:

```
./alternetwork-db.sh add
```

The following is log output from one of the instances of the Connections' Posts service, showing that it went from serving traffic to only performing retries:

```
2019-02-18 04:05:55.986  ... connections = 2,3
2019-02-18 04:05:55.989  ... getting posts for user network cdavisafc
2019-02-18 04:05:55.995  ... connections = 2,3
2019-02-18 04:05:56.055  ... getting posts for user network cdavisafc
2019-02-18 04:05:56.056  ... getting posts for user network cdavisafc
2019-02-18 04:05:56.059  ... On (0) request to unhealthy posts service  I/O
➥ error on GET request for "http://posts-svc/posts": Connect to posts-
➥ svc:80 [posts-svc/10.19.252.1] failed: connect timed out; nested
➥ exception is org.apache.http.conn.ConnectTimeoutException: Connect to
➥ posts-svc:80 [posts-svc/10.19.252.1] failed: connect timed out
2019-02-18 04:05:56.060  ... connections = 2,3
2019-02-18 04:05:56.060  ... connections = 2,3
2019-02-18 04:05:56.070  ... getting posts for user network cdavisafc
2019-02-18 04:05:56.074  ... connections = 2,3
2019-02-18 04:05:56.092  ... On (1) request to unhealthy posts service  I/O
➥ error on GET request for "http://posts-svc/posts": Connect to posts-
➥ svc:80 [posts-svc/10.19.252.1] failed: connect timed out; nested
➥ exception is org.apache.http.conn.ConnectTimeoutException: Connect to
➥ posts-svc:80 [posts-svc/10.19.252.1] failed: connect timed out
2019-02-18 04:05:56.093  ... On (2) request to unhealthy posts service  I/O
➥ error on GET request for "http://posts-svc/posts": Connect to posts-
➥ svc:80 [posts-svc/10.19.252.1] failed: connect timed out; nested
➥ exception is org.apache.http.conn.ConnectTimeoutException: Connect to
➥ posts-svc:80 [posts-svc/10.19.252.1] failed: connect timed out
2019-02-18 04:05:56.229  ... On (0) request to unhealthy posts service  I/O
➥ error on GET request for "http://posts-svc/posts": Connect to posts-
➥ svc:80 [posts-svc/10.19.252.1] failed: connect timed out; nested
➥ exception is org.apache.http.conn.ConnectTimeoutException: Connect to
➥ posts-svc:80 [posts-svc/10.19.252.1] failed: connect timed out
2019-02-18 04:05:56.232  ... On (0) request to unhealthy posts service  I/O
➥ error on GET request for "http://posts-svc/posts": Connect to posts-
➥ svc:80 [posts-svc/10.19.252.1] failed: connect timed out; nested
➥ exception is org.apache.http.conn.ConnectTimeoutException: Connect to
➥ posts-svc:80 [posts-svc/10.19.252.1] failed: connect timed out
2019-02-18 04:05:56.310  ... On (0) request to unhealthy posts service  I/O
```

```
⇒ error on GET request for "http://posts-svc/posts": Connect to posts-
⇒ svc:80 [posts-svc/10.19.252.1] failed: connect timed out; nested
⇒ exception is org.apache.http.conn.ConnectTimeoutException: Connect to
⇒ posts-svc:80 [posts-svc/10.19.252.1] failed: connect timed out
2019-02-18 04:05:56.343  ... On (6) request to unhealthy posts service  I/O
⇒ error on GET request for "http://posts-svc/posts": Connect to posts-
⇒ svc:80 [posts-svc/10.19.252.1] failed: connect timed out; nested
⇒ exception is org.apache.http.conn.ConnectTimeoutException: Connect to
⇒ posts-svc:80 [posts-svc/10.19.252.1] failed: connect timed out
```

The following shows the JMeter output from this experiment, annotated with three points in time. When the trial begins, the Connections' Posts app is returning results with 0.0% error. Then at time marker 1, when you run the ./alternetwork-db.sh add command, you can see that quickly, the error rate goes to 100%. The Connections' Posts service never returns, JMeter times out on the request (and counts the attempt as an error), yet the Connections' Posts apps continue retrying the Posts service indefinitely.

```
START Running Jmeter on Mon Feb 18 20:08:18 UTC 2019
JVM_ARGS=-Xmn402m -Xms1608m -Xmx1608m
jmeter args=-n -t /etc/jmeter/jmeter_run.jmx
Feb 18, 2019 8:08:20 PM java.util.prefs.FileSystemPreferences$1 run
INFO: Created user preferences directory.
Creating summariser <summary>
Created the tree successfully using /etc/jmeter/jmeter_run.jmx
Starting the test @ Mon Feb 18 20:08:21 UTC 2019 (1550520501121)
Waiting for possible Shutdown/StopTestNow/Heapdump message on port 4445
summary +      67 in 00:00:08 =    8.2/s Err:      0 (0.00%) Active: 67
summary +     501 in 00:00:30 =   16.7/s Err:      0 (0.00%) Active: 314
summary =     568 in 00:00:38 =   14.9/s Err:      0 (0.00%)
summary +     999 in 00:00:30 =   33.3/s Err:      0 (0.00%) Active: 562
summary =    1567 in 00:01:08 =   23.0/s Err:      0 (0.00%)
summary +    1493 in 00:00:30 =   49.8/s Err:      0 (0.00%) Active: 810
summary =    3060 in 00:01:38 =   31.2/s Err:      0 (0.00%)
summary +    1992 in 00:00:30 =   66.4/s Err:      0 (0.00%) Active: 1059
summary =    5052 in 00:02:08 =   39.4/s Err:      0 (0.00%)
summary +    2488 in 00:00:30 =   82.9/s Err:      0 (0.00%) Active: 1307
summary =    7540 in 00:02:38 =   47.7/s Err:      0 (0.00%)
summary +    2929 in 00:00:30 =   97.7/s Err:      0 (0.00%) Active: 1500
summary =   10469 in 00:03:08 =   55.7/s Err:      0 (0.00%)
summary +    2997 in 00:00:30 =   99.9/s Err:      0 (0.00%) Active: 1500
summary =   13466 in 00:03:38 =   61.7/s Err:      0 (0.00%)

<time marker 1 - I have broken the network between Posts and MySQL>

summary +    2515 in 00:00:30 =   83.8/s Err:   2239 (89.03%) Active: 1500
summary =   15981 in 00:04:08 =   64.4/s Err:   2239 (14.01%)
summary +    3000 in 00:00:30 =  100.0/s Err:   3000 (100.00%) Active: 1500
summary =   18981 in 00:04:38 =   68.2/s Err:   5239 (27.60%)
summary +    2961 in 00:00:30 =   98.7/s Err:   2961 (100.00%) Active: 1500
summary =   21942 in 00:05:08 =   71.2/s Err:   8200 (37.37%)
summary +    2970 in 00:00:30 =   99.0/s Err:   2970 (100.00%) Active: 1500
summary =   24912 in 00:05:38 =   73.7/s Err:  11170 (44.84%)
summary +    3007 in 00:00:30 =  100.1/s Err:   3007 (100.00%) Active: 1500
```

```
summary =   27919 in 00:06:08 =   75.8/s Err: 14177 (50.78%)
summary +    2968 in 00:00:30 =   99.0/s Err:  2968 (100.00%) Active: 1500
summary =   30887 in 00:06:38 =   77.6/s Err: 17145 (55.51%)

<time marker 2 - I have repaired the network between Posts and MySQL>

summary +    3007 in 00:00:30 =  100.2/s Err:  3007 (100.00%) Active: 1500
summary =   33894 in 00:07:08 =   79.2/s Err: 20152 (59.46%)
summary +    2995 in 00:00:30 =   99.8/s Err:  2995 (100.00%) Active: 1500
summary =   36889 in 00:07:38 =   80.5/s Err: 23147 (62.75%)
summary +    2997 in 00:00:30 =   99.9/s Err:  2997 (100.00%) Active: 1500
summary =   39886 in 00:08:08 =   81.7/s Err: 26144 (65.55%)
summary +    3000 in 00:00:30 =   99.9/s Err:  3000 (100.00%) Active: 1500
summary =   42886 in 00:08:38 =   82.8/s Err: 29144 (67.96%)

<another 6 minutes of 100% error!!>

summary +    3011 in 00:00:30 =  100.4/s Err:  3011 (100.00%) Active: 1500
summary =   78913 in 00:14:38 =   89.9/s Err: 65171 (82.59%)
summary +    2982 in 00:00:30 =   99.4/s Err:  2982 (100.00%) Active: 1500
summary =   81895 in 00:15:08 =   90.2/s Err: 68153 (83.22%)
summary +    3057 in 00:00:30 =  101.9/s Err:  2999 (98.10%) Active: 1500
summary =   84952 in 00:15:38 =   90.6/s Err: 71152 (83.76%)
summary +    3054 in 00:00:30 =  101.8/s Err:  2390 (78.26%) Active: 1500
summary =   88006 in 00:16:08 =   90.9/s Err: 73542 (83.56%)
summary +    2982 in 00:00:30 =   99.3/s Err:  2442 (81.89%) Active: 1500
summary =   90988 in 00:16:38 =   91.2/s Err: 75984 (83.51%)
summary +    3025 in 00:00:30 =  101.0/s Err:  2418 (79.93%) Active: 1500
summary =   94013 in 00:17:08 =   91.4/s Err: 78402 (83.39%)
summary +    2991 in 00:00:30 =   99.7/s Err:  2374 (79.37%) Active: 1500
summary =   97004 in 00:17:38 =   91.7/s Err: 80776 (83.27%)
summary +    3106 in 00:00:30 =  103.5/s Err:  2253 (72.54%) Active: 1500
summary =  100110 in 00:18:08 =   92.0/s Err: 83029 (82.94%)
summary +    3017 in 00:00:30 =  100.6/s Err:  1825 (60.49%) Active: 1500
summary =  103127 in 00:18:38 =   92.2/s Err: 84854 (82.28%)
summary +    2997 in 00:00:30 =   99.9/s Err:  1839 (61.36%) Active: 1500
summary =  106124 in 00:19:08 =   92.4/s Err: 86693 (81.69%)
summary +    2987 in 00:00:30 =   99.5/s Err:  1787 (59.83%) Active: 1500
summary =  109111 in 00:19:38 =   92.6/s Err: 88480 (81.09%)
summary +    3036 in 00:00:30 =  101.3/s Err:  1793 (59.06%) Active: 1500
summary =  112147 in 00:20:08 =   92.8/s Err: 90273 (80.50%)
summary +    2985 in 00:00:30 =   99.5/s Err:  1795 (60.13%) Active: 1500
summary =  115132 in 00:20:38 =   93.0/s Err: 92068 (79.97%)
summary +    2988 in 00:00:30 =   99.6/s Err:  1786 (59.77%) Active: 1500
summary =  118120 in 00:21:08 =   93.1/s Err: 93854 (79.46%)
summary +    3009 in 00:00:30 =  100.1/s Err:  1859 (61.78%) Active: 1500
summary =  121129 in 00:21:38 =   93.3/s Err: 95713 (79.02%)
summary +    3021 in 00:00:30 =  100.9/s Err:  1829 (60.54%) Active: 1500
summary =  124150 in 00:22:08 =   93.5/s Err: 97542 (78.57%)
summary +    3001 in 00:00:30 =  100.1/s Err:  1802 (60.05%) Active: 1500
summary =  127151 in 00:22:38 =   93.6/s Err: 99344 (78.13%)
summary +    3121 in 00:00:30 =  104.0/s Err:  1308 (41.91%) Active: 1500
summary =  130272 in 00:23:08 =   93.8/s Err: 100652 (77.26%)
summary +    3096 in 00:00:30 =  103.1/s Err:  1036 (33.46%) Active: 1500
summary =  133368 in 00:23:38 =   94.0/s Err: 101688 (76.25%)
```

```
summary +    2976 in 00:00:30 =   99.3/s Err:   596 (20.03%) Active: 1500
summary = 136344 in 00:24:08 =   94.2/s Err: 102284 (75.02%)
summary +    3005 in 00:00:30 =  100.1/s Err:   583 (19.40%) Active: 1500
summary = 139349 in 00:24:38 =   94.3/s Err: 102867 (73.82%)
summary +    3002 in 00:00:30 =  100.1/s Err:   634 (21.12%) Active: 1500
summary = 142351 in 00:25:08 =   94.4/s Err: 103501 (72.71%)
summary +    2999 in 00:00:30 =  100.0/s Err:   596 (19.87%) Active: 1500
summary = 145350 in 00:25:38 =   94.5/s Err: 104097 (71.62%)
summary +    3013 in 00:00:30 =  100.4/s Err:   580 (19.25%) Active: 1500
summary = 148363 in 00:26:08 =   94.6/s Err: 104677 (70.55%)
summary +    3016 in 00:00:30 =  100.5/s Err:   579 (19.20%) Active: 1500
summary = 151379 in 00:26:38 =   94.7/s Err: 105256 (69.53%)
summary +    2999 in 00:00:30 =  100.0/s Err:   600 (20.01%) Active: 1500
summary = 154378 in 00:27:08 =   94.8/s Err: 105856 (68.57%)
summary +    2999 in 00:00:30 =  100.0/s Err:   571 (19.04%) Active: 1500
summary = 157377 in 00:27:38 =   94.9/s Err: 106427 (67.63%)
summary +    2988 in 00:00:30 =   99.6/s Err:   600 (20.08%) Active: 1500
summary = 160365 in 00:28:08 =   95.0/s Err: 107027 (66.74%)
summary +    3107 in 00:00:30 =  103.6/s Err:    58 (1.87%) Active: 1500
summary = 163472 in 00:28:38 =   95.1/s Err: 107085 (65.51%)
summary +    2995 in 00:00:30 =   99.8/s Err:     0 (0.00%) Active: 1500
summary = 166467 in 00:29:08 =   95.2/s Err: 107085 (64.33%)
summary +    3007 in 00:00:30 =  100.2/s Err:     0 (0.00%) Active: 1500
summary = 169474 in 00:29:38 =   95.3/s Err: 107085 (63.19%)
```

At time marker 2 in the preceding output, after 3 minutes of having the MySQL service disconnected, you repair the network by running the following command:

```
./alternetwork-db.sh delete
```

What you're looking for now is how long it will take before the system returns to a steady state—one where the Connections' Posts service is experiencing 0.0% error.

As you can see, the output is rather lengthy. Approximately 9 minutes after the network was restored, you see the first signs of recovery. Then it takes another 12–13 minutes before the system is fully recovered. *This is a retry storm.* The system was so overwhelmed from the queued retries that it took well over a quarter of an hour to recover. Imagine Amazon unable to complete sales transactions for that period of time. That would be an expensive outage!

And as bad as that seems, what I've demonstrated here remains a small example. In a system with hundreds of connected service instances, a short network blip can result in hours-long outages that can go so far as to even crash application instances. Remember the story that started this book? That Amazon outage was ultimately caused by a retry storm that occurred after a short network outage.

**WARNING**    A retry storm can have catastrophic effects on a complex, distributed system.

Before moving on to covering mitigations of retry storms, I'd like you to run the same test but with retries turned off. This time, when the attempt to access the Posts service times out, the Connections' Posts service will return an error with no result, but it will return. To turn off retries, change the value of the env variable CONNECTIONPOSTCONTROLLER_IMPLEMENTRETRIES in the cookbook-deployment-kubernetes-connectionposts.yaml file to `false` and update the deployment with the following command:

```
kubectl apply -f cookbook-deployment-kubernetes-connectionposts.yaml
```

You can then create the JMeter pod as you've previously done with the `kubectl create` command (if you hadn't already deleted the prior deployment, please do so first with the `kubectl delete deploy` command). The following is the output of JMeter, with two time markers inserted:

```
START Running Jmeter on Mon Feb 18 20:58:54 UTC 2019
JVM_ARGS=-Xmn528m -Xms2112m -Xmx2112m
jmeter args=-n -t /etc/jmeter/jmeter_run.jmx
Feb 18, 2019 8:58:56 PM java.util.prefs.FileSystemPreferences$1 run
INFO: Created user preferences directory.
Creating summariser <summary>
Created the tree successfully using /etc/jmeter/jmeter_run.jmx
Starting the test @ Mon Feb 18 20:58:56 UTC 2019 (1550523536966)
Waiting for possible Shutdown/StopTestNow/Heapdump message on port 4445
summary +     18 in 00:00:02 =    7.9/s Err:     0 (0.00%) Active: 18
summary +    401 in 00:00:30 =   13.4/s Err:     0 (0.00%) Active: 263
summary =    419 in 00:00:32 =   13.0/s Err:     0 (0.00%)
summary +    890 in 00:00:30 =   29.7/s Err:     0 (0.00%) Active: 506
summary =   1309 in 00:01:02 =   21.0/s Err:     0 (0.00%)
summary +   1378 in 00:00:30 =   46.0/s Err:     0 (0.00%) Active: 752
summary =   2687 in 00:01:32 =   29.1/s Err:     0 (0.00%)
summary +   1877 in 00:00:30 =   62.6/s Err:     0 (0.00%) Active: 1000
summary =   4564 in 00:02:02 =   37.3/s Err:     0 (0.00%)
summary +   2369 in 00:00:30 =   79.0/s Err:     0 (0.00%) Active: 1249
summary =   6933 in 00:02:32 =   45.5/s Err:     0 (0.00%)
summary +   2869 in 00:00:30 =   95.6/s Err:     0 (0.00%) Active: 1498
summary =   9802 in 00:03:02 =   53.8/s Err:     0 (0.00%)
summary +   3004 in 00:00:30 =  100.2/s Err:     0 (0.00%) Active: 1500
summary =  12806 in 00:03:32 =   60.3/s Err:     0 (0.00%)
summary +   2998 in 00:00:30 =   99.9/s Err:     0 (0.00%) Active: 1500
summary =  15804 in 00:04:02 =   65.2/s Err:     0 (0.00%)
summary +   3001 in 00:00:30 =  100.0/s Err:     0 (0.00%) Active: 1500
summary =  18805 in 00:04:32 =   69.1/s Err:     0 (0.00%)

<time marker 1 - I have broken the network between Posts and MySQL>

summary +   2951 in 00:00:30 =   98.4/s Err:  2662 (90.21%) Active: 1500
summary =  21756 in 00:05:02 =   72.0/s Err:  2662 (12.24%)
summary +   2999 in 00:00:30 =  100.0/s Err:  2999 (100.00%) Active: 1500
summary =  24755 in 00:05:32 =   74.5/s Err:  5661 (22.87%)
summary +   3001 in 00:00:30 =  100.0/s Err:  3001 (100.00%) Active: 1500
summary =  27756 in 00:06:02 =   76.6/s Err:  8662 (31.21%)
summary +   3000 in 00:00:30 =  100.0/s Err:  3000 (100.00%) Active: 1500
summary =  30756 in 00:06:32 =   78.4/s Err: 11662 (37.92%)
summary +   3001 in 00:00:30 =  100.0/s Err:  3001 (100.00%) Active: 1500
```

```
summary =  33757 in 00:07:02 =   80.0/s Err: 14663 (43.44%)
summary +   3000 in 00:00:30 =  100.0/s Err:  3000 (100.00%) Active: 1500
summary =  36757 in 00:07:32 =   81.3/s Err: 17663 (48.05%)
summary +   2999 in 00:00:30 =  100.0/s Err:  2999 (100.00%) Active: 1500
summary =  39756 in 00:08:02 =   82.4/s Err: 20662 (51.97%)

<time marker 2 - I have repaired the network between Posts and MySQL>

summary +   3051 in 00:00:30 =  101.7/s Err:  1473 (48.28%) Active: 1500
summary =  42807 in 00:08:32 =   83.6/s Err: 22135 (51.71%)
summary +   2999 in 00:00:30 =  100.0/s Err:     0 (0.00%) Active: 1500
summary =  45806 in 00:09:02 =   84.5/s Err: 22135 (48.32%)
```

As you can see, while the network is disrupted, the Connections' Posts service reports 100% error. But most important, as soon as the network is reestablished, at time marker 2, the system immediately returns to a stable state with 0.0% error. There are no queued retries overwhelming the system.

> **NOTE**  When employing retries, the system took 15 minutes to recover from a 3-minute network disruption. When *not* employing retries, the recovery from a 3-minute network disruption was immediate.

So you're faced with a paradox. Retries can cause catastrophic effects, yet they can also provide great benefits, particularly when failed calls are only intermittent. Is there a way to take advantage of the benefits of retries without the risk of a retry storm wreaking havoc on the system? Indeed there is. There are several. In this chapter, I'll talk about being smarter about the way we do retries—about being a kinder client. The next chapter covers putting up protections in front of a service to keep less-kind clients from causing problems in the system.

### 9.1.6   *Avoiding retry storms: Kind clients*

Despite the dramatically negative consequences that you saw with retries in the previous section, their value remains obvious. For intermittent connectivity issues in particular, retries will often work, thereby snuffing an error that could otherwise have propagated widely through the distributed system that makes up our cloud-native software. The trick then is to balance the tension between the potential negative effects and the positive ones.

The first observation we can make is that for the issues that present themselves only sporadically and for limited durations, it rarely takes more than one or two repeat attempts to have a successful exchange. Therefore, the first control you could put in place on our retry loop is to limit the total number of such retry attempts. So, for example, instead of having a while loop that runs indefinitely, you could implement a counter and stop the retries when you've hit a threshold.

But then, what happens when a connection is only momentarily unavailable, but all retry attempts have been exhausted before connectivity is reestablished? You've just lost out on the benefits of retries because you were overzealous on repeating your requests. Introducing a delay between retry attempts lends a bit of balance here.

### 9.1.7 *Let's see this in action: being a kinder client*

Let's apply two controls, limiting the number of retry attempts and slowing the rate of retries, to our implementation and see how this changes the behavior of our software, particularly while under load.

I won't repeat all of the setup and build instructions again; my presentation here is just an extension to that of the preceding section. To access the new implementation, check out the following tag from the Git repo:

```
git checkout requestretries/0.0.3
```

In the next listing, you'll see that in the place where you formerly had the naïve retry implementation, you now have the following code.

> **Listing 9.2  Excerpt from ConnectionsPostsController.java**

```java
try {
    postSummaries = postsServiceClient.getPosts(ids, restTemplate);
    response.setStatus(200);
    return postSummaries;
} catch (HttpServerErrorException e) {
    logger.info(utils.ipTag() + "Call to Posts service returned 500");
    response.setStatus(500);
    return null;
} catch (ResourceAccessException e) {
    logger.info(utils.ipTag() + "Call to Posts service timed out");
    response.setStatus(500);
    return null;
} catch (Exception e) {
    logger.info(utils.ipTag() + "Unexpected Exception: Exception Class "
        + e.getClass() + e.getMessage());
    response.setStatus(500);
    return null;
}
```

Notice that the only difference in the various catch blocks is the message that's logged, so logically, the implementation is now as follows:

```java
try {
    postSummaries = postsServiceClient.getPosts(ids, restTemplate);
    response.setStatus(200);
    return postSummaries;
} catch (Exception e) {
    logger.info(utils.ipTag() + e.getMessage());
    response.setStatus(500);
    return null;
}
```

You'll also notice that calling the Posts service is now facilitated through a new class, PostsServiceClient, which is a client for the Posts service. Creating this class provides a surface area against which the Spring Retry annotations can be applied.

With the preceding code, if the call to the Posts service is successful, you return the set of posts obtained through the `postsServiceClient.getPosts` invocation. Otherwise, set HTTP status to 500 (an error) and return nothing. Let's have a look at the implementation of this Posts service client.

**Listing 9.3    Method from PostsServiceClient.java**

```java
@Retryable( value = ResourceAccessException.class,
            maxAttempts = 3,
            backoff = @Backoff(delay = 500))
public ArrayList<PostSummary> getPosts(String ids,
    RestTemplate restTemplate) throws Exception {

    ArrayList<PostSummary> postSummaries = new ArrayList<PostSummary>();
    String secretQueryParam = "&secret=" + utils.getPostsSecret();
    logger.info("Trying getPosts: " + postsUrl + ids + secretQueryParam);

    ResponseEntity<ConnectionsPostsController.PostResult[]> respPosts
        = restTemplate.getForEntity(postsUrl + ids + secretQueryParam,
                        ConnectionsPostsController.PostResult[].class);
    if (respPosts.getStatusCode().is5xxServerError()) {
        throw new HttpServerErrorException(respPosts.getStatusCode(),
                                "Exception thrown in obtaining Posts");
    } else {
        ConnectionsPostsController.PostResult[] posts
            = respPosts.getBody();
        for (int i = 0; i < posts.length; i++)
            postSummaries.add(
                new PostSummary(
                    getUsersname(posts[i].getUserId(),restTemplate),
                            posts[i].getTitle(), posts[i].getDate())));
        return postSummaries;
    }
}
```

This code uses a project that's part of the Spring Framework, Spring Retries (https://github.com/spring-projects/spring-retry). I find it interesting that the retry patterns now encapsulated in this project were originally embedded within the Spring Batch project. Having been extracted into its own project allows it to be used in many scenarios; as a case in point, the first line of the README for the Spring Retry project says, "It is used in Spring Batch, Spring Integration, Spring for Apache Hadoop (amongst others)." Retries are so ubiquitous in cloud-native software that it makes sense to have a library so that you can easily use them in many use cases.

I want to draw your attention to two parts of this code. First, notice that the `@Retryable` annotation includes attributes that reflect exactly the controls I talked about previously: limiting the number of retries, and giving some time between retry attempts (you'll wait half a second between attempts). Notice also that you can specify that retries should be attempted for only certain exceptions—in this case, an access (connect or read timeout) exception.

The other thing that you'll notice in studying the code is that you're no longer responsible for the looping logic. This code simply implements the happy path. It makes the HTTP request to Posts, and if that returns an error HTTP status code, it passes that error up. Otherwise, it processes the response body and returns those values. There's no try/catch, no loop. If, however, this code were to generate a `ResourceAccessException`, which can be thrown by the `restTemplate`, the Spring Retry implementation would catch it, and based on the annotation values, perhaps execute the method again. On a side note, Spring Retry achieves this via aspects; hence, the inclusion of the AOP (Aspect-Oriented Programming) dependency along with the Spring Retry one.

---

**Listing 9.4   Excerpt from pom.xml for the Connections' Posts service**

```
<dependency>
    <groupId>org.springframework.boot</groupId>
    <artifactId>spring-boot-starter-aop</artifactId>
</dependency>
<dependency>
    <groupId>org.springframework.retry</groupId>
    <artifactId>spring-retry</artifactId>
    <version>1.2.2.RELEASE</version>
</dependency>
```

Let's see what this implementation does in our load scenario from the previous section. If you want to follow along, you'll, of course, have to redeploy the software. If you ran the examples in the previous section, you can run the `deployApps.sh` bash script. You'll then place exactly the same load against this deployment as you did for the previous. The following is the output (as can be seen in the logs for the JMeter pod), once again with two time markers inserted:

```
START Running Jmeter on Mon Feb 18 21:58:55 UTC 2019
JVM_ARGS=-Xmn502m -Xms2008m -Xmx2008m
jmeter args=-n -t /etc/jmeter/jmeter_run.jmx -l resultsconnectionsposts
Feb 18, 2019 9:58:57 PM java.util.prefs.FileSystemPreferences$1 run
INFO: Created user preferences directory.
Creating summariser <summary>
Created the tree successfully using /etc/jmeter/jmeter_run.jmx
Starting the test @ Mon Feb 18 21:58:57 UTC 2019 (1550527137576)
Waiting for possible Shutdown/StopTestNow/Heapdump message on port 4445
summary +     14 in 00:00:02 =    8.1/s Err:      0 (0.00%) Active: 14
summary +    394 in 00:00:30 =   13.2/s Err:      0 (0.00%) Active: 259
summary =    408 in 00:00:32 =   12.9/s Err:      0 (0.00%)
summary +    887 in 00:00:30 =   29.6/s Err:      0 (0.00%) Active: 508
summary =   1295 in 00:01:02 =   21.0/s Err:      0 (0.00%)
summary +   1388 in 00:00:30 =   46.3/s Err:      0 (0.00%) Active: 756
summary =   2683 in 00:01:32 =   29.3/s Err:      0 (0.00%)
summary +   1887 in 00:00:30 =   62.9/s Err:      0 (0.00%) Active: 1005
summary =   4570 in 00:02:02 =   37.6/s Err:      0 (0.00%)
summary +   2377 in 00:00:30 =   79.3/s Err:      0 (0.00%) Active: 1253
```

```
summary =    6947 in 00:02:32 =   45.8/s Err:     0 (0.00%)
summary +    2878 in 00:00:30 =   95.9/s Err:     0 (0.00%) Active: 1500
summary =    9825 in 00:03:02 =   54.1/s Err:     0 (0.00%)
summary +    2993 in 00:00:30 =   99.7/s Err:     0 (0.00%) Active: 1500
summary =   12818 in 00:03:32 =   60.6/s Err:     0 (0.00%)
summary +    3006 in 00:00:30 =  100.2/s Err:     0 (0.00%) Active: 1500
summary =   15824 in 00:04:02 =   65.5/s Err:     0 (0.00%)

<time marker 1 - I have broken the network between Posts and MySQL>

summary +    2645 in 00:00:30 =   88.2/s Err:  2354 (89.00%) Active: 1500
summary =   18469 in 00:04:32 =   68.0/s Err:  2354 (12.75%)
summary +    3002 in 00:00:30 =  100.0/s Err:  3002 (100.00%) Active: 1500
summary =   21471 in 00:05:02 =   71.2/s Err:  5356 (24.95%)
summary +    3000 in 00:00:30 =  100.0/s Err:  3000 (100.00%) Active: 1500
summary =   24471 in 00:05:32 =   73.8/s Err:  8356 (34.15%)
summary +    3006 in 00:00:30 =  100.2/s Err:  3006 (100.00%) Active: 1500
summary =   27477 in 00:06:02 =   76.0/s Err: 11362 (41.35%)
summary +    3015 in 00:00:30 =  100.5/s Err:  3015 (100.00%) Active: 1500
summary =   30492 in 00:06:32 =   77.9/s Err: 14377 (47.15%)
summary +    3051 in 00:00:30 =  101.7/s Err:  3051 (100.00%) Active: 1500
summary =   33543 in 00:07:02 =   79.6/s Err: 17428 (51.96%)

<time marker 2 - I have repaired the network between Posts and MySQL>

summary +    3002 in 00:00:30 =  100.0/s Err:  3002 (100.00%) Active: 1500
summary =   36545 in 00:07:32 =   80.9/s Err: 20430 (55.90%)
summary +    2942 in 00:00:30 =   98.1/s Err:  2942 (100.00%) Active: 1500
summary =   39487 in 00:08:02 =   82.0/s Err: 23372 (59.19%)
summary +    3323 in 00:00:30 =  110.8/s Err:   378 (11.38%) Active: 1500
summary =   42810 in 00:08:32 =   83.7/s Err: 23750 (55.48%)
summary +    3021 in 00:00:30 =  100.6/s Err:     2 (0.07%) Active: 1500
summary =   45831 in 00:09:02 =   84.6/s Err: 23752 (51.83%)
summary +    2998 in 00:00:30 =  100.0/s Err:     0 (0.00%) Active: 1500
summary =   48829 in 00:09:32 =   85.4/s Err: 23752 (48.64%)
summary +    3001 in 00:00:30 =  100.0/s Err:     0 (0.00%) Active: 1500
summary =   51830 in 00:10:02 =   86.1/s Err: 23752 (45.83%)
```

When you begin the test, you're seeing 0.0% errors coming from Connections' Posts. The calls to the Posts service, and all other processing, are all completing successfully. At time marker 1, you disconnect the Posts and MySQL services by using the same route commands in the MySQL containers via the following command:

```
./alternetwork-db.sh add
```

As you can see, the error quickly reaches 100% because the Connections' Posts service will return a server error if it doesn't receive a result from the Posts service, even while retries are implemented. But now look at what happens after time marker 2, when you reestablish the network by running this:

```
./alternetwork-db.sh delete
```

You see the first signs of recovery in only 1 minute and are fully recovered in less than 3. You avoided the retry storm, even in the most extreme conditions where the network was lost for minutes.

This might leave you wondering whether this implementation provides value in the more intermittent error scenarios. Let's simulate this by disconnecting only one of the Posts services from the network. You can do this by executing a single one of the kubectl commands from the alternetwork-db.sh script. For example:

```
kubectl exec mysql-57bdb878f5-dhlck -- route $1 -host 10.36.4.11 reject
```

What you've done is broken only a single connection from one instance of a Posts service to the MySQL service, exactly as shown in figure 9.5.

Looking at the JMeter log output, you can see that although the Posts service is having trouble because of the lack of connectivity to MySQL (starting at time marker 1), many of the resultant failed attempts from Connections' Posts are being washed completely away by the retries. You've disconnected only a single instance of the Posts service from MySQL. On average, 25% of the requests from Connections' Posts to Posts will fail. But as you can see in the following output, the overall error is far smaller—less than 1%. And when connectivity is restored at time marker 2, the error rate immediately returns to 0.0%:

```
START Running Jmeter on Mon Feb 18 22:16:50 UTC 2019
JVM_ARGS=-Xmn524m -Xms2096m -Xmx2096m
jmeter args=-n -t /etc/jmeter/jmeter_run.jmx -l resultsconnectionsposts
Feb 18, 2019 10:16:52 PM java.util.prefs.FileSystemPreferences$1 run
INFO: Created user preferences directory.
Creating summariser <summary>
Created the tree successfully using /etc/jmeter/jmeter_run.jmx
Starting the test @ Mon Feb 18 22:16:52 UTC 2019 (1550528212234)
Waiting for possible Shutdown/StopTestNow/Heapdump message on port 4445
summary +      58 in 00:00:07 =    8.2/s Err:     0 (0.00%) Active: 58
summary +     483 in 00:00:30 =   16.1/s Err:     0 (0.00%) Active: 304
summary =     541 in 00:00:37 =   14.6/s Err:     0 (0.00%)
summary +     982 in 00:00:30 =   32.7/s Err:     0 (0.00%) Active: 553
summary =    1523 in 00:01:07 =   22.7/s Err:     0 (0.00%)
summary +    1477 in 00:00:30 =   49.3/s Err:     0 (0.00%) Active: 802
summary =    3000 in 00:01:37 =   30.9/s Err:     0 (0.00%)
summary +    1974 in 00:00:30 =   65.8/s Err:     0 (0.00%) Active: 1049
summary =    4974 in 00:02:07 =   39.2/s Err:     0 (0.00%)
summary +    2473 in 00:00:30 =   82.4/s Err:     0 (0.00%) Active: 1298
summary =    7447 in 00:02:37 =   47.4/s Err:     0 (0.00%)
summary +    2920 in 00:00:30 =   97.4/s Err:     0 (0.00%) Active: 1500
summary =   10367 in 00:03:07 =   55.4/s Err:     0 (0.00%)

<time marker 1 - I have broken a single connection between Posts and MySQL>

summary +    2998 in 00:00:30 =   99.9/s Err:     3 (0.10%) Active: 1500
summary =   13365 in 00:03:37 =   61.6/s Err:     3 (0.02%)
summary +    2999 in 00:00:30 =  100.0/s Err:     0 (0.00%) Active: 1500
summary =   16364 in 00:04:07 =   66.3/s Err:     3 (0.02%)
summary +    2993 in 00:00:30 =   99.8/s Err:     1 (0.03%) Active: 1500
```

```
summary =  19357 in 00:04:37 =   69.9/s Err:    4 (0.02%)
summary +   3001 in 00:00:30 =  100.1/s Err:    1 (0.03%) Active: 1500
summary =  22358 in 00:05:07 =   72.8/s Err:    5 (0.02%)
summary +   2994 in 00:00:30 =   99.8/s Err:    1 (0.03%) Active: 1500
summary =  25352 in 00:05:37 =   75.2/s Err:    6 (0.02%)
summary +   3005 in 00:00:30 =  100.1/s Err:    2 (0.07%) Active: 1500
summary =  28357 in 00:06:07 =   77.3/s Err:    8 (0.03%)
summary +   3001 in 00:00:30 =  100.1/s Err:    1 (0.03%) Active: 1500
summary =  31358 in 00:06:37 =   79.0/s Err:    9 (0.03%)

<time marker 2 - I have repaired the connection between Posts and MySQL>

summary +   2999 in 00:00:30 =  100.0/s Err:    1 (0.03%) Active: 1500
summary =  34357 in 00:07:07 =   80.5/s Err:   10 (0.03%)
summary +   3000 in 00:00:30 =  100.0/s Err:    1 (0.03%) Active: 1500
summary =  37357 in 00:07:37 =   81.7/s Err:   11 (0.03%)
summary +   3009 in 00:00:30 =  100.3/s Err:    0 (0.00%) Active: 1500
summary =  40366 in 00:08:07 =   82.9/s Err:   11 (0.03%)
```

What you see here is that with only a few simple controls, limiting the number of retry attempts and taking some time between them, you can realize the benefits of retries while avoiding worsening conditions in an already degraded system.

### 9.1.8  *When not to retry*

You've just clearly seen the benefits of retries, and you should use them liberally in your software designs. Except when you shouldn't. There will be many nuanced reasons that you may want to avoid retries (using caching as an alternative may boost performance, for example), and I won't cover those here. But I'd like to spend a moment circling back to a topic I introduced at the start of this chapter: times that it's unsafe to perform retries (when you don't receive a response after clicking the Purchase button, for example).

I chose the word "safe" here quite intentionally because there's a formal definition of *safety* in HTTP that gets at precisely the point I want to make. Here are two definitions from the HTTP spec (www.w3.org/Protocols/rfc2616/rfc2616-sec9.html):

- A *safe* method is one that may be invoked *zero* or more times with the same effect. The method must not have any side effects.
- An *idempotent* method is one where invoking the method *one* or more times will have the same effect. Side effects are permitted in this case, but all repeated invocations must have the same side effect as the first.

What you're doing with retries is addressing the "or more" part of those statements. But which one of these statements applies to our pattern? In short, it's the former—*only safe methods should be retried*. When you make a request over the network, there's no guarantee that any of your requests will reach their intended recipient, so you may end up in a situation where *zero* of your attempts are successful. Therefore, as a general rule, only safe methods should be retried. If you wish to implement any failure handling around nonsafe methods, you must implement compensating behaviors such as Sagas.

Here's an important point: it's up to you, the developer, to know whether the invocations you're making are safe or not. Referring back to the HTTP specification, you see that the HTTP requests that are safe are GET, HEAD, OPTIONS, and TRACE. But Spring Retry doesn't have visibility into any of the HTTP requests you make from within `@Retryable` methods, so it's up to you to add that annotation only to methods that are safe. If you had a method that encapsulated a POST request that deducted $100 from your bank account, you'd be disappointed with retries. Apply retries only when it's safe to do so.

## 9.2　*Fallback logic*

*Design for failure.* This is a mantra for cloud-native software that I hope you've already been learning throughout reading this book. As a case in point, retrying a request when the first fails is a good design. But what do you do when your attempts at recovery are also unsuccessful? What happens when you retry several times and still get no response? What you've done in the preceding examples of this chapter is return an error, but you can do better.

One of the most fundamental patterns in designing for failure is to implement fallback methods—code that's executed when the main logic fails. Sure, sometimes when the software can't complete its task, the right thing is to return an error. But in this world of highly distributed, constantly changing software deployments with an abundance of failure scenarios, you need to build new muscle. You need to establish a habit of thinking about alternative results, even if less than ideal.

The example that has been running through this chapter provides an excellent opportunity to exercise that muscle, and extending the retry logic is the perfect place to do it. When designing fallback behaviors (and any of the resilience patterns described in this book), you need to think through the real-world scenario your software is addressing. In the part of the implementation that you'll extend, you're trying to get the list of blog posts for a set of users. Although some of those users may be rather prolific, perhaps posting several times a week or even more than once a day, the creation of new blog posts is something that still happens rather infrequently. If a user were to access their aggregated feed at a time when the MySQL database storing the posts were unavailable, it might be better to return a set of posts that may be missing only the newest entries instead of returning nothing at all. I can tell you personally, when I'm accessing an aggregated set of recipes to decide what to make for dinner this eve, I can still produce something pretty tasty even if I don't have the absolute latest recipe that Food52 has posted.

### 9.2.1　*Let's see this in action: Implementing fallback logic*

Let's look at this in practice. Check out the following tag from the repository:

```
git checkout requestretries/0.0.4
```

I won't repeat the optional build instructions here. Please see the earlier examples in this chapter (and book) if you want to change the code and do deployments yourself. As always, I've prebuilt everything and have made Docker images available in Docker Hub.

Before testing it, let's have a look at the implementation. For fallback in the case when the Posts service isn't providing a valid result, your Connections' Posts service will simply return the latest Posts that it has previously seen. To do this, you've added simple caching to the implementation. Recall that our Connections' Posts implementation already binds to a Redis key/value store, a database ideally suited for caching. So now when a call to Posts yields a result, the logic in Connections' Posts will store that result in Redis before returning it. That store sets you up to be able to then implement the fallback behavior when the Posts service is in a bad way. The upper part of figure 9.6 shows the flow that caches results when the Posts service is reachable and delivering results. The lower part of figure 9.6 shows the flow that reads results from the cache when Posts is experiencing trouble.

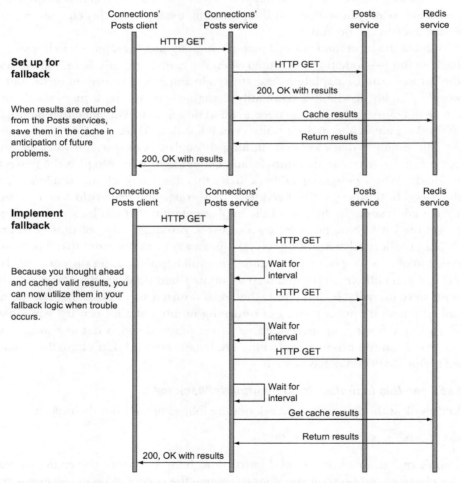

**Figure 9.6   Thinking ahead, you cache results when they're available, so that when you later experience trouble, you have those cached values to use as a part of your fallback logic.**

Adding the fallback implementation then is simple. With Spring Retry, you add a method to your service with the `@Recover` annotation, and Spring will invoke that method after all retry attempts have been exhausted. The method signature must match that of the method implementing the main logic, with the addition of an exception type as the first argument. The recover method will be called only under certain circumstances, as defined by the type of error.

**Listing 9.5  Method from PostsServiceClient.java**

```
@Recover
public ArrayList<PostSummary> returnCached(
                        ResourceAccessException e,
                        String ids, RestTemplate restTemplate)
                                            throws Exception {
  logger.info("Failed ... Posts service - returning cached results");

  PostResults postResults = postResultsRepository.findOne(ids);
  ObjectMapper objectMapper = new ObjectMapper();
  ArrayList<PostSummary> postSummaries;
  try {
    postSummaries = objectMapper.readValue(
                        postResults.getSummariesJson(),
                        new TypeReference<ArrayList<PostSummary>>() {});
  } catch (Exception ec) {
    logger.info("Exception on deserialization " + ec.getClass()
                + " message = " + ec.getMessage());
    return null;
  }
  return postSummaries;
}
```

Although it may seem obvious as you look at this simple example, I do want to draw your attention to the fact that in most cases your fallback behavior requires some setup. In this example, the preceding code isn't all that's required for fallback. The logic that caches results when they're successfully obtained is needed setup for this. Our `@Retryable` method is the place where you're thinking ahead to darker days.

**Listing 9.6  Method from PostsServiceClient.java**

```
@Retryable( value = ResourceAccessException.class,
            maxAttempts = 3, backoff = @Backoff(delay = 500))
public ArrayList<PostSummary> getPosts(String ids,
                                    RestTemplate restTemplate)
                                            throws Exception {

  ArrayList<PostSummary> postSummaries = new ArrayList<PostSummary>();

  String secretQueryParam = "&secret=" + utils.getPostsSecret();

  logger.info("Trying getPosts: " + postsUrl + ids + secretQueryParam);
```

```
ResponseEntity<ConnectionsPostsController.PostResult[]> respPosts
   = restTemplate.getForEntity(
       postsUrl + ids + secretQueryParam,
       ConnectionsPostsController.PostResult[].class);
if (respPosts.getStatusCode().is5xxServerError()) {
   throw new HttpServerErrorException(respPosts.getStatusCode(),
               "Exception thrown in obtaining Posts");
} else {
   ConnectionsPostsController.PostResult[] posts = respPosts.getBody();
   for (int i = 0; i < posts.length; i++)
      postSummaries.add(
         new PostSummary(getUsersname(posts[i].getUserId(), restTemplate),
         posts[i].getTitle(), posts[i].getDate())));
   // thinking ahead to darker days, cache the result
   ObjectMapper objectMapper = new ObjectMapper();
   String postSummariesJson =
             objectMapper.writeValueAsString(postSummaries);
   PostResults postResults = new PostResults(ids, postSummariesJson);
   postResultsRepository.save(postResults);
   return postSummaries;
}
}
```

Let's now have a look at the effect that adding fallback behavior has on the stability of our implementation. You're going to run the same load test that you've done previously. If you wish to follow along, please update your deployment by rerunning the application deployment script:

```
./deployApps.sh
```

You now run the load test with our usual command:

```
kubectl create -f loadTesting/jmeter-deployment.yaml
```

As always, after the load test has reached full capacity, you break the network between all instances of the Posts service and the MySQL service for 3 minutes (time marker 1) and then restore the network (time marker 2). Before you look at the results of the test run, let's look at the log output for one of the Connections' Posts services:

```
(the network is currently broken...)

... : [10.36.4.11:8080] getting posts for user network cdavisafc
... : Trying getPosts: http://posts-svc/posts?userIds=2,3&secret=newSecret
... : Failed to connect to or obtain results from Posts service - returning
      cached results
... : Failed to connect to or obtain results from Posts service - returning
      cached results
... : [10.36.4.11:8080] connections = 2,3
... : Trying getPosts: http://posts-svc/posts?userIds=2,3&secret=newSecret
... : Failed to connect to or obtain results from Posts service - returning
      cached results
```

```
(after restoring the network)

...  : Trying getPosts: http://posts-svc/posts?userIds=2,3&secret=newSecret
...  : [10.36.4.11:8080] getting posts for user network cdavisafc
...  : Trying getPosts: http://posts-svc/posts?userIds=2,3&secret=newSecret
...  : [10.36.4.11:8080] connections = 2,3
...  : Trying getPosts: http://posts-svc/posts?userIds=2,3&secret=newSecret
...  : [10.36.4.11:8080] getting posts for user network cdavisafc
...  : [10.36.4.11:8080] connections = 2,3
...  : Trying getPosts: http://posts-svc/posts?userIds=2,3&secret=newSecret
...  : [10.36.4.11:8080] getting posts for user network cdavisafc
...  : [10.36.4.11:8080] connections = 2,3
...  : Trying getPosts: http://posts-svc/posts?userIds=2,3&secret=newSecret
...  : Trying getPosts: http://posts-svc/posts?userIds=2,3&secret=newSecret
```

While the network is disrupted, Spring Retry first repeats the access attempt three times and then calls the @Recover method, returning cached results. After the network is restored, live results are once again returned.

Let's now have a look at how this implementation fares under load. The following is the log output from the JMeter test:

```
START Running Jmeter on Mon Feb 18 23:10:22 UTC 2019
JVM_ARGS=-Xmn506m -Xms2024m -Xmx2024m
jmeter args=-n -t /etc/jmeter/jmeter_run.jmx -l resultsconnectionsposts
Feb 18, 2019 11:10:24 PM java.util.prefs.FileSystemPreferences$1 run
INFO: Created user preferences directory.
Creating summariser <summary>
Created the tree successfully using /etc/jmeter/jmeter_run.jmx
Starting the test @ Mon Feb 18 23:10:24 UTC 2019 (1550531424214)
Waiting for possible Shutdown/StopTestNow/Heapdump message on port 4445
summary +    194 in 00:00:19 =   10.0/s Err:    0 (0.00%) Active: 159
summary +    687 in 00:00:30 =   22.9/s Err:    0 (0.00%) Active: 406
summary =    881 in 00:00:49 =   17.8/s Err:    0 (0.00%)
summary +   1184 in 00:00:30 =   39.5/s Err:    0 (0.00%) Active: 655
summary =   2065 in 00:01:19 =   26.0/s Err:    0 (0.00%)
summary +   1682 in 00:00:30 =   56.1/s Err:    0 (0.00%) Active: 904
summary =   3747 in 00:01:49 =   34.2/s Err:    0 (0.00%)
summary +   2176 in 00:00:30 =   72.6/s Err:    0 (0.00%) Active: 1151
summary =   5923 in 00:02:19 =   42.5/s Err:    0 (0.00%)
summary +   2676 in 00:00:30 =   89.2/s Err:    0 (0.00%) Active: 1400
summary =   8599 in 00:02:49 =   50.8/s Err:    0 (0.00%)
summary +   3000 in 00:00:30 =  100.0/s Err:    0 (0.00%) Active: 1500
summary =  11599 in 00:03:19 =   58.2/s Err:    0 (0.00%)

<time marker 1 - I have broken the network between Posts and MySQL>

summary +   2752 in 00:00:30 =   91.7/s Err:    0 (0.00%) Active: 1500
summary =  14351 in 00:03:49 =   62.6/s Err:    0 (0.00%)
summary +   3000 in 00:00:30 =   99.9/s Err:    0 (0.00%) Active: 1500
summary =  17351 in 00:04:19 =   66.9/s Err:    0 (0.00%)
summary +   3001 in 00:00:30 =  100.1/s Err:    0 (0.00%) Active: 1500
summary =  20352 in 00:04:49 =   70.3/s Err:    0 (0.00%)
summary +   2998 in 00:00:30 =   99.9/s Err:    0 (0.00%) Active: 1500
summary =  23350 in 00:05:19 =   73.1/s Err:    0 (0.00%)
```

```
summary +   3038 in 00:00:30 =  101.3/s Err:      0 (0.00%) Active: 1500
summary =  26388 in 00:05:49 =   75.5/s Err:      0 (0.00%)
summary +   3039 in 00:00:30 =  101.3/s Err:      0 (0.00%) Active: 1500
summary =  29427 in 00:06:19 =   77.6/s Err:      0 (0.00%)
summary +   3000 in 00:00:30 =  100.0/s Err:      0 (0.00%) Active: 1500
summary =  32427 in 00:06:49 =   79.2/s Err:      0 (0.00%)

<time marker 2 - I have repaired the network between Posts and MySQL>

summary +   3089 in 00:00:30 =  102.9/s Err:      0 (0.00%) Active: 1500
summary =  35516 in 00:07:19 =   80.8/s Err:      0 (0.00%)
summary +   3080 in 00:00:30 =  102.7/s Err:      0 (0.00%) Active: 1500
summary =  38596 in 00:07:49 =   82.2/s Err:      0 (0.00%)
```

It's exactly as you'd expect. Because Connections' Posts is returning cached results when the downstream dependent Posts service isn't producing results, the client of Connections' Posts (JMeter) never sees an error during the outage. Yet as you saw in the preceding Connections' Posts log, as soon as the network is restored, live values are returned.

> **NOTE** This is pretty solid. The users of your software saw *no* errors, even while parts of the system were experiencing trouble. Trouble in one part of your software didn't cascade through the distributed system.

Reflecting back on the series of tests you've just run, table 9.1 summarizes the results.

**Table 9.1  Employing a simple retry with other patterns can eliminate or lessen negative impacts.**

| Version of Connections' Posts service | During network outage | Time to initial signs of recovery | Time to full recovery |
|---|---|---|---|
| Naïve retries | 100% error | 9 minutes | 12–13 minutes |
| Kind retries using Spring Retry and no fallback | 100% error | 1 minute | 3 minutes |
| Kind retries using Spring Retry with fallback method | 0.0% error | N/A—no failure during network outage | N/A |

As is clear from this summary, employing an otherwise good cloud-native pattern in an overly simplistic way can generate additional problems. But by using the simple retry with other patterns, the negative impacts can be significantly lessened or even entirely eliminated.

As you can see, the various compensating behaviors you've implemented have had a tremendous positive impact on the stability of the system and the user experience. Designing for failure makes a difference!

Now that you've implemented several patterns on the client side of the interaction, let's look back at the opening diagram of the chapter and fill in a few details. In figure 9.7, you can see that the client side has implemented both retries and fallback behavior. In chapter 10, you'll turn to the other end of the interaction.

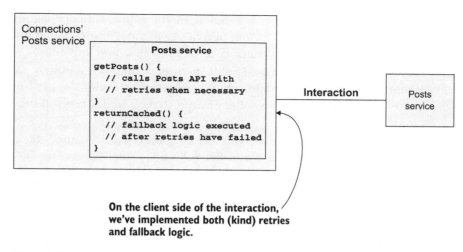

On the client side of the interaction, we've implemented both (kind) retries and fallback logic.

**Figure 9.7 Implementation of client-side patterns such as retries and fallbacks yields a far more robust system. (You'll turn to the services side of the interaction in the next chapter.)**

## 9.3 *Control loops*

Despite their seeming simplicity, I've just spent a great deal of time covering retries for two reasons. First, they're an essential tool for building resilient distributed systems, and as you saw, can be tricky to get just right. But even more important, I use them as a concrete example of a more generic pattern that I want to say more about now: control loops.

### 9.3.1 *Understanding types of control loops*

The retries you've been studying here aren't the first example of redundant actions in this text, though up until now I mentioned them only briefly. For instance, by deploying your apps into a Kubernetes environment, you're taking advantage of at least one of the control loops built into that runtime platform: the replication controller. The Kubernetes replication controller implements a control loop that allows you to specify your app deployment declaratively, and Kubernetes will create and maintain that application topology. The control loop never expects to reach a *done* state. It's designed to constantly be looking for the inevitable change and to respond appropriately.

This isn't a book on Kubernetes, so I won't cover them in detail, but the controllers are constantly (in a control loop) comparing the actual state of workloads running in the Kubernetes cluster to the desired state of those workloads, which it obtains (in the control loop) from the Kubernetes API server, the source of truth for desired cluster state. Here's a small sampling of some of the control loops implemented by that platform:

- *Replication controller*—This controller is in the business of managing deployments (see the YAML files for our app deployments), ensuring that the desired number of replicas remain running through failures and upgrades.
- *Daemonset controller*—A Kubernetes daemonset defines pods; exactly one will be running on each worker node (physical or virtual machine) of the Kubernetes cluster. The daemonset controller ensures that all nodes have all desired daemonsets deployed.
- *Endpoints controller*—As workloads are deployed and assigned IP addresses dynamically, the endpoints controller will update the Kubernetes DNS service (among other things).
- *Namespaces controller*—Namespaces may be used as a tenancy within a Kubernetes cluster, and certain policies may be applied to namespaces upon their creation. For example, a network segment may be created and assigned to isolate network traffic for apps deployed into that namespace. The namespaces controller watches for changes in the list of Kubernetes namespaces and performs any necessary actions.

Let me home in on that last example for a moment. I've been talking about control *loops*. Why do you need a loop? Can't your system simply perform the necessary actions when, for example, someone issues the `kubectl create namespace` command? In theory, yes. But as you saw in the example of the first part of this chapter, it's quite possible that this code may not be accessible when the command is executed. If that happens, do you fail to create the namespace? Do you automatically retry a time or two? The controller pattern is explicitly designed to handle these types of problems, and it does this so well that its use permeates throughout a modern distributed system such as Kubernetes. So too should you apply it liberally in your cloud-native software.

### 9.3.2  Controlling the control loop

Earlier in the chapter, I talked about controlling the retry loop. The controls you applied did things like limit the number of times the loop was executed, control its cadence, and select the conditions under which an action would be initiated (the type of exception). Again, just as the retry loop generalizes to a basic control loop, so too do some of the parameters you can apply to them.

For example, the type of exception that a `@Retryable` method is applied to is akin to a data type. Notice that the Kubernetes controllers I listed previously each applied to different types of Kubernetes objects. Although in a general sense a controller loops indefinitely, it's perfectly acceptable to change this tenet, as you did when limiting the total number of retries for a particular remote request. And finally, let's look at the cadence at which actions are taken as a result of the control loop.

When talking about request retries, I showed you an example; you slowed the rate of retries (to half a second) but kept the interval consistent. You might have noticed the `@Backoff` annotation in the `@Retryable` declaration. This annotation hints at the ability to customize the backoff algorithm. You could implement any linear or nonlinear backoff policy of your choice, but Spring Retry already has some common ones built in. You already saw an example of the former, when you waited half a second between retry attempts. Let me now show you a nonlinear example in action. To start, if you haven't already done so, please check out the following tag from your Git repo:

```
git checkout requestretries/0.0.5
```

The app deployment manifests describe a smaller deployment of our software, suitable for deployment into your Minikube cluster. You can deploy the appropriate version of the sample by executing the `deployApps.sh` bash script. Although you can certainly send `curl` commands against the Connections' Posts service at this point, what I want to focus on here is the behavior of the Kubernetes replication controller—the control loop that's watching and maintaining the state of your app deployments.

Have a look at the output of the `kubectl get pods` command. I'd like you to watch it continuously, so type the command `watch kubectl get pods`. You'll see something like this:

```
$ kubectl get pods
```

| NAME | READY | STATUS | RESTARTS | AGE |
|------|-------|--------|----------|-----|
| connection-posts-67d8db4c7b-tscf8 | 1/1 | Running | 0 | 10h |
| connections-748dc47cc6-7bzzr | 1/1 | Running | 0 | 10h |
| mysql-64bd6d89d8-ggwss | 1/1 | Running | 0 | 1d |
| posts-649d88dff-kmmx8 | 1/1 | Running | 0 | 9h |
| redis-846b8c56fb-8k8f7 | 1/1 | Running | 0 | 1d |
| sccs-84cc988f57-fjhzx | 1/1 | Running | 0 | 1d |

It's a fresh installation with one instance each of our sample microservices. What I'd like you to do now is infect the Posts service; you'll make it unhealthy. You can do this by issuing the following command:

```
curl -i -X POST $(minikube service --url posts-svc)/infect
```

And now just watch the `get pods` output. After approximately 15–30 seconds, you'll see the Posts service getting restarted. If it goes fast, you may notice only that the counter in the RESTARTS column is incremented:

```
$ kubectl get pods
```

| NAME | READY | STATUS | RESTARTS | AGE |
|------|-------|--------|----------|-----|
| connection-posts-67d8db4c7b-tscf8 | 1/1 | Running | 0 | 10h |
| connections-748dc47cc6-7bzzr | 1/1 | Running | 0 | 10h |
| mysql-64bd6d89d8-ggwss | 1/1 | Running | 0 | 1d |
| posts-649d88dff-kmmx8 | 1/1 | Running | 1 | 9h |
| redis-846b8c56fb-8k8f7 | 1/1 | Running | 0 | 1d |
| sccs-84cc988f57-fjhzx | 1/1 | Running | 0 | 1d |

Now infect that instance again by issuing the same `curl` command. After approximately 15–30 seconds, you'll see the app restart again. Keep re-infecting it every time it comes back. After you've done this four or five times, instead of the app restarting, the status will read `CrashLoopBackOff`. The replication controller has noticed that the app has repeatedly become unhealthy and will wait a bit longer before attempting another restart. It has implemented a nonlinear backoff policy.

```
$ kubectl get pods
NAME                              READY   STATUS            RESTARTS   AGE
connection-posts-67d8db4c7b-tscf8 1/1     Running           0          10h
connections-748dc47cc6-7bzzr      1/1     Running           0          10h
mysql-64bd6d89d8-ggwss            1/1     Running           0          1d
posts-649d88dff-kmmx8             1/1     CrashLoopBackOff  5          9h
redis-846b8c56fb-8k8f7            1/1     Running           0          1d
sccs-84cc988f57-fjhzx             1/1     Running           0          1d
```

What I hope you take away from this dialogue, and the chapter as a whole, is the need to start looking for the control loops in your cloud-native software designs. Although for many of us an imperative style of programming feels natural, in a distributed system problems abound. They may not show themselves initially, but lurking beneath seemingly sound implementations are hairy edge cases and implementations that fail when unexpected changes occur. An eventually consistent, control-loop-driven software design will fare far better in the distributed systems that make up our cloud-native software.

## *Summary*

- Retrying requests that time out can absorb errors that otherwise would have propagated through the system.
- If not done right, queued retry requests can overload a system even after connectivity problems are corrected.
- Properly configured retries can dramatically reduce the risk of these retry storms, while still providing significant benefits in less-dramatic outages.
- It's your responsibility as a developer to use retries only when it's *safe* to do so.
- You should make a habit of implementing not only the core flow of your service, but also the fallback logic for when the happy path is failing.
- Retries are but one example of a control-loop pattern.
- Control loops are an essential technique for the distributed systems that make up cloud-native software.

# Fronting services: Circuit breakers and API gateways

10

**This chapter covers**

- The service side of an interaction between two microservices
- Circuit breakers
- API gateways
- Sidecars and service mesh

I began talking about interactions between services in chapter 8, with a focus on dynamic routing and service discovery; I was talking about how clients can find and access a service they depend on. After the client finds and addresses the needed service, it initiates an interaction. The previous chapter and this one come together to consider both sides of that interaction—as shown in figure 10.1. In chapter 9, I talked about the resilience of this interaction; I was largely talking about request redundancy, something the client is responsible for and applies controls to. Now I want to turn to the service side of that client/service interaction and the essential design patterns that play a role here.

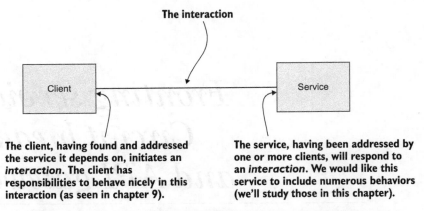

**The interaction**

Client

Service

**The client, having found and addressed the service it depends on, initiates an *interaction*. The client has responsibilities to behave nicely in this interaction (as seen in chapter 9).**

**The service, having been addressed by one or more clients, will respond to an *interaction*. We would like this service to include numerous behaviors (we'll study those in this chapter).**

**Figure 10.1   Just as the client can and should implement certain patterns to act as a good participant in the interaction, so too should the service. These are the patterns covered in this chapter.**

As the developer of the service, you have to account for many interaction-related concerns:

- In the previous chapter, I presented a solution to the retry storm problem that was implemented on the client side of the interaction (*kind retries*, I called them). But the service developer can't depend on clients always being kind and must therefore guard against retry storms. From the service perspective, a *retry storm* is simply a case of having more incoming requests than it can handle. The service is ultimately responsible for protecting itself from intentional or inadvertent denial-of-service attacks.
- I previously talked about techniques for deploying a new version of a service—blue/green and rolling upgrades in particular. You'll recall that I also talked about parallel deployments, whereby multiple versions of a service are running at the same time, with some requests being served by one of those services and some requests being served by another. In most cases, decisions on which service version should respond to a given request are handled on the service side of the client/service interaction.
- The service should respond only to requests from authorized parties.
- A service is also responsible for making monitoring and logging information available (a foreshadow of the next chapter).

This chapter covers two patterns that address these concerns: circuit breakers and API gateways. Circuit breakers explicitly target the first of these concerns and are used to protect the service from being overwhelmed with too much traffic. API gateways are used to address all of these concerns, and then some. Although API gateways have been in use for some time, I specifically cover the needs brought by the cloud-native architectures that have been in use only recently.

I close the chapter by covering a recently popularized implementation approach for the patterns of both the server side and the client side of the interactions: sidecars. Yes, I'll be talking about Istio and friends here.

## 10.1  Circuit breakers

The concept of a *circuit breaker* in your software is exactly the same as that of the electrical system in your home. You have any number of potentially power-drawing sources in your home—lights, outlets, appliances, and so forth. The more power that's simultaneously drawn on your wires, the hotter the wires will get, and if there's enough load, the wires could get hot enough to light the walls through which they run on fire. To keep this from happening, the wires are run through a circuit breaker that will detect when the power draw gets dangerously high and will open the circuit so that all power will be cut off. Better to have no power than to light the house on fire.

### 10.1.1  The software circuit breaker

In your software, circuit breakers operate in essentially the same way. When the load is too high, a circuit opens and keeps traffic from flowing through. But two differences exist. First, the mechanism for detecting when the circuit should open is based on actual failures, not a prediction of possible failures (you wouldn't want an electrical circuit to trip only after a small fire was detected). And second, the software circuit breaker usually has a self-healing mechanism built in (as opposed to having a human stumble through a dark house to find the electrical panel to manually flip the breaker).

The basic idea is this: If a service starts to fail more than a little bit, you stop all traffic to that service for a while, hopefully giving it time to recover from whatever is causing it to fail. Then, after some time, you check to see how it's doing by allowing a single request through. If that request fails, you keep the protection in place, not allowing further traffic. If that request succeeds, you treat the service as healthy and allow traffic to flow freely again.

We can model this behavior by defining three states that a circuit breaker can be in (Closed, Open, or Half-Open), as shown in figure 10.2. We can then describe the events that drive changes in state, as follows:

- The ideal state of your circuit breaker is *Closed*: traffic is flowing through the circuit, to the service that the circuit is protecting.
- The circuit breaker sits in that flow of traffic and looks out for failures. A small number of failures is not a problem; indeed, resilience to such "blips" is part of a good cloud-native design. When the failure rate gets too high, the state of the circuit breaker will become *Open*.
- While the circuit breaker is Open, no traffic will be allowed through to the service that the circuit breaker is protecting. If the service had started failing because it was overwhelmed with request load, or an intermittent network outage was causing trouble, the break from handling load may allow the service to return to a healthy state.

- After some time has passed, you want to try the service again to see whether it has recovered. You do this by putting the circuit breaker into a *Half-Open* state.
- When in the Half-Open state, the circuit breaker implementation will test the service by allowing a single request or a small number of requests through to the service.
- If the test requests are successful, the circuit will transition back to the Closed state. If the test fails, the circuit will transition back to the Open state and wait it out just a bit longer.

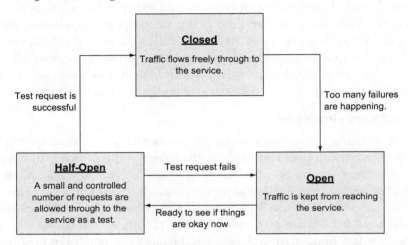

**Figure 10.2    You model the operation of the circuit breaker via three states and define the conditions or events that cause transitions between them. When the circuit is Closed, traffic flows freely. When the circuit is Open, requests won't reach the service. The Half-Open state is transitory, the means by which the circuit can be reset to Closed.**

I've described the circuit breaker intuitively, but you and/or the circuit breaker implementation need to concretely define the specifics for the state changes. What constitutes "too many failures," for example? In a moment, you'll look at a concrete implementation and study these details. First, I want to draw your attention to one concept that's not depicted in this diagram: how the use of a circuit breaker affects the client/service interaction that's so central in this and the previous chapter.

The sequence diagram in figure 10.3 shows three scenarios of a single interaction between a client and a service at a time when the service is experiencing trouble. In the first case, no circuit breaker is in use. In the second, you have a circuit breaker, and the state is Closed. Finally, you have a circuit breaker with an Open state.

In the first two cases, you can see that the behavior is effectively identical: the client makes a request, and because of the trouble the service is experiencing, it times out waiting for a response. But in the last case, when the circuit is open because the circuit breaker has detected trouble, the client will quickly receive a response. The key here is that delays are disastrous in a complex distributed system, and the circuit breaker significantly reduces the length and frequency thereof. I like to think of circuit breakers as a "kindness" pattern implemented on the service side.

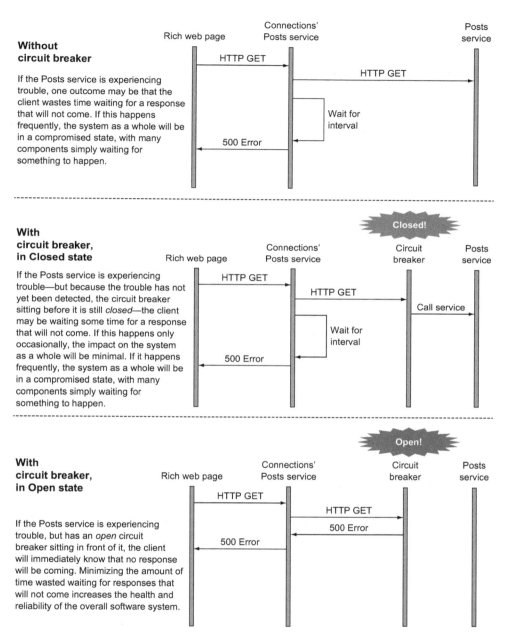

**Without circuit breaker**

If the Posts service is experiencing trouble, one outcome may be that the client wastes time waiting for a response that will not come. If this happens frequently, the system as a whole will be in a compromised state, with many components simply waiting for something to happen.

**With circuit breaker, in Closed state**

If the Posts service is experiencing trouble—but because the trouble has not yet been detected, the circuit breaker sitting before it is still *closed*—the client may be waiting some time for a response that will not come. If this happens only occasionally, the impact on the system as a whole will be minimal. If it happens frequently, the system as a whole will be in a compromised state, with many components simply waiting for something to happen.

**With circuit breaker, in Open state**

If the Posts service is experiencing trouble, but has an *open* circuit breaker sitting in front of it, the client will immediately know that no response will be coming. Minimizing the amount of time wasted waiting for responses that will not come increases the health and reliability of the overall software system.

**Figure 10.3  At times when a service is unavailable—because of network outages, trouble with the service itself, or another issue—one of the main benefits of circuit breakers is that they significantly reduce the amount of time wasted while waiting for responses that are at that moment unlikely to come.**

Let's now look at an implementation of the circuit breaker in our running example. This will demonstrate basic use and configurability, and allow you to think a bit more deeply about the structure of your service implementations.

### 10.1.2 *Implementing a circuit breaker*

As is usual, you can run the code examples by checking out the Git repository, two specific tags for the examples herein, and deploying to a Kubernetes cluster. As I've done all along, I've built the code samples and bundled them in Docker images that are available to you in Docker Hub, so you needn't build the code from source. If you do want to build from source, I've included the Maven and Docker build files for your convenience. Before running the examples, let's have a look at the code.

Assuming you've already cloned the repository, please check out your first chapter 10 tag with the following command:

```
git checkout circuitbreaker/0.0.1
```

The code is all located in the cloudnative-circuitbreaker directory, so change into that now. You'll notice that there are implementations only for the Posts and the Connections services, because the Connections' Posts service is the client side of the interaction and is unchanged from that of the previous chapter.

The service you'll protect with the circuit breaker is the Posts service, so let's start by looking at the code in the source directory for that service. The first thing you'll notice is a new Java class: PostsService. The circuit breaker implementation fronts an actual service, and the way that it's implemented here, you have the circuit breaker running within the same process as the main service implementation; the circuit breaker is close to the actual service (spoiler alert—I'll explain this more when I talk about Istio at the end of this chapter).

You originally had a lot of logic in the Posts controller itself. But what you've done now is put the core of the service implementation into that new PostsService class, and you now have the controller handling only the front edge of the service interaction. The controller still handles tasks like request parsing and response generation, as well as some of the basic authentication and authorization logic. The new PostsService doesn't deal with the HTTP protocol and instead focuses only on the core logic of the service, which for our simple example is only a database query and response object generation.

Most pertinent to our discussion is the addition of an annotation around the PostsService's get method, as shown in the listing 10.1.

---

**Listing 10.1    Method from PostsService.java**

```java
@HystrixCommand()
public Iterable<Post> getPostsByUserId(String userIds,
                            String secret) throws Exception {

    logger.info(utils.ipTag() + "Attempting getPostsByUserId");
```

```
Iterable<Post> posts;

if (userIds == null) {
    logger.info(utils.ipTag() + "getting all posts");
    posts = postRepository.findAll();
    return posts;
} else {
    ArrayList<Post> postsForUsers = new ArrayList<Post>();
    String userId[] = userIds.split(",");
    for (int i = 0; i < userId.length; i++) {
        logger.info(utils.ipTag() +
                    "getting posts for userId " + userId[i]);
        posts = postRepository.findByUserId(Long.parseLong(userId[i]));
        posts.forEach(post -> postsForUsers.add(post));
    }
    return postsForUsers;

}
}
```

The `@HystrixCommand()` indicates that this method is to be fronted with a circuit breaker, and the Spring Framework will insert the implementation. It does so with an aspect that intercepts all incoming requests and implements the protocol I described previously.

Okay, so let's see this in action—in particular, through the lens of the retry-storm scenario you learned about in the previous chapter. I want to take the naïve retry implementation of Connections' Posts, the one that caused the system to remain unhealthy for an extended period of time after the network was reestablished, and couple that with a circuit breaker protecting the Posts service. See figure 10.4. You'll run the same load tests as you did before.

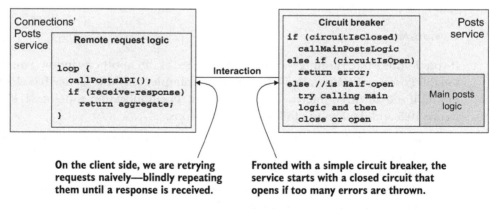

Figure 10.4   For your first test run, you'll be running with the naïve retries on the client side of the interaction, and a simple circuit breaker at the front of the service.

SETTING UP

Once again, I refer you to the setup instructions for running the samples in earlier chapters in this text. There are no new requirements for running the sample in this chapter.

You'll be accessing files in the cloudnative-circuitbreaker directory, so in your terminal window, change into that directory.

And as I've described in previous chapters, I've already prebuilt Docker images and made them available in Docker Hub. If you want to build the Java source and Docker images and push them to your own image repository, I refer you to earlier chapters (the most detailed instructions are in chapter 5).

RUNNING THE APPS

As you progress through the chapter, you'll have different versions of the circuit breaker, so to start, you'll need to check out the right tag on the GitHub repo:

```
git checkout circuitbreaker/0.0.1
```

You'll need a Kubernetes cluster with sufficient capacity, as I described in chapter 9. If you still have the examples running from the previous chapter, no need to clean up and start again; the commands you'll run here will update the versions of all microservices appropriately. If you do want to start from scratch, you may use `deleteDeploymentComplete.sh` as I've previously described. This simple bash script allows you to keep MySQL, Redis, and SCCS running. Calling it with no options deletes only the three microservice deployments; calling the script with `all` as an argument deletes MySQL, Redis, and SCCS as well.

Given that you've checked out the Git tag as described previously, you can deploy or update the running services by running the following script (or issuing the `kubectl apply` commands contained therein):

```
./deployApps.sh
```

If you do this while running `watch kubectl get all` in another window, you'll either see the Posts service upgraded—for this first example, only this service has changed—or you'll see all three microservices deployed. The application topology is shown in figure 10.5 and deploys the following app versions:

- *Connections' Posts*—This is the version from the request resilience project (of chapter 9) that has the naïve retry implementation, the one that blindly retries timed-out requests forever.
- *Connections*—This is the version from the request resilience project and is the standard connections implementation.
- *Posts*—This is a new version of the app that has been refactored to separate the controller from the main logic of the service. The main method in the latter has now been wrapped in a Hystrix circuit breaker.

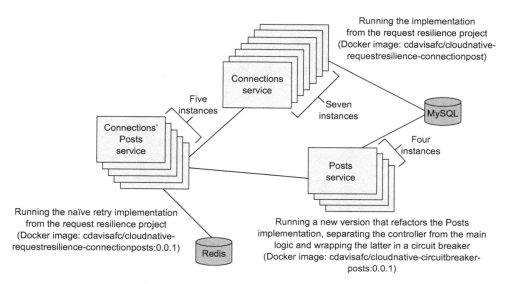

**Figure 10.5 The deployment topology has versions of the Connections' Posts and Connections services from the previous chapter and provides a new version of the Posts service. This implementation wraps the main Posts logic in a circuit breaker.**

Let's now send some load to this implementation. You do so by issuing the following two commands:

```
kubectl create configmap jmeter-config \
  --from-file=jmeter_run.jmx=loadTesting/ConnectionsPostsLoad.jmx
kubectl create -f loadTesting/jmeter-deployment.yaml
```

If you ran the first command during the experiments of chapter 9, rerunning it here is unnecessary, as the config map for the Apache JMeter deployment will already exist. Now let's look at the output of the load test:

```
$ kubectl logs -f <name of your jmeter pod>
START Running Jmeter on Sun Feb 24 05:21:46 UTC 2019
JVM_ARGS=-Xmn442m -Xms1768m -Xmx1768m
jmeter args=-n -t /etc/jmeter/jmeter_run.jmx -l resultsconnectionsposts
Feb 24, 2019 5:21:48 AM java.util.prefs.FileSystemPreferences$1 run
INFO: Created user preferences directory.
Creating summariser <summary>
Created the tree successfully using /etc/jmeter/jmeter_run.jmx
Starting the test @ Sun Feb 24 05:21:48 UTC 2019 (1550985708891)
Waiting for possible Shutdown/StopTestNow/Heapdump message on port 4445
summary +     85 in 00:00:10 =    8.1/s Err:     0 (0.00%) Active: 85
summary +    538 in 00:00:30 =   18.0/s Err:     0 (0.00%) Active: 332
summary =    623 in 00:00:40 =   15.4/s Err:     0 (0.00%)
summary +   1033 in 00:00:30 =   34.5/s Err:     0 (0.00%) Active: 579
summary =   1656 in 00:01:10 =   23.5/s Err:     0 (0.00%)
summary +   1529 in 00:00:30 =   51.0/s Err:     0 (0.00%) Active: 829
summary =   3185 in 00:01:40 =   31.7/s Err:     0 (0.00%)
```

```
summary +   2029 in 00:00:30 =   67.6/s Err:      0 (0.00%) Active: 1077
summary =   5214 in 00:02:10 =   40.0/s Err:      0 (0.00%)
summary +   2520 in 00:00:30 =   84.1/s Err:      0 (0.00%) Active: 1325
summary =   7734 in 00:02:40 =   48.2/s Err:      0 (0.00%)
summary +   2893 in 00:00:30 =   96.4/s Err:      0 (0.00%) Active: 1500
summary =  10627 in 00:03:10 =   55.8/s Err:      0 (0.00%)
summary +   3055 in 00:00:30 =  101.8/s Err:      0 (0.00%) Active: 1500
summary =  13682 in 00:03:40 =   62.1/s Err:      0 (0.00%)
summary +   3007 in 00:00:30 =  100.2/s Err:      0 (0.00%) Active: 1500
summary =  16689 in 00:04:10 =   66.7/s Err:      0 (0.00%)

<time marker 1 - I have broken the network between Posts and MySQL>

summary +   2510 in 00:00:30 =   83.6/s Err:   2084 (83.03%) Active: 1500
summary =  19199 in 00:04:40 =   68.5/s Err:   2084 (10.85%)
summary +   3000 in 00:00:30 =  100.0/s Err:   3000 (100.00%) Active: 1500
summary =  22199 in 00:05:10 =   71.5/s Err:   5084 (22.90%)
summary +   3000 in 00:00:30 =  100.0/s Err:   3000 (100.00%) Active: 1500
summary =  25199 in 00:05:40 =   74.0/s Err:   8084 (32.08%)
summary +   2953 in 00:00:30 =   98.4/s Err:   2953 (100.00%) Active: 1500
summary =  28152 in 00:06:10 =   76.0/s Err:  11037 (39.21%)
summary +   2916 in 00:00:30 =   96.9/s Err:   2916 (100.00%) Active: 1500
summary =  31068 in 00:06:40 =   77.6/s Err:  13953 (44.91%)
summary +   3046 in 00:00:30 =  101.7/s Err:   3046 (100.00%) Active: 1500
summary =  34114 in 00:07:10 =   79.3/s Err:  16999 (49.83%)
summary +   3019 in 00:00:30 =  100.7/s Err:   3019 (100.00%) Active: 1500
summary =  37133 in 00:07:40 =   80.7/s Err:  20018 (53.91%)

<time marker 2 - I have repaired the network between Posts and MySQL>

summary +   2980 in 00:00:30 =   99.3/s Err:   2980 (100.00%) Active: 1500
summary =  40113 in 00:08:10 =   81.8/s Err:  22998 (57.33%)
summary +   3015 in 00:00:30 =  100.5/s Err:   3015 (100.00%) Active: 1500
summary =  43128 in 00:08:40 =   82.9/s Err:  26013 (60.32%)
summary +   3020 in 00:00:30 =  100.7/s Err:   3020 (100.00%) Active: 1500
summary =  46148 in 00:09:10 =   83.8/s Err:  29033 (62.91%)
summary +   3075 in 00:00:30 =  102.5/s Err:   3072 (99.90%) Active: 1500
summary =  49223 in 00:09:40 =   84.8/s Err:  32105 (65.22%)
summary +   3049 in 00:00:30 =  101.6/s Err:   2395 (78.55%) Active: 1500
summary =  52272 in 00:10:10 =   85.6/s Err:  34500 (66.00%)
summary +   3191 in 00:00:30 =  106.4/s Err:   2263 (70.92%) Active: 1500
summary =  55463 in 00:10:40 =   86.6/s Err:  36763 (66.28%)
summary +   2995 in 00:00:30 =   99.7/s Err:   1203 (40.17%) Active: 1500
summary =  58458 in 00:11:10 =   87.2/s Err:  37966 (64.95%)
summary +   3031 in 00:00:30 =  101.1/s Err:   1193 (39.36%) Active: 1500
summary =  61489 in 00:11:40 =   87.8/s Err:  39159 (63.68%)
summary +   3009 in 00:00:30 =  100.3/s Err:   1182 (39.28%) Active: 1500
summary =  64498 in 00:12:10 =   88.3/s Err:  40341 (62.55%)
summary +   3083 in 00:00:30 =  102.8/s Err:    859 (27.86%) Active: 1500
summary =  67581 in 00:12:40 =   88.9/s Err:  41200 (60.96%)
summary +   3110 in 00:00:30 =  103.7/s Err:    597 (19.20%) Active: 1500
summary =  70691 in 00:13:10 =   89.4/s Err:  41797 (59.13%)
summary +   2999 in 00:00:30 =   99.9/s Err:      0 (0.00%) Active: 1500
summary =  73690 in 00:13:40 =   89.8/s Err:  41797 (56.72%)
summary +   3001 in 00:00:30 =  100.1/s Err:      0 (0.00%) Active: 1500
summary =  76691 in 00:14:10 =   90.2/s Err:  41797 (54.50%)
```

Just as you did for the tests in the previous chapter, after all the load has been established (at time marker 1 in the preceding log), you break the network between all instances of the Posts service and the MySQL database. As you can see, this results in all requests to Connections' Posts failing (this is what you're calling from the JMeter tests). After a roughly 3-minute outage, you reestablish the network, at time marker 2. Studying the log output, you can see that it took only about 1 minute for the first signs of recovery, and another 3.5 to 4 minutes for full recovery. Table 10.1 shows these results side by side with the results of having the naïve retry implementation (an unkind client indeed) with no protection around the service.

**Table 10.1   A circuit breaker provides significant protections against retry storms.**

| Version of Connections' Posts service | Version of Posts service | Time to initial signs of recovery | Additional time to full recovery |
|---|---|---|---|
| Naïve retries | No circuit breaker | 9 minutes | 12–13 minutes |
| Naïve retries | Circuit breaker protecting the service | 1–2 minutes | 4–5 minutes |

That's already a stark difference! I'll point out that the circuit breaker provides protection not only from retry storms, but from excessive load or other error conditions, regardless of the cause. But in this case, how did the circuit breaker change the interaction between the Connections' Posts and the Posts service that allowed the system to recover so much faster? It goes back to figure 10.3; you've implemented the third scenario, so that instead of Connections' Posts timing out for every one of the retries, after the circuit is open, it quickly receives a response from the Posts service, a response that clearly indicates a problem (with a 500 status code), so the retry backlog, if you will, is then much smaller.

Let's explore this first implementation. As you can imagine, the @HistrixCommand() annotation allows numerous configuration options to control how it behaves. In this first example, you've simply accepted the defaults. Looking at the simple state diagram, in figure 10.6, I've annotated it with those defaults. The circuit breaker will trip when 50% of the requests to the service fail and will remain open for 5 seconds before entering the Half-Open state.

Numerous other configuration options can be used for the Hystrix circuit breaker.[1] You can, for example, set a minimum number of failures before the circuit will trip. But the one that I want to focus on here is setting a fallback method. Remember how, when you implemented the kinder request redundancy with Spring Retry in the preceding chapter, you added a fallback method whereby you cached previous results and used those when the Posts service wasn't responding? Same idea here: when the circuit is open, instead of returning an error as your implementation currently does, you'll return something to stand in for the real result.

---

[1]These configuration options are available on GitHub at http://mng.bz/O2rK.

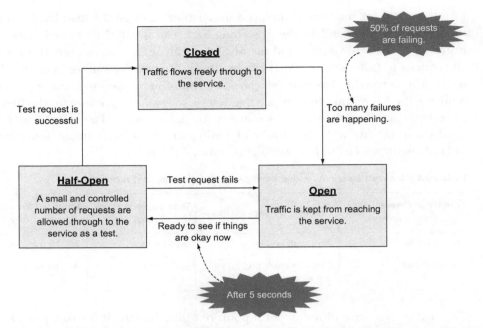

**Figure 10.6   The default Hystrix implementation trips the circuit when 50% of requests fail and moves from the Open state to a Half-Open state seconds after entering the Open state. Successful or unsuccessful requests made while in the Half-Open state will transition the circuit breaker to Closed and Open states, respectively.**

> **NOTE**   The subtitle of this book is *Designing Change-tolerant Software*. One of the single most important things you must do when designing your software is always be thinking, "What should the software do in the event the operation I'm invoking isn't successful?"

It's quite telling that frameworks that help you implement resiliency patterns have built-in primitives for fallback, on both sides of an interaction; figure 10.7 shows this clearly.

The context for each of these fallback methods differs. On the left side of figure 10.7, the Connections' Posts service is the *consumer* of information sought via the interaction, and can decide what it should do when live information isn't available. Is stale content better than no content? In our final implementation in chapter 9, you made the call that it was and returned cached content. On the right-hand side of figure 10.7, the Posts service is the *provider* of information sought via the interaction and must decide whether any type of "success" response is better than an outright failure. Whatever the alternate success return is, this behavior must be well documented so that clients aren't lured into believing they have one set of data when, in fact, they're receiving an alternate set.

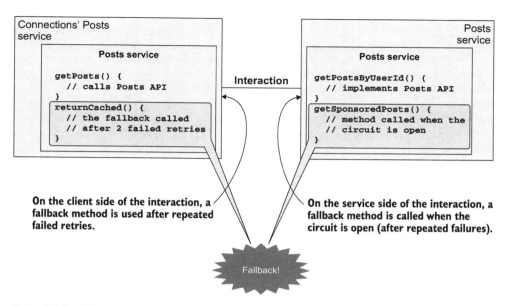

**Figure 10.7  Failures can occur on either side of an interaction, and fallbacks provide safeguards.**

Let's check this out with a running implementation. You'll make only minor changes to our previous example. To see them, please check out the next Git tag with the following command:

```
git checkout circuitbreaker/0.0.2
```

Looking at the code for the Posts API, and the PostsService class specifically, you see that now a fallback method is provided, and the @HystrixCommand annotation points to it. In listing 10.2 you see that the fallback implementation returns precanned results, sponsored content in the event that live data isn't available:

**Listing 10.2  Methods from PostsService.java**

```java
@HystrixCommand(fallbackMethod = "getSponsoredPosts")
public Iterable<Post> getPostsByUserId(String userIds,

                                 String secret) throws Exception {

    logger.info(utils.ipTag() + "Attempting getPostsByUserId");

    Iterable<Post> posts;

    if (userIds == null) {
        logger.info(utils.ipTag() + "getting all posts");
        posts = postRepository.findAll();
        return posts;
    } else {
        ArrayList<Post> postsForUsers = new ArrayList<Post>();
        String userId[] = userIds.split(",");
        for (int i = 0; i < userId.length; i++) {
```

```
            logger.info(utils.ipTag() +
                        "getting posts for userId " + userId[i]);
        posts = postRepository.findByUserId(Long.parseLong(userId[i]));
        posts.forEach(post -> postsForUsers.add(post));
        }
    return postsForUsers;
    }
}

public Iterable<Post> getSponsoredPosts(String userIds,
                                        String secret) {
    logger.info(utils.ipTag() +
                "Accessing Hystrix fallback getSponsoredPosts");
    ArrayList<Post> posts = new ArrayList<Post>();
    posts.add(new Post(999L, "Some catchy title",
                "Some great sponsored content"));
    posts.add(new Post(999L, "Another catchy title",
                "Some more great sponsored content"));
    return posts;
}
```

I want to draw your attention to two points here:

- The fallback method is called anytime an error is returned from the Hystrix-protected command (the `getPostsByUserId` method, in this case), even when the circuit is closed. The Hystrix library favors attempting fallbacks in all cases of failure, even if they're never part of a major failure.
- Hystrix fallback methods can be chained; if the primary method fails, `fallbackMethod1` can be called. This could, for example, attempt to calculate its results by using cached data or load data via an alternate channel. If `fallbackMethod1` were to fail, control could be passed to `fallbackMethod2`, and so on. This is a powerful abstraction at your disposal.

You'll notice that our fallback implementation is very, very naïve. It even hardcodes content (in the code!) rather than drawing it from a data store; this is purely to keep your implementation simple. Please don't hardcode content into your source code!

### RUNNING THE APPS

I assume that you already have running the example from earlier in this section, and that you have checked out the Git branch as I described previously. If your previous load test is still running, stop it with the following command:

```
kubectl delete deploy jmeter-deployment
```

You can update your deployment to the version that implements the fallback behavior by running the following bash script or by executing the commands contained therein:

```
./deployApps.sh
```

Again, if you're watching a `kubectl get all` command, you'll see both the Connections and the Posts services being updated. An update was needed for Connections only to preload the sponsor's user ID. The Connections' Posts service wasn't updated. You'll still be running the naïve retry implementation from chapter 9. And finally, let's place some load against this deployment:

```
kubectl create -f loadTesting/jmeter-deployment.yaml
```

And now you'll have a look at the logs for this deployment:

```
START Running Jmeter on Sun Feb 24 04:39:23 UTC 2019
JVM_ARGS=-Xmn542m -Xms2168m -Xmx2168m
jmeter args=-n -t /etc/jmeter/jmeter_run.jmx -l resultsconnectionsposts
Feb 24, 2019 4:39:25 AM java.util.prefs.FileSystemPreferences$1 run
INFO: Created user preferences directory.
Creating summariser <summary>
Created the tree successfully using /etc/jmeter/jmeter_run.jmx
Starting the test @ Sun Feb 24 04:39:25 UTC 2019 (1550983165958)
Waiting for possible Shutdown/StopTestNow/Heapdump message on port 4445
summary +    217 in 00:00:21 =   10.4/s Err: 0 (0.00%) Active: 171
summary +    712 in 00:00:30 =   23.7/s Err: 0 (0.00%) Active: 419
summary =    929 in 00:00:51 =   18.3/s Err: 0 (0.00%)
summary +   1209 in 00:00:30 =   40.3/s Err: 0 (0.00%) Active: 667
summary =   2138 in 00:01:21 =   26.4/s Err: 0 (0.00%)
summary +   1706 in 00:00:30 =   57.0/s Err: 0 (0.00%) Active: 916
summary =   3844 in 00:01:51 =   34.7/s Err: 0 (0.00%)
summary +   2205 in 00:00:30 =   73.5/s Err: 0 (0.00%) Active: 1166
summary =   6049 in 00:02:21 =   43.0/s Err: 0 (0.00%)
summary +   2705 in 00:00:30 =   90.2/s Err: 0 (0.00%) Active: 1415
summary =   8754 in 00:02:51 =   51.2/s Err: 0 (0.00%)
summary +   2998 in 00:00:30 =   99.9/s Err: 0 (0.00%) Active: 1500
summary =  11752 in 00:03:21 =   58.5/s Err: 0 (0.00%)

<time marker 1 - I have broken the network between Posts and MySQL>

summary +   3004 in 00:00:30 =  100.0/s Err: 0 (0.00%) Active: 1500
summary =  14756 in 00:03:51 =   63.9/s Err: 0 (0.00%)
summary +   2997 in 00:00:30 =   99.9/s Err: 0 (0.00%) Active: 1500
summary =  17753 in 00:04:21 =   68.1/s Err: 0 (0.00%)
summary +   3001 in 00:00:30 =  100.1/s Err: 0 (0.00%) Active: 1500
summary =  20754 in 00:04:51 =   71.4/s Err: 0 (0.00%)
summary +   3000 in 00:00:30 =  100.0/s Err: 0 (0.00%) Active: 1500
summary =  23754 in 00:05:21 =   74.0/s Err: 0 (0.00%)
summary +   3000 in 00:00:30 =  100.0/s Err: 0 (0.00%) Active: 1500
summary =  26754 in 00:05:51 =   76.3/s Err: 0 (0.00%)
summary +   3000 in 00:00:30 =  100.0/s Err: 0 (0.00%) Active: 1500
summary =  29754 in 00:06:21 =   78.1/s Err: 0 (0.00%)
summary +   2995 in 00:00:30 =   99.9/s Err: 0 (0.00%) Active: 1500
summary =  32749 in 00:06:51 =   79.7/s Err: 0 (0.00%)

<time marker 2 - I have repaired the network between Posts and MySQL>

summary +   3005 in 00:00:30 =  100.2/s Err: 0 (0.00%) Active: 1500
summary =  35754 in 00:07:21 =   81.1/s Err: 0 (0.00%)
summary +   2997 in 00:00:30 =   99.9/s Err: 0 (0.00%) Active: 1500
summary =  38751 in 00:07:51 =   82.3/s Err: 0 (0.00%)
```

As usual, time marker 1 indicates the time that you broke the network connection between the Posts service and the MySQL database, and time marker 2 indicates when you reestablished the connections. And as you can see, calls to Connections' Posts never failed, even during the network outage. This is exactly as you'd expect given that the fallback method for the circuit breaker returns sponsored content on any failures of the Posts service.

Perhaps a more interesting metric is how quickly live content is returned after the network is reestablished. Any guesses? Yes, you're right: less than 5 seconds. Recall that the default setting for `sleepWindowMilliseconds` is 5000, meaning the circuit state will be set to Half-Open 5 seconds after being set to Open. As soon as that happens, the trial request that you allow through to the Post service logic will succeed, and the circuit will close, returning the application back to a stable state. You can see this transition in the log output for one of the Posts service instances:

```
2019-02-23 02:59:03.084   getting posts for userId 2
2019-02-23 02:59:03.148   Attempting getPostsByUserId
2019-02-23 02:59:03.148   getting posts for userId 2
2019-02-23 02:59:03.167   Attempting getPostsByUserId
2019-02-23 02:59:03.167   getting posts for userId 2

<time marker 1 - I have broken the network between Posts and MySQL>

2019-02-23 02:59:03.213   Accessing Hystrix fallback getSponsoredPosts
2019-02-23 02:59:03.237   Accessing Hystrix fallback getSponsoredPosts
2019-02-23 02:59:03.243   Accessing Hystrix fallback getSponsoredPosts
2019-02-23 02:59:03.313   Accessing Hystrix fallback getSponsoredPosts
2019-02-23 02:59:03.351   Accessing Hystrix fallback getSponsoredPosts
2019-02-23 02:59:03.357   Accessing Hystrix fallback getSponsoredPosts
2019-02-23 02:59:03.394   Accessing Hystrix fallback getSponsoredPosts
... (there are many more of these log lines)

<time marker 2 - I have repaired the network between Posts and MySQL>

... (another 5 seconds or so of Hystrix mentioning messages)
(then, ...)

2019-02-23 03:02:33.705   Accessing Hystrix fallback getSponsoredPosts
2019-02-23 03:02:33.717   Accessing Hystrix fallback getSponsoredPosts
2019-02-23 03:02:33.717   Accessing Hystrix fallback getSponsoredPosts
2019-02-23 03:02:33.898   getting posts for userId 3
2019-02-23 03:02:33.898   getting posts for userId 3
2019-02-23 03:02:33.899   getting posts for userId 3
2019-02-23 03:02:33.899   getting posts for userId 3
2019-02-23 03:02:33.900   getting posts for userId 3
2019-02-23 03:02:33.905   Accessing Hystrix fallback getSponsoredPosts
2019-02-23 03:02:33.911   Accessing Hystrix fallback getSponsoredPosts
2019-02-23 03:02:33.943   Accessing Hystrix fallback getSponsoredPosts
2019-02-23 03:02:34.080   Accessing Hystrix fallback getSponsoredPosts
2019-02-23 03:02:34.100   Accessing Hystrix fallback getSponsoredPosts
2019-02-23 03:02:34.113   Accessing Hystrix fallback getSponsoredPosts
2019-02-23 03:02:34.216   Accessing Hystrix fallback getSponsoredPosts
2019-02-23 03:02:34.225   Accessing Hystrix fallback getSponsoredPosts
```

```
2019-02-23 03:02:34.300  Accessing Hystrix fallback getSponsoredPosts
2019-02-23 03:02:34.368  Accessing Hystrix fallback getSponsoredPosts
2019-02-23 03:02:34.398  Attempting getPostsByUserId
2019-02-23 03:02:34.398  getting posts for userId 2
2019-02-23 03:02:34.400  getting posts for userId 3
2019-02-23 03:02:34.433  Attempting getPostsByUserId
2019-02-23 03:02:34.433  getting posts for userId 2
2019-02-23 03:02:34.434  Attempting getPostsByUserId
2019-02-23 03:02:34.434  getting posts for userId 2
2019-02-23 03:02:34.435  getting posts for userId 3
2019-02-23 03:02:34.437  getting posts for userId 3
2019-02-23 03:02:34.472  Attempting getPostsByUserId
2019-02-23 03:02:34.472  getting posts for userId 2
2019-02-23 03:02:34.475  getting posts for userId 3
2019-02-23 03:02:34.556  Attempting getPostsByUserId
2019-02-23 03:02:34.556  getting posts for userId 2
2019-02-23 03:02:34.559  getting posts for userId 3
2019-02-23 03:02:34.622  Attempting getPostsByUserId
(and operation has returned to normal)
```

Table 10.2 shows the results from each of the tests you've run through the previous chapter and this one. Each case simulated the same 3-minute network outage between Connections' Posts and Posts, but with different patterns applied to the client side (in chapter 9) or the server side (in chapter 10) of the interaction.

**Table 10.2  Results from the network outage simulations show the benefit of applying certain cloud-native patterns to service interactions.**

| Version of Connections' Posts service | Version of Posts service | During network outage | Time to initial signs of recovery | Time to full recovery | Test run in chapter |
|---|---|---|---|---|---|
| Naïve retries | No circuit breaker | 100% error | 9 minutes | 12–13 minutes | 9 |
| Kind retries using Spring Retry and no fallback | No circuit breaker | 100% error | 1 minute | 3 minutes | 9 |
| Kind retries using Spring Retry with fallback method | No circuit breaker | 0% error | N/A—no failure during network outage | N/A | 9 |
| Naïve retries | Circuit breaker protecting the service—no fallback method | 100% error | 1–2 minutes | 4–5 minutes | 10 |
| Naïve retries | Circuit breaker protecting the service—with fallback method | 0% error | N/A—no failure during network outage | < 5 seconds  Considering "full recovery" the time when actual results, not sponsor results, are again returned | 10 |

This summary is interesting indeed. Implementing patterns focused on resilience of interactions makes a big difference in the overall health of your software. Although, clearly, patterns are applicable both on the client and on the server side of an interaction, you often won't be responsible for implementations on both sides. Therefore, particularly if you're implementing a consumer, it's crucial that you fully understand the contract for the API—whether the service you're consuming will alter results when execution deviates from the "happy path." And when you're providing a service, make sure to fully specify that contract.

Reflecting on what a circuit breaker does, and particularly in light of the use of aspects in the Hystrix implementation, you can see that the circuit breaker is essentially acting as a gateway to the Posts service. Ah, but the circuit breaker is but one example of functionality you may want to place in front of a service. Let's now have a look at the API gateway as a more generic pattern.

## 10.2 API gateways

The availability of both open source and commercial API gateways predates the rise of microservice and cloud-based architectures. For example, Apigee (since acquired by Google) and Mashery (since acquired by Intel and then sold to TIBCO) were companies both founded in the early 2000s, and both focused on API gateways.

The role of the API gateway in a software architecture has always been exactly what the title of this chapter says, to sit in front of bits of implementation and provide a whole host of services. These services might include the following:

- *Authentication and authorization*—Controlling access to the service the API gateway fronts. The mechanisms for this access control vary and can include secrets-based approaches such as the use of passwords or tokens, or could be network-based, either integrating with or implementing firewall-type services.
- *Encryption of data in flight*—The API gateway can handle decryption and is therefore the place where certificates must be managed.
- *Protecting the service from load spikes*—Configured properly, the API gateway becomes the only way that clients can access a service. Therefore, load-throttling mechanisms implemented here can provide significant protections. You might be thinking that what we just covered with circuit breakers sounds a bit like this, and you'd be right.
- *Access logging*—Because all traffic into the service comes through the API gateway, you have the ability to log all access. These logs can support a myriad of use cases, including auditing and operations observability.

Any of these concerns could be addressed within the service itself, yet it's obvious that these are cross-cutting concerns that needn't be implemented over and over again. Use of API gateways relieves the developer of functionality that could just be viewed as plumbing, allowing them to focus on business needs. But perhaps even more important, it provides a point where enterprise controls can be uniformly applied. Certainly, one of the most challenging things for IT operations is to demonstrate that security and compliance requirements are met on everything—centralized control is key.

The API gateway can perform its duties by interfacing with many other services. For example, the gateway doesn't itself store the users that need to be authenticated and authorized. Instead, it depends on an identity and access management solution and identity store (for example, LDAP) for those services; it simply enforces the policies expressed therein.

Figure 10.8 depicts a simple scenario: an API gateway is fronting a couple of services, all access to those services comes through the gateway, and it interfaces with other components to support the functionality it offers. An IT systems administrator, using an interface for the API gateway, will configure the needed policies. The figure also depicts an auditor reviewing access logs for each of the services.

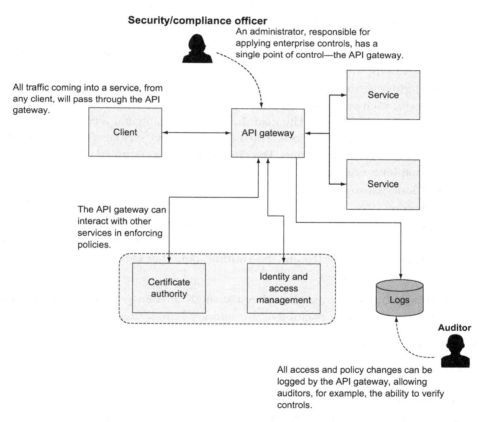

**Figure 10.8   The API gateway fronts all services and becomes the policy configuration and enforcement point for them.**

### 10.2.1  *The case for API gateways in cloud-native software*

If API gateways have been around and in use for more than 15 years, why am I covering them in this book? Well, as you can imagine, just as with many other topics we've discussed so far, the evolution to cloud-native software architectures introduces new requirements on the API gateway:

- It's pretty clear that the componentization of software that yields many more independent (micro) services increases the number of services to control by several orders of magnitude. Although it certainly wasn't ideal even then, it was at least theoretically possible for IT staff to manage service access without a centralized control plane. When you have thousands or even tens of thousands of service instances, this is no longer possible.

- The constant change being exerted on the service instances as they're re-created during outages and scheduled upgrades similarly means that any manual configurations that may have been done when deployments changed only annually or biannually (firewall rules, for example) are now completely intractable without a software solution to assist.

- Highly distributed systems have led to the implementation of other resilience patterns, such as the retries you've just been studying, which brings different load profiles to a service. The load that will be coming at a service is less predictable than it had been before. You need to protect services from unexpected and extreme request volumes. The circuit breaker you studied in the early part of this chapter is one type of this protection that has made its way into the API gateway.

- Cloud-native architectures have played a role in truly enabling new business models that allow for fee-based consumption of services. An API gateway enables the necessary metering, possibly with load throttling.

- In earlier chapters, I talked about parallel deploys. The API gateway is an excellent place to implement the routing logic that's so critical to things like safe upgrade processes.

Whereas API gateways may have been strongly advised yet not mandatory a decade ago, the characteristics of cloud-native software render them absolutely critical now.

### 10.2.2  *API gateway topology*

I hope at this point you're thinking something like, "Okay, I get why they're needed, but I don't like your figure 10.8. A centralized gateway sure seems like a cloud-native antipattern." You're right! You need consistent application of policies across all of your services—that's one of the value props of API gateway patterns. But that doesn't mean the implementation must be centralized. Yes, 15 years ago the API gateway was often deployed as a centralized, even if clustered, component, but that has changed in cloud-native architectures.

As I've already alluded to several times, the circuit breaker you studied and implemented in the first section of this chapter is an example of a gateway pattern, and the implementation certainly was distributed. In fact, it was compiled into the binary for the service itself (remember the inclusion of the `@HystrixCommand` annotation?). To get right to the punch line, what you need is distributed implementations of API gateway patterns. To get a visual of this, look at figure 10.9. There you can see that each of the services has had a gateway tacked to the front of it, and this gateway, just as in the previous diagram, interfaces with the set of components that support or are needed for its operations.

You'll also notice that I've depicted many more service instances than in the previous picture. You can imagine that if you had that many services with a centralized API gateway, and *all* interaction flowed through that gateway, you'd have to concern yourself with ensuring that the gateway was sized properly to handle the traffic to a heterogeneous and therefore difficult-to-predict set of app instances. By distributing the processing, each gateway instance handles the load for its service alone, and the proper sizing of the gateway is far more tractable.

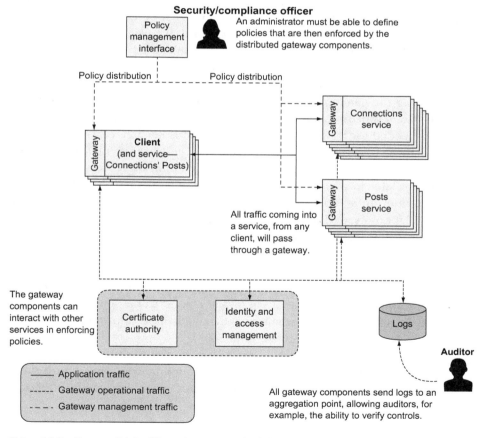

**Figure 10.9  You can think of the gateway as a single logical entity, something that's needed for administration. But for cloud-native architectures, the implementation is best distributed.**

I'd like to take a moment for you to explore an open source API gateway that has become popular in the last few years. It comes from our microservice heroes, Netflix. Zuul (named after a gatekeeper figure in the movie *Ghostbusters*), is described as "an edge service that provides dynamic routing, monitoring, resiliency, security, and more." These are the very things I've been attributing to the API gateway pattern. Zuul uses or embeds several other components from the Netflix microservices framework, including Hystrix (circuit breakers), Ribbon (load balancing), Turbine (metrics), and more.

Zuul, written in Java and therefore running in the JVM, is configured to front services via a URL. For example, to configure it to act as the gateway for our Posts service, you'd provide configuration data such as the following:

```
zuul.routes.connectionPosts.url=http://localhost:8090/connectionPosts
server.port=8080
```

The question then is how to include Zuul in your software topology. It's absolutely possible to create a deployment that looks like that of figure 10.8, but in a highly distributed software architecture, one closer to that of figure 10.9 is advised. In fact, Spring Cloud provides a way for Zuul to be embedded in your service in much the same way that the circuit breaker was embedded in our earlier example.[2] In doing so, you achieve the deployment topology shown in figure 10.9.

Having the gateway embedded into the service carries some obvious advantages: there's no network hop between the gateway and the service itself, the host name is no longer needed for configuration, only the path is needed, cross-origin resource sharing (CORS) concerns go away, and so on. But there are several disadvantages as well.

First, recall from the earlier discussions on application lifecycle that binding configuration later in the cycle offers more flexibility. If you've included the preceding configuration in an application.properties file, a change in configuration requires a recompilation. As we discussed, property values can be injected later via environment variables, but that still requires a restart of the JVM (or at least a refresh of the application context).

Second, if you're embedding a Java component, that pretty much means your service implementation must also be in Java, or at least be running in the JVM. Although all of the code examples here are in Java, the patterns I espouse are applicable to and should be implemented in whatever language is most appropriate in your scenario. I'm not a huge fan of Java-only solutions.

And finally, one of the goals of the API gateway pattern is to separate the concerns of the service developer from those of the operator. You want to give the latter the ability to apply consistent controls across all of the running services and offer them a control plane that makes this manageable.

---

[2] As is typical with Spring Boot, including Zuul is as straightforward as including `spring-cloud-starter-netflix-zuul` in your Maven or Gradle dependencies: http://mng.bz/YP4o.

How then do you achieve something like this gateway pattern in a way that's programming-language agnostic, more loosely coupled, and manageable? Enter the service mesh.

## 10.3 The service mesh

We don't have to go all the way to the service mesh in one step, so let me back up a little bit and start with a primitive that plays the central role in the service mesh. Then I will go on to introduce the service mesh and the role it's increasingly playing in the cloud-native software architecture.

### 10.3.1 The sidecar

Going back to the question that I just posed—how to provide distributed API gateway functionality that avoids the disadvantages of an embedded Java component—the answer is the sidecar. At the simplest level, a *sidecar* is a process that runs alongside your main service. If you look back at figure 10.9, you can imagine that the gateway services could be thought of as running alongside the services, not necessarily embedded. To meet the requirement that it not be compiled into the service binary, this, of course, means that the gateway sidecar is running as a separate process alongside the main service process.

Brilliantly, Kubernetes offers an abstraction that makes this work beautifully: the Kubernetes pod. A *pod* is the smallest unit of deployment in Kubernetes, and it contains one or more containers. You can host your main service in one container and the gateway services in another, both running in the same pod. We can now redraw our earlier diagram to use these constructs; see figure 10.10.

Each container has its own runtime environment, so the main service could, say, be running in a JVM, and the gateway sidecar could be implemented in, say, C++. Check—one disadvantage addressed. But now the communication between the gateway and the main service is interprocess, and even intercontainer; that means a network hop. Again, the architecture of Kubernetes comes to our assistance. All services running in a Kubernetes pod are hosted at the same IP address, meaning they can address each other over `localhost` and the network hop is therefore minimal.

One of the most popular sidecar implementations in use today is Envoy (www.envoyproxy.io). Originally built by ride-share company Lyft, Envoy is a distributed proxy written in C++, making it extremely efficient. It can be used within various deployment topologies, though the most common is having each instance front a single instance of a service (in a topology such as the one reflected in figure 10.10).

But this description is a bit disingenuous. Notice that I described Envoy as a proxy, not a gateway. Envoy does more than act as a gateway; it also proxies clients. I want to draw your attention all the way back to figure 10.7, which depicts both a client and a service that are participating in an interaction. That diagram specifically shows that you added retry behaviors to the outbound interaction on the client side and added a circuit breaker at the front of the inbound to the service-side code. The

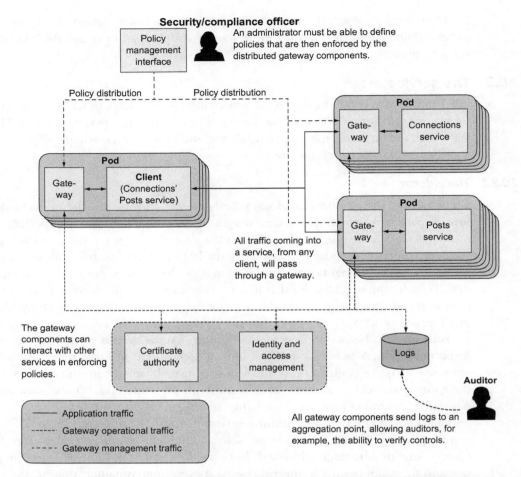

**Figure 10.10   The distributed gateway runs as a sidecar to each service. In Kubernetes this is achieved by running two containers in a single pod—one that's the primary service  and the other a gateway sidecar.**

latter is implementing a gateway pattern; the former is a proxy. The punch line? Envoy implements a proxy on the client side and a reverse-proxy/gateway on the service side of the interaction.

Okay, so that's pretty cool.

Redrawing figures 10.7 and 10.10 in figures 10.11 and 10.12, respectively, you can now see that a key element in cloud-native architectures, the interaction, is programmed through sidecars. Envoy implements a host of patterns at the edges of these interactions, including retries, circuit breakers, rate limiting, load balancing, service discovery, observability, and more. As I've said many times before, although you, the application developer or architect, must understand the patterns covered throughout this book, you aren't always responsible for implementing them. I'll say it again: this is pretty cool.

Notice that the interaction is now between proxies; the same is true in figure 10.12.

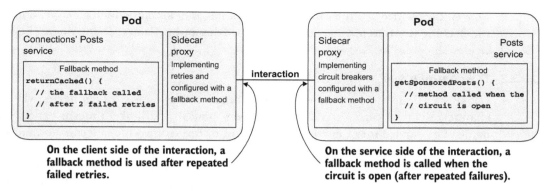

**Figure 10.11** Figure 10.7 redrawn with retry behavior on the client side of the interaction implemented in a sidecar, and the circuit breaker on the service side also implemented in a sidecar.

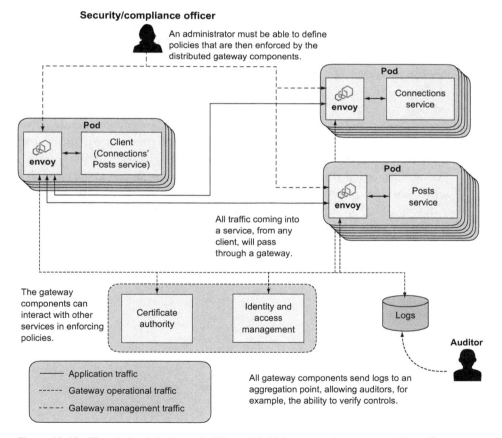

**Figure 10.12** The abstract "gateway" of figure 10.10 is now made concrete with an Envoy sidecar, one of several sidecar implementations.

I haven't yet addressed the other two disadvantages of an embedded gateway, both of which come down to manageability of the proxies and gateways. That's where the service mesh comes in.

### 10.3.2  *The control plane*

Looking at figure 10.12, you see a whole bunch of Envoy proxies connected via the channels that will carry interactions between them. It looks like a mesh; hence, the name. The service mesh encompasses the set of interconnected sidecars and adds a control plane for management of those proxies.

One of the most widely used service meshes available today comes from Istio (https://istio.io/), an open source project that was incubated by Google, IBM, and Lyft. It extends Kubernetes, using the pod primitive as the deployment mechanism for Envoy sidecars. Istio's tagline is "Connect, secure, control, and observe services," and it does so by supporting automatic sidecar injection and providing components that support configuration of the Envoy proxies, certificate handling, and policy enforcement. A control plane API offers the interface to this management control plane.

Figure 10.13 completes the picture that we've been deriving through the chapter.

This chapter and the preceding one have focused on the two sides of an interaction between services. Because the interaction crosses processes and sometimes even network boundaries, a variety of patterns are necessary to provide a robust software implementation that's tolerant to the inevitable changes in these distributed, cloud-based deployments. I've covered two of the key ones, retries on the client side and circuit breakers on the service side, the latter generalizing to a gateway pattern. Most notably, the service mesh has emerged as an essential part of the platform for running cloud-native applications. I strongly encourage you to use this technology.

I want to cover one final topic that centers on interaction: troubleshooting. Whether the main flow is request/response or event driven, the experience that a user has with the software is a reflection of the operation of dozens or even hundreds of services, all interacting with one another. When something doesn't go quite right, how on earth do we find the root cause of the trouble? This is covered in the next chapter.

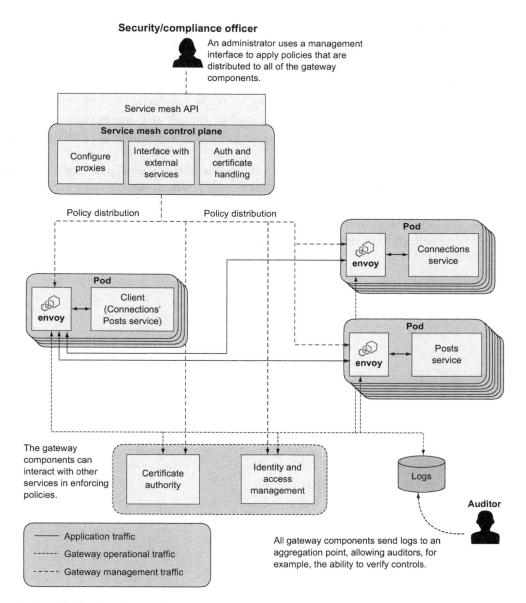

**Figure 10.13   A service mesh brings together sidecars and a control plane for their management.**

## Summary

- A host of patterns are designed to sit at the front edge of a service, which control the way an interaction with that service is handled.
- Circuit breakers are an essential pattern for protecting a service from being overwhelmed by load, including for traffic produced through retry storms.
- API gateways, which predate cloud-native software architectures, have evolved to operate well in the new context of highly distributed, constantly changing software deployments.
- Patterns applied on both the client side and the service side of an interaction can be encapsulated in and deployed as a sidecar proxy.
- The service mesh adds to the sidecar proxy a management plane that allows an operator to control security, offer observability, and allow configuration of the collection of services/apps that make up the cloud-native software.

# Troubleshooting: Finding the needle in the haystack

Back in 2013, I was working with one of the first enterprise customers of the Cloud Foundry open source platform. I visited a particular client every couple of weeks to check on their progress and to help explain capabilities that at that time were really quite new to the industry. And no matter how cool the feature set I was describing, one of the engineers from that organization invariably responded with something along the lines of "Cornelia, you are giving me a Ferrari without a dashboard." You see, we hadn't yet done a good job of adding capabilities in the area of observability, and there was simply no way that this customer (or any customer, really) could put a system in production without the ability to adequately monitor its health and the health of the applications running on the platform. That customer engineer, Srini, was absolutely right!

Solutions for system and application observability are nothing new. A big part of the operational practices for a piece of software, often captured in a runbook, is centered on how to assess if that software is running well, and how to, as early as possible, recognize when something goes awry. Over the past decades, tools along with best practices have been established that have helped turn the task of observability into a robust and dependable practice. But just as with many other well-established aspects of software, a cloud-native architecture brings with it a new set of challenges for which we must establish a new set of tools and practices. What are some of the new concerns for our highly distributed, constantly changing software?

As you've now seen many times, the constant change I speak of manifests itself as an ephemerality of the running apps and the environment in which they reside. The container a service is running in is constantly in flux—deleted and replaced by new instances during lifecycle operations such as an upgrade, or to recover instances that have had some type of catastrophic event (such as out of memory). This poses problems for many of the familiar troubleshooting practices of the past, which often involved poking around the runtime environment for clues. Now that you can't count on that runtime environment being around, how do you ensure access to the information you need to diagnose potential problems?

And the highly distributed nature of our software also brings new challenges. When a single user request fans out into dozens or hundreds of downstream requests, how can you pinpoint the cause of trouble in that complex hierarchy? Where you once had many components running in a single process and could therefore navigate through a call stack with relative ease, you now have calls that span a large number of distributed services, yet you'd still like to understand what that "call stack" looks like.

This chapter focuses on both of these elements. You'll see how to generate and handle log and metric data in a way that accounts for ephemeral runtime environments. And you'll learn about distributed tracing—a set of techniques and tools that mimic the intraprocess tracing techniques of the past, allowing an operator to follow the flow of related requests throughout a distributed network of microservices.

## 11.1   *Application logging*

I won't spend any time convincing you to write entries to logs; that's table stakes. But some of you may have performed log management from within an application; for example, you might have opened files and written to them. What I will argue for is that management of logs should be completely outside the application code.

Truth be told, this isn't an argument specific to cloud-native apps. It's a good idea for all software. The app code should express what should be logged, and the location where that log entry appears should be entirely controlled by the application deployment, not the app itself. Plenty of frameworks support this approach: Apache Log4j and its successor, Logback (https://logback.qos.ch/), for example, do just that; we've been using the latter in our code samples throughout this book. These allow the application code to simply have statements such as the following:

```
logger.info(utils.ipTag() + "New post with title " + newPost.getTitle());
```

Whether that log message then appears in a particular file, or in a console, or in something else is determined as part of the deployment.

For cloud-native applications, that deployment configuration should send the log lines to stdout and stderr. I know that's a pretty opinionated statement, so let me lend it a bit of support:

- Files are off-limits. The local filesystem lives only as long as the container does. You're going to need to access logs even after (dare I say, particularly after) an app instance and its container are gone. True, some container orchestration systems do support allowing a container to connect to an external storage volume whose lifecycle is independent from that of the container, but the semantics for doing so are complex, and the risk for contention issues with many other applications and application instances is significant.
- Driven in large part by the surge in popularity of open source and its accompanying resistance to proprietary solutions, we aim for some level of standardization wherever we can get it. We don't want to do logging one way if we deploy on JBoss, another way if we deploy on WebSphere, and yet another way on WebLogic. Stdout and stderr are ubiquitous; there's no vendor lock-in there.
- Stdout and stderr are not only vendor agnostic, but operating system agnostic. The concepts are the same whether on Linux, Windows, or another OS, and implementations deliver the same capabilities.
- Stdout and stderr are streaming APIs, and logs are most definitely streams. They don't have a start or end; instead, entries just keep flowing. As those entries appear in the stream, a stream-processing system can appropriately handle them.

Okay, then, application developers don't need to concern themselves with more than making a method call on a logger object (for example), but let's talk for just a moment about how the logs are then handled. As with many other topics we've already discussed, platforms are your friends. Case in point: you've already had ample practice as a user of the log-handling features of Kubernetes. Our app instances use SLF4J (a façade for logging frameworks such as Logback) objects to create log entries that are sent to the stdout and stderr streams. When you execute a command such as `kubectl logs -f pod/posts-fc74d75bc-92txh`, the Kubernetes CLI will connect into and present the stream entries to your terminal.

What I haven't spent any time talking about is how logging works when you have many instances of a service. For the most part, I've had you stream the logs for a single application instance. But in some situations, you may be interested in looking at the logs for an app, regardless of the number of instances running. For example, you may want to check whether a specific request was handled by any of your application instances without having to check the logs for each instance individually. Kubernetes will allow you to do this with a command such as the following:

```
$ kubectl logs -l app=posts
2018-12-02 22:41:42.644   ... s.c.a.AnnotationConfigApplicationContext ...
2018-12-02 22:41:43.582   ... trationDelegate$BeanPostProcessorChecker ...

  .   ____          _            __ _ _
 /\\ / ___'_ __ _ _(_)_ __  __ _ \ \ \ \
( ( )\___ | '_ | '_| | '_ \/ _` | \ \ \ \
 \\/  ___)| |_)| | | | | || (_| |  ) ) ) )
  '  |____| .__|_| |_|_| |_\__, | / / / /
 =========|_|==============|___/=/_/_/_/
 :: Spring Boot ::        (v1.5.6.RELEASE)


2018-12-02 22:41:44.309   ... c.c.c.ConfigServicePropertySourceLocator ...

...

2018-12-02 22:42:38.098   : [10.44.4.61:8080] Accessing posts using secret
2018-12-02 22:42:38.102   : [10.44.4.61:8080] getting posts for userId 2
2018-12-02 22:42:38.119   : [10.44.4.61:8080] getting posts for userId 3
2018-12-02 22:42:40.806   : [10.44.4.61:8080] Accessing posts using secret
2018-12-02 22:42:40.809   : [10.44.4.61:8080] getting posts for userId 2
2018-12-02 22:42:40.819   : [10.44.4.61:8080] getting posts for userId 3
2018-12-02 22:42:43.399   : [10.44.4.61:8080] Accessing posts using secret
2018-12-02 22:42:43.399   : [10.44.4.61:8080] getting posts for userId 2
2018-12-02 22:42:43.408   : [10.44.4.61:8080] getting posts for userId 3
2018-12-02 22:53:27.039   : [10.44.4.61:8080] Accessing posts using secret
2018-12-02 22:53:27.039   : [10.44.4.61:8080] getting posts for userId 2
2018-12-02 22:53:27.047   : [10.44.4.61:8080] getting posts for userId 3
2018-12-02 22:41:21.155   ... s.c.a.AnnotationConfigApplicationContext ...
2018-12-02 22:41:22.130   ... trationDelegate$BeanPostProcessorChecker ...

  .   ____          _            __ _ _
 /\\ / ___'_ __ _ _(_)_ __  __ _ \ \ \ \
( ( )\___ | '_ | '_| | '_ \/ _` | \ \ \ \
 \\/  ___)| |_)| | | | | || (_| |  ) ) ) )
  '  |____| .__|_| |_|_| |_\__, | / / / /
 =========|_|==============|___/=/_/_/_/
 :: Spring Boot ::        (v1.5.6.RELEASE)


2018-12-02 22:41:23.085   ... c.c.c.ConfigServicePropertySourceLocator ...

...

2018-12-02 22:42:46.297   : [10.44.2.57:8080] Accessing posts using secret
2018-12-02 22:42:46.298   : [10.44.2.57:8080] getting posts for userId 2
2018-12-02 22:42:46.305   : [10.44.2.57:8080] getting posts for userId 3
2018-12-02 22:53:30.260   : [10.44.2.57:8080] Accessing posts using secret
2018-12-02 22:53:30.260   : [10.44.2.57:8080] getting posts for userId 2
2018-12-02 22:53:30.266   : [10.44.2.57:8080] getting posts for userId 3
```

Taking a closer look at this output, you'll notice that the first part shows log entries from one pod instance, followed by entries from the second instance; the logs from multiple instances aren't interleaved. In many cases, it may be helpful to see the messages in time order, across all instances. For example, here's an ordering of the previous logs:

```
2018-12-02 22:41:21.155  ... s.c.a.AnnotationConfigApplicationContext ...
2018-12-02 22:41:22.130  ... trationDelegate$BeanPostProcessorChecker ...


  .   ____          _            __ _ _
 /\\ / ___'_ __ _ _(_)_ __  __ _ \ \ \ \
( ( )\___ | '_ | '_| | '_ \/ _` | \ \ \ \
 \\/  ___)| |_)| | | | | || (_| |  ) ) ) )
  '  |____| .__|_| |_|_| |_\__, | / / / /
 =========|_|==============|___/=/_/_/_/
 :: Spring Boot ::        (v1.5.6.RELEASE)

2018-12-02 22:41:23.085  ... c.c.c.ConfigServicePropertySourceLocator ...
2018-12-02 22:41:42.644  ... s.c.a.AnnotationConfigApplicationContext ...
2018-12-02 22:41:43.582  ... trationDelegate$BeanPostProcessorChecker ...


  .   ____          _            __ _ _
 /\\ / ___'_ __ _ _(_)_ __  __ _ \ \ \ \
( ( )\___ | '_ | '_| | '_ \/ _` | \ \ \ \
 \\/  ___)| |_)| | | | | || (_| |  ) ) ) )
  '  |____| .__|_| |_|_| |_\__, | / / / /
 =========|_|==============|___/=/_/_/_/
 :: Spring Boot ::        (v1.5.6.RELEASE)

2018-12-02 22:41:44.309  ... c.c.c.ConfigServicePropertySourceLocator ...


...


2018-12-02 22:42:38.098  : [10.44.4.61:8080] Accessing posts using secret
2018-12-02 22:42:38.102  : [10.44.4.61:8080] getting posts for userId 2
2018-12-02 22:42:38.119  : [10.44.4.61:8080] getting posts for userId 3
2018-12-02 22:42:40.806  : [10.44.4.61:8080] Accessing posts using secret
2018-12-02 22:42:40.809  : [10.44.4.61:8080] getting posts for userId 2
2018-12-02 22:42:40.819  : [10.44.4.61:8080] getting posts for userId 3
2018-12-02 22:42:43.399  : [10.44.4.61:8080] Accessing posts using secret
2018-12-02 22:42:43.399  : [10.44.4.61:8080] getting posts for userId 2
2018-12-02 22:42:43.408  : [10.44.4.61:8080] getting posts for userId 3
2018-12-02 22:42:46.297  : [10.44.2.57:8080] Accessing posts using secret
2018-12-02 22:42:46.298  : [10.44.2.57:8080] getting posts for userId 2
2018-12-02 22:42:46.305  : [10.44.2.57:8080] getting posts for userId 3
2018-12-02 22:53:27.039  : [10.44.4.61:8080] Accessing posts using secret
2018-12-02 22:53:27.039  : [10.44.4.61:8080] getting posts for userId 2
2018-12-02 22:53:27.047  : [10.44.4.61:8080] getting posts for userId 3
2018-12-02 22:53:30.260  : [10.44.2.57:8080] Accessing posts using secret
2018-12-02 22:53:30.260  : [10.44.2.57:8080] getting posts for userId 2
2018-12-02 22:53:30.266  : [10.44.2.57:8080] getting posts for userId 3
```

Although it can be helpful to see the logs aggregated in this way, with entries inter-leaved in time order, it's almost always important that log entries can be attributed to specific instances of the app. In these log entries, you can see this through the IP address: one instance has IP address 10.44.4.61, and the other has 10.44.2.57. Ide-ally, the instance designation would be added by the framework or platform so that the application code can be agnostic of the runtime environment.

Kubernetes doesn't do this. The IP address and port you see here are added through the Utils package in our implementation. I have, using the guidance from chapter 6 on application configuration, taken care to abstract the details of the plat-form, injecting the IP address through an environment variable, but I'd much rather have the platform include designation such as this with absolutely no effort from the developer. The takeaway is that as an application developer, you may need to place attention on ensuring that your log output includes information that identifies which app instance the entry is attributed to.

When I talk about a platform for handling logs, aggregation is only one of the nec-essary elements. Logs need to be ingested at scale and must be stored, and interfaces must support search and analysis of these potentially large volumes of data. The ELK stack (www.elastic.co/elk-stack) draws together three open source projects—Elastic-search, Logstash, and Kibana—to meet these requirements. Commercial offerings such as Splunk provide comparable capabilities. When you send your logs to stdout and stderr and ensure that the entries are attributable to specific app instances, you're doing all that's needed to allow systems such as these to provide powerful observability features. And you'll allow for the preservation of log entries even when application containers disappear.

## 11.2    *Application metrics*

In addition to log data, application metrics are needed for holistic application moni-toring. Metrics generally provide finer-grained insight into running applications than log files do; metrics are structured, whereas log files are usually unstructured or semi-structured at best. Frameworks are virtually always used to both automatically generate a default set of metrics and allow for custom metrics to be emitted. Default metrics generally include values around memory and CPU consumption, as well as HTTP interactions (when appropriate). For a language such as Java, metrics around garbage collection and the class loader are often included as well.

You've already been using the Spring Framework for metrics, simply by including the actuator dependency. In addition to the /actuator/env endpoint that you previ-ously used, the actuator provides an /actuator/metrics endpoint that emits the stan-dard and custom metrics for your Spring Boot apps. The following shows output served by this endpoint on the Connections' Posts service:

```
$ curl 35.232.22.58/actuator/metrics | jq
{
  "mem": 853279,
  "mem.free": 486663,
```

```
  "processors": 2,
  "instance.uptime": 2960448,
  "uptime": 2975881,
  "systemload.average": 1.33203125,
  "heap.committed": 765440,
  "heap.init": 120832,
  "heap.used": 278776,
  "heap": 1702400,
  "nonheap.committed": 90584,
  "nonheap.init": 2496,
  "nonheap.used": 87839,
  "nonheap": 0,
  "threads.peak": 43,
  "threads.daemon": 41,
  "threads.totalStarted": 63,
  "threads": 43,
  "classes": 8581,
  "classes.loaded": 8583,
  "classes.unloaded": 2,
  "gc.ps_scavenge.count": 1019,
  "gc.ps_scavenge.time": 8156,
  "gc.ps_marksweep.count": 3,
  "gc.ps_marksweep.time": 643,
  "httpsessions.max": -1,
  "httpsessions.active": 0,
  "gauge.response.metrics": 1,
  "gauge.response.connectionPosts": 56,
  "gauge.response.star-star": 20,
  "gauge.response.login": 2,
  "counter.span.accepted": 973,
  "counter.status.200.metrics": 3,
  "counter.status.404.star-star": 1,
  "counter.status.200.connectionPosts": 32396,
  "counter.status.200.login": 53
}
```

In addition to the values reported for memory, threads, and the class loader, notice that this instance has successfully served a great many (32,396) results on the /connectionsposts endpoint, several (53) on the /login endpoint, and three on the very /actuator/metrics endpoint you're using to get this data. It also responded once with a 404 status code.

Application metrics have been in widespread use for far longer than cloud-native applications, and once again, I want to focus on what changes in this new cloud context. Just as with logs, a key concern is ensuring that metrics data is available even after a runtime environment is no longer available. You need to get the metrics out of the app and runtime context, and two basic approaches are available: a pull-based model and a push-based one.

### 11.2.1  *Pulling metrics from cloud-native applications*

In a *pull-based approach*, a metrics aggregator is implemented as a collector that requests metrics data from each of the application instances and stores those metrics in a time-series database (figure 11.1). It's a bit like the `curl` to the `/actuator/metrics` endpoint that you saw just a moment ago; the collector as a client makes a request, and the app instance responds with the needed data.

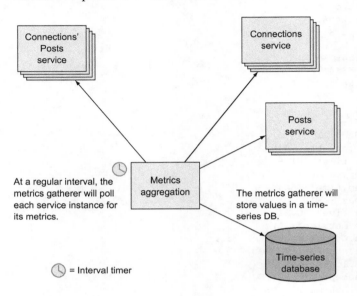

**Figure 11.1   With a pull-based metrics-gathering approach, each service implements a metrics endpoint that's accessed at a regular interval to capture and store the values for subsequent search and analysis.**

But what you've done with that `curl` isn't quite right. In the days where you had only a single application instance, or you treated each of a handful of instances as a separate entity, making a request via HTTP was fine; you could target each app instance directly. But now, when you have multiple app instances that are load balanced, you'll be getting metrics from only one of the app instances, and further, you don't know which one. This sounds familiar, right? It's the same issue you had with log entries not being associated with a specific instance, a problem you at least partially solved with the use of the `Utils` package that included an instance identity in the log entries. But it's more than that; in collecting metrics, you want to consistently gather values for each of the instances at a regular interval, and load balancers typically won't distribute requests as uniformly as you need.

The solution is to have the collector fully control which app instances it will pull from and at what interval. That collector wants to control where requests are made rather than allowing a load balancer to choose; again, I hope this sounds familiar. This is akin to client-side load balancing that you learned about in chapter 8, and part of client-side load balancing is service discovery. Figure 11.2 depicts the flow:

- At every interval, the collector requests metrics data from each instance.
- The set of instances is found through a service-discovery protocol, and how often the collector invokes this protocol to get the latest instance identities can vary. Doing so at every interval can be expensive, yet ensures that any changes in application topology are reflected as soon as possible. If it's acceptable that metrics for a new instance to be left out of the collection for a short time, the service discovery protocol can be executed less frequently.
- Performing service discovery at an interval separate from the metrics collection one yields a more loosely coupled solution.

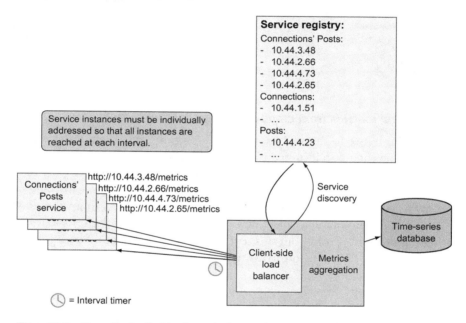

**Figure 11.2**  **The collector that implements the metrics aggregator must reach each service instance at every interval and must therefore control the load balancing. It will interact through a service discovery protocol to keep up to date with IP address changes.**

One complication with a pull-based approach is that the collector must, of course, have access to each of the instances from which it will request data. The IP address for each of the instances must be addressable from the metrics aggregator. Often, service instances are only individually addressable from well within an execution environment. You've seen this in our sample deployments, where only the Connections' Posts service was available from outside the cluster—and therefore the metrics gatherer must also be deployed within that network space. A common deployment topology for Kubernetes-based environments is to deploy Prometheus (https://prometheus.io/) *inside* the Kubernetes cluster itself. With this deployment topology, Prometheus uses the embedded DNS service and has direct access to the application instances (figure 11.3).

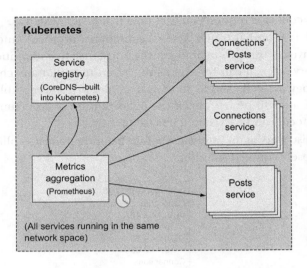

**Figure 11.3   The metrics gatherer must address each service instance individually, and because those IP addresses are accessible only from *within* a runtime environment such as Kubernetes (external access is via load balancer), the metrics gather is also generally deployed within that network space. In the case of Kubernetes, this also allows you to use the built-in DNS service for service discovery.**

### 11.2.2   *Pushing metrics from cloud-native applications*

An alternative to the pull-based model for gathering app metrics is a push-based one, whereby each app instance is responsible for delivering metrics to a metrics aggregator at a regular interval (figure 11.4). As an application developer, you might have an aversion to taking on the burden of delivering metrics data—working on code for that takes you away from the core business logic that's delivering value to your customers and organization. The good news is that like many of the cross-cutting concerns I've spoken about throughout this text, much of the work of metrics generation and delivery is taken care of by our trusty frameworks and platforms.

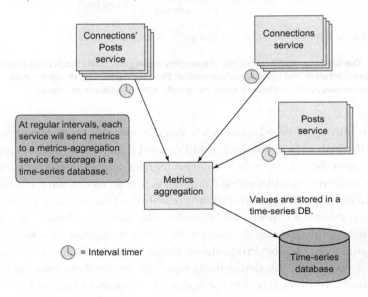

**Figure 11.4   In a push-based metrics solution, each service sends metrics to an aggregation and storage service at a certain interval.**

Frameworks delivering push-based metrics implementations generally do so with the use of an agent that takes care of gathering and delivering metrics to the metrics aggregator. The agent is usually compiled into the application binary with the inclusion of a dependency in something like a POM or Gradle build file. What is trickier, because of the constantly changing environment our apps and the agents live in, is proper configuration of that agent on deployment and during ongoing systems management.

For example, the IP address of the metrics aggregator must be configured into the running app so the agent knows where to send metrics. Using the best practices described in chapter 6, this is straightforward for initial deployment, but making configuration changes to an already running application must be done with care, as covered in chapter 7. You might be thinking this sounds like standard service discovery (also discussed earlier, in chapter 8), but because metrics delivery often is fairly resource intensive, adding a service discovery protocol into the flow of delivering metrics may generate unacceptable latency.

One more backward reference: in chapter 10, I talked about the sidecar providing API gateway functionality and implementing protocols around retries and circuit breakers. But the sidecar is also ideally suited for metrics collection. Recall that the sidecar is addressable from other containers in the pod via `localhost`, effectively shielding the app from changes in the metrics-gathering service. The in-app agent simply delivers metrics to the sidecar, and the sidecar then assumes responsibility for forwarding the data on to an external collector (figure 11.5). If the coordinates of the collector change, the app configuration doesn't change, and therefore no app lifecycle operations are needed. The sidecar/service mesh is specially designed to handle the constant change present in cloud-native applications and now takes on that responsibility. For example, the control plane for the service mesh may push any new IP address out into the mesh, updating all the sidecars. And sidecars such as Envoy are designed to adapt to application configuration changes more easily with capabilities such as hot restarts.

Did you notice? In the preceding discussion, I made a whole host of references to earlier chapters. Solving the metrics management problem for cloud-native apps is best done by applying cloud-native patterns. The example in this section is a great example.

Finally, having a sidecar proxy can provide value over and above simply proxying outbound metric pushes from the app, as it can also provide some level of observability even when no agent is installed into the application. Because it proxies traffic coming into and going out of the application, it can generate many metrics on behalf of the application. For example, counts of HTTP status codes, latencies, and more can be gathered or calculated, and delivered without anything being done within the application code.

This is an outstanding example of clever architectures and innovative frameworks allowing the separation of business concerns in the application from operational ones. Using the right platform can relieve the application developer of a great many concerns, allowing them to focus on the business outcomes of their code.

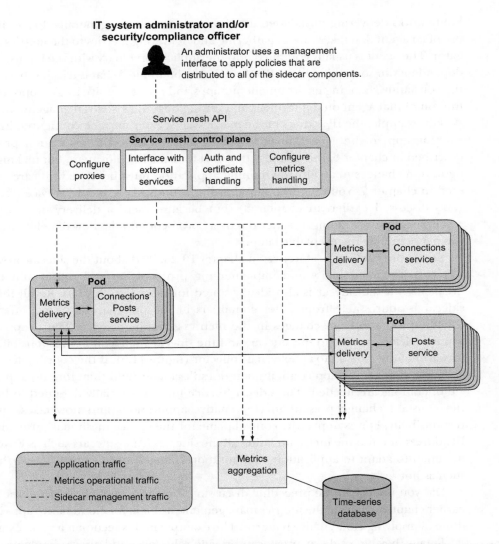

**Figure 11.5   When a service mesh is used, the application services are simply configured to connect to the local sidecar proxy, and the service mesh control plane is used to keep the configuration of the metrics delivery components up to date.**

## 11.3   *Distributed tracing*

Let's look at another capability that a combination of application frameworks and cloud-native platforms can bring. This capability, *distributed tracing*, is critically important for the highly distributed cloud-native application.

In an environment where our code is all running within the same process, we can use well-established tools to follow and troubleshoot the execution flow of an application. Source-level debugging will jump from method to method, and when configured correctly will even step into code that's brought into the application via inclusion of a library (code that you haven't written). When exceptions occur, the call stack that's printed to the console and/or output to logs shows the sequence of calls that were made, something that's often helpful in diagnosing problems.

But now an invocation of your application can result in a cascade of downstream requests that are usually running out of process and, in fact, are most often running in totally different runtime contexts (in different containers or on different hosts). How can you see the equivalent of a call stack, or simply get a view into what is happening as a result of an application invocation in this distributed scenario? The technique that has become prevalent in the industry and has solid tooling behind it is distributed tracing.

Distributed tracing, exactly as it sounds, is about tracing program flow across a distributed set of components. It's what allows us to gain visibility into the fan-out of all of the downstream requests that result from, for example, a Netflix homepage access. In figure 11.6, the point on the left side represents the homepage request, and the lines to other points represent calls to additional services made to gather the contents of a user's homepage display.

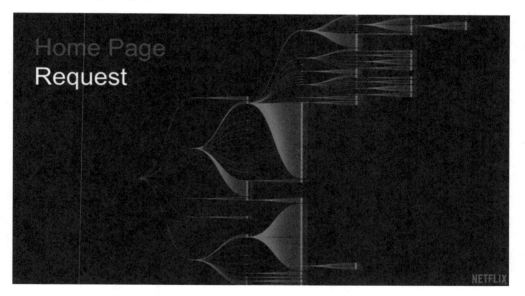

**Figure 11.6**  Diagram appearing in a presentation from Scott Mansfield of Netflix shows a request to the Netflix homepage results in a series of downstream service invocations. Distributed tracing allows you to gain visibility into this complex call tree.

A rather popular technology being used today is Zipkin (https://zipkin.io/), a project modeled after the research on distributed tracing that was first published in the Google Dapper paper in 2010.[1] At the core of the technique are the following:

---

[1]The paper, "Dapper, a Large-Scale Distributed Systems Tracing Infrastructure," is available from Google at http://mng.bz/178V.

- The use of *tracers*, unique identifiers that are inserted into requests and responses so that related app invocations can be found
- A control plane that uses these tracers to assemble the call graph for a set of what otherwise are independent (by design!) invocations

When a service is invoked and that service makes a downstream request to another service, any tracer included in the request to the former will be passed on to the latter. That tracer is then available in the runtime context of each of the services and—*here's the key*—can be included in any metrics or log output. Using that tracer along with other data from the services context (timestamps, for example) allows you to piece together the flow through a set of services that in combination build the response to a service request.

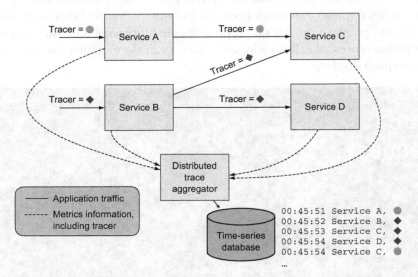

**Figure 11.7   Requests carry tracers that are propagated in downstream requests. The tracers are then available in the runtime context of a service invocation and annotates data that's aggregated into a distributed tracing service.**

In figure 11.7, you can see a set of services and invocations that carry these tracers. Also depicted in this diagram is a database that collects output from each of the services—data that includes the tracer values. From the data stored in there, you can rebuild the "call stack" for the set of related component invocations. For example, you can see that a request coming into service A created a subsequent call to service C; and an unrelated request to service B also led to a downstream request to service C, followed by a request to service D.

To make this more concrete, let's get our sample code running and look at new output.

## SETTING UP

Once again, I refer you to the setup instructions for running the samples in earlier chapters. Running the sample in this chapter carries no new requirements.

You'll be accessing files in the cloudnative-troubleshooting directory, so in your terminal window change into that directory.

And as I've described in previous chapters, I've already prebuilt Docker images and made them available in Docker Hub. If you want to build the Java source and Docker images and push them to your own image repository, I refer you to earlier chapters (the most detailed instructions are in chapter 5).

## RUNNING THE APPLICATION

You'll need a Kubernetes cluster with sufficient capacity, as described in the first example of chapter 9. If you still have the examples running from the previous chapter, let's get those cleaned up. Run the script I've provided as follows:

```
./deleteDeploymentComplete.sh all
```

Running this deletes all instances of the Posts, Connections, and Connections' Posts services, as well as MySQL, Redis, and SCCS that are running. If you have other things running in your Kubernetes cluster, you may want to clear some of that out. Just make sure you have enough capacity.

A slight start order dependency exists. After creating the MySQL server, you need to create the actual databases therein, so let's get it and the other backing services running first:

```
./deployServices.sh
```

After the MySQL database is up and running, which you can see by running `kubectl get all`, you'll create the database by using the MySQL CLI as follows:

```
mysql -h <public IP address of your MySQL service> \
 -P <port for your MySQL service> -u root -p
```

The password is `password`. After you're in, you'll run the command to create the database:

```
create database cookbook;
```

Now you can start the microservices, which you do by running the following script:

```
./deployApps.sh
```

I'll go into the details of the implementation in just a moment, but let's start by invoking our Connections' Posts service and viewing log output. You'll first log in with the following command:

```
curl -i -X POST -c cookie \
  <connectionsposts-svc IP>/login?username=cdavisafc
```

And then get your Connections' Posts with the following:

```
curl -b cookie <connectionsposts-svc IP>/connectionsposts | jq
```

Now let's look at the logs for each of our microservices. As I talked about in earlier sections, because you have multiple instances of each microservice, some type of log aggregation would be helpful, and although that offered in Kubernetes could be better, it's sufficient for our purposes here. Run each of the following commands, and then you'll study the results:

```
kubectl logs -l app=connectionsposts
kubectl logs -l app=connections
kubectl logs -l app=posts
```

### 11.3.1  *Tracer output*

The following three log output listings are excerpts from the output of each of these commands.

**Listing 11.1   Log output from Connections' Posts**

```
2019-02-25 02:20:11.969 [mycookbook-connectionsposts,2e30...,2e30...]
➡ getting posts for user network cdavisafc
2019-02-25 02:20:11.977 [mycookbook-connectionsposts,2e30...,2e30...]
➡ connections = 2,3
```

**Listing 11.2   Log output from Connections**

```
2019-02-25 02:20:11.974 [mycookbook-connections,2e30...,9b5f...] getting
➡ connections for username cdavisafc
2019-02-25 02:20:11.974 [mycookbook-connections,2e30...,9b5f...] getting
➡ user cdavisafc
...
2019-02-25 02:20:11.987 [mycookbook-connections,2e30...,b915...] getting
➡ user 2
...
2019-02-25 02:20:11.994 [mycookbook-connections,2e30...,990f...] getting
➡ user 3
```

**Listing 11.3   Log output from Posts**

```
2019-02-25 02:20:11.980 [mycookbook-posts,2e30...,33ac...] Accessing posts
➡ using secret ...
2019-02-25 02:20:11.980 [mycookbook-posts,2e30...,33ac...] getting posts
➡ for userId 2
2019-02-25 02:20:11.981... [mycookbook-posts,2e30...,33ac...] getting posts
➡ for userId 3
```

The log output now includes new values enclosed in square brackets. The first is the application name. The second is the trace ID; this is exactly the tracer that I've been talking about. The third value is the span ID, used to identify each unique invocation of an app;

for example, in the preceding log output, the Connections app was invoked three times, as indicated by the three span IDs (9b5f..., b915... and 990f...). The span ID can be used to correlate metrics or log outputs that are part of a single service execution.

Studying the preceding output, which truncates the trace IDs and span IDs to the first four digits of hex numbers generated by the Spring Framework, you can see the following:

- When you `curl` the Connections' Posts service, a trace ID starting with 2e30 is generated.
- Because the call is the outermost invocation, that number is also the span ID (2e30...) and represents the work being done to generate the list of posts for the people that `cdavisafc` follows.
- Any log output from the Connections' Posts service has these values for trace ID and span ID.
- The Connections service was invoked three times:
  - Because all the outputs include a trace ID of 2e30, you know that these invocations were all downstream requests from your `curl` to Connections' Posts.
  - Because this output has three span IDs, you know that the Connections service was invoked three times.
- The Posts service was invoked once. Because the trace ID is 2e30, you know that the invocation is a downstream request from your original `curl` command.
- Finally, at the beginning of each line of log output is a timestamp.

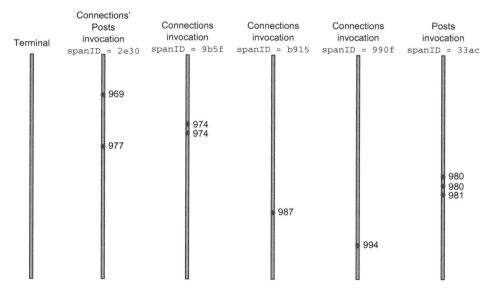

Figure 11.8  From the annotated log output, you can piece together some of the flow of a single request—that with trace ID 2e30. Notice that you can't see where the calls to the services came from.

This data allows you to piece together part of the flow, as depicted in figure 11.8. The dots are accompanied with a timestamp showing moments when log output was generated. This diagram shows the following:

- (With your original `curl`) the Connections' Posts service is called.
- The Connections service is called (to get a list of the users I follow).
- The Posts service is called (with the list of those connections to get a list of posts for those connections).
- (For each post returned from there, and there are two), the Connections service is called (to obtain the name of the user that made the post).

I've parenthesized parts of the preceding flow because those are the semantics that you and I know about our sample application, but the nonparenthesized parts of the phrases are what can be seen in the trace output. This is interesting; in figure 11.8, you're blind to the details that are within the parentheses in the preceding description. Figure 11.9 fills in the details that come from these additional phrases.

Note that the data represented in the arrows of figure 11.9 could also be inserted into log output, but that's not done with the Spring Cloud libraries.

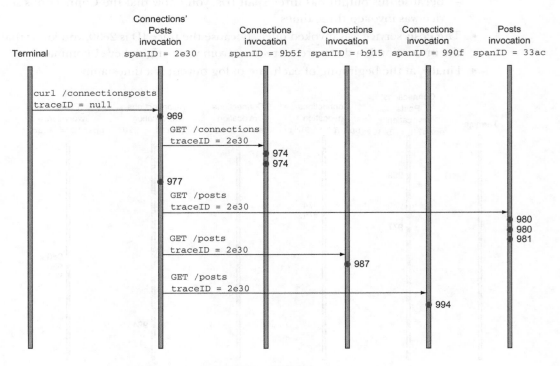

Figure 11.9  Here, the service invocations are overlaid on the time, trace ID, and span ID stamped log output shown in the previous figure. This information isn't currently appearing in your logs.

### 11.3.2 *Assembling traces via Zipkin*

I've had you explore what is happening with the trace and span IDs by inspecting the logs, but tooling such as Zipkin allows you to analyze these types of values more effectively. Zipkin provides a data store for trace- and span-annotated metrics, and a user interface that displays data and supports navigation through that data.

Services are responsible for delivering the data to the Zipkin store, and this brings us to an important consideration. The act of sending data out of a service takes resources; it consumes memory, CPU cycles, and I/O bandwidth. The metrics that I spoke of earlier were scoped to a service. You were gathering data about how the running service was operating. The metrics I'm now covering are scoped to a service invocation. With the former, you could decide to gather metrics once a second, but if a service is responding to 100 requests per second and you're gathering metrics for every invocation, that's two orders of magnitude more resource intensive. As a result, the best practice for distributed tracing is to gather metrics for only a subset of all service requests.

I've covered this nuance here because I want you to apply the use of distributed tracing to experiments we ran in chapters 9 and 10. You're going to put our application under load, but you want to limit the impact that the act of tracing has on our system, so you need to configure it so that it emits tracing info for only a subset of the calls. In the deployment for each of our services, you'll see a configuration such as the following:

```
- name: SPRING_SLEUTH_SAMPLER_PERCENTAGE
  value: "0.01"
```

This will cause 1% of requests to generate tracing metrics and send them to Zipkin (I will explain Spring Cloud Sleuth in a moment). Let's now place load on the system. I've changed the volume of requests in our simulation, so I need you to upload a new JMeter configuration into Kubernetes with the following:

```
kubectl create configmap zipkin-jmeter-config \
  --from-file=jmeter_run.jmx=loadTesting/ConnectionsPostsLoadZipkin.jmx
```

You can then start the simulation running:

```
kubectl create -f loadTesting/jmeter-deployment.yaml
```

This is now repeating the accesses of the Connections' Posts service, and for a subset of these requests, trace data is being stored in the Zipkin database. To access the URL for the Zipkin user interface, look up the IP address and port for the Zipkin service with the following command:

```
echo http://\
$(kubectl get service zipkin-svc \
-o=jsonpath={.status.loadBalancer.ingress[0].ip})"/"\
$(kubectl get service zipkin-svc \
-o=jsonpath={.spec.ports[0].port})
```

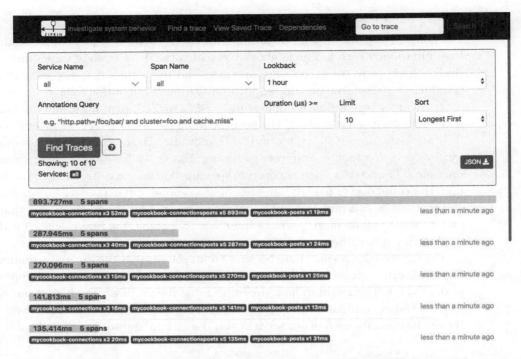

**Figure 11.10    Zipkin provides a user interface that allows for search through the data stored in the distributed metrics database and pulls together entries that are related through a common trace ID. This display shows five such traces, each of which draws together five individual service requests, represented as *spans*.**

Access that URL in your browser and click the Find Traces button. This will show results such as in figure 11.10.

Displayed here are five traces through our distributed application. Each of these results corresponds to a separate `curl` to the Connections' Posts service. The first took almost 900 ms to complete; the second and third, less than 300 ms; and the last two, less than 150 ms. Clicking on the light-grey bar for the fourth displayed invocation, the one that reads "141.813ms 5 spans," renders the display shown in figure 11.11.

This display lays out the spans that make up a single invocation, those spans having been gathered together because they share the same trace ID. Recall the log output you looked at just a moment ago and pieced together in figure 11.8; in fact, figure 11.11 is similar to figure 11.8 laid on its side. You can see that the span for the Connections' Posts service stretches for the full 141 ms, and you also see the spans for the downstream requests—the request to Connections to obtain the list of followed users, the request to the Posts service to get the list of posts, and the two requests back to the Connections service to get the names of the post authors. This is exactly the flow derived from the earlier log output.

**Figure 11.11** **Zipkin display showing the details of a single request to the Connections' Posts service. This service request resulted in four downstream requests: one to the Connections service, one to the Posts service, and then two more requests to the Connections service. The latency for each request, represented as a span, is also shown.**

Now let's disrupt our system with a network outage, just as you did in chapters 9 and 10. I've provided you with a script that will break the network connections between the instances of our Posts service and the MySQL database. You'll have to update that script to point to your MySQL pod and to include the IP addresses of your Posts service instances. You can then invoke this script with the following command:

```
./loadTesting/alternetwork-db.sh add
```

Leave the network broken for 10–15 seconds and then restore the network by executing the following command:

```
./loadTesting/alternetwork-db.sh delete
```

Let's now return to the main Zipkin dashboard and click the Find Traces button. You'll see something that looks like figure 11.12.

The bars that represent the full length of a specific invocation (those reading "26.488s 22 spans") have turned light red, giving you the first indication of trouble. Looking at the details, you see that each invocation has more than the five spans that you saw when the system was healthy. Clicking on one of these red bars shows the details shown in figure 11.13.

Here you see the retries! Because of the network disruption between the Posts service and its database, the Posts service is unable to generate a response, and the request coming from the code of the Connections' Posts service times out. You can now see that the version of the code that I pulled from chapter 9 into this project is that which does brute-force, or very unkind, retries. After the network connection is reestablished, the call to the Posts service succeeds, and the execution of the Connections Posts concludes.

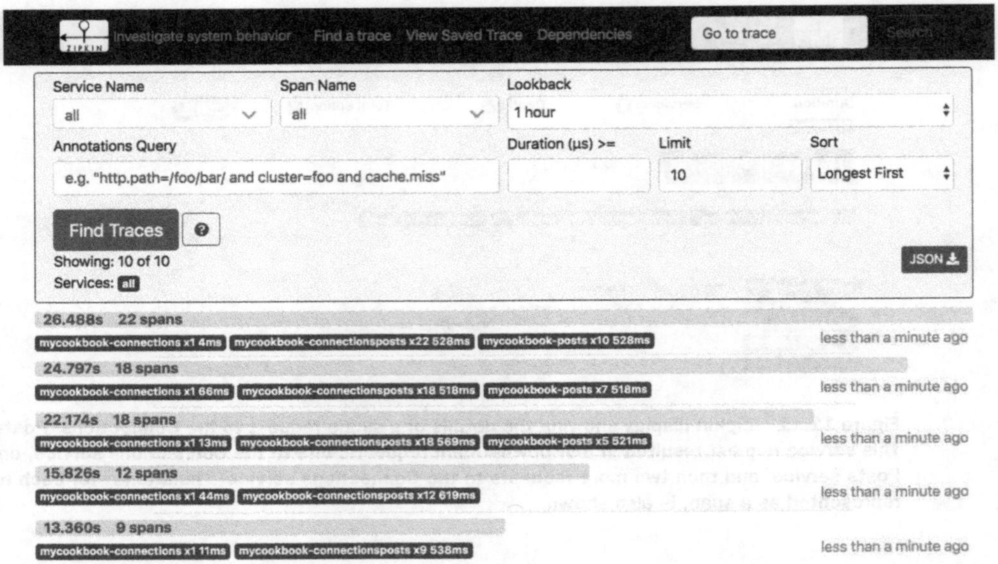

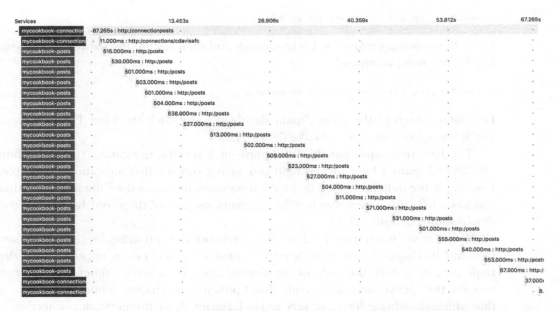

**Figure 11.12    While the network was disrupted, requests to the Connections' Posts service resulted in failed downstream requests. You see, for example, that what normally was satisfied with four downstream requests resulted in many more requests/spans. The bars reporting the time and number of spans (for example, "26.488s 22 spans") are also now colored red, indicating that some of those downstream requests returned errors.**

**Figure 11.13    The details of one of the request traces show repeated failed calls to the Posts service, each taking roughly 500 ms. This is the value of the request time-out on the HTTP invocations made from the Connections' Posts service.**

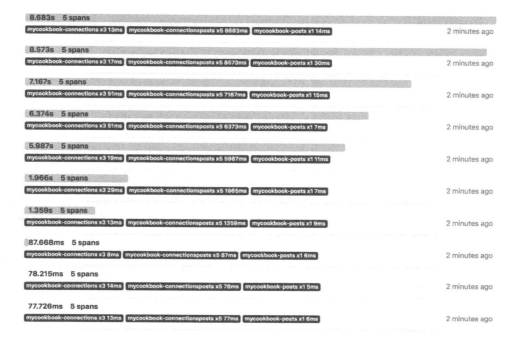

**Figure 11.14** When the network is restored, downstream requests again succeed, but you can see from the time taken to fulfill Connections' Posts requests that a backlog of traffic had been generated and required time to dissipate.

Finally, returning to the Zipkin homepage and viewing the list of traces shortly after the restoration of the network, you see displayed the data shown in figure 11.14.

This shows that the time needed for Connections' Posts processing returns to normal after the traffic from the retry storm dissipates.

By using distributed tracing techniques, you gained valuable insight into how our cloud-native application was performing. You were able to quickly see when and where errors were thrown, and you were able to track the route back to stability following the repair of an earlier outage. And the good news is that when using something such as the Spring Framework, these capabilities are easily added to an implementation.

### 11.3.3 Implementation details

Recall that at the core of distributed tracing are two specific techniques:

- Insertion of trace IDs
- A control plane that collects metrics that include these trace IDs, and uses them to link together related service invocations

These two concerns are addressed with the inclusion of two dependencies in your project POM files:

**Listing 11.4    Added to pom.xml of each of the three microservices**

```xml
<dependency>
    <groupId>org.springframework.cloud</groupId>
    <artifactId>spring-cloud-starter-sleuth</artifactId>
    <version>2.0.3.RELEASE</version>
</dependency>
<dependency>
    <groupId>org.springframework.cloud</groupId>
    <artifactId>spring-cloud-sleuth-zipkin</artifactId>
    <version>2.0.3.RELEASE</version>
</dependency>
```

Spring Cloud Sleuth instruments the generation and propagation of trace and span IDs. Including the first of the preceding dependencies causes these values to be included in the log files that you studied earlier. The second of these dependencies adds the delivery of the metrics to a Zipkin server, the address of which is configured into each of your services by setting the `spring.zipkin.baseUrl` property. You can see this setting, along with the sampler rate, in the Kubernetes deployment files for each of the services. (Notice that you're addressing the Zipkin service via name; the service discovery protocol built into Kubernetes assists with the actual binding.)

**Listing 11.5    Added to deployment yaml file for each of the three microservices**

```yaml
- name: SPRING_APPLICATION_JSON
  value: '{"spring":{"zipkin":{"baseUrl":"http://zipkin-svc:9411/"}}}'
- name: SPRING_SLEUTH_SAMPLER_PERCENTAGE
  value: "0.01"
```

I've included a Zipkin service in the sample application deployment with the zipkin-deployment.yaml file.

And that's it. That's right—you don't need to change anything else in the code to enable distributed tracing. It's entirely handled by the Spring Framework. The value that distributed tracing brings is worth this level of effort, and even a bit more, should you be programming in a language that doesn't provide the same level of support as this. At the time of writing, Zipkin libraries exist for Java, JavaScript, C#, Golang, Ruby, Scala, PHP, Python, and more. This broadly adopted technology is also included in other fabrics such as Istio (see section 10.3.2 in chapter 10.)

## Summary

- Both metrics and log entries must be proactively pulled out of the runtime context in which our services are executing, because those execution environments are often unavailable after a service has either experienced trouble or has been upgraded. Execution environments for our services should be thought of as ephemeral.

- Aggregation of log entries from multiple instances of a service is important for observability. A solution that interleaves, in time order, entries from the different services is usually preferred.

- Collection of observability information, logs, metrics, and tracing data is effectively implemented in sidecar proxies, which allows the application to focus on business logic and concentrates the operational needs into the service mesh.

- Well-established distributed-tracing techniques, and implementations thereof, provide valuable insight into the health and performance of your distributed applications.

- Many of the patterns covered earlier in this book are used in the solutions that offer the necessary observability. Application configuration, application lifecycle, service discovery, gateways, and service mesh all come into play.

# Cloud-native data:
# Breaking the data monolith

*12*

Remember how I defined *cloud-native* in chapter 1? There I did a lightweight analysis that took us from high-level requirements for modern software to a set of four characteristics: cloud-native software is redundant, adaptable, modular, and dynamically scalable (figure 12.1). And for the bulk of the book, you've studied these characteristics in the context of the services and interactions that make up our software. But recall that the third entity in the mental model that I also laid out in chapter 1 was *data*. The characteristics of cloud-native software apply just as much to the data layer.

Take, for example, redundancy. Although the value of having multiple copies of data has been long understood, the patterns for achieving it in the past were often bolted on, and sometimes came through operational practices. For example, in active/passive deployment topologies, the active node is serving all read and write traffic, while the passive node is being updated with writes behind the scenes. If something happens to the active node, the whole system could fail over to what had been the passive node. Modern cloud-native data services (recall that in section 5.4.1, I talked about the special types of services that are the stateful ones) have redundancy built deeply into their multinode designs and employ patterns such as Paxos and leader/follower to drive the consistency and availability characteristics they deliver.

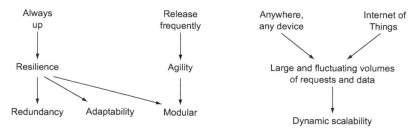

**Figure 12.1  User requirements for software drive our development toward cloud-native architectural and management tenets. For cloud-native data, we'll turn our focus to modularity and the autonomy that comes from it.**

For scalability, we've also seen significant changes in the patterns that rule the day. Traditional databases were most often scaled vertically, by providing larger and larger hosts and storage devices to serve expanding needs. But as you've seen throughout the text, with cloud-native horizontal scalability rules, most modern databases such as Cassandra, MongoDB, and Couchbase have this model designed into the core of their systems. As data volumes increase, new nodes can be joined to the database cluster, and existing data and requests will be redistributed across all of the old and new nodes.

Although we could study a great deal about all four characteristics shown at the bottom of figure 12.1, in this final chapter I place the bulk of our attention on *modularity*. Clearly, having many individual (micro)services brought together to form our software is central to cloud-native architectures. But the name *microservice* is a bit misleading (hence, I've used it only sparingly throughout the text). It encourages us to focus too much on the size of the service, rather than on the most valuable thing it brings: autonomy. When done right, microservices can be built by independent teams and can be independently managed (scaled). Further, they're the primary entity against which many of the other cloud-native patterns are applied (circuit breakers, service discovery) and they're at the endpoints of cloud-native interactions.

We used to have monolithic applications that we've now decomposed into many individual services, and this has given us modularity. Or has it? Those monolithic applications had at the backend monolithic databases, and all too often we see new

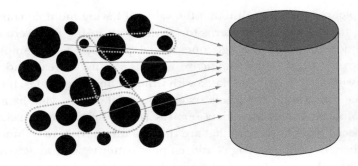

Figure 12.2   Independent microservices that share a single database are not autonomous.

cloud-native designs that look like figure 12.2. We've broken the compute portion of our software into individual services but have left a centralized, monolithic data tier.

This simple diagram makes it clear that such designs offer only the illusion of modularity; a shared database creates transitive dependencies between otherwise independent services. For example, if one service wants to change a database schema, it must coordinate with all other services that share any part of that database schema. Further, with a shared database, many individual services are all competing for concurrent access, creating additional bottlenecks. Alas, our microservices aren't all that autonomous after all.

As the chapter title suggests, ultimately, our goal is to break up that data monolith. You may already have heard it said that every microservice should own its own database, but that might sound dangerous. How will you maintain integrity of your data across dozens or hundreds of stores? How will different teams coordinate across this complex network? Just as breaking the compute monolith apart brought new challenges—challenges we've systematically addressed with the set of patterns presented throughout this text—breaking the data monolith also brings challenges. And those challenges will be addressed with patterns—cloud-native data patterns.

Many in the industry believe that event sourcing is the ultimate answer to these problems, and this chapter covers that topic. But just as with all of the other patterns covered in this book, it's not all or nothing. I would like to take us on a journey that starts with basic, familiar design patterns and work our way up to event sourcing. My hope is that presenting the topic in this manner will not only deepen your understanding of the key elements of cloud-native data handling, but also provide a practical way for you to get there in steps.

I'll start with caching, a technique that has been in use for some time and remains relevant in cloud-native software architectures; remember what happened when we added a cache as part of our fallback behaviors when studying resiliency patterns? We'll have another look at caching here. Then I'll do a brief review of chapter 4, where we turned request/response on its head and sent events flowing through our services topology instead. I'll enhance that event-driven design by adding an event log, and then I'll finally introduce the concept of event sourcing. As we go through this design evolution, I'll use an analysis of request successes and failures under different outage conditions as a measure of autonomy, and you'll see the important role that data design plays in our cloud-native architectures.

## 12.1 Every microservice needs a cache

To see the value that caching brings—and it goes beyond just performance—let's start with a design that doesn't yet use a cache. Figure 12.3 shows our usual example, in which the Connections' Posts service aggregates content from our two other services: Connections, which manages users and who they follow, and Posts, which manages blog posts. In this diagram, we're using the familiar request/response protocol to interact between these services.

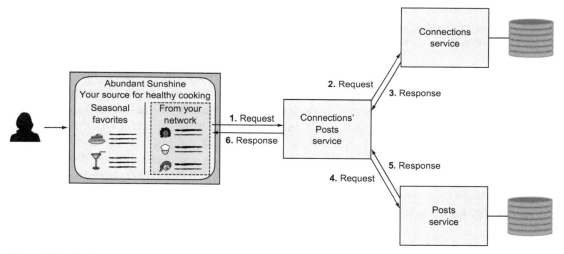

**Figure 12.3  A simple topology with an aggregating service communicating with dependent services via request/response.**

Using this simple architecture as a baseline for the analysis that runs through the rest of the chapter, let's look at the system's resiliency in the face of partial outages. Figure 12.4 shows the four compute components of our software: the rich web application and the three services depicted with the horizontal lines. When solid, these lines represent a time that the service is available and producing results, and breaks in those lines indicate when the service is unavailable or not functioning properly.

You'll note that I haven't depicted any downtime for the rich web application or the Connections' Posts service. This is not to imply that they never go down. Rather, I want to focus only on the dependencies between microservices and with the request/response protocol; those interactions exist only when the aggregating service is being called and is functioning.

Coming in vertically are requests from the web application to the Connections' Posts service, and then cascading to the dependent services. Whenever either the Connections service or the Posts service is down, the aggregating service fails to generate a result.

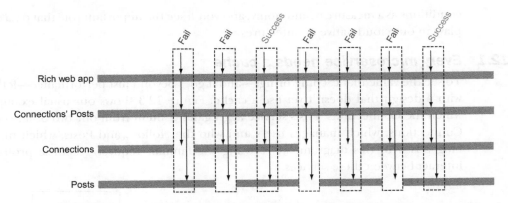

**Figure 12.4   Whenever one of the dependent services is unavailable or otherwise not functioning correctly, the Connections' Posts service will also fail to generate a result.**

Now let's add a cache to the Connections' Posts service (figure 12.5). This cache may be populated in numerous ways. With *look-aside caching*, the cache client (in this case, the Connections' Posts service) is responsible for implementing the caching protocol: when data is needed, it will check the cache for a value, and if it's not present, will make a request to the downstream service and write the result into the cache before itself returning a result. With *read-through caching*, the Connections' Posts service accesses only the cache, and the cache implements the logic of obtaining the value from the downstream service when necessary. Regardless of the protocol, a value is stored locally following a successful downstream request.

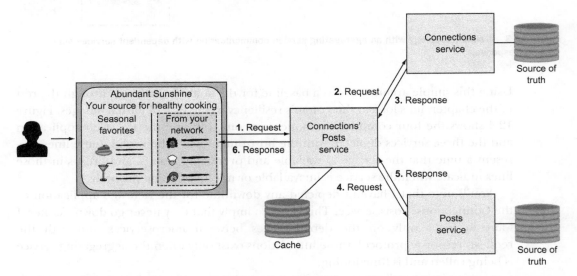

**Figure 12.5   A cache added to the Connections' Posts service will store the responses from successful requests to dependent services. The source of truth for the data remains in the databases tied to each of the downstream services; the storage local to the Connections' Posts service is not an authoritative copy.**

Let's now look at whether our system has become more resilient with this addition. Figure 12.6 adds another horizontal bar alongside that of the Connections' Posts service. To simplify things a bit, assume that the cache is available anytime the Connections' Posts service is. We can see that initially the request results are exactly what we previously saw: when either of the downstream services is unavailable, the aggregating service will be unable to generate a full response. But after the cache is populated, it insulates the consumer, the web app, from failures of the downstream services.

I want to draw your attention to one subtlety in figure 12.6. Compared to the scenario depicted in figure 12.4, notice that you can start seeing success on incoming requests as soon as each downstream service has been reached at least once, and that successful downstream requests needn't all come at the same time. It should be clear that the level of resilience is directly tied to our system components' degree of autonomy.

That's all pretty compelling, and clearly you achieved far greater levels of resilience when you made Connections' Posts more autonomous by adding a cache. Why isn't this enough? The answer is that everything I've shown here is a significant oversimplification of caching. You can see a hint of that in figure 12.6, where I make the point that the second request *could* succeed *if* the first request happened to load the data needed for the second one. How do you know, for example, if a lack of any cached posts for Food52 means there are no new posts on that site, or that a successful Posts request including that site has yet to happen? And if the cache has an entry, how do you know whether it's up to date?

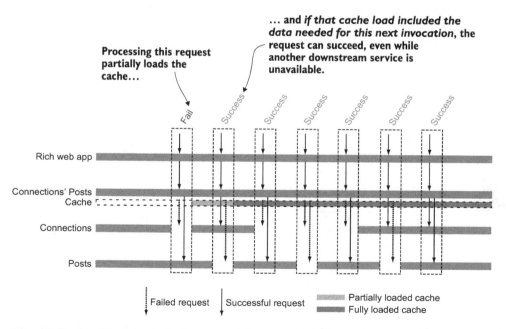

**Figure 12.6   By adding a cache to Connections' Posts, you add a degree of autonomy to the service and achieve greater resilience as a result.**

The way we've historically used caching, and even the motivating factors for using it, were different from our present aims for its use in microservice architectures. Often used to achieve a certain level of performance gain, the data we cached tended to be more static (website images and zip-code-to-city mappings, for example), so expiring the cache based on a timer was usually sufficient. A cache miss was a consistent indicator that it hadn't yet been loaded, and processes were often put in place to warm or preload the cache when an app using it was started. Trying to use a cache in these microservice-centric scenarios requires that we rethink the patterns, and front and center is the concern around cache freshness. Ideally, whenever something changes in a downstream service, we'd like to have those changes reflected in our local data store as soon as possible.

Aha! You see where I'm going with this?

## 12.2   *Moving from request/response to event driven*

As I suggested, we began our journey to this better way of handling local storage in chapter 4, when we turned request/response on its head, moving to an event-driven interaction protocol. Figure 12.7 looks similar to the diagrams earlier in the chapter, but with one important distinction: the interaction between Connections' Posts and its related services is initiated from the opposite end. Connections' Posts does have its own local storage, reminiscent of the cache from the previous example, but it's now updated anytime one of the downstream services broadcasts a change.

Gone is the need to worry about cache expiry. Gone is the need to wonder whether a lack of data truly means that such data doesn't exist. Assuming that the mechanism for delivery of downstream events is functioning (and you'll see shortly how we assure

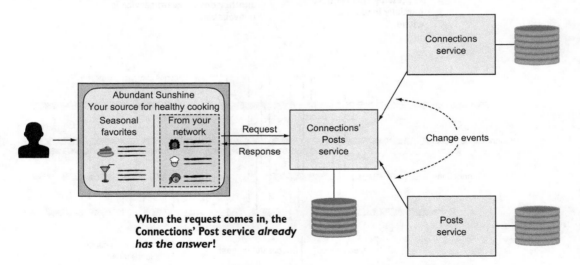

**Figure 12.7   When changes occur in downstream services, events describing those changes are sent to interested parties where their local storage is updated.**

this), the Connections' Posts service can operate in its own bounded context and not worry about what's happening elsewhere in the system. This is indeed a thing of beauty!

Let's look at what this does to our system's resilience. Figure 12.8 updates our earlier diagrams. You can now see that the events coming from Posts and Connections are sent to Connections' Posts, and when a request comes in from the web page, whether the dependent services are up or down doesn't matter; Connections' Posts has its own local storage and is operating autonomously. But what happens if Connections' Posts is unavailable when one of the other services has an event to deliver? As implemented in chapter 4, that event would be lost. Sure, we can use some of the other patterns we've studied, such as retries, to compensate for some of the failures, but in some cases those won't work. The net result is bad.

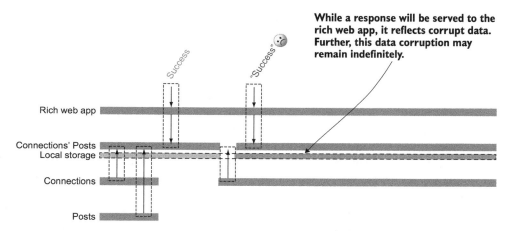

**Figure 12.8   The event-driven approach allows the Connections' Posts service to operate with complete autonomy, using the data in the local storage. Missed events, however, can corrupt that local storage, "successfully" returning incorrect results.**

To Connections' Posts, everything seems right in the world. It will return a result based on the data in its local storage, exactly as it should. It has no idea that the data is now not accurate. And it gets worse. It's not usually the case that an event is of interest to only a single party; instead, many other entities may care if a user in the system changes their username, for example. If that change event doesn't reach many intended participants, inconsistencies can propagate widely through your system, as shown in figure 12.9.

In essence, local stores, possibly many of them, are now corrupt. Even worse, they may remain so indefinitely! The event-driven approach promised to eliminate the question of cache freshness, but it has failed.

Remember that comment about the mechanism for delivering downstream events being sound? Clearly, we don't yet have a sound system. So, let's continue.

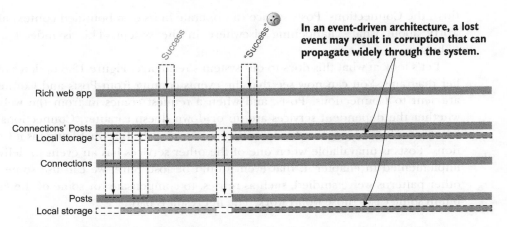

**Figure 12.9  Events are usually of interest to numerous parties, so when they're not properly delivered, this can cause inconsistencies to propagate throughout the system.**

## 12.3   *The event log*

You have to eliminate the need for Connections' Posts to be available when an event it cares about is being sent. Yes, you guessed it—you'll use some type of asynchronous messaging system. Instead of Connections sending events directly to Connections' Posts, it will deliver those events to a system that's responsible for the delivery thereof. Of course, your software will then depend on that messaging system being available, but concentrating messaging semantics within a system specially designed for that purpose not only allows for consistent implementation of the patterns, but also allows you to focus resiliency efforts in the messaging fabric rather than across the vast network of interrelated services. If the messaging system is itself designed in a cloud-native way, with redundancy and dynamic scaling, it will be dependable. Figure 12.10 shows the event log added to your software architecture.

Let's see how this impacts the resilience of the software as a whole. Figure 12.11 adds another component: the event log. As the Connections and Posts services generate events, they're sent to the log, and the parties interested in the event will pick them up and process them. Notice that the first message, sent from the Connections service, is picked up by both the Posts and Connections' Posts services. The second event, however, generated by the Posts service, makes its way only to Connections' Posts. And an event that's produced when consumers are unable to immediately respond is maintained in the event log, (at least)[1] until all interested parties have consumed it, even if those consumers come online at vastly different times. As a result, we can see that the availability of the aggregating service is strong even while outages are occurring throughout the system.

---

[1] Stay tuned—I'll address this phrase, "at least," when I talk about event sourcing.

Event log
Connections service
Abundant Sunshine
Your source for healthy cooking
Seasonal favorites
From your network
Request
Response
Connections' Posts service
Posts service

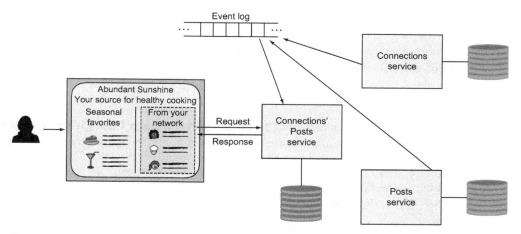

**Figure 12.10 With the addition of an event log, you've now completely decoupled each of the three services from one another. Events are produced into and consumed from the event log, and the event log is responsible for retaining the events until they're no longer needed.**

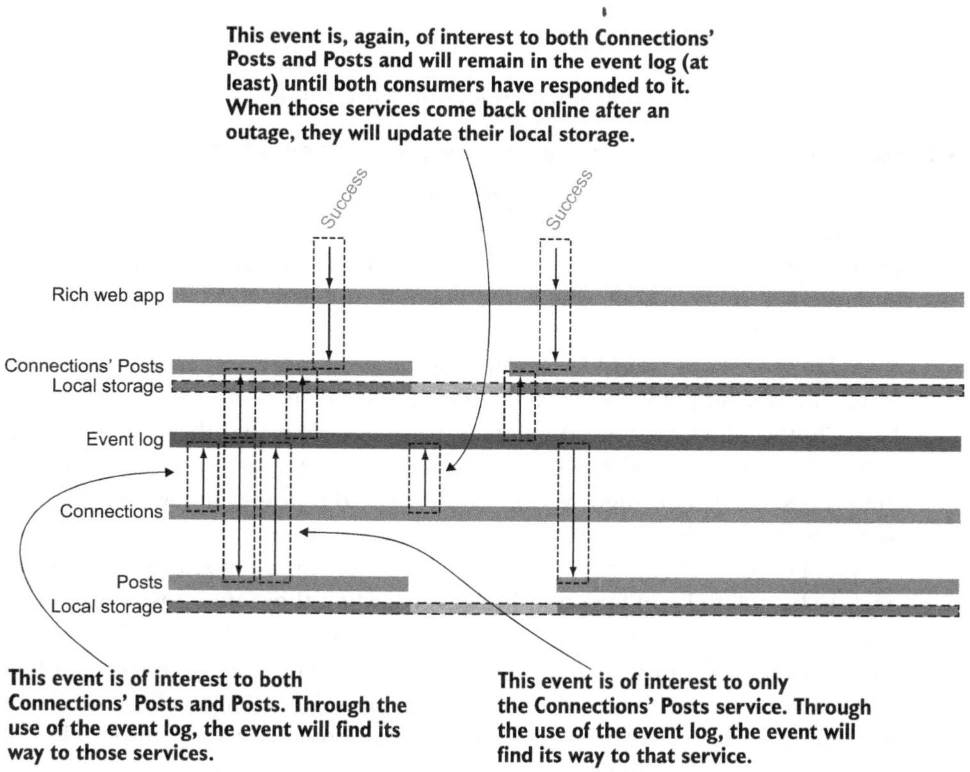

This event is, again, of interest to both Connections' Posts and Posts and will remain in the event log (at least) until both consumers have responded to it. When those services come back online after an outage, they will update their local storage.
Success
Success
Rich web app
Connections' Posts
Local storage
Event log
Connections
Posts
Local storage
This event is of interest to both Connections' Posts and Posts. Through the use of the event log, the event will find its way to those services.
This event is of interest to only the Connections' Posts service. Through the use of the event log, the event will find its way to that service.

**Figure 12.11 Events are produced into and consumed from the event log, which maintains those events as long as they're needed. Through use of the event log, you've entirely decoupled the services from one another.**

One note on consistency: Previously, you saw a case where, because of a missed event, your cache could become corrupt. Arguably, even here, in the time between the production of an event and the consumption thereof, the local storage of the consumer is out of date. When I talk about event sourcing later in this chapter, I will address this concern.

> **Connecting to a messaging fabric usually happens through a client library**
>
> Note that producing and consuming messages from code is usually done with some type of client library, and that library will often implement some of the resiliency patterns you've been studying. For example, if the event log can't be reached with a first request, the client library may retry. And if the connectivity continues to fail, the library code may invoke a service-discovery protocol to find alternative endpoints to contact.
>
> Developers needn't be concerned with the details of the protocol. Instead, they need only specify the type of service level they need from the interaction. For example, if the implementation requires guaranteed delivery of events (the software must report an error if the message can't be delivered), that will be specified through the client API. If, on the other hand, the implementation can tolerate some event loss, that too can be specified.

It's high time we looked at some code, don't you think?

### 12.3.1   *Let's see this in action: Implementing event-driven microservices*

The implementation for this chapter builds on that of chapter 4, where I had challenged our natural inclination toward request/response, instead providing an event-driven solution. But there you still had the tight coupling between the services, as described in section 12.2, where the client sent events directly to consumers. Figure 12.7 depicts that implementation.

What I do here is add the event log, thereby more loosely coupling the services from one another. I'm basically headed in the direction of the depiction in figure 12.10, but when we get into the details, the example is slightly more complicated. Not only is the Connections' Posts service interested in the generated events, but so too is the Posts service. This slightly more sophisticated topology allows us to explore details in a more comprehensive way.

The Posts service has the responsibility for managing blog posts—allowing for new posts to be created and for publishing events when those new posts come in. The posts it stores include the title, body, and date of the post, as well as the ID for the user who made the post. In our system, the Connections service is responsible for managing users, as well as the connections between them. In order to allow a user to change their details, username, or given name, for example, queries in your code will refer to that user only by ID. But the user ID is an implementation detail, an internal identifier that should not be leaked out through any API. Therefore, through the API, you refer to users via their username. For example, when adding a new post, you send a POST request to the Posts service with a payload that looks something like this:

```
{
    "username":"madmax",
    "title":"I love pho",
    "body":"Yesterday I made my mom a beef pho that was very close to what I
    ➥ ate in Vietnam earlier this year ..."
}
```

A user with the username madmax has published a post about the pho he recently cooked. When you store this in the database, however, you don't want to store the username, because if Max later changes it, you'll have difficulty finding his older posts. As such, you store the post with his user ID, as shown in the following output of a SQL query:

```
mysql> select * from cookbookposts.post;
+----+--------------------+---------------------+------------+---------+
| id | body               | date                | title      | user_id |
+----+--------------------+---------------------+------------+---------+
|  1 | Yesterday I made...| 2018-10-30 11:56:05 | I love pho |       2 |
...
```

Because of this level of indirection, the Posts service needs to map user IDs to user-names. The Posts service doesn't manage users (the Connections service does), but in order to remain decoupled from the Connections service, it must keep in its own data-base an up-to-date copy of some of the data managed by the Connections service; namely, the correlation of ID to username. You can see that table through the follow-ing SQL query:

```
mysql> select * from cookbookposts.user;
+----+-----------+
| id | username  |
+----+-----------+
|  1 | cdavisafc |
|  2 | madmax    |
|  3 | gmaxdavis |
+----+-----------+
```

Okay, so in figure 12.12, both the Connections and the Posts services are generating events, and the Posts and the Connections' Posts services are consuming events. In that diagram, you can also see the data stores associated with each of your services. The Connections and Posts services each own data that's stored in a source-of-truth database, and the Posts and Connections' Posts services store copies of data owned by another service in local storage databases. These local databases are kept up to date through eventing.

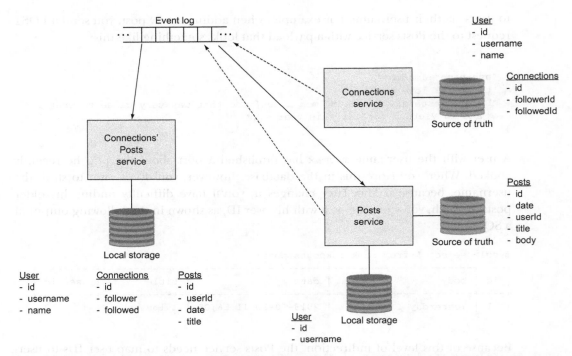

**Figure 12.12    The full event and data topology of our implementation. The Posts and Connections services both "own" data (source of truth) and produce events (dotted arrows) when changes occur in that data. Posts and Connections' Posts both store data they don't own (local storage) and update that data by handling events (solid arrows).**

Table 12.1 sums up the roles that each service plays in the overall software architecture.

**Table 12.1    Service roles in our event-driven software architecture**

| Role | Connections service | Posts service | Connections' Posts service |
|------|---------------------|---------------|----------------------------|
| *Source of truth*—A dedicated database to store data owned by the service. | This service owns users and connections between users. | This service owns posts. | |
| *Write and event producer*—HTTP endpoint implementations update source-of-truth databases and deliver events to Kafka. | Generates user event anytime a user is created, updated, or deleted. | Generates a post event anytime a post is created. | |
| | Generates connection event anytime a connection is created or deleted. | | |

**Table 12.1  Service roles in our event-driven software architecture (continued)**

| Role | Connections service | Posts service | Connections' Posts service |
|---|---|---|---|
| *Event handler*—Subscribes to events and updates local storage databases accordingly. | | Updates local storage databases when users are created, updated, or deleted. | Updates local storage when users, connections, and posts are created, updated, or deleted. |
| *Local storage*—A dedicated database to store data not owned by this service. | | This service stores mappings of username to user ID. | This service stores user and connection data as well as post summaries. |
| *Read*—HTTP endpoint implementations that serve the domain entities for the service. | Users. Connections. | Posts. | Posts made by users followed by an individual. |

Turning now to the project, you can see the preceding details reflected in the directory and package structure. So that you can look at this yourself, let me get you set up with that project.

Assuming you've already cloned the repository, check out the following tag:

```
git checkout eventlog/0.0.1
```

You can now change into the directory for this chapter:

```
cd cloudnative-eventlog
```

Figure 12.13 shows the key parts of the directory structure of the project, as described in the preceding table:

- Read APIs are implemented as controllers that are located in packages with the suffix read. All three services support read APIs.
- Any source-of-truth data is implemented with JPA classes located in a package with the suffix sourceoftruth. This package exists for both the Posts and Connections services.
- Write APIs, supporting HTTP methods such as POST, PUT, and DELETE, are implemented as controllers that are located in packages with the suffix write. In addition to persisting data into the source-of-truth database for the service, these write controllers produce events into our messaging fabric. This package exists for both the Posts and Connections services.
- Event consumers are implemented within packages with the suffix eventhandlers. This package exists for both the Posts and the Connections' Posts services.
- The local storage for data obtained through events is implemented with JPA classes located in a package with the suffix localstorage. This package exists for both the Posts and Connections' Posts services.

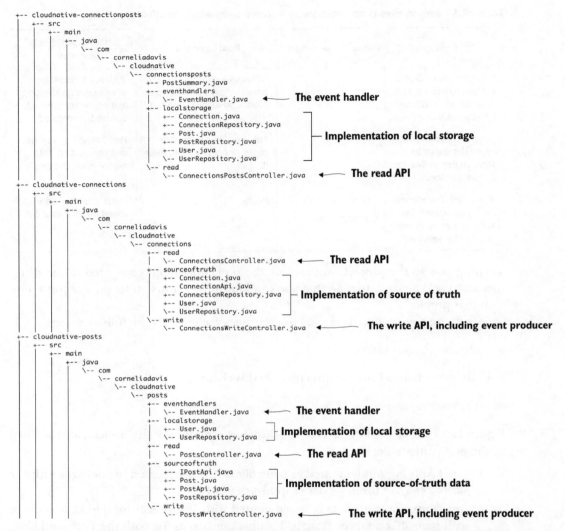

**Figure 12.13   The directory structure for our three microservices, showing the organization of event-producing and -consuming code, as well as read APIs and both "owned" data storage and "local" data storage.**

Figure 12.14 offers another way to view microservices structured in this way—using the Posts service as an example. The post data (date, title, body, and author ID) is owned by the service and stored in the source-of-truth database. The user-ID-to-username mapping data is only a copy of data owned by another service and is stored in the local storage database. We have a write controller that performs two steps; it both persists source-of-truth data and delivers events into the event log. The event handler performs a single task that consumes events of interest and persists data into the local storage database. And finally, the read controller performs a single task that queries both databases to generate lists of posts.

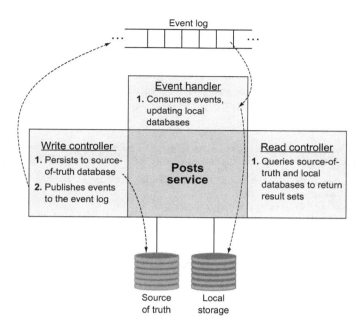

**Figure 12.14 A service implements a write controller that's responsible for taking changes to the first-class entities of the service, an event handler that's responsible for maintaining a local database of nonprimary entity data that's nevertheless part of the bounded context, and a read controller that supports querying data across these databases.**

With an understanding of this structure established, let's now take a closer look at a few parts of the implementation, starting with the write controller for the Connections service. The code in the following listing executes when a new user is created.

**Listing 12.1   Method from ConnectionsWriteController.java**

```
@RequestMapping(method = RequestMethod.POST, value="/users")
public void newUser(@RequestBody User newUser,
                    HttpServletResponse response) {

    logger.info("Have a new user with username " + newUser.getUsername());

    // persist this user in our DB          Stores data into
    userRepository.save(newUser);           source-of-truth DB

    // send event to Kafka
    UserEvent userEvent =
    new UserEvent("created",
                  newUser.getId(),
                  newUser.getName(),                  Delivers
                  newUser.getUsername());              change event
    kafkaTemplate.send("user", userEvent);
}
```

First, the new user is stored in your source-of-truth database, and then an event is sent to the event log (you can see from the comment that you're using Kafka—I'll talk a bit more about Kafka when we get to running the example). You send out a user event that captures that a user has been created with a particular ID, name, and username, and you deliver that event to a topic called user. I'll say more about topics (and queues) in just a moment, but for now just think of these as the topics you're familiar with from your prior message-driven implementations. A *topic* is simply a channel onto which messages are delivered and from which messages are consumed.

Let's compare this to code from the event-driven implementation of chapter 4 in listing 12.2 (you can find this code in this cloudnative-eventlog module by looking at the repo tag eventlogstart).

**Listing 12.2   Method from ConnectionsWriteController.java**

```
@RequestMapping(method = RequestMethod.POST, value="/users")
public void newUser(@RequestBody User newUser,
                    HttpServletResponse response) {

    logger.info("Have a new user with username " + newUser.getUsername());

    // persist this user in our DB
    userRepository.save(newUser);          ⟵── Persists the data

    // let interested parties know about this new user
    // posts needs to be notified of new users
    try {
                                                               ⎤ Sends event to
        RestTemplate restTemplate = new RestTemplate();    ⟵─┘ Posts service
        restTemplate.postForEntity(postsControllerUrl+"/users",
                                   newUser, String.class);
    } catch (Exception e) {
        // for now, do nothing - when we add the event log this known bad
        // will go away
        logger.info("problem sending change event to Posts");
    }

    // connections posts needs to be notified of new users
    try {                                                      ⎤ Sends event to
                                                               ⎥ Connections'
        RestTemplate restTemplate = new RestTemplate();    ⟵─┘ Posts service
        restTemplate.postForEntity(connectionsPostsControllerUrl+"/users",
                                   newUser, String.class);
    } catch (Exception e) {
        // for now, do nothing - when we add the event log this known bad
        // will go away
        logger.info("problem sending change event to ConnsPosts");
    }
}
```

A snippet of this code shows that after saving the user in the database, events were delivered both to the Posts and the Connections' Posts services. With the introduction of an event log, you were able to remove this coupling—the event producer needn't know anything about the consumers—and the code is also obviously far simpler and therefore far more maintainable.

Let's now turn to an implementation of an event consumer. The next listing shows a portion of the event handler code for the Connections' Posts service.

**Listing 12.3   Methods from EventHandler.java**

```java
@KafkaListener(topics="user",
                groupId = "connectionspostsconsumer",
                containerFactory = "kafkaListenerContainerFactory")
public void userEvent(UserEvent userEvent) {

    logger.info("Posts UserEvent Handler processing - event: " +
                userEvent.getEventType());

    if (userEvent.getEventType().equals("created")) {

        // make event handler idempotent.
        // If user already exists, do nothing
        User existingUser
            = userRepository.findByUsername(userEvent.getUsername());
        if (existingUser == null) {

            // store record in local storage
            User user = new User(userEvent.getId(), userEvent.getName(),
                                 userEvent.getUsername());
            userRepository.save(user);

            logger.info("New user cached in local storage " +
                        user.getUsername());
            userRepository.save(new User(userEvent.getId(),
                                         userEvent.getName(),
                                         userEvent.getUsername()));
        } else
            logger.info("Already existing user not cached again id " +
                        userEvent.getId());
    } else if (userEvent.getEventType().equals("updated")) {
        // ... handle updated event
    }


}


@KafkaListener(topics="connection",
                groupId = "connectionspostsconsumer",
                containerFactory = "kafkaListenerContainerFactory")
public void connectionEvent(ConnectionEvent connectionEvent) {

    // ... handle changes to connections - who follows who.
    // it is created and deleted events
}

@KafkaListener(topics="post",
                groupId = "connectionspostsconsumer",
                containerFactory = "kafkaListenerContainerFactory")
public void postEvent(PostEvent postEvent) {

    // ... handle changes to posts - that is, new posts.

}
```

There are several interesting things in this implementation:

- You can see from this, and the previous code showing the event producer, that the details of interfacing with the event log are abstracted away from the developer. Including the Spring Kafka dependency in the POM file draws in a Kafka client, allowing the developer to use a simple API to designate topics and other details so that events are easily delivered and consumed.
- The Connections' Posts service event handler consumes messages from three topics. These topics organize change events for users, connections, and posts. Although the producer simply provided a topic name, consumers must also provide a `groupId` that controls how messages are consumed.
- From both this and the producer code previously shown, you can see references to event schema: `UserEvent`, `ConnectionEvent`, and `PostEvent`. Events published to and consumed from an event log must have a format, and both the producer and consumer must know the details.
- You can see a comment in this code about making the consumer logic for the user-created event idempotent. In a distributed system, guaranteeing exactly once delivery of events can be complex and expensive from a performance standpoint. Making services idempotent relieves some of this burden.

We will drill into each of these topics in just a moment, but first let's run the code.

### SETTING UP
One last time, I refer you to the setup instructions for running the samples in earlier chapters in this text; there are no new requirements for running the sample in this chapter.

You'll be accessing files in the cloudnative-eventlog directory, so in your terminal window change into that directory.

And as I've described in previous chapters, I prebuilt Docker images and made them available in Docker Hub. If you want to build the Java source and Docker images and push them to your own image repository, I refer you to earlier chapters (the most detailed instructions are in chapter 5).

### RUNNING THE APPLICATION
This example can be run on a small Kubernetes cluster, so if you'd like, you may use Minikube or something similar. If you still have the examples running from the previous chapter, get those cleaned up; run the script I've provided as follows:

```
./deleteDeploymentComplete.sh all
```

Running this deletes all instances of the Posts, Connections, and Connections' Posts services, as well as any MySQL, Redis, or SCCS services that are running. If you have other apps and services running in your Kubernetes cluster, you may want to clear some of those out too; just make sure you have enough capacity. In earlier chapters, deleting the services was optional, but in this case, I encourage you to delete all of them. Some of them are not used here (SCCS), and I'd like you to use a fresh MySQL instance because the database topology is fairly different.

There is a slight start-order dependency in that after creating the MySQL server, you need to create the actual databases therein. So get it and the event log running first:

```
./deployServices.sh
```

Once the MySQL database is up and running, which you can see by running `kubectl get all`, you'll create the databases using the `mysql` CLI as follows:

```
mysql -h $(minikube service mysql-svc --format "{{.IP}}")
➥ -P $(minikube service mysql-svc --format "{{.Port}}") -u root -p
```

The password is `password`, and after you're in, you'll run the following three commands:

```
create database cookbookconnectionsposts;
create database cookbookposts;
create database cookbookconnections;
```

Notice that you're now creating databases for each of the services; until now, you always created only a single database. That means that you were implementing exactly the design depicted in figure 12.2!

Now you can start the microservices, which you do by running the following script:

```
./deployApps.sh
```

Everything is now up and running, and you can load data. But hang on. If you've been running the examples all along, you might note that I've never asked to you load data before. Why now?

The reason is that you've broken the database apart and have both source-of-truth databases and local storage databases, and I want you to use the very eventing that you've built into your services to load data into all of these data stores. And I want you to watch what happens when this data is loaded, so please stream the logs from each of your microservices, one each in three different terminal windows, with the following command (remember, you can get your pod names with a `kubectl get all`):

```
kubectl logs -f po/<name of your pod instance>
```

If you look at the end of the log for your Posts service, you'll see a line that includes this:

```
o.s.k.l.KafkaMessageListenerContainer  : partitions assigned:[user-0]
```

And if you look at the end of the log for your Connections' Posts service, you'll see lines that include these:

```
o.s.k.l.KafkaMessageListenerContainer  : partitions assigned:[post-0]
o.s.k.l.KafkaMessageListenerContainer  : partitions assigned:[connection-0]
o.s.k.l.KafkaMessageListenerContainer  : partitions assigned:[user-0]
```

This shows that the Posts service is listening for events on the user topic, and the Connections' Posts service is listening for events on each of the user, connection, and post topics. Ah, you see our eventing topology coming to life! Now load some data and see that flow in action. Run the following command:

```
./loadData.sh
```

If you look in that file, you'll see that I created same sample data that you've been using all along. Look again at the logs.

The log for the Connections service shows exactly the entries you expect—creation of three users and connections between them:

```
...ConnectionsWriteController   : Have a new user with username madmax
...ConnectionsWriteController   : Have a new user with username gmaxdavis
...ConnectionsWriteController   : Have a new connection: madmax is
➥ following cdavisafc
...ConnectionsWriteController   : Have a new connection: cdavisafc is
➥ following madmax
...ConnectionsWriteController   : Have a new connection: cdavisafc is
➥ following gmaxdavis
```

The log output of the Posts service is a bit more interesting; you see the listener being invoked to handle three user-created events and to create three users in your local user storage:

```
...EventHandler   : Posts UserEvent Handler processing - event: created
...EventHandler   : New user cached in local storage cdavisafc
...EventHandler   : Posts UserEvent Handler processing - event: created
...EventHandler   : New user cached in local storage madmax
...EventHandler   : Posts UserEvent Handler processing - event: created
...EventHandler   : New user cached in local storage gmaxdavis
```

Later in the same log, you see messages that posts are being created:

```
...PostsWriteController   : Have a new post with title Cornelia Title
...PostsWriteController   : find by username output
...PostsWriteController   : user username = cdavisafc id = 1
...PostsWriteController   : Have a new post with title Cornelia Title2
...PostsWriteController   : find by username output
...PostsWriteController   : user username = cdavisafc id = 1
...PostsWriteController   : Have a new post with title Glen Title
...PostsWriteController   : find by username output
...PostsWriteController   : user username = gmaxdavis id = 3
```

In the implementation for the Posts writer, I've included a log message that shows the lookup of the user ID from the username, the latter of which is supplied as a part of the post; of course, this lookup is happening against our local user storage database.

Finally, looking at the logs for the Connections' Posts service, you can see what I hope you have now come to expect—messages showing the user, connection, and post events being processed and data being stored in your local databases:

```
...EventHandler.   : Posts UserEvent Handler processing - event: created
...EventHandler.   : New user cached in local storage cdavisafc
...EventHandler.   : Posts UserEvent Handler processing - event: created
...EventHandler.   : New user cached in local storage madmax
...EventHandler.   : Posts UserEvent Handler processing - event: created
...EventHandler.   : New user cached in local storage gmaxdavis
...EventHandler.   : Creating a new connection in the cache:2 is following 1
...EventHandler.   : Creating a new connection in the cache:1 is following 2
...EventHandler.   : Creating a new connection in the cache:1 is following 3
...EventHandler.   : Creating a new post in the cache with title Max Title
...EventHandler.   : Creating a new post in the cache with title Cornelia
 ⮡ Title
...EventHandler.   : Creating a new post in the cache with title Cornelia
 ⮡ Title2
...EventHandler.   : Creating a new post in the cache with title Glen Title
...EventHandler.   : Posts UserEvent Handler processing - event: created
```

Let's run a few more commands to watch them in action.

When you now ask Connections' Posts for the posts of people I follow

```
curl $(minikube service \
        --url connectionsposts-svc)/connectionsposts/cdavisafc | jq
```

you see the following result:

```
[
  {
    "date": "2019-01-22T01:06:19.895+0000",
    "title": "Chicken Pho",
    "usersName": "Max"
  },
  {
    "date": "2019-01-22T01:06:19.985+0000",
    "title": "French Press Lattes",
    "usersName": "Glen"
  }
]
```

Let's now change a username. With the following, change the username for cdavis-afc to cdavisafcupdated:

```
curl -X PUT -H "Content-Type:application/json" \
     --data '{"name":"Cornelia","username":"cdavisafcupdated"}' \
     $(minikube service --url connections-svc)/users/cdavisafc
```

One more time, let's have a look at the logs. First, notice that each of the Posts and Connections' Posts logs has processed that event. Each log shows an entry such as this:

```
...: Updating user cached in local storage with username cdavisafcupdated
```

Now requests both to the Connections' Posts service and the Posts service (recall that all three services implement read controllers) reflect that change:

```
curl $(minikube service --url \
    connectionsposts-svc)/connectionsPosts/cdavisafc
curl $(minikube service --url \
    connectionsposts-svc)/connectionsPosts/cdavisafcupdated
curl $(minikube service --url posts-svc)/posts
```

I encourage you to explore this event flow topology by issuing more commands, watching the logs, and seeing what the results yield. I'll remind you that Posts and Connections also have read APIs, including endpoints that allow you to see each of the collections of objects they control:

```
curl $(minikube service --url connections-svc)/users
curl $(minikube service --url connections-svc)/connections
curl $(minikube service --url posts-svc)/posts
```

Figure 12.15 shows the event topology in a bit more detail. You can see the various producers, consumers, and topics, and how they relate to one another.

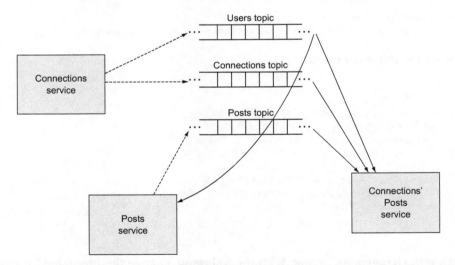

Figure 12.15   The event topology defines the topics that will hold events and the producers and consumers of each. The Connections service produces users and connection events. The Posts service produces post events and consumes user events. The Connections' Posts service consumes user, connection, and post events.

One final comment before I move on to three more event-log architectural topics: You might have noticed the `sleep` command in the `loadData.sh` script. Yes, it's a bit hacky, but it's in there to avoid a race condition whereby the `curl` command to create a post reaches the Posts service before the events for creating the user have been processed by that Posts service. You can handle this scenario in a less hacky way, such as a simple retry from within the code, sending the event into a "retry" topic to attempt the processing again at a later time, or even failing to create the post. Analyzing these options and choosing the right one is an interesting topic for sure but is beyond the scope of this chapter. Have a look at the reference I point you to at the end of this chapter.

Okay, now go back to the three topics that I queued up for further discussion:

- Different types of messaging channels and their applicability in cloud-native software
- The event payload
- The value of idempotent services

### 12.3.2 *What's new with topics and queues?*

Those of you who have worked with or are familiar with the basics of the messaging systems of the past, very possibly JMS (Java Messaging Service) systems, will know about queues and topics. But in case it's been some time ago, let me jog your memory. Both abstractions have publishers and subscribers, the actors that produce messages to and consume messages from a named channel (the topic or queue), but the way messages are handled, both by the messaging fabric and by the consumers, differs.

For *queues*, which can have multiple subscribers, a single message will be processed by only *one* of the subscribers. Further, if no subscribers are available at the time a message appears in the channel, the message will be retained until a subscriber consumes it. After it has been consumed, the message disappears.

For *topics*, which can also have multiple subscribers, a single message will be sent to *all* subscribers at the time it's produced. The message will be processed by any number of consumers, even zero. Consumers will receive messages only if they're attached to the topic at the time the message is produced. If a consumer isn't connected to the topic when the message is produced, it will never see it. If there are no subscribers on a topic, messages delivered there will simply disappear. You can think of the topic as providing more of a message-routing function. Figure 12.16 depicts both queues and topics.

Although the newer *event log* shares some of the same concepts as those from the JMS days (brokers, producers, consumers, and even topics), the semantics around some of these are subtly different and can result in vastly different behaviors. From a developer perspective, the broker looks essentially the same as it did before; it's the conduit to having producers and consumers connect to an event log. The implementation of a modern event-logging system such as Apache Kafka, however, is generally more cloud-native, allowing for brokers to come in and out of existence as the infrastructure changes and/or the event log cluster is scaled up and down. The role of a

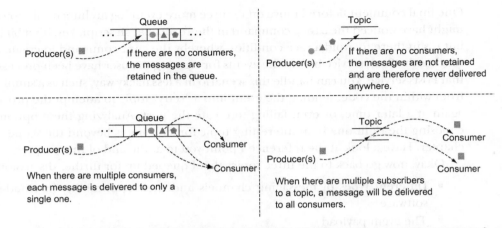

**Figure 12.16   Messaging systems, largely standardized with JMS, provide support for queues and topics. Queues retain messages until each one is consumed. Topics don't retain any messages, instead simply delivering them to all available subscribers.**

producer is also much the same as before; it will connect to the event log via a broker and deliver events.

It's when it comes to topics and consumption from those topics that things change. Consumers indicate an interest in events that are published to a particular topic. But the way events are picked up when multiple consumers exist is where it gets interesting. As you've seen in abundance, in our cloud-native architectures, we will have many different microservices, each of which will have multiple instances deployed. The consumption patterns of the event log are optimized for this use case.

> **NOTE**   What we need is a semantic that allows for different microservices to be able to consume the same event, but have only one instance of each process the event.

With Kafka, this semantic is supported with two abstractions: the *topic* and the *group ID*. Any microservice that has an interest in a particular event will create a listener for the topic that carries the event, and any new event will be delivered to *all* listeners—all microservices. The `groupId` is used to ensure that only one instance of a particular microservice receives a message; it will be delivered to only one of all instances sharing the same `groupId`.

The easiest way to understand this is in the context of our sample application.

Recall that events that capture the creation of a new user, or changes to an existing one, need to be consumed by both the Posts service and the Connections' Posts service. Therefore, both the Posts and the Connections' Posts services will listen on the user topic. But then, because you want only one instance of the Posts service, and only one instance of the Connections' Posts service to process an event, you set the `groupId` uniformly over all Posts instances and set the `groupId` uniformly over all Connections' Posts instances as shown here—from the Posts event handler:

```
@KafkaListener(topics="user", groupId="postsconsumer")
public void listenForUser(UserEvent userEvent) {
    ...
}
```

and from the Connections' Posts event handler:

```
@KafkaListener(topics="user", groupId = "connectionspostsconsumer",
               containerFactory = "kafkaListenerContainerFactory")
public void userEvent(UserEvent userEvent) {
    ...
}
```

In essence, an event topic is a bit of a hybrid between an old-school topic and an old-school queue; the event topic acts as a topic across consumers with different group IDs, and as a queue across consumers sharing the same group ID. Figure 12.17 shows this event consumption topology.

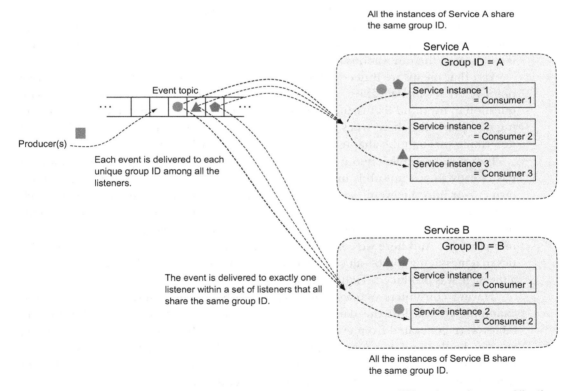

**Figure 12.17  Event topics in Kafka have behaviors that are a hybrid between JMS topics and queues. Like the old-school topics, events are delivered to all unique group IDs—there are multiple subscribers. But within a set of listeners that share the same group ID, the behavior is like a queue, delivering the event to one of the listeners.**

An event log topic is different from a messaging topic in one other way, and the name provides a hint—specifically, the word "log." Whether it's an application log being routed to Splunk or a database write log, we generally think of logs as something in which the entries are kept around, possibly indefinitely. Preservation of the event log is a fundamental principle of our event-log-based architectures. Events are kept around for any consumers that might be interested in them, even if the consumer isn't connected at the time of event production. You've already seen this in the analyses of our resilience and resultant service autonomy characteristics from earlier in the chapter; in figure 12.11, you saw that the parties interested in an event can pick them sometime after they are produced.

I want to take a concept here to an extreme, an extreme that I assert isn't actually outlandish at all. The events in the event log are kept for any consumer that might at any point in the future be interested in them—*even consumers that we haven't even thought of and don't yet exist!* That's right, we want to keep events around so that when we have an idea of something we want to do (train a machine learning model to come up with suggestions for food-blogging sites you might like based on the history of users, connections, and posts from the last two years), you can develop that software and it can consume all the events of interest. Preserving the two-year history of events is supporting the innovations of today.

Yes, that means we'll need a lot of storage, but storage costs have decreased to a point where it's manageable, and the opportunity gained well outweighs it. There's no question in my mind that virtually any organization should be thinking about generating and persisting these types of event logs, both for the immediate needs I've been describing through the chapter, as well as these forward-looking ones.

I want to be explicit about one last thing when it comes to topics, even though it has already shown up subtly in our discussions so far: each consumer maintains their own cursor into the event log/topic. A *cursor* is the position in the event log at which they have consumed preceding events. As a result, each consumer can process events on their own schedule—even those yet-to-be imagined consumers I talked about a moment ago! And here we come back to this notion of autonomy. Recall the semantics of a messaging topic—all consumers needed to be online at the very moment that a message was produced. Tight coupling!

Having consumers manage their own cursors enables interesting patterns. For example, say you lost the database for the Connections' Posts service. Because all tables were generated from event log data, to recover the Connections' Posts service, you need only stand up a new, empty database, set the cursor back to the beginning of the event log, and reprocess all the events. No need for mainline code that is different from failure-recovery code; the results will be predictably the same.

Or will they? As is often the answer to such open-ended questions, it depends. Our next topic has an impact.

### 12.3.3 *The event payload*

I want to touch upon several aspects related to event payloads here, but I'll start with what I had in mind when I posed the predictability question a moment ago. You want to be able to re-create your state, the state of the Connections' Posts service, for example, entirely from the messages in the event log. All the data needed to derive that state must be carried in the events—no references to outside sources are allowed.

Let me illustrate this with an example. Say when the Posts service publishes an event to a topic, in order to save space in the event log, you decide not to include the body of the blog post, but instead only the URL to the blog post. Any consumers know that this is the format of the event, so if they need to process the body of the post, perhaps to do some sentiment analysis, they can retrieve the body by following the link. Although this may work initially, what happens if the blog post is taken down? Reprocessing the event log at a later date won't allow you to generate the same result you initially did. This brings us to the first rule.

> **EVENT PAYLOAD, RULE #1**    An event that's published to an event log should be described *in its entirety*.

I know what you're thinking: "There's no way that I am putting high-resolution images into an event log!" And I don't disagree—you shouldn't. I suggest that asynchronous image processing is not a use case for the type of event-driven workflow that I've just described. Yes, you want some processing to occur as the result of an image showing up in a specific location on the filesystem, for example. You'll want to land a notification of this new image in a topic (or more likely, a queue), but I suggest that what is dropped onto the topic, a URL to where the image can be found, is a message rather than an event. I assert that if the payload isn't a complete representation of an event from which state can be derived, that it's instead a message. Of course, it's completely acceptable to continue using message-passing patterns even as you use event-logging patterns in other parts of your system; it's all about choosing the right pattern for the job.

Now let's dig a bit deeper into the details of an event—in particular, the schema. Events have structure, and it's essential that consumers know that structure so that they can appropriately process the payload. The question, then, is who is responsible for that structure. In the early 2000s, one of the answers that was quite en vogue was the enterprise service bus (ESB). The idea was that a canonical data model would be defined and, if you will, "installed" into the ESB. Producers would then transform their message into the canonical model as a part of the on-ramp into the ESB, and consumers would similarly transform from the canonical model into their own off-ramp. ESBs had entire frameworks around the production and management of the canonical models and the transformations. It was all very hard, and very nonagile.

I've come to think of the ESB as a slight incremental evolution of the centralized, canonical, corporate database. Look back at figure 12.2. All of the "independent" microservices in that picture aren't very independent at all when tethered to a single, centralized database. It turns out that moving that centralization into the messaging fabric didn't make our systems any less coupled than they were before. What we want instead is to allow producers to deliver events in the form that's native to their domain. Consumers, who had to adapt to the canonical model in the past anyway, will adapt to the model from the producer.

**EVENT PAYLOAD, RULE #2**   There's no canonical event model for the event log. Producers have control over the data format of the events they deliver, and consumers will adapt to that.

The most observant of you will notice that the cloudnative-eventlog project has another module in it called cloudnative-eventschemas, and it looks a little bit like a centralized data model. Guilty. I've created this single module and used it for events across all three of our microservices only as a convenience to keep our sample project as simple as possible. In reality, the Connections, Posts, and Connections' Posts services would have their own repositories, and each service would define the schemas for the events they generate and the schemas for the data of interest in events produced by other services.

And this leads me to the final point I want to make about event payloads: the schemas for these payloads must be managed. Producers who "own" the schemas for the events they produce must adequately describe *and version* those schemas, and the descriptions must be made available to any interested parties in a formalized way. This is why Confluent, the company providing a commercial offering based on Apache Kafka, has a schema registry.[2] The schema registry can then also be used to serialize and deserialize events—payloads needn't be JSON in the event log. To sum it up, just because we aren't centralizing schema into a single canonical model doesn't mean we have the wild, wild west; there still needs to be order.

**EVENT PAYLOAD, RULE #3**   All events published to an event log must have an associated schema that may be accessed by all interested parties, and schemas must be versioned.

The content I've covered here only begins to scratch the surface on the topic of event payloads, but I hope that it has adequately highlighted some of the key tenets and how they differ from those of the message-based systems you might be familiar with from the past. As with everything else in cloud-native systems, the focus is on autonomy rather than centralization, evolution rather than prediction, and adaptation rather than strictness.

### 12.3.4   *Idempotency*

Now, let's go back to that comment in the event handler code in the Connections' Posts service:

```
// make event handler idempotent.
```

---

[2]The Confluent Schema Registry provides a host of services that support both creators and consumers of events: http://mng.bz/GWAM.

For just a moment, let's think about the flow that's happening across our three micro-services without the complications that come with them being distributed. New users, connections, and posts come into the Connections and Posts services, which in turn will deliver events to the event log. Consumers pick up these events and process them, writing entries into their respective local storage database. It's a simple flow. But we know that plenty can go wrong as soon as we distribute the components.

For starters, a producer may experience trouble delivering an event to the event log. Say the producer sends an event to the log but doesn't get an acknowledgement that it was received. In this case, it will try again. On the second attempt, it receives an acknowledgment, and the producer is done. But consider this: when its first attempt to write to the log wasn't acknowledged, it's possible that it was in fact recorded but that the acknowledgment was lost before being received by the producer. In this case, the second attempt could well have put a second event into the log.

You can avoid having duplicate log entries in various ways (most messaging fabrics support *exactly once* delivery, for example), but this can be expensive in terms of performance. As a result, *at-least-once* delivery is generally preferred, effectively shifting the responsibility for deduplication to the consumer.

And that's where idempotency comes in. An *idempotent* operation is one that can be applied one *or more* times, yielding the same result. When creating a new record in a local database, for example, checking to see whether it was already created and doing nothing in this case makes the operation idempotent. A delete operation is usually idempotent because if you delete an object once, or more than once, in the end the state is the same—the object is deleted. Updates of entities are also usually idempotent.

If you write a consumer that's not idempotent, this places restrictions on the way it may be used. It forces exactly once (or at-most-once) semantics on the event-delivery protocol, for example. If, on the other hand, you write a consumer that's idempotent, it affords its use in a broader range of use cases.

> **EVENT CONSUMER, RULE #1**  If at all possible, make the operations of your event consumers idempotent.

## 12.4 Event sourcing

Whew. We've just covered was lot—some new things to think about and a lot of new ways of applying familiar concepts. Yet we're not quite done. Before launching into this final topic, however, I want to remind you of where we began and where we're aiming to go in this discussion.

### 12.4.1 The journey so far

This chapter is about cloud-native *data*. At the core, we're talking about breaking up the data monolith, because without doing this, componentizing the compute mono-lith gives us only the illusion of autonomy. The microservice, which has a bounded context, is a natural place for us to also draw the lines for data storage, so the first step is that every microservice will get its own database. The question then is how those local data stores are populated. One option is caching, and we see immediate gains in autonomy and resultant resilience. But caching works far better for infrequently changing content than for the often-changing content associated with my microservices. The latter entails many complexities for keeping the data up to date. This leads us to an event-driven approach, where changes are proactively propagated through the network of services that make up our software. But events can be done in a way that too tightly couples different services to one another, so we use the familiar pub/sub pattern. But rather than calling it *messaging*, we call it an *event log* because, among other important differences, the event log should be thought of as something that persists entries indefinitely, and all consumers can work their way through the log in the way that meets their needs. Figure 12.18 depicts this progression.

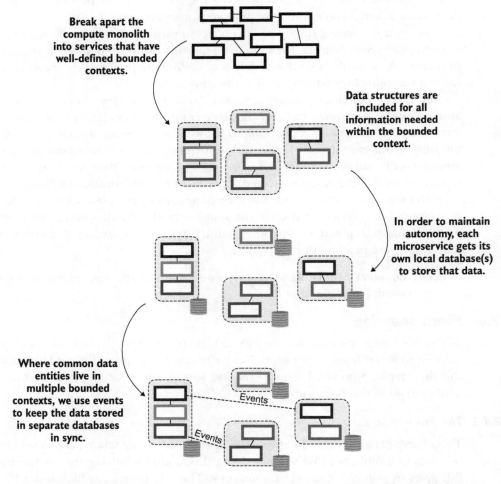

**Break apart the compute monolith into services that have well-defined bounded contexts.**

**Data structures are included for all information needed within the bounded context.**

**In order to maintain autonomy, each microservice gets its own local database(s) to store that data.**

**Where common data entities live in multiple bounded contexts, we use events to keep the data stored in separate databases in sync.**

**Figure 12.18   Our derivation of cloud-native data begins by breaking apart the data monolith so that the data supports the bounded contexts of the microservices. Microservices get their own databases, and where needed, data is kept consistent across the distributed data fabric through eventing.**

Despite what I believe seems a reasonable progression that addresses more and more of the challenges of distributing the data through our cloud-native software, I hope that you have at least a vague sense of discomfort. More hairy edge cases exist than the ones I talked about in the previous "Idempotency" section, for example. And the brief overview on payload handling might have left you with more questions than answers. But an even bigger cloud is looming over the architecture I've derived thus far: *who "owns" what data?*

## 12.4.2 *The source of truth*

In our sample application, figuring out who owns what data is pretty simple. The Connections service owns users and connections, and the Posts service owns posts. But in a more realistic setting, the question is far more difficult to answer. Does the software running in the bank's branch location "own" a customer record, or is it the mobile banking application? Or is it perhaps the premiere-customer web application?

At issue here is, what is the source of truth for each and every piece of data in your system? When a discrepancy exists in the email address for a customer across different apps and data stores, which is the right one?

What if I were to tell you it's *none* of the apps? And here we come to the explanation for the title of this section: *the source of truth for all data is the event store/log.*

This is what is behind the term *event sourcing*. The basic pattern for event sourcing is that all sources of record data writes are made *only* to the event store, and all other stores are simply holding projections or snapshots of state derived from the events stored in the event log. Recall figure 12.14; it showed the three interfaces to the Posts service: the read controller, the write controller, and the event handler. The write controller did two things, persisted new posts in the Posts database and delivered an event to the event log for any other microservice that cares about that event. At the time, I intentionally glossed over what happens when the record is written successfully to the database. But then the event isn't successfully delivered, or we don't know that it has been successfully delivered, to the event log. Egad, another hairy edge case.

In a way, the problem is that a two-phase commit doesn't work across this heterogeneous and distributed set of components; I can't create a transaction around the database write and the delivery of the event. The solution is this: rather than coordinate across two operations, do only one thing. Figure 12.19 updates figure 12.14 to reflect exactly that:

- The write controller is responsible only for delivering events to the event log. Looking back at figure 12.14, you can see that the write controller had been responsible for two things—storing data and delivering events. That it is now responsible for only one of these functions yields a more robust system.
- The event handler is responsible only for reading events and projecting those events into the local data store.
- The read controller is responsible only for returning results based on the state in the local data store.

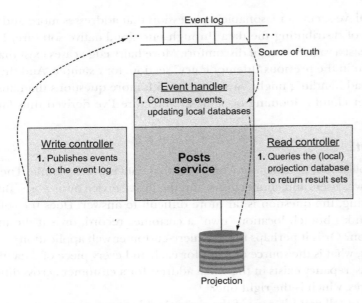

Figure 12.19   **The write controller *only* writes to the event log, which is now the source of truth. The local database for the microservice stores only projections derived from the event log data; this derivation is implemented in the event handler.**

Notice that in this diagram it appears as though some of the data in the local store is being updated it a roundabout way. The event goes into the event store and then comes out of the event store into the projection store. But rather than think of this as a deficiency, I challenge you to think of the write controller as being separate from the Posts service. That's why I've drawn the box not touching the Posts service; each part of the service does only one thing, and we achieve our desired outcomes though composition. What might seem like an inefficiency is offset by a corresponding increase in the robustness of our system.

Figure 12.20 updates the earlier event-driven figure 12.12 to reflect the event-sourcing approach. You can see the resulting simplification in the data topology. No longer do some services have both source-of-truth databases and local/projection databases while others don't; all services have only their projection data stores, and the means for keeping those stores up to date is also uniform. Elegant designs are more robust and dependable designs.

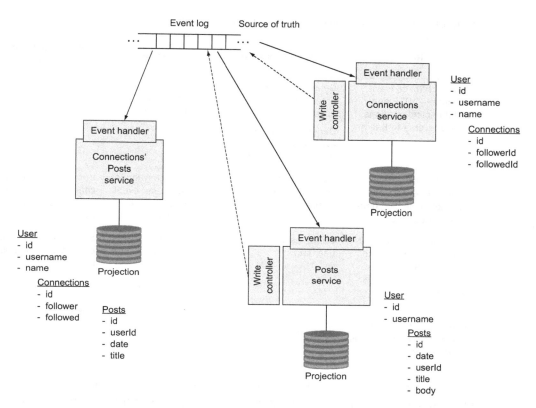

**Figure 12.20** **The event log is the single source of truth. All microservice-local stores are projections derived from the events in the event log, by the event handlers. The microservice-local stores are only projections.**

### 12.4.3 Let's see this in action: Implementing event sourcing

Let's look at the code changes that take our earlier event-log-based implementation all the way to an event-*sourced* one. Check out the following tag from the Git repo:

```
git checkout eventlog/0.0.2
```

As discussed previously, we've simplified the set of roles that any given service might fulfill. This is reflected in table 12.2; the consistency of patterns across the different services is stark.

Because it was the most sophisticated of all of the services, let's study the Posts service in more detail.

First, you'll see that all database functionality has been consolidated from the `localstorage` and `sourceoftruth` packages into a single one that I've named *projectionstorage*; all data is now stored in the projection store. This isn't to say that you couldn't have more than one projection store. You could, for example, project events

**Table 12.2    Service roles in our event-sourced software architecture**

| Role | Connections service | Posts service | Connections' Posts service |
|---|---|---|---|
| *Write controller/event producer*—HTTP endpoint implementations deliver events to Kafka. | Generates user event anytime a user is created, updated, or deleted.<br><br>Generates connection event anytime a connection is created or deleted. | Generates a post event anytime a post is created. | |
| *Event handler*—Subscribes to events and updates projection databases accordingly. | Invoked anytime a user or connections event appears in the event log. | Invoked anytime a post or user event appears in the event log. | Invoked anytime a user, connection, or post event appears in the event log. |
| *Projection database*—A dedicated database to store all data of the bounded context of the service. | Stores user and connection data. | Stores a subset of user data. | Stores subsets of user, connection, and post data. |
| *Read*—HTTP endpoint implementations that serve the domain entities for the service. | Users.<br>Connections. | Posts. | Posts made by users followed by an individual. |

into a relational database to support relational queries, and project events into a graph database to support graph queries. The emphasis in this refactor is that there's now only projection data management.

Second, the read controller is largely unchanged, except to accommodate the data store refactoring I've just described.

Third, you can see in listing 12.4 that the write controller no longer writes to local storage, but only sends the create or update event to the event log. You'll also notice that I've moved the ID generation out of the database because I want to assign an ID when the event is produced, not when the projection is created.

**Listing 12.4    Method from PostsWriteController.java**

```java
@RequestMapping(method = RequestMethod.POST, value="/posts")
public void newPost(@RequestBody PostApi newPost,
                    HttpServletResponse response) {

    logger.info("Have a new post with title " + newPost.getTitle());

    Long id = idManager.nextId();
    User user = userRepository.findByUsername(newPost.getUsername());
    if (user != null) {
        // send out new post event
        PostEvent postEvent
          = new PostEvent("created", id, new Date(), user.getId(),
```

```
                        newPost.getTitle(), newPost.getBody());
        kafkaTemplate.send("post", postEvent);
    } else
        logger.info("Something went awry with creating a new Post - user with
    ⮑ username "
            + newPost.getUsername() + " is not known");
}
```

And finally, added to the event handler is a new method for processing post events. It essentially contains the logic that you removed from the original write controller; in the next listing, you persist the post data in the projection store.

**Listing 12.5   Method from EventHandler.java**

```
@KafkaListener(topics="post",
                groupId = "postsconsumer",
                containerFactory = "kafkaListenerContainerFactory")
public void listenForPost(PostEvent postEvent) {

    logger.info("PostEvent Handler processing - event: "
                + postEvent.getEventType());

    if (postEvent.getEventType().equals("created")) {
        Optional<Post> opt = postRepository.findById(postEvent.getId());
        if (!opt.isPresent()){
            logger.info("Creating a new post in the cache with title "
                        + postEvent.getTitle());
            Post post = new Post(postEvent.getId(),
                            postEvent.getDate(),
                            postEvent.getUserId(),
                            postEvent.getTitle(),
                            postEvent.getBody());
            postRepository.save(post);
        } else
            logger.info("Did not create already cached post with id "
                        + existingPost.getId());
    }
}
```

Similar changes were made to the Connections service, but no changes were needed for the Connections' Posts service because it had no source-of-record data, or write controller to start. After studying the code, I encourage you to run the deployApps.sh script to update the deployment to this latest implementation. Run through some examples to see this in action (create a user, create connections and posts, delete a connection), watch the logs, and read the resultant state by using each service's read controllers:

```
curl $(minikube service --url connections-svc)/users
curl $(minikube service --url connections-svc)/connections
curl $(minikube service --url posts-svc)/posts
curl $(minikube service --url connections-svc)/connectionsPosts/<username>
```

This event-sourcing approach, while perhaps different from the way you might think about implementing services such as the examples in this book, is a critical part of a microservices architecture. It's a pattern that allows you to lose a projection database and any backups thereof and still recover the state of your software by replaying the logs to generate them anew. It allows for microservices that might previously have been beholden to a deep dependency hierarchy for their functionality to operate autonomously, even in the event of network or other infrastructure failures or hiccups. It allows teams to evolve their services without needing to be in lockstep evolution with other services. This pattern is an essential tool to building change-tolerant software.

## 12.5   *We're just scratching the surface*

Although we've covered a lot of ground in this chapter, there are still so many more things to talk about when it comes to cloud-native data:

- We haven't talked about partitioning the event log, which is required for scale. When you have 10 million users, you're going to need to organize the users into subsets. Do you do this by grouping user events by the first letter of their last name, or some other characteristic?
- We haven't talked about event ordering very much, which is essential to using the event log to derive state projections. Event log technologies implement sophisticated algorithms to ensure proper ordering and may at times tell a producer that it couldn't record an event because of certain ordering constraints not being met; the event producer must accommodate this.
- We haven't talked about how to evolve event schemas or techniques such as schema resolution (supported by Apache Avro) that allow old events to impersonate new events.
- We haven't talked about a practice of taking periodic snapshots of the projection data stores so that if you need to rebuild a projection store from the log, you needn't go all the way back to the beginning of time.

The topic of cloud-native data is so involved that it deserves its own volume, and I have a recommendation for you. In 2017, Martin Kleppmann, computer science researcher and one of the originators of Apache Kafka at LinkedIn, published *Designing Data-Intensive Applications* (O'Reilly Media). I could not give this a stronger endorsement!

### Summary

- When you give a microservice a database to store the data that it needs to fulfill its job, it realizes a significant gain in autonomy. As a result, your system as a whole will be more resilient.
- Although in many scenarios it's far better than nothing, using caching to fill this local database is rife with challenges; caching isn't a pattern that works well for frequently changing data.

- Proactively pushing data changes into these local data stores via events is a far better approach.
- The familiar pub/sub pattern is used as the backbone of this technique, though the entities that we produce and consume are events rather than messages.
- Making the event log the single source of truth for data, with all service-local databases holding only projections, achieves consistency in a way that works in the highly distributed, constantly changing environment that our cloud-native software runs in.

# *index*

## P

parallel deployments 179–181
partition tolerance 132
PID (process ID) 157
PII (personally identifiable information) 69
ping 211
pipelines 75
Pivotal Cloud Cache 118
pods 121, 225, 289
POM files 317
pom.xml files 113
post event 341
POST request 103, 257, 331
PostEvent 338
Posts microservice 92–94, 98, 103, 106, 112, 121,
    150, 158, 174, 181, 194, 196, 202, 209, 228,
    233, 240, 260, 274, 309–310, 323, 327, 336, 348
posts package 92
Posts service, configuring and deploying
    122, 124–129
Posts URL 124, 151, 167, 191
PostsController class 103
PostsController.java file 146, 160, 187, 201
PostsService class 272, 279
PostsServiceClient class 251
postsServiceClient.getPosts 252
PostSummary class 92
PostsWriteController 101
Process ID (PID) 157
production instability 28, 34
Prometheus 303
property files 41, 140, 144–146, 148, 165
pull-based approach 302
PUT operation 103

## Q

queues 343–346

## R

RabbitMQ 106
read controller 351
Read role 333, 354
read-through caching 324
Ready to Ship software 37
recommendations service 63
@Recover annotation 259, 261
recovery point objectives (RPOs) 132
recovery time objectives (RTOs) 132
Redis 113, 135–136, 190–191, 228–229, 235,
    274, 338
Redis IP 151, 192

Redis port 151, 192
redis-cli 149, 189, 235
redis-svc 229
redundancy 13, 108, 328
/refresh URL 175
regions 53
repeatability 40–44
    control of deployable artifact 41–42
    control of environment 40–41
    control of process 42–44
replica sets 121
replication controller 264
request durability 233
request resilience 233
request retries 233–257
    kind clients 250–256
    retry storms 238–250
        running apps 241–250
        setting up 240–241
    simple retries 233–238
        running apps 235–238
        setting up 234–235
    when not to retry 256–257
request/response pattern 84, 86, 112
request/response programming model 88–94
    cloud-native data 326–327
    event-driven programming model versus
        105–107
    microservices
        obtaining and building 90
        running 90–91
    setting up 89
    studying code 92–94
resilience 15, 19, 172
resiliency patterns 278
resilient interactions 266
    control loops 263–266
        controlling 264–266
        types of 263–264
    fallback logic 257–262
    request retries 233–257
        kind clients 250–256
        retry storms 238–250
        simple retries 233–238
        when not to retry 256–257
ResourceAccessException 253
responsiveness 172
RESTful service 103
restricted networks 239
restTemplate 224–225, 253
retry behavior 291
retry logic disabled 244
retry logic enabled 244
retry pattern 106–107

System.out 195
system/environment values 148–157
  building microservices 149
  running apps 150–157
  setting up 149
systemEnvironment key 156

**T**

targetPort 229
TCP liveness probes 201
TCP/UDP protocol level 214
theFirstSecret 174
theSecondSecret 174
tight coupling 346
tokens 116, 133
Tomcat container 90, 95, 114
topics 343–346
trace ID 310–311, 313
TRACE request 257
tracers 308
traditional load-balancing 210
troubleshooting 319
  application logging 296–300
  application metrics 300–305
    pulling metrics from cloud-native
      applications 302–303
    pushing metrics from cloud-native
      applications 304–305
  distributed tracing 306–319
    assembling traces via Zipkin 313–317
    implementation details 317–319
    running apps 309–310
    setting up 309
    tracer output 310–312
Twelve-Factor App 144, 195

**U**

UAT (user acceptance testing) 29
unauthenticated 126
unified log 16
upgrading 75–77
user acceptance testing (UAT) 29
user event 341
User Profile app 17–18

user-ID-to-username mapping data 334
UserEvent 338
Users URL 124, 151, 167, 192
Utils class 154, 186, 188–189, 300, 302
Utils.java file 154, 186

**V**

valid login token 133
@Value annotation 146, 154
Vault, HashiCorp 166, 173
vent log topic 346
Version of Deployable Artifact 181
Version of the App Config 181
VERSIONING_TRIGGER 193–194
vertical scaling 110
VMs (virtual machines) 58, 78
vulnerability patching 75–77

**W**

watch kubectl get all command 274
watch kubectl get pods command 193, 265
WebLogic 52, 297
WebSphere 52, 297
while loop 238, 250
Write and Event Producer 332
write controller 335, 351, 354
write logic (commands) 104

**Y**

YAML files 149, 197

**Z**

zero downtime 175, 178, 184
  as application requirement 7
  updating application configuration with
    142–143
zero-downtime credential rotation pattern 188
Zipkin 307, 313–317
Zuul 288